The Delinquent Girl

The Delinquent Girl

Edited by
Margaret A. Zahn

TEMPLE UNIVERSITY PRESS
Philadelphia

TEMPLE UNIVERSITY PRESS
1601 North Broad Street
Philadelphia PA 19122
www.temple.edu/tempress

Library of Congress Cataloging-in-Publication Data

   The delinquent girl / edited by Margaret A. Zahn.
     p. cm.
   Includes bibliographical references and index.
   ISBN 978-1-59213-951-4 (cloth : alk. paper)
   ISBN 978-1-59213-952-1 (pbk. : alk. paper)
   1. Female juvenile delinquents.   I. Zahn, Margaret A.

HV6046.D39 2009
364.36082—dc22   2008012509

2 4 6 8 9 7 5 3 1

To all girls whose futures depend on the support we give them *now*.

And to all of those who gave me support along the way, especially my sisters, my brother, and their families, and my son Christopher— all of whom have made my world a better place.

And to the memory of my mother, whose determination and support led me to study delinquency rather than practice it.

Contents

List of Figures and Tables

FIGURES

TABLES

Acknowledgments

A book of this magnitude required work and support from many quarters. First, I would like to thank the Office of Juvenile Justice and Delinquency Prevention, its administrator Robert Flores, and grant managers, Barbara Allen-Hagen and Janet Chiancone. Without their vision and support from the cooperative agreement, the resources to support this work would not have been available. Second, incalculable thanks to the authors who worked so tirelessly, not only reviewing massive amounts of research literature but also making multiple revisions based on reviews from peers, editors, and the Temple University Press. Then, too, there are the people at RTI International (RTI) who created the reference database, especially Loraine Monroe, and people who helped edit at various stages, including Sharon Barrell, Jeff Novey, and colleague Angela Browne. Assistance from Mark Pope of RTI, Jake Day and Lisa Tichavsky, graduate students at North Carolina State University, in keeping many details on track, is also greatly appreciated.

On a personal note, during the course of the project I sustained a significant injury. Special thanks to colleagues in the Crime, Violence, and Justice Program at RTI, and in the Department of Sociology at North Carolina State University, and to Jacob Day, Lisa Tichavsky, and Pat DeSomma who went above and beyond the call of duty to help get things done. Friends, Phillip and Elisa Stiles, Larry and Nancy Monteith, Mary Beth Kurz, and John and Belinda Hester were significant support during that time. And very special thanks to my sisters Beverly and Judith, my son Christopher, and my brother Dick, all of whom provided inestimable support.

I would also like to acknowledge Rosemary and Karen, two girls who I met forty years ago when serving as an intern in a girls' detention facility. Their experiences and the experiences of girls in detention that I have met over the recent past have kept the meaning of this work alive. This book is dedicated to those girls, with the hope that our work represents their lives and provides for them a better future.

Finally, this project was supported by Grant No. 2004-JF-FX-K001 awarded by the Office of Juvenile Justice and Delinquency Prevention, Office of Justice Programs, U.S. Department of Justice. Points of view or opinions in this document are those of the authors and do not necessarily represent the official position or policies of the U.S. Department of Justice.

The Delinquent Girl

Introduction

MARGARET A. ZAHN, ROBERT AGNEW, AND ANGELA BROWNE

With some exceptions, extensive recent scholarship focusing on gender and crime has tended to concentrate on women, not on girls. Longitudinal studies have been conducted with great impact on fields of knowledge; however, most of these, also, did not focus on girls (for example, Farrington 1994; Loeber, Keenan, and Zhang 1997; Thornberry and Krohn 2005). Moffitt and others (2001) and Widom (1995) are notable exceptions. In addition, while existing treatises have provided important windows into girls' involvement in delinquency (see, for example, Chesney-Lind and Pasko 2004), no comprehensive review exists of empirical evidence for the causes and correlates of girls' delinquency.

Over the past decade and a half, girls' involvement in the juvenile justice system has increased. It is estimated that there were over 640,000 arrests of females under eighteen in 2006.[1] Arrests were most common for minor crimes, particularly larceny-theft, simple assault, disorderly conduct, and running away from home. A substantial number of girls, however, were arrested for more serious offenses, such as aggravated assault and burglary. Self-report surveys of juveniles suggest that the extent of female offending is much higher. According to the 2006 *Monitoring the Future* survey, for example, 26 percent of female high school students reported involvement in shoplifting, while 32 percent admitted to some sort of theft, and 15 percent reported having been involved in a gang fight (Lloyd et al. 2007). Further, some data suggest that girls' delinquency is increasing faster than boys' delinquency (although see the discussion of this idea in Chapter 3). In 1980, girls accounted for 18 percent of all juvenile arrests for index crimes. Today, girls account for 29 percent of such arrests. Many of these female offenders come to the attention of the juvenile justice system. For example, almost fifteen thousand girls were in residential facilities in October 2003 (Snyder and Sickmund 2006). Female delinquency, then, is not uncommon and sometimes results in serious sanction by the justice system.

Despite the extensive involvement of girls in delinquency, for many years criminologists neglected the topic of female delinquency. Theories of delinquency were often developed with males in mind and there was little effort to conduct research on females. The juvenile justice system also focused its efforts on male offenders. This has started to change in recent years. Scholars have critiqued much of the theory and research on girls' delinquency and have turned a critical eye toward the treatment of female offenders in the justice system. These critiques have most often focused on adult women, with less attention to adolescent females. (For an important exception, see Chesney-Lind and Pasko 2004.) Likewise, organizations such as the National Institute of Justice and the Office of Juvenile Justice and Delinquency Prevention (OJJDP) have become increasingly concerned about female juvenile offenders. A volume on adolescents and female delinquency is sorely needed. This book represents an effort by leading criminologists to meet that need.

This compilation is the result of a year-long effort in which members of the "Girls Study Group" reviewed large bodies of research on the extent and nature of girls' delinquency, the causes and correlates of such delinquency, and the juvenile justice system's response to this delinquency. The Girls Study Group is a multidisciplinary group of academics and practitioners, convened and funded by the OJJDP to determine the state of knowledge in the field of girls' delinquency and, ultimately, recommend effective prevention and intervention programs for girls. (A list of the study group members appears in the Appendix.)

The eleven chapters in this book provide an overview of the research on girls' delinquency, discuss policy implications, and point to areas where further research is critically needed. The book begins with an examination of the major theories or explanations of female delinquency and the "gender gap" in delinquency, that is, the higher rate of male versus female offending. In particular, the Agnew and the Miller and Mullins chapters discuss, in general terms, the effect of a broad range of factors on female and male offending. The Steffensmeier and Schwartz chapter then examines the extent of, and especially recent trends in, female delinquency. Subsequent chapters in the book examine the specific causes of female delinquency in more detail. These causes include biopsychological factors and various features of the social environment, including family, school, peer, gang, and community-level factors. The final chapter considers the role of the juvenile justice system and changes in justice policies in the commitment of girls to treatment or correctional facilities.

Chapter 1, by Agnew, focuses on "mainstream" theories of delinquency, such as strain, control, social learning, and integrated theories. Many of these theories were developed with males in mind, but Agnew argues that recent versions of these theories have become more sensitive to issues of gender and have much to say about the causes of female offending and the gender gap in crime. At the same time, Agnew acknowledges that such theories are in need of further revision if they are to explain the complex relationship between gender and crime.

Miller and Mullins (Chapter 2) examine feminist theories of girls' delinquency. Although some feminist theorists have questioned the applicability of mainstream theories to the explanation of girls' delinquency, Miller and Mullins argue that "the most promising approach for understanding girls' delinquency is to develop scholarship that draws from the important insights of broader criminological thought, but does so while critically examining the gendered life situations of girls and boys and their impact on delinquency" (p. 33). Miller and Mullins describe the various ways in which feminist approaches can help us better understand female delinquency. Among other things, such approaches point to those social forces that influence the standing of females (and males) on the major causes of crime, the meaning of these causes for females and males, and the response to these causes. Miller and Mullins then describe several recent explanations of female delinquency and the gender gap that effectively draw on both mainstream theories and feminist insights. It is important to note that Agnew and Miller and Mullins discuss many of the same recent theories of delinquency, pointing to the increasing potential for integration between mainstream and feminist theories in recent scholarship.

Steffensmeier and Schwartz (Chapter 3) set the context by providing an assessment of the extent of recent trends in girls' delinquency and the gender gap in boys' and girls' offending. In particular, they focus on an evaluation of the claim that girls' violence is increasing more rapidly than boys'. Based on statistical evidence and data from police, juvenile justice officials, and agency personnel who work with juvenile offenders and delinquent girls, they question whether the increases in girls' violence signify that girls' underlying behavior is changing. Rather, they argue that girls are being arrested for behavior that in the past would have been ignored, would have been handled informally, or would have resulted in less serious charges. While examining the possibility of increased social control of girls' behavior, they take into account how the relative invisibility of girls' delinquency in the past and the gendered nature of violence and delinquency intersect with recent shifts in penal philosophy and enforcement practices.

The Fishbein and others chapter (Chapter 4) focuses on the effect of several major "biopsychological factors" on girls' delinquency. Many psychological and biopsychological factors could be considered. In fact, an entire book could be devoted to these factors. However, Fishbein and others focus on stress reactivity, attention deficit-hyperactivity disorder, conduct disorder, intellectual deficits, early pubertal maturation, and mental health problems as particularly germane to delinquent girls in custody. The authors examine gender differences in the level of and sensitivity to these factors, suggesting that it is this differential sensitivity that is most important to understanding gender differences. It is important to note that, while Fishbein and others stress the importance of biological and psychological factors, they readily acknowledge that such factors are intimately connected with social factors. Biopsychological and social factors work together to influence offending, although these connections have yet to be explored fully.

Much of the rest of the book focuses on factors related to the social environment. Kruttschnitt and Giordano (Chapter 5) examine a range of family factors associated with girls' delinquency. They review research on the effect of family structure, family processes, and parental criminality on delinquency, paying special attention to whether there are gender differences in such effects. The area of physical and sexual abuse is given special consideration, as victimization experiences have been identified by some as influential precursors of girls' pathways into delinquency. After discussing methodological shortcomings in the research, including the lack of control groups and use of convenience samples, they conclude that sexual abuse is related to delinquency. However, it is not clear whether sexual abuse has a greater effect on delinquency than other forms of maltreatment. There is little evidence that gender conditions the relationship between sexual abuse and delinquency. Furthermore, since peers become increasingly important during adolescence, they suggest that studies connecting extrafamilial influences with familial ones are critical to understanding pathways to girls' delinquency.

In addition to family influences, peer influences have been shown to be important factors in delinquency. Giordano (Chapter 6) reviews the research on the influence of peers, peer groups, and romantic partners on girls' and boys' delinquency. Special attention is given to how these relationships may influence girls and boys differently. They find that some processes influence both genders equally. However, cross-gender relationships appear to be especially important in fostering female delinquency. The implications of these findings for delinquency prevention program development are detailed, with suggestions for offering relationship-focused curricula to supplant some of the health-based programs currently in use.

Peer relationships often take place within the larger social institution of the school. Sociostructural factors related to school are examined by Payne, Gottfredson, and Kruttschnitt in Chapter 7. Here, as in other chapters, the authors note that research has firmly established that certain school-related factors, for example, academic achievement and attachment to school, influence delinquency for both girls and boys. Very few firm conclusions, however, can be drawn regarding gender differences in the magnitude of the effects. School achievement is important for both boys and girls, as is school bonding, with a slightly greater impact of achievement for boys and attachment for girls. Deeper understanding of these differences for varying ethnic and age groups remains an important issue, especially as they intersect with gender.

Of course, individuals, schools, peers, and families are nested in communities. Chapter 8, by Zahn and Browne, distills the extensive literature in this area. While there is a burgeoning literature on neighborhood effects on crime, studies

specifically examining gender differences in neighborhood effects and delinquency are small in number. The Moving-to-Opportunity (MTO) studies and
the Project on Human Development in Chicago Neighborhoods (PHDCN)
study are two notable exceptions, with each showing substantial differences for
girls and boys in terms of impacts of neighborhood environments. In the MTO
studies, decreases in violent behavior were seen for all youths who moved to
more advantaged neighborhoods. However, suppression effects on property
offenses over time occurred only among girls. Other positive effects (e.g., better
performance in school and subsequent college attendance) were found for girls
but not for boys. Analyses of the mechanisms underlying these gender differences
are unclear, however. We also need more information on "good girls" who come
from bad, or highly disadvantaged, neighborhoods (Elliott et al. 2006).

Chapters 1 through 8 review primarily quantitative studies and do not focus
on specific forms of delinquency. Chapter 9 by Morash and Chesney-Lind reviews
the qualitative literature and focuses more specifically on violence and how the
various contexts of peers, schools, and communities shape girls' violent responses.
It is in this chapter, and in Chapter 10 on gangs by Miller, that the voices of girls
can actually be heard and their various situations more specifically understood.
Morash and Chesney-Lind contend that, although girls and boys both fight to
maintain status or for self-protection, girls fight to defend their reputation, particularly from sexual accusations, and out of anger at being victimized.

In Chapter 10, Miller dispels popular claims of "new violent female offenders" and outlines both historical and contemporary knowledge about girls'
involvement in gangs—both their extent and type of participation. Drawing on
a range of studies examining different types of gangs from different ethnic groups
and different locales, Miller evaluates our current knowledge of girls in gangs.
She includes the level of gang involvement, girls' risk factors and pathways into
gang membership, and the consequences for girl gang members, such as further
risk of victimization and long-term costs of gang involvement for girls.

The book's final chapter by Feld analyzes changes in the treatment of girls in
the juvenile justice system. After three decades of deinstitutionalizing status
offenders, the juvenile justice system, Feld says, remains committed to protecting
and controlling girls, but without providing resources necessary to respond to
their real needs. The failure to provide services creates substantial pressures to
circumvent restrictions on the disposition of status offenders by relabeling them
or "transinstitutionalizing" them into mental health or chemical dependency
treatment facilities. In sum, the increasing confinement of girls appears to be
driven by a relabeling of minor forms of girls' violence from "incorrigibility" to
simple assault. The lack of real resources to deal with girls' needs is a chronic
underlying problem.

This book summarizes large bodies of research on the causes and correlates
of female delinquency. The evidence suggests that girls and boys are similarly
impacted by many causal factors. However, there are different rates of exposure
to some causal factors (e.g., sexual assault) and also differential sensitivity to a

number of factors. For example, while associating with delinquent peers increases the likelihood of delinquency for both girls and boys, girls are more affected by romantically involved peers, especially when less serious delinquent acts are considered. Our theories, our research, and our prevention and intervention programs, then, need to be gender informed.

The comprehensive review also identifies enormous research gaps. For instance, although the Girls Study Group had envisioned including research findings on race, class, and ethnic differences in each chapter, the research to support that ambition was not sufficient. Where it was possible to include this information, it is included, although this area remains a research frontier yet to be traversed. There also is a huge gap in distinguishing the causes of delinquency from the causes of arrest and incarceration. Analysis of general populations and the correlates of delinquency for girls are not necessarily the same as correlates of delinquency in girls who are in juvenile justice custody. Sorting out the reasons for this difference is crucial to our ultimate understanding and control of the problem.

In the end, the importance of knowing the causes and correlates of girls' pathways to delinquency is in their implications for preventing offending and treating juvenile offenders. Some of these factors, such as family dysfunction, have similar relevance for girls and boys. Others, such as the impact of dating partners, may have special relevance for girls. Although there has been discussion of gender-responsive programming for females, to date almost all of that discussion relates to adults. While there are similarities between adolescent and adult females, there are also substantial differences. Adolescent girls are subject to school and parental social control, are developmentally immature in brain development and social experience, and experience increasing importance of peers as they go through adolescence. All of these differences require consideration.

While subsequent work of the study group will focus on programs for girls, the foundation for that programming is found in this book. It is the causes and correlates of girls' pathways to delinquency that serve as the necessary background for successful intervention. We invite our readers to enter the world that shapes the formation of delinquent girls and hope they leave with the understanding necessary to improve that world.

1

The Contribution of "Mainstream" Theories to the Explanation of Female Delinquency

ROBERT AGNEW

T his chapter describes the contribution of "mainstream" theories of crime to the explanation of female delinquency and the gender gap in delinquency. Such theories include strain theory; social learning theory; control theory; labeling theory; deterrence, rational choice, and routine activities theories; Moffitt's theory of life-course persistent offending; and selected integrated theories. These theories tend to explain crime in terms of characteristics of the individual and the individual's immediate social environment. (Chapter 8, this volume, by Zahn and Browne focuses on the effect of the larger social environment, particularly the community, on female delinquency.) This chapter examines contributions of each theory in turn and concludes by listing the key insights from these theories.

As noted by several criminologists, most mainstream theories were developed to explain male delinquency, and most tests of these theories devote little or no attention to gender (Kruttschnitt 1996; Miller and Mullins 2006; Morash 1999; Morris 1987; Steffensmeier and Allan 1996; Steffensmeier and Broidy 2001). However, some researchers in recent years have applied these theories to the explanation of female delinquency and the gender gap in delinquency. Data suggest that the causal factors identified by these theories do apply to females and that these theories can explain much of the gender gap in delinquency (Jensen 2003; Jensen and Eve 1976; Lanctot and Le Blanc 2002; Moffitt et al. 2001; Rowe, Vazsonyi, and Flannery 1995; Simons, Miller, and Aigner 1980; Smith 1979; Smith and Paternoster 1987).

At the same time, these theories are somewhat limited in the explanations they provide. In particular, they often fail to account for the complex relationship between gender and delinquency. For example, many fail to explain why gender differences in delinquency vary by type of delinquency (e.g., why gender differences are greatest for serious violence). Also, they offer little insight into gender differences in the context or nature of particular crimes (e.g., gender differences in the motivation, victim characteristics, and level of injury for violent crimes). Further, they often fail to consider fully the varied mechanisms by which gender may influence delinquency (e.g., gender differences in socialization, social control, social position, power/resources, interactional dynamics, and opportunities). Finally, they fail to consider the ways in which gender interacts with race, class, and age to affect delinquency.

To be fair, these problems affect many feminist theories as well, but they are particularly common among mainstream theories. Clearly, a complete explanation of female delinquency will require that the insights of mainstream theories be integrated with those of feminist theories and the research on gender and crime. Describing the contributions of mainstream theories is a first step toward that integration.

The Contribution of Mainstream Theories

The examination here focuses on the best-supported version of each theory or a generic version that combines the best elements from the different versions. I briefly describe (a) the major arguments of the theory, (b) how the theory explains the gender gap in delinquency, and (c) how the theory explains female delinquency. I summarize the evidence for each theory and note areas where further research is needed.

General Strain Theory

Major Arguments
General strain theory (GST) argues that a range of strains or stressors increases the likelihood of delinquency (Agnew 1992, 2006). These strains fall into three broad groups: the failure to achieve positively valued goals (e.g., autonomy, masculine status, monetary success), the loss of positive stimuli (e.g., property, romantic partners), and the presentation of negative stimuli (e.g., verbal and physical abuse). Such strains lead to negative emotions such as anger and frustration. And individuals may cope with these strains and negative emotions through delinquency. Delinquency may be a way of reducing or escaping from strains (e.g., theft to achieve monetary goals, running away to escape from abusive parents), seeking revenge against the source of the strains or related targets, or alleviating negative emotions (e.g., through illicit drug use).

Certain strains are said to be more conducive to criminal coping than others. These strains (a) are seen as high in magnitude, (b) are seen as unjust, (c) are associated with low social control, and (d) create some incentive or pressure to engage in crime. Such strains include parental rejection; parental supervision/discipline that is erratic, excessive, or harsh; child abuse and neglect; negative secondary school experiences (e.g., low grades, negative relations with teachers); abusive peer relations (e.g., verbal and physical abuse); the failure to achieve selected goals, including thrills/excitement, autonomy, masculine status, and money; criminal victimization; residence in economically deprived communities; homelessness; and discrimination based on race/ethnicity and gender. Data suggest that these strains do increase the likelihood of delinquency, although many of these strains, such as peer abuse and discrimination, have not been well researched. Further, limited data suggest that certain of these strains increase delinquency through their effect on negative emotions such as anger (Agnew 2006).

GST also argues that some individuals are more likely than others to cope with strains through crime. Five general sets of characteristics are said to increase the likelihood of criminal coping: (a) poor coping skills and resources (e.g., poor social and problem-solving skills, the personality trait of low self-control); (b) low levels of conventional social support; (c) low social control; (d) association with criminal others and beliefs favorable to crime; and (e) exposure to situations where the costs of crime are low and the benefits are high. These factors increase the likelihood of criminal coping since they reduce the ability to cope in a legal manner, reduce the costs of crime, and increase the disposition for crime. Certain of these factors also influence the individual's perception of and sensitivity to strains. Data on whether these factors increase the likelihood of criminal coping are mixed, a fact that may reflect the difficulty of detecting interaction or conditioning effects in survey research (Agnew 2006; Mazerolle and Maahs 2000).

Explaining the Gender Gap in Delinquency

Males and females experience similar amounts of strains (Broidy and Agnew 1997). Males, however, may be more likely to engage in delinquency because they are more likely to experience strains conducive to delinquency and more likely to cope with strains through delinquency. Although the data are somewhat mixed, there is reason to believe that males are more likely to experience the following strains conducive to delinquency: harsh parental discipline; negative secondary school experiences, such as low grades and negative relations with teachers; peer abuse, with males more likely to report that their relations with peers are characterized by conflict, competition, jealousy, and imbalance; difficulty achieving several goals conducive to delinquency, such as autonomy, thrills/excitement, money, and masculine status; criminal victimization; and homelessness (Agnew 2006; Agnew and Brezina 1997; Bottcher 2001; Broidy and Agnew 1997; Cernkovich and Giordano 1979; Giordano, Cernkovich, and Pugh 1986; Hagan and McCarthy 1997; Hay 2003; McCarthy, Felmlee, and Hagan 2004; Messerschmidt 1993).

Further, females are more likely than males to experience certain strains that may inhibit other-directed delinquency. These strains include close supervision by parents and others; the burdens associated with the care of others, especially family members; problems in forming and maintaining close relationships; and pressure to conform to traditional gender roles, with such pressure increasing during adolescence (Agnew 2006; Agnew and Brezina 1997; Berger 1989; Broidy and Agnew 1997; Chesney-Lind and Shelden 2004; Gove and Herb 1974). The extent to which these gender differences in strains explain gender differences in offending is unknown. No currently available data set contains measures of delinquency and measures of all or even most of these strains. A few studies, however, provide partial support for GST. Eitle and Turner (2002), for example, found that gender differences in crime were partly explained by the higher rates of violent victimization "both experienced and witnessed" among males.

GST also suggests that males are more likely to cope with strains through other-directed crime (Agnew and Brezina 1997; Broidy 2001; Broidy and Agnew 1997; Cloward and Piven 1979; Hay 2003; Piquero and Sealock 2004; Robbers 2004). There are several reasons for this. While females are as likely as or more likely than males to respond to strains with anger, the anger of females is more often accompanied by feelings of depression, guilt, and anxiety. This may be because females are more likely to blame themselves for the strains they experience, be concerned about hurting others, and view their anger as inappropriate. The anger of males, however, is more often characterized by moral outrage. Males are more likely to blame others for the strains they experience and view their anger as an affirmation of their masculinity. The moral outrage of males is more conducive to other-directed crime than the type of anger experienced by females. (The anger of females, however, may be especially conducive to self-directed crimes and deviant acts [e.g., drug use, eating disorders] [Broidy 2001; Broidy and Agnew 1997; Obeidallah and Earls 1999].)

Males are also more likely to cope with strains through other-directed crimes because they have poorer coping skills and resources, are lower in certain types of social support, are lower in social control, are more likely to associate with other criminals, and are more likely to hold beliefs conducive to criminal coping. Cloward and Piven (1979), for example, point to those gender-related beliefs that proscribe that "women endure rather than deviate" (p. 663). In addition, males are physically larger and stronger than females, which increases their ability to engage in several types of criminal coping. However, the "sexualization and commodification of the young, female body" increases the likelihood that females will engage in selected crimes, like prostitution (Chesney-Lind 1989; Gaarder and Belknap 2002; Steffensmeier and Allan 2000).

A number of studies have examined whether males are more likely to cope with selected strains through delinquency. Most such studies find that this is the case, although some studies find that strains have comparable effects on delinquency among males and females and a few find that certain strains have larger effects on females (Agnew 2006; Agnew and Brezina 1997; Broidy 2001; Broidy and Agnew 1997; Cernkovich and Giordano 1979; Datesman, Scarpitti, and Stephenson 1975; Hay 2003; Piquero and Sealock 2004; Robbers 2004; Smith and

Paternoster 1987). More research is needed in this area, particularly research that examines a broader range of strains, that looks at different types of crime (e.g., violence versus drug use), and that more systematically examines the possible reasons for any gender differences in coping that are found.

Explaining Female Delinquency

GST explains female delinquency by arguing that many females do experience strains conducive to delinquency, such as parental rejection, harsh discipline, negative secondary school experiences, peer abuse, homelessness, a strong need for money, and criminal victimization. To illustrate, females are encouraged to focus on their appearance and are the target of massive advertising campaigns for products such as cosmetics and clothing. Many females lack the money to purchase such products and turn to shoplifting as a result (Chesney-Lind and Shelden 2004). Further, females are more likely than males to experience certain strains conducive to delinquency, including sexual abuse, gender discrimination, and, possibly, partner/dating violence and certain types of romantic disputes—such as those involving the infidelity and emotional detachment of one's partner (Agnew 2006; Bottcher 2001; Miller and White 2003).

Chesney-Lind (1989) describes the effects of sexual abuse on female delinquency, arguing that some females run away to escape from abuse at home. These females often must engage in crimes like theft and prostitution to survive on the street, and they are frequently abused by a new set of males, further increasing the strains they experience. Several studies support these arguments, suggesting that sexual abuse plays a central role in the generation of serious female offending (Acoca 1998b; Chesney-Lind and Shelden 2004; Daly 1992; Gilfus 1992; Hubbard and Pratt 2002). The effects of gender discrimination, partner abuse, and romantic disputes on offending have not been well examined, but limited quantitative and qualitative data suggest that they too increase the likelihood of crime (Bottcher 2001; Eitle 2002; Gaarder and Belknap 2002; Katz 2000; Miller and White 2003). Note that lower-class females and the members of certain racial and ethnic groups, like African Americans and Latinos, are more likely to experience most of the aforementioned strains (Chesney-Lind and Shelden 2004; Gaarder and Belknap 2002; Gilfus 1992; Miller and White 2003).

Further, some females do possess characteristics conducive to criminal coping. Among other things, criminal coping is expected to be more likely among females who are poor, are low in self-control, are low in conventional social support, associate with criminal others, hold beliefs favorable to crime, and reject traditional gender beliefs. Little research has been conducted in this area.

Social Learning Theory

Major Arguments

Social learning theory argues that individuals learn to be delinquent from others, including family members, friends, neighborhood residents, and media figures

(Akers and Sellers 2004; Akers 1998). These others teach the individual to engage in delinquency in three major ways. They model delinquent behavior, which the individual then imitates, especially if the delinquency is modeled by close others and results in reinforcement. They reinforce the individual's delinquency in certain circumstances, leading the individual to anticipate further reinforcement in similar circumstances. And they teach beliefs favorable to delinquency. These beliefs do not involve the unconditional approval of all delinquent acts. Rather, individuals are typically taught that delinquency is desirable, justifiable, or excusable in certain conditions. For example, violence may be presented as a justifiable response to a broad range of provocations (Anderson 1999). Individuals are also taught certain general values conducive to delinquency, like the importance of being tough. And individuals may be taught to unconditionally approve of select, minor delinquent acts such as underage drinking, sexual intercourse, and marijuana use (Agnew 2005a).

Data provide a fair degree of support for social learning theory (Agnew 2005a; Akers and Sellers 2004; Akers 1998). Associating with delinquent peers, especially gang members, is one of the strongest predictors of delinquency. It should be noted, however, that the effect of delinquent peers is only partly explained by the mechanisms listed by social learning theory: exposure to criminal models, the reinforcement of delinquency, and beliefs favorable to delinquency (Krohn 1999; see Warr 2002 for additional mechanisms by which delinquent peers may contribute to delinquency). Having criminal parents and siblings is a relatively strong predictor of delinquency. Some data also suggest that exposure to media violence increases violent behavior, although the effect is modest in size (Agnew 2005a). Further, most data suggest that individuals who hold beliefs favorable to delinquency are more likely to engage in delinquent acts.

Explaining the Gender Gap

Social learning theorists argue that males have higher levels of delinquency than females primarily because they are more likely to associate with delinquent peers and belong to gangs. Data provide some support for this argument, with gender differences in delinquent peer association explaining a significant part of the gender gap in delinquency (Jensen 2003; Liu and Kaplan 1999; Mears, Ploeger, and Warr 1998; Moffitt et al. 2001; Moore and Hagedorn 2001; Morash 1986; Rowe, Vazsonyi, and Flannery 1995; Warr 2002). Males are said to be more likely to associate with delinquent peers because they are subject to less parental supervision, are less often confined to the home, are more attracted to delinquent peers because of their values and individual traits, and are less likely to be excluded from delinquent peer groups because of their greater physical strength and other factors (Steffensmeier 1983). Further, most studies suggest that delinquent peers have a larger effect on delinquency among males than females, perhaps because females are more constrained by their moral beliefs and are higher in self-control (Crosnoe, Erickson, and Dornbusch 2002; Elliott, Huizinga, and Ageton 1985;

Johnson 1979; Mears, Ploeger, and Warr 1998; Moffitt et al. 2001; Piquero et al. 2005; Simpson and Elis 1995; Smith 1979; Warr 2002).

Related to the studies mentioned, a few recent studies suggest that all-female peer groups are less conducive to delinquency than mixed-gender or all-male peer groups (Bottcher 1995, 2001; Giordano, Cernkovich, and Pugh 1986; McCarthy, Felmlee, and Hagan 2004). Female peers provide less pressure, reinforcement, and models for delinquency than do male peers. Also, female peers may be less likely to abuse one another and more likely to function as sources of support.

Social learning theorists also explain the gender gap in delinquency by arguing that males are more likely to hold beliefs favorable to delinquency. Data provide some support for this argument (Jensen 2003; Liu and Kaplan 1999; Mears, Ploeger, and Warr 1998). For example, Heimer and De Coster (1999) found that males were more likely to agree with statements such as "It is alright to beat up another person if he/she called you a dirty name" and "It is alright to beat up another person if he/she started the fight."

Further, social learning theorists argue that males are more likely to be taught identities that are conducive to delinquency. In particular, male identities are said to emphasize competitiveness, independence, risk-taking, and strength. Female identities are said to emphasize concern for others, dependence, caution, passivity, and submissiveness. Research on the relationship between gender identities and delinquency has produced mixed results, for reasons that are not entirely clear (Bottcher 1995, 2001; Chesney-Lind and Shelden 2004; Costello and Mederer 2003; Giordano and Cernkovich 1979; Heimer 1995, 1996; Heimer and De Coster 1999; Jensen 2003; Norland, Wessel, and Shover 1981; Shover et al. 1979). Some researchers suggest, however, that gender-linked identities may be related to crime when one focuses on those aspects of identity most directly relevant to crime. Jensen (2003), for example, found that males were somewhat more likely to view themselves as tough, mean, unforgiving, and prone to trouble; while females were more likely to view themselves as nice, prone to avoid trouble, caring about others, and forgiving. These differences in identity partly explained gender differences in delinquency. (It should be noted that some evidence suggests that delinquent beliefs and gender identities may differ by class and race/ethnicity, although more research is needed in this area before definitive conclusions can be drawn [Bottcher 2001; Heimer and De Coster 1999; Simpson and Elis 1995].)

Explaining Female Delinquency

According to social learning theory, some females are more likely than others to engage in delinquency because they are more likely to associate with others who provide exposure to delinquent models, reinforce delinquent behavior, and teach beliefs favorable to delinquency. Also, some females are more likely to be taught identities favorable to delinquency.

Association with delinquent peers and gang members is a critical variable, with one recent meta-analysis suggesting that such association, along with a prior history of antisocial behavior, is the strongest predictor of female delinquency (Elliott, Huizinga, and Ageton 1985; Heimer 1996; Hubbard and Pratt 2002; Jensen 2003; Johnson 1979; Laundra, Kieger, and Bahr 2002; Liu and Kaplan 1999; Moore and Hagedorn 2001; Piquero et al. 2005; Smith and Paternoster 1987; Warr 2002; and see Chapter 6 in this book). Several factors increase the likelihood of delinquent peer association in females, including poor parental supervision, sexual abuse by family members, running away from home, poverty, school problems, early puberty, limited prospects for the future, and residence in economically deprived communities (Acoca 1998b; Chesney-Lind and Shelden 2004; Elliott, Huizinga, and Ageton 1985; Joe and Chesney-Lind 1999; Moffitt et al. 2001; Morash 1986).

In addition, research suggests that females are more likely to engage in delinquency if they associate with older males, including romantic partners, and are part of mixed-sex or all-male peer groups (Agnew and Brezina 1997; Bottcher 2001; Giordano 1978; Giordano and Cernkovich 1979; Haynie et al. 2005; Heimer and De Coster 1999; McCarthy, Felmlee, and Hagan 2004; Moffitt et al. 2001; Warr 2002; and see Chapter 6 in this book). Further, data suggest that females are more likely to engage in delinquency if they have criminal parents or siblings, hold beliefs favorable to delinquency, and, possibly, have identities emphasizing "masculine" traits such as toughness and meanness (Heimer 1996; Heimer and De Coster 1999; Jensen 2003; Johnson 1979; Lanctot and Le Blanc 2002; Laundra, Kieger, and Bahr 2002; Miller 2002a; Shover et al. 1979; Steffensmeier and Broidy 2001; and see Chapter 6 in this book).

Control Theory

Major Arguments

Control theorists do not ask why individuals engage in delinquency, but rather why they conform. According to control theorists, delinquency requires no special explanation. It is frequently the easiest or most expedient way for individuals to satisfy their needs and desires. What requires explanation, then, is conformity. Control theorists contend that people conform because of the controls or restraints to which they are subject (Agnew 2005a; Gottfredson and Hirschi 1990; Hirschi 1969; Sampson and Laub 1993). These controls are of three types.

The first is external control. Here individuals conform because they fear they will be sanctioned by others if they do not. These others include parents, friends, school officials, neighbors, and police. External control is enhanced to the extent that these others set clear rules that forbid delinquency and related behaviors, monitor the individual's behavior, and consistently sanction rule violations in a meaningful but not overly harsh manner.

The second type of control involves the individual's "stake in conformity." Some individuals are less likely to engage in delinquency because they have a lot to lose through delinquent acts. In particular, they have strong emotional bonds to conventional others, like parents and teachers, that may be jeopardized by delinquency. And they have a large investment in conventional activities, like getting an education. Individuals who are doing well in school, devote more time to homework, and anticipate obtaining a good education and job are less likely to engage in delinquency because it might jeopardize their accomplishments and future plans.

The third type of control is internal control, which refers to the individual's ability to restrain him- or herself from responding to temptations and provocations with delinquency. Internal control is partly a function of the individual's beliefs regarding delinquency. Some individuals have been taught to condemn delinquency and are less likely to engage in delinquency as a result. Other individuals, however, have an amoral orientation toward delinquency (control theorists contend that few individuals are deliberately taught beliefs favorable to delinquency). And internal control is partly a function of several related personality traits that influence the individual's ability to exercise self-restraint. Those traits conducive to delinquency include impulsivity, a preference for immediate versus delayed rewards, a preference for risky activities, high activity levels, little ambition or motivation, and an irritable disposition. Individuals with these traits are said to be low in self-control.

Explaining the Gender Gap

Control theorists argue that males have higher rates of offending than females because they are lower in the three major types of control (Costello and Mederer 2003; Gottfredson and Hirschi 1990; Heimer and De Coster 1999; McCarthy, Felmlee, and Hagan 2004; Shover et al. 1979). Males are subject to less external control; most notably, they are less well supervised by parents and less strongly tied to the household than females. Also, males are less likely to be sanctioned by parents, peers, and others for aggressive and delinquent behavior. Males are less strongly attached to conventional others such as parents and teachers. Males do less well at school, spend less time on homework, and dislike school more. Males are less likely to condemn crime. And males are lower in self-control. These gender differences in control are explained in several ways, including the greater desire of parents and others to regulate the sexual behavior of females (reflecting the double standard for sexual behavior). Also, some researchers have said that females need to show more concern for others and exercise greater self-control since they are the primary caregivers in society (Bottcher 1995; Costello and Mederer 2003).

Some criminologists also argue that certain control variables have a stronger effect on delinquency among females or males. Most notably, emotional bonds to others are said to have a stronger effect among females, since females attach greater importance to establishing and maintaining close relationships with others. School performance, however, is said to have a stronger effect among males, given their greater concern with achievement (Canter 1982a; Heimer and De Coster 1999; Rankin 1980).

Data provide a fair degree of support for control theory explanations of the gender gap. Most studies suggest that male adolescents are less well supervised by parents, are less strongly tied to the household through chores and family-care responsibilities, are less constrained from crime by peers, have lower grades in school, like school less, are less likely to condemn crime, and are much lower in self-control (Bottcher 1995, 2001; Canter 1982a; Cernkovich and Giordano 1987, 1992; Chesney-Lind and Shelden 2004; Costello and Mederer 2003; Crosnoe, Erickson, and Dornbusch 2002; Hagan and McCarthy 1997; Hagan, Simpson, and Gillis 1979; Jensen and Eve 1976; LaGrange and Silverman 1999; McCarthy, Felmlee, and Hagan 2004; Moffitt et al. 2001; Richards and Tittle 1981; Rowe, Vazsonyi, and Flannery 1995; Simons, Miller, and Aigner 1980; Singer and Levine 1988; Smith and Paternoster 1987; Thornberry et al. 1991). These gender differences in levels of control, particularly self-control, explain a significant portion of the gender gap in delinquency. Less evidence exists for the proposition that males have weaker emotional bonds to conventional others. Data on whether certain types of control have stronger effects on delinquency among males or females are somewhat mixed (Canter 1982a; Cernkovich and Giordano 1987, 1992; Heimer and De Coster 1999; Johnson 1979; Krohn and Massey 1980; Kruttschnitt 1996; Laundra, Kieger, and Bahr 2002; Rankin 1980; Smith and Paternoster 1987). Most studies suggest that the different types of control generally have similar effects among males and females, although a meta-analysis of studies about control types and gender effects would be quite useful.

Explaining Female Delinquency

Some females are more likely to be delinquent than others because they are lower in the forms of control described earlier. That is, they are lower in parental supervision, are less tied to their homes and families, are weakly bonded to conventional others such as parents and teachers, do poorly in school, spend little time on homework, are in peer groups in which the constraints against delinquency are lower (e.g., delinquent peer groups, mixed-gender or all-male groups), do not condemn crime, and are low in self-control. Data suggest that these types of control affect female as well as male delinquency (Elliott, Huizinga, and Ageton 1985; Fleming et al. 2002; Friedman and Rosenbaum 1988; Heimer 1995; Hubbard and Pratt 2002; Huebner and Betts 2002; Jensen and Eve 1976; Johnson 1979; Krohn and Massey 1980; LaGrange and Silverman 1999; Lanctot and Le Blanc 2002; Mason and Windle 2002; Smith 1979; Smith and Paternoster 1987; and see Chapters 5 and 7 in this book). It should be noted, however, that certain types of control have a stronger effect on delinquency than others, with some data suggesting that parental supervision, the nature of peer relations, and self-control are among the more important predictors of delinquency (Agnew 2005a).

Labeling Theory

Major Arguments

Labeling theory focuses on the reaction to delinquency, both the formal reaction by the juvenile justice system and the informal reaction by parents, friends, teachers, and community residents. The key insight of labeling theory is that others often react to the individual's delinquency in ways that increase the likelihood of further delinquency (Agnew 2005b; Braithwaite 1989; Cullen and Agnew 2003; Heimer and Matsueda 1994; Matsueda 1992; Schur 1984; Sherman 1993). In particular, others often treat individuals who are labeled delinquent in a harsh and rejecting manner. Among other things, labeled individuals may be severely punished by parents, school officials, and the justice system. They may be viewed with suspicion and mistrust. They may be denied certain opportunities; for example, their schooling may be interrupted and their future educational and occupational plans may be jeopardized. And conventional others may be reluctant to associate with them.

These reactions increase the likelihood of delinquency for four reasons. First, they increase the labeled individual's strain, since the individual is subject to much negative treatment by others. Second, they reduce the individual's level of control, since bonds to conventional others such as parents and teachers are weakened. Also, the individual's stake in conformity is threatened. Third, they foster the social learning of crime. Labeled individuals often associate with other delinquents, since conventional others do not want to associate with them. Finally, labeled individuals may eventually come to see themselves as delinquents and act in accord with this self-image.

The evidence on labeling theory is mixed. Data suggest that labeling by parents and teachers may increase the likelihood of further delinquency, partly by affecting the juvenile's relations with others and self-concept (Adams and Evans 1996; Matsueda 1992; Triplett and Jarjoura 1994). And several studies find that individuals who are arrested or officially sanctioned by the justice system are more likely than comparable individuals to engage in subsequent delinquency, although not all studies find this (Agnew 2005b; Huizinga et al. 2003; Stewart et al. 2002b). Part of the reason for these mixed findings may be that some labeled individuals are more subject to the harsh and rejecting reactions described than others. Also, some individuals may be more likely than others to respond to this reaction with crime. Recent work on labeling theory has focused on these issues, with some attention being devoted to the ways in which gender influences the labeling process and the response to labeling.

Explaining the Gender Gap

Labeling theorists argue that males are more likely than females to be labeled delinquents, because of the cultural stereotype of males as troublemakers and the fact that males engage in more delinquency (Gove and Herb 1974). Males are also more likely to be treated in a harsh and rejecting manner by others once they are labeled, because they are viewed as more threatening and are less likely to have close ties to others (Braithwaite 1989). Further, males are more likely to respond to this harsh and rejecting treatment with crime for the same reasons they are more likely to respond to strains in general with crime. A major exception to these arguments, however, is said to involve status offenses, especially those linked to sexual behavior or the possibility of sexual behavior. Female status offenders are said to be more likely to be labeled delinquent and treated in a harsh and rejecting manner because of the sexual double standard, with sexual behavior on the part of female adolescents being more strongly condemned (Bartusch and Matsueda 1996; Chesney-Lind and Shelden 2004).

Research provides some support for these arguments. Males are more likely to be informally labeled as delinquents/troublemakers by others such as parents and teachers, primarily because they are more likely to engage in delinquency (Adams and Evans 1996; Bartusch and Matsueda 1996; Giordano et al. 1999; Liu and Kaplan 1999; Simons, Miller, and Aigner 1980). Males are also more likely to be falsely labeled as delinquents, although some females are falsely labeled as well (Bartusch and Matsueda 1996). Among females, false accusations are most common against the poor, African Americans, and those from broken homes. It is important to note, however, that Bartusch and Matsueda (1996) found that females are more likely than males to be labeled delinquent by parents and others for *a given delinquent act,* but *not* for a given status offense (Liu and Kaplan 1999; Schur 1984). Bartusch and Matsueda (1996) speculate that this may occur because "female offending is inconsistent with gender-specific expectations and readily violates parents' stereotypical conceptions of delinquency as a male enterprise" (p. 154). Related to this, Hagan, Simpson, and Gillis (1979) present data to the effect that women are more often the objects of informal social control.

Bartusch and Matsueda further found that being labeled a rule violator by parents increases the likelihood that juveniles will label themselves as rule violators, which in turn increases the likelihood of delinquency (see also Jensen 2003). This effect was stronger for males than females. In addition, they found that being labeled a rule violator by parents has a direct effect on delinquency among males, but not among females. Bartusch and Matsueda speculated that labeling by parents may be more likely to act as a deterrent to females, who are more concerned with maintaining a positive image and a positive relationship with others. Also, as Braithwaite (1989) suggests, labeled females may be less subject to harsh and rejecting reactions from others, given their closer ties to conventional others. Rather, labeled females may be more subject to "reintegrative shaming." Further, labeled females may be more responsive to such shaming. In this area, Jensen and Erickson (1978) found that females were more concerned than males about the negative consequences of labeling (Heimer 1996).

In summary, data suggest that males are more likely than females to be negatively labeled by parents and others, because of their higher levels of delinquency and, possibly, increased susceptibility to false labeling (although females may be more likely to be labeled for a given delinquent act). This labeling leads to delinquent self-concepts among both males and females, although males are more likely to have delinquent self-concepts since they are more often labeled (Jensen 2003). Further, labeling may be more likely to lead to delinquency among males. These gender differences in informal labeling explain a significant part of the gender gap in delinquency.

Several studies have examined official labeling, with most attempting to determine whether gender influences the likelihood of arrest, court referral, court processing, and sanctioning. The data here are mixed, but there is reason to believe that in some jurisdictions females who commit status offenses and selected minor crimes may be treated more severely than males. This may be especially true for poor females and the members of certain minority groups (for overviews, see Chesney-Lind and Shelden 2004; and MacDonald and Chesney-Lind 2001). A few studies have examined the impact of official labeling on future life changes. These studies suggest that such labeling typically has a negative effect on both males and females, although there are some gender differences in effects. Both males and females report negative educational consequences, but males also report negative occupational consequences (Moffitt et al. 2001; Tanner, Davies, and O'Grady 1999). Those few studies that have examined the effect of official labeling on future offending typically do not report results separately by gender. Clearly, more research is needed on the likelihood and impact of both informal and formal labeling on males and females.

Explaining Female Delinquency

Labeling theory argues that some females are more delinquent than others because they have been informally labeled as delinquents by parents, teachers, and others; they have been formally labeled by the juvenile justice system (i.e., they have been arrested, detained, formally or informally processed by the court, and sanctioned); or both. Delinquency should be more likely among those who have been severely labeled by a broad range of individuals and groups (e.g., treated in the harsh and rejecting manner described earlier, severely sanctioned by the juvenile justice system). Related to this, delinquency should be more likely among those females who see themselves as delinquents, troublemakers, and the like. As suggested, there is some support for these arguments.

Deterrence, Rational Choice, Routine Activities Theories

Major Arguments

Deterrence, rational choice, and routine activities theories differ from one another in important ways (Agnew 2005a; Cornish and Clarke 1986; Cullen and Agnew 2003; Felson 2002; Miethe and Meier 1994; Piquero and Tibbetts 2002). But these theories are all based on the idea that individuals consider somewhat the costs and benefits of crime and choose to engage in crime if they believe it is to their advantage. Deterrence theorists focus on the legal costs of crime and argue that individuals are more likely to engage in crime when they believe that the certainty and severity of official sanctions are low. Rational choice theorists focus on a broad range of costs and benefits. The benefits of crime may be both monetary and nonmonetary (e.g., thrills, social approval), and the costs may be both legal and nonlegal (e.g., disapproval from parents, guilt). Rational choice theorists do *not* argue that individuals carefully consider all of the potential costs and benefits of crime. Rather, individuals are said to give at least some consideration to certain of the costs and benefits, even though this consideration may be hurried and based on incomplete or inaccurate information. Crime is said to be more likely when benefits are seen as outweighing costs.

The data provide some support for these arguments. Individuals are more likely to engage in crime when (a) the perceived certainty and, to a lesser extent, severity of official sanction are low; (b) the perceived likelihood and severity of informal sanction are low; (c) the anticipated moral costs of crime, such as guilt and shame, are low; and (d) the anticipated pleasure associated with crime is high (Agnew 2005a, 2005b; Cullen and Agnew 2003; Piquero and Tibbetts 2002). Rational choice theorists have discussed those factors that influence the perceived costs and benefits of crime, and they draw heavily on the theories described in this area. For example, the perceived costs and benefits of crime are said to be influenced by such things as the individual's level of monetary strain, parental supervision, moral beliefs, self-control, and association with delinquent peers. The costs and benefits of crime are also influenced by a range of situational factors, most of which are specific to particular types of crime. For example, individuals contemplating burglary are likely to conclude that the costs of burglary are low if they encounter an isolated, unguarded home with easy entry.

The routine activities perspective is also built on the idea that offenders take into account the potential costs and benefits of crime. This perspective focuses on the factors that influence the calculation of costs and benefits, and its core idea is that crime is most likely when motivated offenders encounter attractive targets for crime in the absence of capable guardians (Felson 2002). The characteristics of attractive targets vary somewhat by type of crime. For property crimes, attractive targets are visible, accessible, easy to move, and valuable. The term "capable guardians" refers to individuals who might intervene if a crime occurs, like parents, teachers, community residents, and police. The likelihood that motivated offenders will encounter attractive targets for crime in the absence of capable guardians is said to be a function of the routine activities in which people engage; that is, what people do, who they do it with, when they do it, and where they do it.

One major finding to emerge from the research on routine activities is that juveniles are more likely to engage in crime if they spend a lot of time engaged in unstructured, unsupervised activities with peers (Osgood et al. 1996; and see Chapter 6 in this book). The costs of crime are likely to be seen as lower in such situations, because capable guardians are absent and peers often lower the perceived costs of crime. In particular, peers may help neutralize the moral costs of crime, provide assistance in committing crimes, and foster a sense of power through the "strength in numbers." The benefits of crime are also likely to be seen as higher in such situations. Individuals are more likely to encounter attractive targets for crime when engaged in unstructured, unsupervised activities with peers. Also, peers frequently reinforce crime, often with social approval.

Explaining the Gender Gap

These theories would argue that males are more likely to engage in crime than females because they are more likely to view the costs of crime as low and the benefits as high (Blackwell and Eschholz 2002; Braithwaite 1989; Costello and Mederer 2003; Richards and Tittle 1981). Several reasons explain why males are more likely to view the costs of crime as low, most of which are related to the theories described earlier in this chapter. Males are not as well supervised as females, so their crimes are less likely to be detected. If detected, male crimes are less likely to be sanctioned by certain others, such as peers. This is mainly because crime is viewed as more appropriate for males, but is also related to such things as the greater physical strength of males. Males have less to lose through crime, since crime is more compatible with male roles and identities. Males are more likely to hold beliefs favorable to crime, thereby lowering the moral costs of crime. Males are lower in self-control, so they give less thought to the possibility of sanctions or the harm that their crimes might cause others. Males spend more time in unstructured, unsupervised activities with peers, which lowers the costs of crime for the reasons indicated. And males are more likely to belong to delinquent peer groups and to engage in crime themselves. This teaches males that the likelihood of sanction for crime is low, since they frequently commit crimes without sanction and see their friends do the same.

Males are also more likely than females to view the benefits of crime as high. This partly stems from the fact that males are lower in self-control, so they are more likely to enjoy engaging in risky and aggressive activities like crime. And it partly stems from the fact that the routine activities of males expose them to more attractive opportunities for crime. Males, in particular, are given more freedom to explore the public sphere, where they might encounter attractive targets for crime. Females, by contrast, are more often involved in conventional activities associated with the home, family, and school, like chores, the care of siblings, homework, and interacting with parents. More freedom allows males to spend more time associating with other males, especially in unsupervised, unstructured settings. Reinforcement for crime is more likely in such circumstances.

Some data support these arguments (Blackwell and Eschholz 2002; Cernkovich and Giordano 1992; Heimer 1996; Jensen and Erickson 1978; McCarthy and Hagan 1999, 2005; Richards and Tittle 1981; Singer and Levine 1988; Smith and Paternoster 1987; Tibbetts and Herz 1996). Males perceive the certainty and severity of official sanctions as lower than females perceive them. Some studies also suggest that the perceived certainty/severity of sanctions may have a larger effect on delinquency among females, although not all studies find this (Cernkovich and Giordano 1992; Smith and Paternoster 1987). Males are less concerned about the reactions of parents and others to their crimes. Males are less concerned about the moral costs of crime, like the guilt and shame that might result from crime. And limited data also suggest that males are more likely to estimate the expected pleasure from crime as high (Hagan, Simpson, and Gillis 1979;

Tibbetts and Herz 1996). Such factors explain a substantial portion of the gender gap in crime.

The reasons for gender differences in these factors are still being examined, but evidence supports many of the aforementioned arguments. Most notably, males have more opportunities for crime since they are away from home more often; interact with more people; have greater access to cars; and spend more time in unstructured, unsupervised activities with peers (Bottcher 1995, 2001; Costello and Mederer 2003; LaGrange and Silverman 1999). While males generally have more opportunities for crime than females, the greater sexual interest in young females creates opportunities for crimes like prostitution. Females may also have much opportunity to engage in crimes involving family violence, including partner violence and petty theft (Chesney-Lind and Shelden 2004; Steffensmeier and Allan 2000).

Explaining Female Delinquency
Not surprisingly, these theories would predict that some females are more likely to engage in crime than other females because they are more likely to estimate the costs of crime as low and the benefits as high. Limited data suggest that estimates of the costs and benefits of crime influence female as well as male delinquency (Piquero and Paternoster 1998; Smith 1979; Smith and Paternoster 1987). Females likely differ in their estimates of the costs and benefits of crime because they differ in such factors as level of supervision; moral beliefs; self-control; time spent in unstructured, unsupervised activities with peers; association with delinquent peers; and prior delinquency (see previous section). For example, some females are more likely to spend unstructured, unsupervised time with peers than others. This is especially true of females who run away from home and spend a lot of time on the "street" (Hagan and McCarthy 1997).

Moffitt's Theory of Life-Course Persistent Offending

Major Arguments
All of the theories discussed focus on the effect of the social environment on delinquency. Moffitt's (1993) theory of life-course persistent offending has played a major role in introducing biological factors and individual characteristics into mainstream criminology. Moffitt's theory states that there are two major types of offenders: life-course persistent and adolescence-limited. Life-course persistent offenders tend to offend at relatively high rates over much of their lives. They commit both minor and serious crimes and, although they comprise only about 5 percent of the population, they account for a majority of all serious crimes. Adolescence-limited offenders limit their offending largely to the adolescent years and they commit primarily minor offenses. The large majority of people are said to be adolescence-limited offenders. Another 10 percent or so of all people are said to refrain from offending. Data provide some support for this

typology, with most studies finding evidence for both life-course persistent and adolescence-limited offenders (D'Unger et al. 1998; Moffitt et al. 2001; Piquero and Tibbetts 2002).

Moffitt argues that the causes of life-course persistent and adolescence-limited offending differ. The causes of adolescence-limited offending are said to be largely social in nature. As juveniles enter adolescence, they physically resemble adults but lack many of the privileges of adults, like the right to stay out late, drink alcohol, and engage in sexual relations. They notice, however, that their delinquent peers engage in these activities. As a consequence, they are attracted to these peers and come to mimic certain of their delinquent behaviors. There has not been much research on this explanation, although some data are compatible with it (Piquero and Brezina 2001). The causes of life-course persistent offending, however, are biological, psychological, and sociological in nature.

Life-course persistent offenders tend to possess a set of individual characteristics that are conducive to crime, with perhaps the most notable of these characteristics being the major personality traits of low constraint and negative emotionality. Individuals low in constraint are impulsive, like risky activities, and have little concern for moral norms and values. Individuals high in negative emotionality are easily upset, have trouble coping with stressors, tend to blame their problems on others, and have an aggressive disposition. (Note: these traits overlap a great deal with low self-control.) These traits form early in life and are fairly stable over time. Individuals with these traits are more likely to respond to temptations and provocations with crime, thereby partly explaining their high rates of offending over the life course. Individuals with these traits are also more likely to impact their environment in ways that increase the likelihood of crime. In particular, individuals with these traits are not pleasant people, and they often elicit negative reactions from others, like parents, teachers, and peers. Parents, for example, may come to reject children with these traits; may treat them in a harsh, abusive manner; or may do both. Also, individuals with these traits often select themselves into environments conducive to crime, like delinquent peer groups, bad jobs, and bad marriages. These environmental effects also help explain high rates of offending over the life course.

The traits of low constraint and negative emotionality are in part biologically based. They are inherited from parents to some degree, and they may also result from certain biological harms, like mothers' drug use during pregnancy, birth complications, head injuries, and exposure to toxic substances like lead. The ways in which such biological factors influence these traits are still being investigated, but there are several promising leads (Fishbein 2001; Moffitt 1993; Rowe 2002). These traits are also influenced by environmental factors, particularly economic disadvantage and family problems. Unfortunately, individuals with a biological predisposition for these traits are frequently exposed to these environmental factors. Among other things, parents who genetically transmit these traits are more likely to be poor and to engage in poor parenting practices (since they are low in constraint and high in negative emotionality). Also, biological harms of the type just described are more common in disadvantaged environments and troubled families.

Data provide some support for Moffitt's theory (Moffitt et al. 2001). Life-course persistent offenders are more likely to show evidence of a biological pre-disposition for crime, they are more likely to possess the personality traits of low constraint and negative emotionality, and these traits have social consequences that increase the likelihood of crime.

Explaining the Gender Gap

Data suggest that males are much more likely than females to be life-course per-sistent offenders (Broidy et al. 2003b; D'Unger, Land, and McCall 2002; Moffitt et al. 2001). This is because males are more likely to experience those biological and environmental factors that contribute to low constraint and negative emo-tionality (Udry 2000). Research does indicate that males are lower in constraint and higher in negative emotionality, and this fact explains a good part of the gender difference in offending, especially serious offending (Hagan, Simpson, and Gillis 1979; Moffitt et al. 2001).

Gender differences in adolescence-limited offending are much less pro-nounced. Females, like males, often experience a gap between their biological maturity and the privileges granted to them. So females frequently engage in adolescence-limited offending. This is especially true of females who reach puberty at an early age and are in environments where they are regularly exposed to older male adolescents and delinquent peer groups (Caspi et al. 1993; Haynie 2003; Moffitt et al. 2001). These facts help explain why gender differences in minor offending are much smaller than differences in serious offending.

Explaining Female Offending

While life-course persistent offending is much more common among males than females, a very small percentage of females become life-course persistent offend-ers. And data suggest that the causes of such offending are similar for males and females (Moffitt et al. 2001). Such offenders should be a high priority for inter-vention, given their high rates of offending, including serious offending (Daly 1992).

Integrated Theories

A good number of theories have been reviewed up to this point, including strain; social learning; control; labeling; deterrence, rational choice, and routine activi-ties; and Moffitt's theories. Several criminologists have attempted to combine some of these theories in an effort to develop more complete explanations of delinquency (Barak 1998; Messner, Krohn, and Liska 1989; Tittle 1995). Some of the more popular integrated theories include those of Catalano and Hawkins (1996); Elliott, Ageton, and Canter (1979); Thornberry (1987); Braithwaite (1989);

Cullen (1994); Tittle (1995); and Colvin (2000). It is not possible to review these theories in this brief chapter. As a consequence, I focus on two recent integrated theories. The first, Agnew's (2005b) general theory of crime and delinquency, draws quite heavily on the integrated theories just listed. The second, Steffensmeier and Allan's (1996, 2000) gendered theory of female offending, draws on both mainstream and feminist theories to explain the gender gap in crime and the causes and nature of female offending.

Agnew's General Theory of Crime and Delinquency (AGTCD)

AGTCD begins with the recognition that many of the theories listed earlier examine the same or similar causal forces. For example, most of these theories argue that erratic and harsh parental discipline increases the likelihood of delinquency. Where these theories most differ from one another is in specifying the reasons *why* these causal forces increase delinquency. For example, strain theory states that harsh/erratic discipline increases delinquency by making juveniles angry; social learning theory states that such discipline models aggressive behavior; and control theory states that such discipline reduces control—including direct control, the emotional bond to parents, and internal control. AGTCD argues that all of these theories are correct. In particular, AGTCD identifies a core set of causal factors and argues that these factors increase delinquency for reasons related to all or most of the leading crime theories.

Four major sets of factors are said to increase the likelihood of delinquency: high irritability and low constraint; poor parenting practices; negative school experiences; and peer delinquency. Adolescents high in irritability and low in constraint are easily upset, blame others for their problems, are impulsive, like risky behavior, care little about others, and hold beliefs favorable to crime. Adolescents high in poor parenting practices are weakly bonded to parents, poorly supervised, subject to harsh or abusive discipline, and have criminal parents and siblings. Adolescents high in negative school experiences dislike school, do poorly in school, spend little time on homework, have low educational and occupational goals, are poorly supervised and disciplined by teachers, and do not get along with teachers. And adolescents high in peer delinquency have close friends who engage in delinquency; spend much time in unsupervised, unstructured activities with their friends; and experience much peer conflict and abuse.

Each of these factors increases strain, fosters the social learning of crime, and reduces control. It is for these reasons that the factors increase delinquency. Further, these factors influence one another. Individuals low in constraint and high in negative emotionality, for example, are more likely to experience poor parenting practices, dislike and do poorly in school, and associate with delinquent peers. To give another example, individuals who experience poor parenting are more likely to be low in constraint and high in negative emotionality, do poorly in school, and associate with delinquent peers. Further, these factors interact with one another in their effect on delinquency. Poor parenting practices, for example, are more likely to lead to delinquency among those who are high in peer delinquency. Finally, engaging in crime, especially crime that is detected by others, can increase the likelihood of subsequent crime for several reasons. Among other things, engaging in crime can contribute to irritability and low constraint, poor parenting practices, and peer delinquency. This is more likely in some conditions than others, however (Agnew 2005b).

Explaining the Gender Gap

AGTCD states that the individual's standing on the four sets of factors affecting delinquency is influenced by a range of factors, particularly the individual's age, gender, socioeconomic status, the socioeconomic status of the individual's community, and race/ethnicity in certain cases (although the effect of race/ethnicity is due largely to its correlation with socioeconomic status). Females are said to score lower on the four factors than males, and that is the primary reason for the gender gap in offending. In particular, females are less likely to be irritable and low in constraint, to experience certain types of poor parenting practices, to have negative school experiences, and to be high in peer delinquency (see previous and Agnew 2005b). Gender differences in irritability/low constraint and peer delinquency are said to be especially important in explaining the gender gap in delinquency.

Explaining Female Delinquency

According to AGTCD, some females are more likely than others to engage in delinquency because they score higher on those four sets of factors that contribute to delinquency. Females who are from poor families and live in poor communities are more likely to fall into this category.

Steffensmeier and Allan's Gendered Theory of Female Offending (SAGTFO)

SAGTFO examines the ways in which gender influences the level and impact of the causal forces identified in many of the aforementioned theories. The theory begins by pointing to the importance of the "organization of gender" and sex differences in biological factors.

The organization of gender refers to gender differences in norms, moral development, and social control. With respect to norms, females are supposed to care for others, especially family members; be subservient to the key males in their lives; act in a weak, submissive manner; and attend to their physical appearance, while protecting their "sexual virtue." With respect to moral development, females are socialized to care for others and be concerned about the maintenance of relationships, while men are socialized to be more independent and competitive. And, with respect to social control, female behavior is more closely monitored and female misbehavior is more likely to be sanctioned. As indicated here, these differences strongly influence gender differences in the motivation for and constraints against crime.

SAGTFO identifies two major sets of sex differences in biological factors. The first involves differences in physical strength, which help account for the much lower rates of violence and certain other types of serious crime by females. The second involves reproductive-sexual differences, along with norms regarding appropriate sexual behavior for males and females. Such differences provide females with greater opportunities for prostitution and reduce their need to commit serious property crimes. These sexual and strength differences also increase the likelihood that females will align themselves with males for protection.

These two sets of factors restrict female opportunities for crime. Females are more often confined to the home and involved in the care of others. Related to this, females are less often involved with delinquent others or engaged in unstructured, unsupervised activities with peers. According to Steffensmeier and Allan (1996), these factors also reduce the motivation for crime among females by "contributing to gender differences in tastes for risk, likelihood of shame and embarrassment, self-control, and assessment of costs versus rewards of crime." Further, opportunities and motivation influence one another: "being able tends to make one more willing, just as being willing increases the prospects for being able" (Steffensmeier and Allan 1996, p. 478).

Finally, gender organization, sex differences in biological factors, and motivations influence the "context of offending," including the circumstances and the nature of the criminal act (e.g., the setting, victim, extent of injury, purpose of the offense). So, for example, females who commit violent crimes are more likely than males to target people they know, are less likely to use weapons, and are less likely to seriously injure their victims.

SAGTFO has not received a formal test, but it helps integrate the gender research with much of the mainstream literature on the causes of crime. Also, the theory provides one model for constructing an integrated theory that combines mainstream and feminist theories. We might, however, expand on SAGTFO by drawing on more recent developments in both feminist and mainstream theories, more explicitly listing the key causes of delinquency, and more fully describing how they affect one another and work together to impact delinquency.

Conclusions

The mainstream theories of delinquency reviewed here have much to say about the causes of female (and male) delinquency and the gender gap in delinquency. A good many causes were listed, but, as indicated, there is reason to believe that some causes may be more important than others. The integrated theories describe certain relationships between these causes and, in the case of Steffensmeier and Allan, describe certain ways in which gender impacts these causes. This concluding section summarizes the major points from the review in terms of a number of "take home points." Such points should be considered by those seeking to develop an integrated theory of female delinquency and to control female delinquency.

Take-Home Points

1. The causes of female delinquency likely include a range of individual characteristics, family factors, school factors, peer factors, perceptions of the costs and benefits of crime, strains or stressors, and a prior history of delinquency. Some of these causes appear to have relatively large, *direct* effects on female delinquency, including low self-control (or low constraint/negative emotionality), parental rejection, poor parental supervision, harsh/erratic discipline, association with delinquent others, time spent in unstructured/unsupervised activities with peers, prior delinquency, delinquent self-image, sexual abuse, and other criminal victimization. These causes should occupy a central place in any integrated theory of female delinquency, and they should be given high priority in efforts to control female delinquency.

2. These causes likely affect delinquency for several reasons. They may lead to negative emotions, such as anger, which create a disposition for delinquency. They may reduce the costs of delinquency. They may foster the impression that delinquency is an appropriate or desirable response in certain situations. And they may lead individuals to believe that they are the type of person who engages in delinquency. It is important to note that, while it is sometimes not possible to alter a cause of delinquency, it may be possible to alter the reason why a cause impacts delinquency. To illustrate, it is not possible to erase a prior history of victimization, but it may be possible to address the anger and depression that such victimization has produced.

3. Most of these causes likely have reciprocal effects on one another. These reciprocal effects are important because they highlight the importance of comprehensive efforts to control delinquency. For example, trying to reduce delinquent peer associations will be quite difficult unless one also addresses those individual characteristics and family problems that help maintain such associations. Further, the causes may sometimes interact with one another in their effect on delinquency. For example, association with delinquent peers is more likely to lead to delinquency among those low in self-control (Wright et al. 2001). Knowledge of such interaction effects also has important policy implications. For example, such knowledge may allow us to reduce the negative effects of delinquent peer association in those situations where it is difficult to reduce contact with delinquent peers.

Mainstream theories, then, have much to say about the causes of female delinquency. Much is still to be learned, however. In particular, there is a strong need for research that (a) considers a broad range of causes, (b) is longitudinal,

(c) includes a good portion of serious offenders, (d) analyzes males separately from females, (e) explores reciprocal and interactive effects, and (f) takes into account possible class and racial/ethnic differences in causal effects (Cernkovich and Giordano 1992; Chesney-Lind and Shelden 2004; Giordano 1978; Heimer 1995; Simpson and Elis 1995; Simpson and Gibbs 2005). In addition, we need research that examines the ways in which the larger social environment, such as the community in which people reside, impacts the causes of delinquency described in this chapter (see Chapter 8 in this book). Further, mainstream theories need to be better integrated with feminist theories and research to provide more complete information on the mechanisms by which gender influences the level and sometimes the effect of the aforementioned causes on delinquency.

2

Feminist Theories of Girls' Delinquency

JODY MILLER AND CHRISTOPHER W. MULLINS

eminist theory provides "a general approach to understanding the status of women [and girls] in society" (Williams 2000, p. 9). In fact,
although there are a range of feminist theories, "all feminist social scientists share the goals of understanding the sources of [gender] inequality
and advocating changes to empower women" (Williams 2000, p. 9). As a
consequence, feminist criminology is distinct from mainstream research on
girls and delinquency because theories of *gender* guide our research, rather
than just theories of delinquency (Daly 1998). Specifically, feminist criminologists examine the role that gender inequality plays in shaping girls' risks
for delinquency, as well as how gender inequality affects the nature of girls'
delinquent activities. In addition, feminist scholars are concerned with how
gender intersects with inequalities based on race, class, and age in shaping
girls' risks and experiences. In this chapter, we provide an overview of feminist approaches to the study of girls' delinquency. Our objective is to highlight why an awareness of gender inequality is crucial to our understanding
girls, delinquency, and violence.

Conceptualizing Gender

To understand the contribution of feminist theoretical insights on girls'
delinquency, it is necessary to start with a general overview of what feminist
theory is, and how our conceptualizations of gender guide our investigation
into the causes of delinquency. Feminist research places the study of delin-

quency and juvenile justice within a framework that recognizes that the social world is thoroughly and systematically shaped by relations of sex and gender. Although feminist scholarship draws from diverse theoretical traditions (Tong 1998), there are a number of central beliefs that guide feminist inquiry. In their influential paper on feminism and criminology, Daly and Chesney-Lind (1988) list five aspects of feminist thought that distinguish it from traditional social inquiry. These include recognition of the following:

- Gender is not a natural fact but a complex social, historical, and cultural product; it is related to, but not simply derived from, biological sex difference and reproductive capacities.
- Gender and gender relations order social life and social institutions in fundamental ways.
- Gender relations and constructs of masculinity and femininity are not symmetrical but are based on an organizing principle of men's superiority and social- and political-economic dominance over women.
- Systems of knowledge reflect men's views of the natural and social world; the production of knowledge is gendered.
- Women (and girls) should be at the center of intellectual inquiry, not peripheral, invisible, or appendages to men (and boys).

In addition, contemporary feminist scholars strive to be attentive to how race and class inequalities intersect with gender inequality, such that girls' experiences vary based on their position in racial and class hierarchies—for example, an impoverished Latina, a working-class white, and a middle-class African American will each have different experiences of gender inequality (Daly and Maher 1998; Maher 1997; Schwartz and Milovanovic 1996; Simpson 1991).

Feminist scholarship on girls' delinquency has been strongly influenced by theoretical developments in other social science disciplines, particularly in sociology (Acker 1990; Connell 2002; Duncan et al. 1997; Fenstermaker and West 2002; Thorne 1994). In this section, we draw from these broader analyses to provide a detailed description of why it is necessary to understand gender—not as a fundamental sex difference, or as an individual-level variable that measures sex differences—as a complex social phenomenon, much like race or class, that is built on structural inequality and shapes individuals' life experiences and outcomes.

Feminist scholars routinely point out that one of the problems with traditional studies of girls and delinquency is that researchers often fail to use adequately sociological conceptualizations of gender and gender inequality in their analyses. Instead, taken-for-granted ideologies about gender are profoundly embedded in social life, and these deeply engrained assumptions often find their way into academic research and theory, as well as into the policies and practices of organizations that deal with delinquent girls. These ideologies include so-called "commonsense" notions of fundamental differences between females and males, coupled with the perception of maleness as the normative standard. This produces scholarship that fundamentally misrepresents and misunderstands the nature of girls' delinquency and produces policies that are misguided at best, and quite harmful at their worst.

Consequently, feminist criminologists have systematically exposed and critiqued the androcentric biases found within traditional criminological theories (Campbell 1991; Smart 1976). Two overarching features of feminist critique are notable. First, much traditional theory has either ignored women and girls—focusing exclusively or implicitly on explaining male participation in crime, and defining females as unimportant or peripheral—or has ignored gender. The tendency to ignore *girls* results in part from the fact that most serious delinquents are male. As a consequence, the field of criminology has been primarily concerned with understanding and explaining boys' and men's offending. Ignoring *gender* results both when theories of male crime don't seek to account for how gender structures and shapes *male* involvement in crime, and when theories assume to be generalizable; that is, theories derived from the study of males are assumed to be able to account for female crime or female offenders. Since theories derived from studies of girls are not seen as generalizable to boys, implicit in this assumption is the notion that females are a subcategory of males (Daly 2000).

A second critique is aimed at theories that do the opposite: theories that are based on beliefs about fundamental differences between females and males—for instance, males are more rational, females more emotional; males are more instrumental, females more relational; males are stronger, females weaker. As taken-for-granted assumptions, these stereotypes about what distinguishes males from females often are reflected in criminological theory and research. It is precisely young women's greater emotional and relational nature, according to these theories, that account for their involvement (or lack thereof) in delinquency, and the nature of their delinquent activities.

Early theories about female delinquency, for example, focused on individual pathologies such as personality disorders and sexual or emotional maladjustment. This is most strongly seen in the work of Thomas (1923a), who ascribed all female offending to individual girls' predilections toward thrill-seeking, and the Gluecks (1934), who claimed the primary cause of girls' delinquencies was girls' inability to control their sexual appetites. Such approaches contrast with theories of male delinquency, which have historically been much more likely to define boys in relation to the broader social world around them. Because many of the gender-based assumptions that have guided criminological theories are hidden or taken for granted, it has taken a feminist lens to bring many of these biases to light. Moreover, while such assumptions about gender are rarely as overt in contemporary research, many recent explanations of girls and delinquency continue to reproduce conventional understandings of gender difference in their search to explain gendered patterns of offending (Miller 2002b). This is especially the case when theories are based on the idea that females and males are fundamentally different.[1]

Even the standard contemporary approaches to studying the causes of delinquency, as illustrated in the various works summarized in this book, approach gender as an individual-level variable, often taking constructs developed to explain male delinquency to examine how these constructs fare in accounting for female delinquency. We'll have more to say on this issue later. For now, suffice it to say that feminist scholars argue that we need to look beyond such dichotomous sex-based approaches, to also examine how the gendered social worlds of youths create unique life experiences for girls and boys, and thus pose unique risks for delinquency. This is not to say that traditional accounts of delinquency are entirely misplaced vis-à-vis girls; instead, we argue that the most promising approach for understanding girls' delinquency is to develop scholarship that draws from the important insights of broader criminological thought, but does so while critically examining the gendered life situations of girls and boys and their impact on delinquency (Simpson 2000).

Consider, for example, sociological analyses of the relationship between race, social class, and delinquency. Popular theoretical approaches include opportunity/strain theories, cultural and social learning theories, and social disorganization theories. Opportunity/strain theories emphasize that disadvantaged groups are denied important legitimate opportunities (for instance, access to good schools, decent jobs) to attain culturally valued success (well-paying, prestigious jobs, for example). The lack of opportunities results in the experience of strain, and some individuals cope with this strain by involving themselves in crime and delinquency (Messner and Rosenfeld 2007). Cultural and learning theories often focus on how living in structurally disadvantaged communities results in cultural adaptations that may favor involvement in crime and delinquency as a means of gaining status and respect (Anderson 1999). Likewise, social disorganization theories focus on deleterious neighborhood conditions that impede community members' ability to control neighborhood crime and delinquency (Bursik and Grasmick 1993a). Although these theories vary in their causal explanations of delinquency, each is grounded in thoroughly social explanations of offending, including recognition of the important role that inequality plays in generating delinquency and crime.

Imagine, by contrast, if studies of the relationships between race, class, and delinquency were conceptualized in the way that studies about gender and delinquency are often approached. It would mean, for example, assuming that African Americans and whites are innately different from one another—that biological, physiological, or psychological differences account for variations in patterns of delinquency, rather than differences that materialize from the structural organization of society. In fact, such theories were prominent in criminological thought in the nineteenth century, but scholars ultimately recognized that such an approach was flawed, precisely because it failed to account for the complex social phenomenon that is racial inequality in society.

Contemporary approaches of girls' delinquency are not so blatantly reductionistic in their orientation as nineteenth-century research on race. However, they are often guided by subtle assumptions about gender that are rooted in notions of natural difference, rather than examining how—as with race—gender-based patterns emerge from structural inequalities and the socially constructed meanings about gender that emerge to account for and justify these inequalities. So what does such a theoretical approach look like? Sociologically, it means studying gender and gender inequality at the macro level[2] (overarching structural patterns of gender inequality and their effects on crime and delinquency), at the meso level (gender inequality within the context of social institutions such as family, school, and neighborhood), and at the micro level (interpersonal relationships within and across gender). Such an approach allows us to examine the ways in which gender structures life chances and opportunities, and generates and legitimates cultural norms of difference and inequality. Examined in this way, the study of gender inequality can yield insights into its impact on girls' and boys' risks for delinquency, their experiences as participants in delinquency, and their treatment by the institutions charged with addressing the problem of delinquency.

All of this may sound a bit abstract for those not familiar with feminist criminology. But hopefully some of the illustrations that follow will help to make it more concrete. The bottom line is that gender inequality has a strong impact on girls' life experiences and life chances, and so it should be at the center of our inquiries as we attempt to understand girls' delinquency. It is only with the inclusion of an understanding of gender inequality that girls' delinquency can be fully understood and theorized. This means that gender must be understood as more than an individual-level variable that measures sex differences. It is a complex social structure in society in much the same ways that social class, race, and age are structural features of society.

Feminist Approaches to Understanding Girls' Delinquency

Two questions have guided mainstream criminological examinations of gender for the last several decades: the question of generalizability and the gender ratio problem. In this section, we will briefly review and critique these approaches for theorizing girls' delinquency, and will then describe more profitable developments within feminist criminology, drawing from Daly's (1998) conceptual schema of *gendered pathways to lawbreaking, gendered crime,* and *gendered lives.*[3] Although feminist theorists have been critical of traditional criminological approaches, there is nonetheless recognition that "many seminal ideas that have emerged in criminological thought can be integrated and/or elaborated in ways that can inform gendered criminological theory" (Simpson 2000). We orient our discussion to emphasize the ways in which feminist analyses challenge and enrich our attempts to understand girls' delinquency.

The Problem of Generalizability

For more than a century, the theories developed to explain why people commit crime have actually been theories of why *males* commit crime. Ironically, the gender gap in offending—that is, males' disproportionate involvement in crime and delinquency—has long been a primary rationale for this focus (Britton 2000). In many cases, this orientation is not outwardly stated; instead theories are presumed to be "gender neutral," and it has been taken for granted that a given theoretical approach can be applied to males or females. Given the recognition of gender as a structuring feature of society, feminists have explicitly posed the questions: "Do theories of men's crime [and boys' delinquency] apply to women [and girls]? Can the logic of such theories be modified to include women [and girls]?" (Daly and Chesney-Lind 1988, p. 514). If not, what alternative explanations can account for female offending? Scholars who have attempted to test whether mainstream theories of delinquency can be generalized to girls have focused on such constructs as the family, social learning, delinquent peer relationships, strain, and deterrence. For the most part, these studies have found mixed results (Broidy 2001; Smith and Paternoster 1987). As Kruttschnitt (1996) summarizes, "it appears that the factors that influence delinquent development differ for males and females in some contexts but not other" (p. 141).

This lack of consistent findings is unsurprising from a feminist perspective. While mainstream theorists who include gender in their analyses often search for generalizable explanations of delinquency, and thus examine whether the same processes are at work in explaining female and male offending, there are several key limitations to this approach. First, they cannot account for the gender ratio of offending—that is, boys' disproportionate involvement in delinquency.[4] Dramatic gender differences in rates of offending suggest that a gender-neutral etiological process is not occurring. This is not to suggest that many of the basic factors included in such analyses are unimportant for understanding crime across gender, but to highlight that it is necessary to examine whether and how such elements influence offending across gender in the same way or with equal force.[5] Moreover, feminist scholars recognize gender as an important feature of the social organization of society and thus of girls' and boys' experiences. Theories that attempt to generalize across gender are unable to address these pivotal social forces (Daly 1998).

For instance, in much of this research, it is often taken for granted that variables or constructs have the same meaning for males and females. While such elements as learning, peer influences, social control, family attachment and supervision, and individual strain and opportunity are essential in the understanding of crime for males and females, recent work shows that, indeed, these factors have variant influence within and across gender (Alarid, Burton, and Cullen 2000; Broidy 2001; Burton et al. 1998; Heimer and De Coster 1999; Katz 2000; Mears et al. 1998). Because of the gendered nature of girls' and boys' lives, important explanatory factors take on different meanings and have different consequences for females and males. For example, Broidy and Agnew's (1997) revision of Agnew's (1992) general strain theory highlights that while broad experiences of strain can produce criminality in both males and females, there are a number of important differences across gender in (a) the sources of strain,

(b) the ways in which strain is interpreted and processed, and (c) the sorts of crimes that result. Moreover, they identify these differences as grounded in gender-based social conditions and processes, rather than merely reflecting individual-level differences between females and males.

This sort of work demonstrates why feminists insist that while some of the theoretical concepts found in presumably "gender-neutral" theories of delinquency may be relevant or useful for understanding girls' offending, gendered theories—that is, those that take gender and gender stratification into account—are preferable to approaches that assume measures or constructs are gender neutral (Daly 2000; Simpson 2000). However, this does not mean that "gender difference" is the sole focus of feminist research. Instead, feminists ask the question: When, how, and why does gender matter? Recent endeavors that examine similarities and differences within and across gender, and especially those that conceptualize gender beyond the individual level, have proven especially fruitful in understanding the causes of crime.

The Gender Ratio of Crime

One problem with attempts to generalize theories across gender is that all of this work begs the question of why it is that females and males have vastly divergent rates of criminal offending. This is the gender ratio problem. Scholars who address this raise the following questions: "Why are women [and girls] less likely than men [and boys] to be involved in crime? Conversely, why are men [and boys] more crime-prone than women [and girls]? What explains [these] gender differences?" (Daly and Chesney-Lind 1988, p. 515). These questions have led scholars to pay attention to gender differences and inequalities, and to develop theories that can account for variations in girls' and boys' delinquency (Bottcher 2001; Hagan, Gillis, and Simpson 1985; Heimer and De Coster 1999).

With boys as the starting point, explanations for the gender ratio of delinquency are typically pursued by asking: What are the factors that limit or block girls' involvement in crime? But to *only* ask this question again reflects an androcentric perspective that makes males the norm upon which females deviate through their limited offending. Inverting this question, and attempting to account for why boys have considerably higher rates of delinquency than girls, raises an important set of additional queries. For instance, a key question is what is it about being male—and about masculinity specifically—that accounts for boys' disproportionate levels of offending?[6]

Moreover, traditional and mainstream approaches typically explain the gender gap by drawing from stereotypical notions of dichotomous gender difference, and treat gender as an individual trait. It does us no good if we merely say "girls are less _____ than boys,"[7] and leave it at that. These general behaviors and perceptions have their roots within structural conditions. Thus, feminist criminologists see as more promising those approaches that treat gender as a key element of social organization (Bottcher 2001; Heimer and De Coster 1999). Not only does such an approach avoid the assumption of essential gender difference, but it also allows for a more complex examination of the gender gap. For instance, data on crime trends reveal that the gender gap remains more persistent for some crimes than others, fluctuates over time (Steffensmeier and Schwartz 2004), and varies by race/ethnicity, class, and age (Sommers and Baskin 1993). Thus, there is no uniform or static gender ratio of offending, leaving the differential gap across offenses an important site for inquiry.

Given that women/girls and men/boys live in diverse structural conditions—conditions that are shaped especially by race and class inequality—approaches that seek simply to address a uniform gender gap miss the opportunity to examine how causal factors differentially shape girls' and boys' offending across crosscutting social positions. For instance, there is evidence of a link between "underclass" conditions and urban African American females' offending that does not hold explanatory power for female offending in other contexts (Hill and Crawford 1990). Likewise, Steffensmeier and Haynie's (2000b) recent structural analysis of homicide reveals variations across gender by age.

The most promising avenues for exploring the complexities of the gender ratio of offending are those that go beyond the reliance on "descriptive and predictive numerical analyses" (Daly 1998, p. 95) for theoretical development. To demonstrate, we draw from Daly's (1998) conceptual schema and examine three areas of inquiry within feminist scholarship that have resulted in a more complex examination of gender and offending:

- *Gendered Pathways to Lawbreaking:* What trajectories (e.g., life events and experiences) bring males and females to offending? What factors and social contexts facilitate entrée to (and desistance from) offending, and in what ways are these gendered?
- *Gendered Crime:* What are the specific contexts and qualities of female and male offending? How are various facets of offending socially organized?
- *Gendered Lives:* How does gender organize the daily lives of females and males, and how does gender structure available courses of action and identities? How do these experiences intersect with crime and criminality?

The typology we draw from here provides a useful means of organizing the primary thematic aspects of feminist research, although much of the research we draw from addresses problems and questions across this categorization, and also speaks to the gender ratio of offending.

Gendered Pathways to Lawbreaking

In the early 1990s, feminist scholars began carefully examining what is now commonly referred to as "gendered pathways." Emphasizing "biographical elements, life-course trajectories and developmental sequences" (Daly, 1998, p. 97), the pathways approach seeks to map the life experiences that lead women and girls to offending as well as desistance (Daly 1992; Giordano, Cernkovich, and Rudolph

2002). One of the important conceptual underpinnings of this research is the recognition of the "blurred boundaries" of victimization and offending. For example, young women who run away from home to escape abuse often inadvertently enter into more dangerous and abusive situations on the streets at the same time that their escape from abusive homes is criminalized. As Chesney-Lind and Pasko (2004) observe, girls' earlier victimization "set[s] the stage for their entry into youth homelessness, unemployment, drug use, survival sex (and sometimes prostitution), and, ultimately, other serious criminal acts" (p. 5).

Gilfus (1992), for example, analyzed life history interviews with incarcerated female offenders. She found that the women's childhoods and adolescence were plagued with abuse and neglect, and many had run away from home in response. Once on the streets, an "onset of drug use, truancy, and stealing" (1992, p. 72) followed, with a large minority entering into juvenile prostitution as a survival strategy. Illegal work was done simply to survive, but further enmeshed the young women in criminal networks. As they transitioned into adulthood, the vast majority experienced continued victimization and many developed drug habits. Thus, this work speaks not only to life contexts that place girls at risk for offending, but also emphasizes the life consequences for young women that can result.

While mainstream criminology has not focused on pathways approaches, developmental and life-course approaches have become increasingly popular. There is also a small but growing literature within this area that expressly compares males and females (Keenan, Stouthamer-Loeber, and Loeber 2004; Moffitt et al. 2001; Silverthorn and Frick 1999; Tibbetts and Piquero 1999). However, similar to the problems noted earlier concerning traditional studies of female offending, these works are rarely done with specific attention to important sociological constructs related to gender. For example, they rarely examine how socialization into gender scripts leads boys and girls to variously interpret sexual or physical victimizations and how these interpretive patterns shape future offending. Instead, the research typically identifies and tests similar causal mechanisms across gender in the search for individual-level gender differences or similarities, rather than examining potentially gender-specific risks related to structural or situational features of gender (Haynie 2003).

Despite the important insights of the "blurred boundaries" approach, including its disruption of the victim/offender dichotomy, some feminist scholars have highlighted that this "leading scenario" of female offending (Daly, 1992, p. 136) needs to be broadened to recognize the diversity of women's and girls' pathways to offending. Moreover, an exclusive emphasis on victimization as the key pathway to female offending can overlook other important facets of women's and girls' lives that put them at risk for offending, including other manifestations of gender inequality. For instance, Gaarder and Belknap's (2002) recent analysis identifies the importance of not only violence and victimization, but also racial and economic marginality, school experiences, structural dislocation, and drug and alcohol use in explaining girls' delinquency.

For example, in-depth analyses of the role of specific social institutions in shaping girls' risks for delinquency are needed, particularly when these studies examine the impact of patterns of gender arrangements within these institutions. Take the family, for instance. Feminist criminologists have focused considerable attention on the impact of family relations in shaping girls' delinquency. As noted, this includes a focus on the effects of incest and sexual abuse on girls' delinquency, patterns of abuse that push girls to run away from home (thus exposing them to delinquent street networks). However, this also includes the study of how patterns of family life can teach young women traditional gender values and behaviors, and thus act as a protective factor vis-à-vis delinquency, even while restricting girls' full participation in public life.

On the other hand, although criminologists routinely examine the role of schooling in explaining youths' risks for offending (Gottfredson 2001), this is an institutional arena that has received limited attention with regard to how gender inequalities within schools shape girls' risks for and patterns of offending (but see Ferguson [2000] regarding race/gender and delinquency among African American boys). Ample evidence exists that schools are an important site of gender inequality (Orenstein 1994). For example, sexual harassment in schools is known to be widespread (AAUW Educational Foundation 2001), but criminologists have not studied whether exposure to sexual harassment and other gender-based inequities in school increases the likelihood that girls will participate in delinquency in response.

It is also the case that studies relying only on female samples cannot sufficiently specify whether and how such risks influence pathways to offending across gender. One area in which feminist pathways analyses have been applied broadly is in the study of youth gangs (Joe and Chesney-Lind 1995; Miller 2001; Moore 1991; Portillos 1999). This research is strengthened by the direct comparison of males and females, or gang and nongang girls, in the same social environments. Such a comparative approach provides a more definitive understanding of how gender impacts on girls' risks for offending. As with other areas of criminological inquiry, research on girls' pathways/risks for gang involvement has generally included two approaches: analyses of etiological risk factors from survey research, and qualitative analyses that focus on girls' accounts of why they joined gangs, and their life contexts both prior to and at the time of joining. Although differing in their approach, most studies include a focus on structural and neighborhood conditions, the family, and peers. In addition, feminist scholarship has focused specific attention to victimization, and this is routinely found to be an important risk for gang involvement among young women (Joe and Chesney-Lind 1995; Miller 2001).

Moore's (1991) work is particularly important, because of her comparative sample. She documents a myriad of family problems that contribute to the likelihood of gang involvement for young women: childhood abuse and neglect, domestic violence among adults (particularly the abuse of female caregivers), alcohol and drug addiction in the family, witnessing the arrest of family members, having a family member who is chronically ill, and experiencing a death in the family during childhood. Her conclusion, based on comparisons of male and female gang members, is that young women are considerably more likely to come from families that have numerous of these problems. Likewise, Miller's (2001) comparison of gang and nongang (but delinquent) girls highlighted the importance of cumulative risks for girls' gang involvement. Portillos' (1999) study of Chicana gang members suggests that girls are also drawn to gang involvement as a means of escaping oppressive patriarchal conditions in the home.

While much of the feminist scholarship described thus far is qualitative, and we have suggested that much quantitative research has not adequately conceptualized gender, we end this section by highlighting a study that significantly raises the bar for quantitative research on how gender shapes risks for delinquency (in this case violence). Heimer and De Coster's (1999) analysis illustrates the tremendous benefit that results from a complex conceptualization of gender. In their "The Gendering of Violent Delinquency," these scholars address two key theoretical problems of interest to feminist criminologists: *within-gender* variability in the use of violence, and variability in violence *across gender* (i.e., the gender ratio of offending). In doing so, Heimer and De Coster provide a theoretical model of the causes of delinquency that can address differences across and within gender, as well as between-gender similarities. They accomplish this by blending insights from a traditional criminological theory—differential association theory—with feminist theory about the definitions, meanings, and impact of gender.

Heimer and De Coster outline a complex theoretical model of violent delinquency based on the differentiated experiences of young women and young men that result from gender inequality. They focus specifically on the interplay between social structure and culture, and argue that different social structural positions—based on gender, race, social class—result in variations in two significant cultural processes: family controls and peer associations. With regard to family controls, Heimer and De Coster differentiate between two types of family controls, which they suggest operate differently for males and females. First, *direct parental controls* include such things as supervision and coercive discipline. On the other hand, *emotional bonding* is a more indirect form of control that results from emotional attachment to families. Particularly as young women are taught to value interpersonal relationships to a greater extent than young men, Heimer and De Coster argue that indirect controls resulting from emotional bonds to the family are the primary controls over girls' behavior, whereas direct controls have a stronger impact on reducing boys' delinquency.

Such findings strongly illustrate our earlier emphasis on precision and contextualization: it is not that boys are less susceptible to parental bonding, as Hirschi (1969) or other individually oriented theories might suggest. Rather, boys' violence does not place the emotional bond between child and parent at risk in the same way that girls' violence does. Quite simply, some level of aggression in boys is both allowed and encouraged. For girls, it is a double deviance— not only have they broken rules of behavior about interpersonal violence, they have also violated the key gender expectations of passivity and attention to inter-personal relationships.

With regard to peer associations, they suggest that boys are more likely to have exposure to friends who engage in aggressive activities. This means boys are also more likely than girls to be exposed to norms favorable to violence. These two cultural processes—family control and peer associations—along with prior histories of violent behavior, influence two cultural outcomes: the extent that youths learn violent definitions (e.g., definitions of violence as an appropriate behavior) and gender definitions (traditional beliefs about the proper behavior of males and females, or of masculinity and femininity). Youths who internalize cultural values accepting of violence are more likely to engage in delinquency. However, cultural definitions of violence also run counter to traditional defini-tions of femininity, which stress "nurturance, passivity, nonaggressiveness, and physical and emotional weakness" (Heimer and De Coster, 1999, p. 283). Thus, the attitudes and beliefs young women learn about appropriate femininity will have a direct effect on their likelihood of engaging in violence.

Through a sophisticated analysis of the National Youth Survey, Heimer and De Coster tested their theoretical model and found strong support for its ability to explain variations in girls' and boys' use of violence, as well as variations in the use of violence within gender, based on the causal pathway of social structural factors (positions tied to race, class, gender) shaping cultural processes (family controls, peer associations), shaping cultural outcomes (violent definitions, gen-der definitions), shaping the likelihood that youths participate in violence. They explain:

> In short, the conclusion of our research is that violent delinquency is "gendered" in significant ways. Adolescent violence can be seen as a prod-uct of gendered experiences, gender socialization, and the patriarchal system in which they emerge. Thus, consistent with feminist arguments, gender differences in violence are ultimately rooted in power differences. (Heimer and De Coster, 1999, p. 305)

Significantly, individual-level character differences across gender do not account for the gender gap in violence; instead, the intersection of gendered meanings with the contexts of family and peer interactions expose males and females to different risks for learning violent definitions and thus engaging in violence (Bottcher 2001).

Gendered Crime
Research on the gendered social organization and situational contexts of crime represents a clear growth area in feminist criminology in recent years. In fact, the analysis of situational contexts of offending has gained momentum in the discipline, both by feminist scholars and by those not using feminist approaches. Among mainstream scholars, the situational turn was partially in response to

the development of a conceptual distinction between the criminal event and criminality as a set of individual characteristics (Cohen and Felson 1979; Cornish and Clarke 1986; Gottfredson and Hirschi 1990). Thus criminologists brought renewed attention to the aspects of social situations that produce criminal events, as well as the individual decision-making and opportunity structures necessary for offending. While such questions date back to Sutherland (1934), they began receiving systematic attention in the 1990s. Most mainstream work in this vein has been grounded theoretically in various opportunity theories (Felson 1998) or within symbolic interactionist approaches (Tedeschi and Felson 1994). Some of this work has relied on qualitative data in order to produce thick descriptions of circumstances and events (Wright and Decker 1994, 1997).

Gendered attention to organizational and situational aspects of crime emerged with Steffensmeier's pioneering analyses in the 1980s of institutional sexism and gender segregation in criminal networks (Steffensmeier 1983; Steffensmeier and Terry 1986). As a logical evolution of feminist criminology, which sees gender as potentially omnirelevant to social behavior and recognizes the situational nature of gender accomplishment, some feminist scholars have turned attention to how situational gender expectations and gendered opportunity structures shape criminal events. This work has taken several notable directions. While most research in this area has focused on adult women, it is nonetheless an important area of inquiry for understanding girls' delinquency as well.

First, as noted in the previous section, an important contribution of feminist criminology has been to highlight the "blurred boundaries" of victimization and offending. While this approach most typically emphasizes the experience of victimization as a background risk for subsequent involvement in crime, feminists have also analyzed victimization as a key situational factor in the foreground of offending. This is most evident in feminist analyses of women who kill their abusive spouses. These events not only involve long-term patterns of serious abuse, but are often triggered by a culminating victimization incident that directly results in the woman's violence (Richie 1996). Likewise, Lisa Maher's (1997) ethnography of a drug economy analyzes one form of female offending—"viccing"—that emerges from the widespread victimization and devaluation of women. Maher's work documents the proliferation of viccing—in which women in the sex trade rob their clients—as a form of resistance against their greater vulnerability to victimization and cheapened sex markets within the drug economy. Comparing viccing with traditional forms of robbery, Maher and Curtis conclude: "The fact that the act [of viccing] itself is little different from any other instrumental robbery belies the reality that the motivations undergirding it are more complex and, indeed, are intimately linked with women's collective sense of the devaluation of their bodies and their work" (1992, p. 246).

In addition to the emphasis on blurred boundaries, recent feminist research also suggests that there are contexts in which situational norms favorable to women's crime and girls' delinquency exist, and these are not just about avoiding or responding to victimization, but also result in economic gain, status, recognition, or emotional rewards such as the excitement, revenge, or alleviation of boredom (Miller 1998; Simpson 1991; Simpson and Elis 1995). Although key motivational factors in these instances may not be explicitly "gendered," this work nonetheless maintains a gendered inquiry by moving beyond individual motivation to examine how women and girls navigate gender-stratified environments, and how they accommodate and adapt to gender inequality in their commission of crime. If a goal of situational crime analysis is to examine "the decision-making process of offenders confronted with specific contexts" (Einstadter and Henry 1995, p. 70), this cannot be accomplished without paying attention to the gendered contexts of the decision-making process, and the ways in which "gendered status structures this participation" (Maher 1997, p. 13).

Still another feminist approach to the study of situational context is reflected in those studies that have used sociological theory on gender as situated accomplishment (West and Fenstermaker 1995; West and Zimmerman 1987). As described above, this perspective emphasizes how women/girls and men/boys "do gender" in response to normative beliefs about femininity and masculinity, and has been incorporated into feminist accounts of crime as a means of explaining differences in female and male offending (Messerschmidt 1993, 2004; Newburn and Stanko 1994; Simpson and Elis 1995). Here, for instance, violence is described as a "'resource' for . . . demonstrating masculinity within a given context or situation" (Simpson and Elis, 1995, p. 50). Although this normative emphasis has primarily been brought to bear on male offending and constructions of masculinity, feminist theorists recently have attempted to account for female crime based on the same framework, but with more limited success (Miller 2002b). Studies of situational context have also included the framing of events within meso-level (e.g., neighborhood) and macro-level (e.g., structural) contexts. Again, an eye to gender enhances our understanding. As noted, extant research highlights that social networks, especially those on the streets, are highly gender-segregated (Anderson 1999; Bourgois 1995; Maher 1997; Miller 1998, 2001; Mullins and Wright 2003; Steffensmeier and Terry 1986). Moreover, concentrated disadvantage strongly shapes the nature of street social networks, which then shapes the interactions within these networks. For example, James, Johnson, and Raghavan (2004) found that residence in a low-income, disorganized community increased girls' and women's exposure to both drugs and violence and this connection was best understood through an examination of how living in this environment shaped their social networks (Simpson 1991; Sommers and Baskin 1993). They note that such neighborhoods "severely restricted [women's and girls'] social networks, both because there were few choices of friends available and because the threat of violence made social activity outside the house unappealing" (2004, pp. 1006–1007; McCarthy, Felmlee, and Haga 2004). In a similar vein, Rountree and Warner (1999) examine how gendered neighborhood social ties affect community crime rates. This work highlights the importance of examining gender beyond the individual level.

Drawing from these various approaches, one of the strongest contributions of situational analysis lies in its ability to examine both similarities and divergences between female and male offending. Much traditional work in criminology—drawing from the character dichotomy noted earlier—suggests that while male violence is instrumental, direct, and highly physical, female violence is expressive, indirect, and relational (Hagan and Foster 2003; Steffensmeier and Allan 1996). Such interpretations embrace rather than challenge taken-for-granted assumptions concerning gendered behaviors. While many scholars have found notable differences between male and female offending, especially in the realm of violence, this binary analytical framework ignores variation within male and female violence. Males *do* engage in relationally focused violence (e.g., fighting in defense of a friend or loved one; see Anderson 1999; Mullins, Wright, and Jacobs 2004) and females engage in instrumental violence (Baskin and Sommers 1997; Miller 1998). In fact, the routine framing of women's and girls' violence as expressive often functions to discredit and undermine their more instrumental goals (Miller and White 2003). Thus, it is through the contextual examination of violent episodes and other offending, with strong attention to situational dynamics, that similarities and differences within and across gender can be uncovered and explained.

Let us return to the area of gang research as an illustration. Miller's (2001) research on young women's participation in street gangs paid particular attention to how gender inequality shaped the nature of girls' activities—including delinquency—within gangs. She found, for instance, that gang girls were much more likely than their non-gang counterparts to be involved in a variety of delinquent activities. Much of this has to do with group processes within gangs themselves, rather than self-selection of delinquent youths into joining gangs (Thornberry 1997). Thus, to understand girls' delinquency within gangs, it was necessary to look at the foreground of gang life. Miller looked not just at comparisons between gang and non-gang girls, but also at variations among young women in gangs, and examined the role that gender-based norms and gender inequality played in girls' delinquency within gangs. She found that only a minority of young women were involved in ongoing serious delinquency, while the majority were not (Fagan 1990). Moreover, young women discussed the ways that gender differentiated young women's gang crime from young men's. They highlighted that gun use was primarily the purview of young men and knives and fists the purview of young women. Many young women expressed moral ambivalence about the gun use and homicides associated with gangs, and also described being excluded from such behavior by young men. Likewise, drug selling, especially crack sales, were also seen as primarily a male endeavor.

Nonetheless, Miller documents important similarities across gender, buttressed by girls' discussions of status issues and gang rivalries. Most notably, although their confrontations with rival gang members tended to manifest themselves in different ways (fistfights, rather than drive-by shootings), girls' confrontations—like boys'—were motivated by gang processes. This finding challenges the tendency to describe girls' use of violence in gangs as resulting only or primarily from protective or defensive responses to gendered vulnerability. Instead, girls described participating in attacks based on retaliation, protection of gang territory, and "being down" for their gangs and gang friends. Even when describing crimes less in keeping with recognized gang motives, girls' accounts highlighted the importance of peer contexts in facilitating their delinquency. Despite the gendered nature of girls' crime, their participation was often an extension of (nongendered) gang processes, suggesting the importance of examining gender inequality in ways that capture its complexity, and also attend to within-gender variations and similarities/differences across gender.

In addition to examining how the foreground of gang participation shapes delinquency, Miller also examined how gangs, delinquency, and gender shaped girls' risks for victimization in gangs. For instance, young women's lesser involvement in serious gang crime decreased their exposure to rival gang violence, but also increased the likelihood that they would be mistreated by their own gang peers when they were seen as unlikely to stand up for themselves. Miller documented the existence of sexual mistreatment within gangs, most notably in the form of sexual initiations and their consequences. The male-dominated structures of girls' gangs shaped their experiences within gangs, as well as their sense of themselves and other young women. And yet, gang participation offered status and recognition not available in other contexts of their lives, allowing them to draw particular advantages from their gang participation, despite the associated costs.

Miller's study illustrates the utility of situational analyses of gender and delinquency. Through close attention to the nature and dynamics of criminal situations, feminist approaches can uncover and elucidate in a more precise fashion how gender operates in both the foreground and background of delinquency events. Through the discovery of contingencies, attention to variations in delinquency within and across gender, and careful examination of the evolution of offending events and the gendered and other contexts in which they emerge, this form of inquiry can more precisely specify dynamic relationships between gender and delinquency.

Gendered Lives
Daly (1998) describes the concept of *gendered lives* as the examination of the "significant differences in the ways that women [and girls] experience society compared with men [and boys]" (p. 98). Compared with the other aspects of feminist criminology we have described, this is perhaps the most challenging, because it requires systematic attention to gender well beyond the analysis of crime. As Daly (1998) notes, "rather than analyze gender as a correlate of crime, one would analyze crime as a correlate of gender" (p. 99). Feminist research has made important inroads in the study of pathways to offending and the gendered nature of offending, but less work has had the scope required to address gendered lives. In this section, we highlight two studies that have accomplished this goal.

Jean Bottcher's (2001) analysis of gender and delinquency focuses not on gender as individual action, but instead on the gendering of social practices. This provides a conceptualization of gender as active and dynamic, and "[m]ost critically, this approach decenters the individual, enabling us to isolate components of social practices, which ... include rules that govern human behavior and the resources that make human activity possible" (p. 897). Based on comparative interviews with male and female siblings, Bottcher's analysis draws from Giddens' structuration theory, and "plac[es] types of activities—activities by which gender was defined—at the center of the analytic frame" (p. 903).

Bottcher (2001) identified three broad types of social practices: making friends and having fun, relating sexually and becoming parents, and surviving hardship and finding purpose. Within these, she also identified more specific gendered dimensions that were related to exposure to and risks for delinquency. For example, gender-segregated friendship groups, boundary maintenance among male peer groups, and male access to privacy and nighttime activities "continuously placed the high-risk males, compared with the high-risk females, at greater risk of delinquent involvement" (p. 910). Likewise, the meanings and rules guiding sexual relationships and childcare responsibilities had similar consequences.

Notable in Bottcher's (2001) approach is that her emphasis on *practices*, rather than individuals, challenges the gender dichotomy often found in studies of gender and crime. She demonstrates that these gendered patterns are not universally applicable to all males or all females:

> Some male-typed social practices appear to encourage or enable delinquent activity for either sex. Conversely, some female-typed social practices appear to discourage delinquent activity for both sexes. Thus, the social practices of gender disclose social conditions and activities that influence delinquent involvement, regardless of sex. (p. 904)

This approach offers a promising avenue for the study of gendered lives, particularly when coupled with analyses of gendered crime, and grounded in how gendered practices may be shaped by other social positions such as race, class, and generation. Moreover, her study demonstrates that the broader examination of gendered lives contributes to our understanding of the gender gap in offending, as well as gendered pathways.

Lisa Maher's (1997) *Sexed Work* also provides a systematic examination of gendered lives, based on several years of ethnography and in-depth interviews with women in a street-level drug economy. Although her research focuses on adult women rather than adolescents, we include it here because it provides an important model for how to examine girls' delinquency in ways that are specifically attentive to gender inequality, as well as inequalities based on race and class. While focused primarily on the foreground of offending, her groundbreaking study goes beyond "gendered crime" through her complex, layered account of women's everyday lives, including their participation in the local drug market. Maher's study is particularly exemplary because of her consistent examination of the intersections of race, class, and gender in shaping women's experiences and lives, and illustrates the strengths of feminist scholarship that moves beyond an exclusive emphasis on gender. Like other feminist scholars whose works we've highlighted, Maher blends feminist analysis with a traditional theoretical approach—in this case, cultural reproduction theory.

Revealing the interdependence of formal and informal economies, including the illicit drug economy, the study focuses on the impact of stratification within formal and informal market economies, and the consequent truncation of women's economic opportunities. This not only provides a broad motivation toward crime, but also limits females to a specific set of criminal activities and methods of crime accomplishment. Although some (primarily nonfeminist) scholars have suggested the drug trade has opened new opportunities for women, Maher's (1997) study provides compelling evidence to the contrary. Gender inequality, as she demonstrates, is institutionalized on the streets: gender segregation and stereotypes of women as unreliable and weak limit women's participation in informal economic street networks. Specifically, the study documents a rigid gender division of labor in the drug economy, shaped as well along racial lines, in which women are "clearly disadvantaged compared to their male counterparts" (p. 54).

Describing the three spheres of income generation on the streets—drug business hustles, nondrug hustles, and sex work—Maher details the ways in which women are excluded from more lucrative opportunities, and find sex work one of their few viable options for making money. Moreover, the introduction of crack cocaine into urban drug markets has further disadvantaged women by increasing competition and drastically reducing market prices, as well as increasing the degradation and mistreatment that women often experience on the streets. In addition, she shows how racial stratification further differentiates the opportunities and experiences of white, African American, and Latina women within street-level sex work. Specifically, clients found white females more desirable (but they were also seen as more easily taken advantage of), Latinas had advantages and costs associated with their being "neighborhood girls," and African American females were seen as less sexually desirable and more dangerous.

Sexed Work challenges several dimensions of previous work on women's participation in drug markets—including both previous feminist studies and traditional criminological approaches. For example, it contradicts "the highly sexualized images of women crack users that dominate the social science literature" (Maher 1997, p. 195). This sexualized imagery—of desperate women willing to do "anything" for their next hit—is part and parcel of the dominant view of drug users (and especially women) as pathological, dependent, and lacking any control over their lives. In contrast, Maher shows that women are involved in a wide array of income-generating activities within the drug economy, with occupational norms governing their activities, despite the rigid division of labor on the streets.

Likewise, Maher's analysis provides a critique of feminist research that overemphasizes women's victimization. When "women's lawbreaking is presented as symptomatic of their victimization" (p. 200), it likewise denies women agency and continues to frame them only in terms of passivity and dependence. Instead, Maher's research displays a complex understanding of the relationship between structure and agency. As she summarizes:

> I have tried to strike a balance between the twin discourses of victimization and volition that inform current understandings of women's drug-related lawbreaking. While this space must be large enough to include the constraints of sexism, racism, and poverty that structure women's lives, it cannot be so big as to overwhelm the active, creative, and often contradictory choices, adaptations, and resistances that constitute women's criminal agencies. (Maher 1997, p. 201)

Maher's work exemplifies the aspects of feminist thought highlighted at the beginning of this chapter, and its scope and depth demonstrates the benefits of a *gendered lives* approach for understanding how gender intersects with cross-cutting structural positions, and how ideologies and social practices reproduce structural inequalities. Her approach provides an important model for how we can better understand the contexts of girls' delinquency, keeping gender and gender inequality at the forefront of our analyses.

Conclusions

Contemporary feminist theory is rich with theoretical development and stimulating research that improves our understanding of girls' delinquency. The fusion of gendered theories with criminological theories has advanced our understanding of the complex ways that gender intersects with crime and criminality. In this chapter, we have broadly explored the major theoretical and empirical directions within feminist criminology, focusing specific attention on research about girls and delinquency, and highlighting studies that bring conceptual attention not just to delinquency but also to gender. Drawing from Daly's (1998) typology, we have examined the central themes that remain current in feminist criminology, including the gender ratio question, gendered pathways, gendered crime, and gendered lives. Some of these have been particularly fruitful in recent years.

With recent qualitative work, we have seen the development of an increasing number of studies that highlight situational contexts and the overall complexity of gender's relation to delinquency. These works have pushed the field well past dichotomous conceptualizations of gender, as is evident as well in recent quantitative analyses of gender (Heimer and De Coster 1999). As these works emphasize the contingent nature of gender, they compel us to envision delinquency similarly. Likewise, feminist pathways research has drawn scholarly attention to those experiences that lead girls into delinquent behaviors and networks, and have also pointed toward critically needed changes in prevention and intervention programs (Acoca 1998b; Henriques and Manam-Rupert 2001). This body of research will be strengthened further with more explicit comparisons across gender. And while the last theme, gendered lives, has received the least systematic attention, it perhaps offers the most promising potential for illuminating the intertwined nature of gendered social structures, behavioral expectations, and identities with delinquency. All of this work will be strengthened with continued systematic attention to the intersections of gender with race, class, generation, and other structuring features of society.

Contemporary guiding questions among feminist researchers have opened up a scholarly space that benefits from the rich theoretical tradition and contemporary developments in criminology, without remaining bound by its often narrow and androcentric conceptualizations of gender. The study of girls' delinquency has much to gain by drawing from feminist conceptualizations of gender. This work continues to advance our understanding of the complex relationship between gender and delinquency. Continuing developments, both qualitative and quantitative, promise to continue the refinement of our understanding not just of delinquency, but of gender as well.

Thus, we conclude our overview by asking readers to keep feminist conceptualizations of gender in mind as they read the chapters in this book. We hope it raises the key questions: Where does our knowledge best seem to capture an understanding of the impact of gender inequality on girls' delinquency? And in what arenas will our scholarship be strengthened further by more critical attention to the gender organization of social life and its effects on young women's lives? As we see it, this is a critical dimension of future studies of girls' delinquency.

3

Trends in Girls' Delinquency and the Gender Gap

Statistical Assessment of Diverse Sources

Darrell Steffensmeier and Jennifer Schwartz

Introduction

One of the most consistent and robust findings in criminology is that, for nearly every category of crime, females commit much less crime and delinquency than males. The gender gap in offending is particularly notable for more serious and violent offenses. In recent years, however, the extent and character of this gender difference in crime is increasingly being called into question by statistics and media reports suggesting a greater involvement of women—and particularly girls—in the criminal justice system. During the past couple of decades, girls' delinquency as reported in *official* sources of data has undergone substantial changes relative to boys' delinquency. *Uniform Crime Report (UCR)* statistics showing marked increases in girls' arrests for aggravated and, especially, simple assault have encouraged the growing perception in the media and among some criminologists that girls' violence is on the rise and that the gender gap in violent offending is closing. For example, between 1980 and 2003 in the United States, girls' arrests nationwide increased 42.7 percent, while arrests of boys actually decreased by 10.2 percent (Federal Bureau of Investigation [FBI] 2004). Within this same time period, arrests of girls for index violent offenses—homicide, rape, robbery, and aggravated assault—increased by 75.2 percent and arrests of girls for "simple assaults" increased by 318.5 percent, whereas boys' arrests declined 11.3 percent for index violent offenses but increased 130.5 percent for simple assault. These arrest trends, along with high-profile cases of female delinquency, are the main source for media headlines such as "Girls getting increasingly violent," "Girls catching up with boys in delinquency and crime," and "Girls not all sugar and spice."

Although little systematic theorizing has been done, commentators have proposed a variety of reasons for what they see as real increases in girls' violence as inferred from the arrest trends. The combination of increased stress and greater female independence is believed to have increased girls' opportunities and motivations for violent crime. However, because arrest counts are a product of both delinquent behavior and responses to it, researchers and policy makers face a dilemma about how to interpret the arrest statistics. Do the arrest gains indicate *real* changes in underlying behaviors of girls—the *Behavior Change Hypothesis*—or are the gains *artifactual*, a product of recent changes in public sentiment and enforcement policies for dealing with youth crime and violence that have elevated the visibility and reporting of girls' "delinquencies" and "violence"—the *Policy Change Hypothesis*.

The statistical information about longitudinal trends in girls' and boys' delinquency and violence comes from three main sources: official, self-report, and victimization surveys (in which the victim identifies the sex and age of the offender). Each source of data has its strengths and weaknesses, and each offers at least a slightly different picture of crime. Official data on delinquency are collected by local government agencies and disseminated by state and national organizations. Arrest data, collected from local police agencies and disseminated by the FBI, are one of the main sources of official data. In contrast, self-report and victimization data are collected independently of the criminal justice system. *Monitoring the Future* (*MTF*), the *National Crime Victimization Survey* (*NCVS*), and the newer *National Youth Risk Behavior Survey* (*NYRBS*) are highly regarded nationally representative, longitudinal surveys.[1]

Because these sources of data differ in how they measure delinquency and violence, they are particularly useful for evaluating whether trends in girls' delinquency are a product of changes in the underlying violent and delinquent behavior of girls or changes in juvenile justice policies that have enhanced the visibility and reporting of girls' delinquency. Our confidence that girls' violence and delinquency have changed is enhanced if all these sources agree on the nature of the trends, despite measurement differences and dissimilar sources of limitations, while that confidence is diminished if the sources disagree.

The *Behavior Change Hypothesis* contends that arrest gains indicate *real* changes in underlying behaviors of girls. Girls' lives and experiences have changed dramatically, perhaps in ways that increase their propensities or opportunities to commit violent crimes. Girls today face greater struggles in maintaining a sense of self and confronting a complex, often contradictory, set of behavioral scripts that specify what is appropriate, acceptable, or possible for girls to do. For example, greater exposure to media messages portraying or condoning girls as violent, such as those in movies like *Charlie's Angels* and *Kill Bill* and video games like *Tomb Raider*, might facilitate changing gender-role expectations toward greater female freedom, assertiveness, and male-like machismo and competitiveness. As it becomes more socially acceptable, girls may increasingly turn to violence as a coping strategy or means of solving interpersonal conflicts with school officials, parents, or other authority figures and peers. The latter may involve arguments with boys in dating contexts but also fights with other girls over ownership of males and defense of one's sexual reputation (Anderson 1999; Campbell 1993; Ness 2004).

In addition to gender-role strain, economic and familial strains may have intensified for girls. Finally catching up to girls may be breakdowns in family, community, and other institutions that once buffered girls against victimization and involvement in violence. Female role models are fewer as mothers are forced back into the job market or are rendered ineffective because of increased substance abuse, particularly in depressed urban areas (Almgren et al. 1998; Brown and Gilligan 1992; Hall 2004). This combination of heightened role strain, changing normative expectations, and increased economic and familial stresses could contribute to girls' greater involvement in physical aggression and violence.

The Policy Change Hypothesis contends that gains are an *artifactual* product of recent changes in public sentiment and enforcement policies for dealing with youth crime and violence that have elevated the visibility and reporting of girls' "delinquencies" and "violence." At least four interrelated policy shifts appear to have escalated the arrest proneness of girls today relative to girls in prior decades and relative to boys (listed in order of their overall importance). For a fuller treatment of these policy shifts, see Steffensmeier and others (2005).

- *Netwidening, or the criminalization of less serious forms of "violence," will escalate female arrests since their violent offending is less serious and less chronic.* Criminalization includes but goes beyond "zero-tolerance" policies to encompass, quite broadly, the (a) targeting of minor or trivial forms of lawbreaking and (b) charging up minor types of lawbreaking into offense classifications representing greater seriousness and harsher statutory penalties.

  Recent enforcement practices have lowered the tolerance for low-level crime and misdemeanors, a policy shift that will disproportionately produce more arrests of less serious offenders. Analysts of crime trends point out that this netwidening has been particularly robust in ambiguous offense categories like simple or aggravated assault, where it is more the practice today that (a) disorderly conduct, harassment, endangering, resisting arrest, and so forth, will be categorized as simple assaults and (b) former simple assaults will be "charged up" to aggravated assault (Blumstein and Wallman 2000; Garland 2001; Steffensmeier and Harer 1999; Zimring 1998). These more expansive definitions of what constitutes "violence" or an "assault" have led to enhanced sanctioning for aggressive conduct among youths overall (Blumstein and Wallman 2000; Fuentes 1998) but even more so among girls who tend to commit the milder, less serious forms of physical attacks or threats (Chesney-Lind 2002; Steffensmeier 1993; Steffensmeier and Schwartz 2004).

What now tends to be dealt with formally was formerly often ignored or dealt with informally.

- *The criminalization of violence occurring between intimates and in private settings such as at home or school will portray levels of female violence that more closely approximate levels of male violence because girls' violence is more likely to take place in this context than in public settings against strangers.* Several recent studies of girls' violence document the trend toward treating domestic and school violence as a criminal matter and establish the impact of these policy shifts on girls' assault arrest trends. A review of girls' "person-to-person" cases referred to Maryland's juvenile justice system revealed the majority to be family-centered "assaults" that involved such activities as a girl hitting or throwing an object at her mother, who subsequently pressed charges (Mayer 1994; as cited in Chesney-Lind 2002). Another study of nearly one thousand girls' files from four California counties concludes that "most of these [assault] charges were the result of nonserious, mutual combat situations with parents" (Acoca 1999, pp. 7–8; see also Schaffner 1999). Case descriptions of girls arrested ranged from "father lunged at daughter while she was calling the police about a domestic dispute [when] daughter hit him" (self-defense) to "throwing cookies at her mother" (trivial argument).

    Heightened public concern about school safety has escalated the vulnerability of girls being arrested for assault as a result of pro-arrest policies for physical confrontations or threats occurring on or near school grounds. Many schools, especially in the large urban centers, have adopted zero-tolerance policies toward violence, employ metal detectors and video cameras, and hire full-time school police. Both male and female youths are being arrested in substantial numbers for behavior that, prior to the creation of these preventive measures, would have likely been handled as a school disciplinary matter (Hagan, Hirschfield, and Shedd 2002). However, the available evidence also suggests that this netwidening in school arrest policies has disproportionately escalated girls' arrests for violent crimes, particularly for assaults involving minor physical confrontations or verbal threats (most frequently with another girl) that in the past would have been ignored, responded to less formally, or resulted in lesser charges such as disorderly conduct or harassment (Hall 2004; Lockwood 1997).

- *Less tolerant family and societal attitudes toward juvenile females will amplify girls' arrests for violence.* Evidence suggests that girls' arrest proneness has been escalated by the gradual spread of due process considerations for girls into the juvenile justice system and curtailment of discretion, while simultaneously maintaining aspects of the traditional "double standard" of seeing girls (but not boys) as needing protection from themselves or from immoral influences (see "bootstrapping" following). Changes over time in the attitudes of the public and the police toward female suspects may also affect girls' arrest rates. An increased emphasis on the legal equality of the sexes, the changing role of girls/women in society, and the perception that they are becoming more violent may produce an increased willingness on the part of victims or witnesses of female crime to report female suspects to the police and for the police to proceed more bureaucratically and formally in processing female suspects.

• *Bootstrapping and relabeling of minor offenses for "girls' protection" will increase girls' arrest levels for assault offenses.* One major focus of research has been the impact of legal reforms that make it more difficult to detain "wayward" or "at-risk" girls for status offenses. A consistent finding across studies has been the increasingly common practice in some jurisdictions to relabel or "boost up" minor offenses and behaviors traditionally categorized as status offenses (sexual misbehavior, running away from home, truancy, in need of supervision, incorrigibility, disorderly conduct) and instead to arrest the girls for assault (or some other felony offense) as grounds for detention or placement in an appropriate program or facility (Chesney-Lind and Paramore 2001; Schaffner 1999).

These policy shifts, taken together, appear to have increased, in particular, the arrest proneness of minority and low-income girls living in depressed urban areas, who, both now and in the past, may employ physical attacks or threats as a coping strategy for dealing with abusive homes and street lives or for confronting interpersonal conflicts with authority figures such as parents or teachers and with peers (Anderson 1999).

Although these two frameworks are broadly applicable to understanding shifts in all sorts of girls' offending trends, we focus in particular on changes in girls' *violence* because of the high-profile nature of this debate and because time-series data are best suited to address the issue of trends in girls' violence. We build on and extend our previous work in this area by also briefly assessing trends in girls' involvement in several forms of *nonviolent* delinquency across arrest and self-report time-series data (Steffensmeier et al. 2005). Although beyond the scope of this chapter, we also assessed whether trends of minority girls differ from those of girls as a whole and found that gender-by-race trends in violence and delinquency overlap considerably.

Using *UCR* Arrest Statistics for Trend Comparisons

The primary source of official data on delinquency comes from the FBI's annual *UCR*. Each *UCR* includes a compilation of thousands of local police precinct reports on crimes that are known to the police via reporting by individuals, schools, or businesses, or via police detection and arrest reports. The FBI compiles additional statistics on roughly thirty categories of crime and the demographic characteristics of arrestees such as age and sex.

We pay disproportionate attention to *UCR* arrest data because of their longevity and high visibility, and because they are at the center of a growing debate about whether girls' delinquency is becoming more serious or violent. However, questions about violence trends for girls are not easily answered because of the intersection between reliability and validity concerns surrounding the data and the gendered character and context of girls' delinquency. We give an overview of these concerns as they relate to understanding trends in girls' violence in particular, although these concerns also apply to understanding and interpreting girls' delinquency trends generally.

Reliability and Validity Concerns

First, the rate of arrests, like any other official measure of crime, is a function of behavior defined as criminal and the control measures established to deal with it. Comparing sex differences in arrest rates over a given period of time is risky because changes in reporting practices and policing may affect one sex more than the other. Citizens, police, and other officials have considerable discretion in defining offenses, so official measures may not reliably reflect the same behaviors over time. For example, whereas definitions of homicide are relatively consistent over time and across place, behaviors on the margins of "violence" are far more variable. Roughly scaled from least to most serious, assault can include such behaviors as throwing something at someone, pushing, grabbing, or shoving; slapping, kicking, biting, hitting with a fist; hitting with an object; choking; threatening with a gun or knife; or using a gun or knife. To distinguish felony from misdemeanor assault and from lesser offenses like harassment and disorderly conduct requires subjective assessments of intent and the degree of bodily injury. More inclusive definitions of what constitutes "violence" or an "assault" have emerged in recent years (Blumstein and Wallman 2000; Steffensmeier 1993; Zimring 1998), so that trends in less serious violence, such as simple assault, will be more affected by policies and practices that expand the sphere of "violence" than trends in homicide or more serious forms of violence.

A second problem with the *UCR* data is that the offense categories are broad and are derived from a *heterogeneous* collection of criminal acts, meaning that between-sex comparisons of a given crime are further complicated by the differing character and context of male and female crime. For example, "larceny-theft" might be shoplifting a fifty dollar item (typically a female crime) or cargo theft amounting to thousands of dollars (typically a male crime). "Burglary" includes both unlawful entry into an ex-partner's apartment to retrieve merchandise as well as safecracking. Qualitatively dissimilar incidents with differing levels of injury may be included in the same *UCR* category. The aggravated assault category includes incidents where the victim was hospitalized because of injuries as well as where the perpetrator brandishes a deadly weapon (e.g., kitchen knife, broken bottle) without inflicting any visible harm. Arrests are not distinguished in terms of offender culpability, such as whether the suspect is a primary or ancillary actor or whether the arrestee was acting antagonistically or defensively. Many females arrested for robbery or burglary act as accomplices to males, and many females arrested for homicide or assault act in response to considerable provocation from males (Mullins and Wright 2003; Steffensmeier and Terry 1986; Steffensmeier and Ulmer 2005). In effect, offenses representing dissimilar events and covering a range of seriousness and level of culpability are included in the same *UCR* category, muddying the comparison of female-to-male crime.

The broadness and subjectivity of *UCR* classification categories have important implications for interpreting trends in girls' arrests for violence, especially in light of elastic definitions of violence that, in more recent years, may have become more encompassing of female forms of "violence." Some evidence suggests that policy changes have increased the arrest probabilities of adolescent females relative to adolescent males in ways that go beyond changes in girls' underlying behavior because recent social control policies inadvertently target the offending patterns of girls. Unless one exercises caution and draws on other sources of evidence to supplement the arrest data, inaccurate or misleading conclusions about girls' delinquency can easily be drawn.

Visibility and Character of Girls' Delinquency

Violence and delinquency have traditionally been defined in male terms and have been seen as mainly, even the sole, property of male adolescents and young men. Until relatively recently, girls' delinquency and violence have been trivialized, minimized, overlooked, and ignored. The reality of girls' delinquency, however, has always been different. Both now and in the past, girls have been involved in delinquency and violence and in some cases in serious forms of crime and violence; there are ample cases of "violent girls" in generations past, just as there are high-profile cases today. While girls are not as delinquent as boys overall, the evidence from self-report surveys and case studies extending back at least three to four decades shows girls committing a long list of illegal acts (Berger 1989; Giordano, Cernkovich, and Pugh 1986).

The second complicating factor involves what is a general axiom about gender variation in crime and its measurement. As noted earlier, *across the spectrum of lawbreaking, girls/women engage in less serious forms of crime and play less culpable roles than boys/men* (see reviews in Steffensmeier 1983; and Steffensmeier and Allan 1996). One important implication of this axiom is that, depending on one's point of reference or *how behaviors are measured,* girls' delinquency can be seen as either very similar or very different from boys' delinquency (see reviews in Berger 1989; Steffensmeier and Allan 1996; and Agnew 2000). On the one hand, they commit similar types of offenses—adolescent girls, like adolescent boys, fight, steal, cheat, lie, vandalize, use drugs, and engage in other delinquent acts. Girls commit some types of delinquencies (shoplifting) about as frequently as boys do. On the other hand, (a) girls in general offend less frequently than boys because there are more male than female offenders and because male offenders commit more offenses than female offenders; (b) boys, more so than girls, commit more serious and more visible delinquencies—thefts of greater value, fights involving greater victim injury and fear, often in street settings and among secondary groups, harder drug use and drug distribution, and much greater predatory sexual deviance; and (c) male youths are also more likely to be chronic or "career" offenders.

A second implication of this axiom is that changes in laws and enforcement toward targeting less serious forms of lawbreaking (e.g., minor acts of physical violence, lowering the blood alcohol content for underage drinking, small amounts of drug use or distribution) will enhance the visibility of girls' offending and increase the risk of arrest for female more so than male offenders. When authorities dip more deeply into the pool of offenders, young women's share of arrests will increase because females tend to be involved disproportionately in the less serious forms of lawbreaking even within a specific offense category. The significance of this general principle—*that the gender gap will be smaller when the measurement taps less serious forms of delinquency or crime, whereas the gap will be larger when more serious forms are included*—is, perhaps, seen most clearly in our treatment assessing trends in girls' violence trends in the following. However, this axiom also applies to other areas of girls' delinquency and the gender gap. With these considerations in mind, we begin our statistical analysis by examining girls' arrest trends across the variety of offense categories contained in the *UCR*. Our aims are to provide an overview of girls' official delinquency in a general sense and to set the stage for the key issue in this chapter of assessing girls' violence trends.

Change in Girls' (and Boys') Delinquency Patterns Based on Arrests

Arrest Rates, Female Percentage (FP) of Arrests, and Female-to-Male Offending Profile

Three principal methods of measuring change in girls' delinquency are used; each takes into account increases in the juvenile population, facilitating comparisons over time.[2] One method involves calculating juvenile male and female *rates* (aged twelve to seventeen) that adjust for the sex and age composition of the population and for variable coverage across jurisdictions in the *UCR* program over the 1980 to 2003 period. Examining girls' and boys' rates yields evidence about (a) sex differences in delinquency in general and by type of offense and (b) whether delinquency levels of either girls or boys are rising, falling, or holding steady.

A second measure is the FP of arrests, which indicates the share of arrests that are female after adjusting for the sex composition of the population at large. The formula to calculate the FP is as follows: Female Rate/(Female Rate + Male Rate) × 100. Therefore, a figure of 50 percent indicates an equal share of arrests for girls and boys. For example, the juvenile female rate for aggravated assault in 2002 was 122/100,000 and the male rate was 375/100,000, so applying the formula: $[122/(122 + 375)] \times 100 = 25$ percent of all juvenile arrestees for aggravated assault were female. Note that an increase in the FP of arrests will occur if female rates increase more than male rates, if female rates are constant but male rates decline, or if female rates decline less than male rates. Examining the FP statistic over time yields evidence as to whether sex differences in crime are narrowing or widening.

The third measure is the *offender-profile percentage*, which is defined as the percentage of all arrests within each sex that are arrests for that particular offense. This part of the analysis examines the distribution of offenses committed by females to determine if the profile of the female arrestee has changed (e.g., toward more violence), that is, if the types of crimes for which girls (or boys) are arrested have changed.

The information provided by these three methods is summarized in Table 3.1 for 1980 (average of 1979–1981), 1990 (1990–1992), and 2000 (2001–2003) for all the offense categories included in the *UCR*.[3]

Trends in Arrest Rates

In the first six columns of Table 3.1, male and female arrest rates per 100,000 for 1980, 1990, and 2000 are shown. Key findings are as follows. For both juvenile females and juvenile males, arrest rates are higher for *less* serious offenses. Over the entire period examined, female rates are highest for larceny, for alcohol/drug violations (DUI, drugs, and liquor law violations), for disorderly conduct, for runaways/curfew, and, in recent years, for simple assault.

Furthermore, in general, the movement of arrest rates over the 1980 to 2003 period was similar for both sexes, but with some divergence over the past decade. As Table 3.1 indicates, since 1990, girls' arrest rates for various offenses have either increased more or decreased less than boys' rates (examples include simple assault, burglary, and disorderly conduct). These somewhat differing patterns of the 1990s from the 1980s suggest that, relative to boys, the nature of what girls are being arrested for has shifted over the past couple of decades, a matter more closely assessed by examining their arrest profiles.

Trends in Arrest Profiles

The last six columns of Table 3.1 compare 1980–2003 male and female arrest profiles, which is the percentage of all arrests within each sex that are arrests for that particular offense. For example, the homicide figures for 2002—0.07 percent for boys and 0.02 percent for girls—indicate that less than 1 percent of all male and all female juvenile arrests were for homicide. In comparison, about 13 percent of male and 21 percent of female juvenile arrests, respectively, were for larceny-theft. And, about 18 percent of all juvenile male arrests and 16 percent of all juvenile female arrests were for "other except traffic"—a residual category that includes mostly criminal mischief, harassment, public disorder, local ordinance violations, and assorted minor law violations.

TABLE 3.1 UCR ARREST TRENDS FOR JUVENILE MALES AND FEMALES ACROSS OFFENSE CATEGORIES FOR 1979–1981, 1990–1992, AND 2001–2003

	Male Rates[a]			Female Rates[a]			Female %[b]			Male Profile[c]			Female Profile[c]		
Offenses	1 1980	2 1990	3 2000	4 1980	5 1990	6 2000	7 1980	8 1990	9 2000	10 1980	11 1990	12 2000	13 1980	14 1990	15 2000
Violent															
Homicide	14.0	30.6	9.2	1.4	1.7	1.1	9.1	5.4	10.5	0.10	0.18	0.07	0.04	0.03	0.02
Rape/sex offenses	127.1	216.6	164.2	7.8	13.4	13.7	5.8	5.8	7.7	0.91	1.31	1.31	0.21	0.26	0.26
Robbery	346.8	398.7	184.9	26.9	39.6	18.6	7.2	9.0	9.1	2.48	2.41	1.47	0.72	0.76	0.35
Aggravated assault	281.3	557.7	374.8	52.6	109.6	122.4	15.7	16.4	24.6	2.02	3.37	2.99	1.40	2.11	2.28
Simple assault	546.4	1,148.1	1,259.3	151.1	382.6	632.4	21.6	24.9	32.8	3.91	6.94	10.04	4.02	7.35	11.79
Weapons	204.0	430.2	259.0	13.1	31.8	33.8	6.0	6.8	11.5	1.46	2.60	2.07	0.35	0.61	0.63
Property/Criminal Mischief															
Larceny-theft	2,614.5	3,168.8	1,616.3	995.0	1,371.8	1,110.2	27.5	30.0	40.7	18.73	19.16	12.89	26.46	26.37	20.69
Stolen property	273.9	380.3	171.5	27.7	45.3	33.8	9.2	10.6	16.4	1.96	2.30	1.37	0.74	0.87	0.63
Motor vehicle theft	466.8	781.8	302.6	55.8	107.0	65.5	10.7	12.0	17.7	3.34	4.73	2.41	1.48	2.06	1.22
Burglary	1,725.0	1,234.7	598.0	121.0	119.7	83.1	6.5	8.8	12.1	12.36	7.46	4.77	3.22	2.30	1.55
Arson	54.4	66.4	53.8	6.5	7.8	8.0	10.7	10.5	13.0	0.39	0.40	0.43	0.17	0.15	0.15
Vandalism	862.1	1,139.5	702.6	78.8	111.5	116.4	8.4	8.9	14.2	6.18	6.89	5.60	2.10	2.14	2.17
Gambling	14.8	10.6	11.9	0.7	0.6	0.4	4.8	5.0	2.9	0.11	0.06	0.09	0.02	0.01	0.01
Fraud/forgery/embezzlement	128.7	162.2	77.7	50.8	74.5	43.6	28.5	31.5	35.9	0.92	0.98	0.62	1.35	1.43	0.81
Drinking/Drugs															
Public drunkenness	307.3	172.8	116.9	51.2	33.9	34.6	14.2	16.5	22.9	2.20	1.04	0.93	1.36	0.65	0.64
Driving under the influence	227.2	142.8	129.3	27.4	24.3	32.3	10.7	14.5	19.9	1.63	0.86	1.03	0.73	0.47	0.60
Liquor laws	935.9	941.9	734.8	283.8	390.1	392.1	23.3	29.3	34.8	6.71	5.69	5.86	7.55	7.50	7.31
Drug abuse violations	760.0	711.7	1,297.5	87.2	49.1	191.1	16.9	11.5	16.6	5.45	4.30	10.35	2.32	0.94	3.56

(continued on next page)

TABLE 3.1 *Continued*

Offenses	Male Rates[a]			Female Rates[a]			Female %[b]			Male Profile[c]			Female Profile[c]		
	1 1980	2 1990	3 2000	4 1980	5 1990	6 2000	7 1980	8 1990	9 2000	10 1980	11 1990	12 2000	13 1980	14 1990	15 2000
Public Order															
Disorderly conduct	853.7	948.9	959.5	185.0	270.1	469.4	17.8	22.2	33.0	6.12	5.74	7.65	4.92	5.19	8.75
Vagrancy	30.3	27.7	13.7	6.3	5.2	4.2	17.1	15.6	23.7	0.22	0.17	0.11	0.17	0.10	0.08
Suspicion	25.1	34.3	6.2	5.7	9.7	2.9	18.9	21.8	30.8	0.18	0.21	0.05	0.15	0.19	0.05
Prostitution	8.9	6.5	3.7	19.0	7.7	8.4	68.2	53.9	69.4	0.06	0.04	0.03	0.51	0.15	0.16
Miscellaneous															
Against family/children	8.8	23.6	39.6	5.1	13.2	25.8	36.3	35.8	39.5	0.06	0.14	0.32	0.14	0.25	0.48
Other except traffic	2,083.7	2,465.8	2,221.3	531.4	687.5	860.7	20.3	21.8	27.9	14.93	14.91	17.72	14.13	13.21	16.04
Curfew/loitering	528.3	620.0	718.4	158.5	245.0	364.6	23.2	28.3	33.7	3.79	3.75	5.73	4.21	4.71	6.80
Runaways	527.6	718.9	404.9	741.8	1,005.7	627.7	58.5	58.3	60.8	3.78	4.35	3.23	19.73	19.33	11.70

[a] Rates represent three-year averages and are adjusted for the sex and age composition of the country and for changes in *UCR* coverage over time. The population base includes people aged twelve to seventeen.

[b] Female Percentage of Arrests = Female Rate/(Female Rate + Male Rate) × 100 percent.

[c] Profile Percentage = (Offense Count/Total Count of All Offenses) × 100 percent. Note: May not sum to 100 percent because of rounding.

We draw the following conclusions from Table 3.1 regarding the nature of girls' delinquency as reflected in their arrest profiles. First, the similarities between the male and female profiles both now and two decades ago are considerable. Girls and boys overlap in five of the six most common arrest categories in 2003: larceny-theft, other except traffic, simple assault, disorderly conduct, and liquor law violations (mostly underage drinking). In total, these offenses account for about two-thirds of all male and three-fourths of all female arrests. All of these offenses involve relatively minor violations. This even appears to be the case with "simple assault," a broad category that includes mostly minor, even trivial, incidents of threat or physical attack against another person such as scratching, biting, throwing objects, shoving, hitting, or kicking (see "Trends in Girls' Violence" following). Girls and boys also overlap in five of the six most rare offense categories, including murder, gambling, embezzlement, suspicion, and vagrancy. Arrests for offenses like aggravated assault and motor vehicle theft (mostly joyriding) represent middling ranks for both sexes. The largest gender difference in arrest profiles is that runaways ranks higher for girls (number 4 versus number 10 for boys), while drug law violations ranks higher for boys (number 3 versus number 8 for girls).

The distribution of offenses for which both girls and boys are arrested has shifted some over the past twenty years, but the changes are comparable for males and females. Note, for example, rank-ordering of boys' and girls' offense distributions are correlated at .80 in 1980 (Table 3.1, columns 10 and 13) as well as in 2000 (columns 12 and 15). (Rank order correlations not shown.) Note also that, of all persons arrested in 2003 versus 1980, larger shares of both male and female arrests are for both assault categories (aggravated, simple) and drug law violations. Relative to her male counterpart, the profile of the adolescent female offender has not changed much in recent decades. As we will see, however, girls have made arrest gains on boys for some offenses.

Trends in the FP of Arrests

The central issue in many discussions of girls' delinquency is whether the gender gap has been narrowing and, if so, for which crimes. The middle columns (columns 7 through 9) in Table 3.1 show the FP of arrests for all the *UCR* offenses.

First, in 2000 (column 9), the female share of arrests for most categories is 20 percent or less and is typically smallest for the most serious offenses such as robbery and homicide, for predatory sex offenses, and for gambling. In turn, the female share of arrests is the largest for prostitution, runaways, larceny-theft, against-family, liquor law violations, and fraud/forgery/embezzlement.

Second, the FP of arrests increased from 1980 to 2003 in the majority of offense categories. The percentage increases were typically small or negligible during the 1980s but with more notable increases in the post-1990s period. As we will discuss, the narrowing gender gap in several offense categories is due to declining arrest rates for boys during the 1990s. (Compare 2000 arrest rates with 1990 and 1980 arrest rates in Table 3.1, columns 1 through 3.)

There were sizable increases in the FP of arrests over the 1980–2003 period for total arrests (from 21 percent to 30 percent) and for the following types of offenses: both aggravated assault and simple assault, larceny-theft and fraud, alcohol-related violations (liquor laws, public drunkenness, DUI), and disorderly conduct (also vagrancy, suspicion). These generally are minor rather than serious types of law violation. Indeed, many arrests in these offense categories can be viewed as "status" violations—behaviors for which juveniles but not adults are arrested.

It is girls' gains in arrests for assault crimes that have most fueled public commentary about the "plague of girls' violence," and assault charges account for a sizable portion of the increasing numbers of girls entering into the juvenile justice system. The "seriousness" of an assault arrest is examined later; however, the consequence of more arrests of girls for *simple assault* is particularly important because its numbers are much larger than those for aggravated assault (rates/100,000 of about 600 for simple assault versus about 100 for aggravated assault). In fact, arrests for simple assault now account for over 10 percent of all girls' (and boys') arrests—a fairly sizable proportion of all arrests.

Third, there are several notable exceptions to the general pattern of increases in the female share of arrests. There was very little change in the FP for homicide, robbery, rape (including sex offenses), arson, gambling, and drug law violations. Note that the female share of drug law violations dropped a bit in the late 1980s/early 1990s (to 12 percent from about 17 percent in 1980), but it ticked up again by the 2002 period to 17 percent, a level at which it has been holding fairly steady for the past several years. This should not obscure the fact, however, that drug arrest rates of both girls and boys increased sharply over the 1990 to 2003 period and at a greater pace than any other crime.

Again we see that girls' share of arrests may rise because their rates are relatively stable or only slightly rising, whereas boys' rates are declining (see Table 3.1). The rise in girls' share of burglary arrests (from about 7 percent to 12 percent) is due to sharply declining burglary rates among male youths, as opposed to stable rates among females. Such is also the case for auto theft (from 11 percent to 18 percent) and stolen property (from 9 percent to 16 percent). A caveat is that the base rate for females arrested for burglary (also auto theft and stolen property) is small so that even a doubling of the FP does not represent a large absolute increase in female offending. For homicide, although the FP is about 10 percent in both 1980 and 2000, this conceals an interesting dip in the FP to about 5 percent in 1990. This dip and subsequent ticking up in the FP reflects a sharp increase in male youth homicides in the late 1980s/early 1990s, brought about in part by the rise in gun- and drug-related violence among young men in large urban areas, followed by an even sharper decrease in homicides committed by young males since the mid-1990s.

In sum, girls have made fairly sizable arrest gains on boys in a number of minor offense categories, although it is the gains in arrest for assaultive violence that have been the most widely recognized by the media, some researchers, and policy makers. It still remains very much the case, however, that national patterns of female offending remain distinct from patterns of male offending. Most juvenile females are arrested for *status* and nonviolent, minor property offenses such as running away and larceny, while males are more often arrested for the more serious violent crimes such as robbery and for drug offenses. These patterns existed in both 1980 and 2003, and they are similar to those found in other comparisons of gender differences in crime (see review by Steffensmeier and Allan 1996).

Trends in Girls' Violence and the Gender Gap: More "Real" Violence by Girls or Widening the Arrest Net?

We begin our assessment of the directionality of girls' and boys' trends in officially recognized violence by more rigorously analyzing the arrest data on violence. We examine the full spectrum of violence, from homicide to simple assault, because the behavior change position just described would anticipate increases in girls' violence across violent offense types; however, we focus more heavily on the assault crimes because, as is made clear shortly, these offenses are driving girls' arrest trends for violence. Our analysis assesses trends from 1980 to 2003 in female and male juvenile arrest rates along with the FP of arrests for a number of violent offenses.[4] Also evaluated are trends in the Violent Crime Index (sum of arrests for homicide, robbery, rape, and aggravated assault) and trends in a composite assault index that combines the figures for aggravated assault and simple assault.

We conducted Dickey-Fuller time-series tests on the data to assess statistically whether the gender gap in arrest trends has been converging, diverging or essentially stable (no change in the gender gap), or trendless (randomly fluctuating gap). Because they overlap in meaning, we use the terms "stable" and "trendless" interchangeably. The Dickey-Fuller tests, especially when combined with figures displaying arrest rates and FPs, provide a solid basis for statistically assessing trends. These methods avoid the convention of arbitrarily picking a few time points, which may lead to inaccurate conclusions. The top panel of Table 3.2 displays Dickey-Fuller results for the arrest data. To better contextualize what a narrowing of the gender gap in violence means and to visually represent whether significant trends in the gender gap are due to increases in female violent crime or declining male rates, Figure 3.1 plots trends in juvenile female and male arrest rates and the FP of arrests for the violent crimes and for the Violent Crime Index. The findings are straightforward.

There is no significant change in the gender gap trend for the following violent crimes: homicide, rape, and robbery. In contrast, the gender gap in arrests has narrowed considerably for both aggravated assault and simple assault, as indicated by positive, significant coefficients (Table 3.2). For simple assault, the female share of arrests rises slowly in the 1980s (from about 21 percent in 1980 to 25 percent in 1990) and then rises at an accelerated pace in the 1990s (to about

TABLE 3.2 TRENDS IN THE JUVENILE GENDER GAP FOR VIOLENCE: AUGMENTED
DICKEY-FULLER TIME-SERIES RESULTS FOR *UCR, NCVS,* AND *MTF,* 1980 [1991]–2003[a]

Violence Indicator	Estimated Value (α)[b]	Trend in the Gender Gap
A. Uniform Crime Report (All Juveniles)		
Homicide	.0078	Trendless
Rape	.0201	Trendless
Robbery	.0122	Trendless
Aggravated assault	.0155*	Convergence
Simple assault	.0262***	Convergence
Assault Index[c]	.0219**	Convergence
Violent Crime Index[d]	.0226**	Convergence
Violent Crime Index minus aggravated assault	.0104	Trendless
B. National Crime Victimization Survey (All Juveniles)		
Rape	—	Stable
Robbery	.0791	Trendless
Aggravated assault	.0209	Trendless
Simple assault	—	Stable
Assault index[c]	—	Stable
Violent Crime Index[d]	—	Stable
C. Monitoring the Future (17- to 18-Year Olds)[c]		
Assault		
Prevalence (1 or more incidents)	—	Stable
High frequency (5 or more incidents)	−.0318	Trendless
Robbery		
Prevalence (1 or more incidents)	−.0153	Trendless
High frequency (5 or more incidents)	—	Stable

*$p < .10$ **$p < .05$ ***$p < .01$ (two-tailed tests)

[a] The gender gap is measured as log(female rate) − log(male rate). The Augmented Dickey-Fuller first differenced equation is based on the following specification: $y_t - y_{t-1} = \alpha + \delta_1(y_{t-1} - y_{t-2}) + \delta_2(y_{t-2} - y_{t-3}) + \ldots + \mu_t$.

[b] One lagged difference is required for the MTF high-frequency assault index. For all other series, the number of lagged differences is zero.

[c] UCR and NCVS assault indexes include aggravated and simple assaults. Items in the MTF assault index (twelfth grade) include (a) hit instructor/supervisor, (b) fight at school/work, and (c) hurt someone badly in a fight. Items in the MTF assault index (all juveniles) include (a) fight at school/work, and (b) hurt someone badly in a fight.

[d] The UCR Violent Crime Index includes homicide, robbery, rape, and aggravated assault. The NCVS Violent Crime Index includes: robbery, rape, and aggravated assault.

34 percent in 2003) (see Figure 3.1). For aggravated assault, the FP remains unchanged during the 1980s (15.5 percent in 1980 versus 15.8 percent in the 1990s), after which the FP rises sharply throughout the 1990s (to about 25 percent in 2003). Increased female representation in arrests for simple assault (13 percent change) moderately outpaces female gains in aggravated assault (9.5 percent), as also indicated by the larger time trend coefficient in the Dickey-Fuller time-series analysis.

The gender gaps for the assault index and the Violent Crime Index have also narrowed significantly, although the Violent Crime Index only because of the swamping effects of the rise in female aggravated assault arrests during the 1990s (see Figure 3.1). The Index gender gap trend (steady over the 1980s with a steep rise in the FP in the 1990s) essentially matches the pattern for aggravated assault, whose large arrest volumes are driving movement of the Index during the 1990s. Also, if aggravated assault counts are omitted from the Violent Crime Index, the gender gap trend is stable in Dickey-Fuller analyses (Table 3.2). This stability is notable because it is sometimes claimed on the basis of the Index that girls' "serious" violence is increasing; however, neither law enforcement nor the citizenry view aggravated assault as approaching the seriousness of other components of the Index, such as homicide or rape.

Movement in violence rates is roughly similar for both sexes across all of the violent crime categories but with some divergence since the mid-1990s (Figure 3.1). Female and male rates rose over much of the past two decades, particularly during the 1986 to 1994 period, but in the late 1990s, male youth rates leveled off or declined, whereas juvenile female rates merely stabilized or continued to inch upward. However, male youth violence rates continues to be much higher than adolescent female rates, particularly for the serious violent index crimes of homicide, rape, and robbery; substantial sex differences in violence still exist.

So far, our analysis shows girls making arrest gains on boys for aggravated and simple assault but not for homicide, rape, and robbery. More rigorous statistical analysis of the arrest trends for the assault offenses support the widely publicized view that girls' violence is rising, but the trends for the other violent crimes do not. There are important theoretical and methodological caveats, however, that call into question whether these assault arrest trends are evidence of a rising tide of adolescent female violence.

The sex-specific changes do not fit with the assertion that, with greater female independence or role strain, female youths will come to engage in more violence. To the contrary, female assault rates have leveled off or declined slightly since the mid-1990s, while male assault rates have declined much further. In this regard, a weakness of the independence/stress thesis comes from the failure to specify how changes in juvenile male behavior as well as juvenile female behavior account for changes in gender gap trends. Moreover, greater female independence and stress should be associated with increased female representation in all types of violent behavior, yet the narrowing gender gap is confined to assault offenses, which are more ambiguously and variably defined than homicide and other more serious forms of violence.

Comparison of Arrest Trends to Unofficial Sources: Victim and Self-Report Surveys

To help resolve the debate over girls' violence, we take a more discerning look at changes in the gender gap by comparing girls' arrest trends to their violence trends as reflected in victimization and self-report data. Unlike the UCRs, these other data are not limited to cases that come to the attention of the police or result in arrests.

Girls' Violence Trends Based on Victim's Reports: NCVS

Victimization surveys provide an important source of information on delinquent or criminal behavior. The logic underlying this data source is somewhat different than official or self-reports, however. The information is not collected from the person who committed the crime, but from the victim of the crime. In the United States, the *NCVS* has been conducted annually since 1973 by the Census Bureau. Each year, members of approximately sixty thousand households

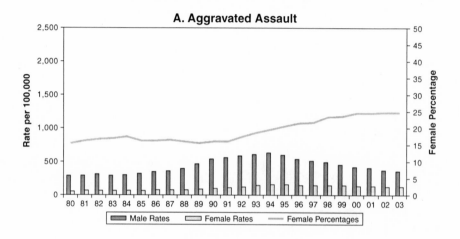

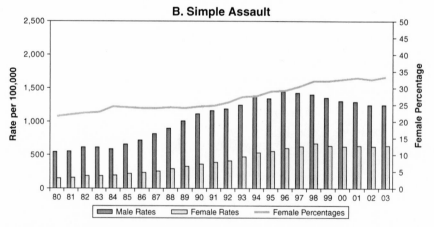

FIGURE 3.1 Trends in juvenile female and male arrest rates[a] (per 100,000) and female percentage of arrests[b] for violent offending: UCR, 1980–2003. *(Continued on facing page.)*

a. Rates are adjusted for the sex composition of the population and for changes in UCR coverage over time. The population base includes juveniles aged twelve to seventeen.
b. Female Percentage = Female Rate/(Female Rate + Male Rate) × 100%.
c. The assault index includes aggravated and simple assaults.
d. The Violent Crime Index includes homicide, aggravated assault, rape, and robbery.

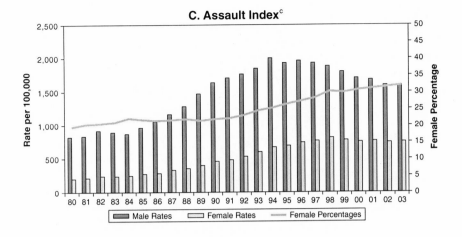

C. Assault Index[c]

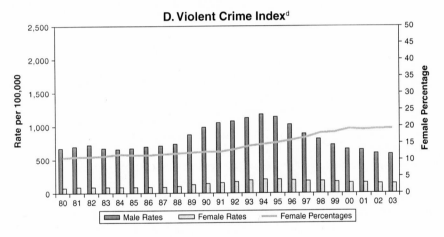

D. Violent Crime Index[d]

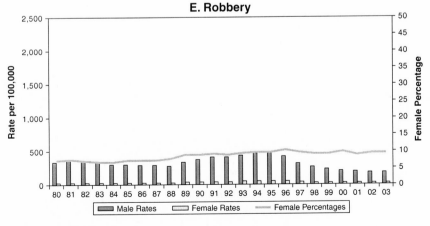

E. Robbery

FIGURE 3.1 *Continued*

are interviewed. Detailed characteristics of the criminal event are obtained when a respondent reports to have been a victim of some crime (i.e., several types of violence, theft, or both). These questions address the time and location of the crime, the level of physical and property damage, and, in the case of violent crime, the perceived characteristics (e.g., age, gender, race) of the offender(s).

The *NCVS* series is such an important source of information on trends in girls' and boys' involvement in violent crime for three reasons. Based on victims identifying the offender's sex and age, the *NCVS* provides trend data for several violent crimes (robbery, sexual assault/rape, aggravated assault, and simple assault) and for the Violent Crime Index among adolescent girls and boys (aged twelve to seventeen). The second reason is that *NCVS* figures are directly comparable to the *UCR* arrest counts because they use the same definitions and coding schemes of violent offenses. Third, many criminologists believe that the *NCVS* provides more reliable estimates of criminal violence than official data sources because of its methodological rigor and because the data are collected independently of police or criminal justice agents.

As with the *UCR* arrest statistics, our analysis of *NCVS* data relies on both Dickey-Fuller tests and illustrative plots of female-to-male trends covering the full 1980 to 2003 period. We focus more heavily on the assault crimes because, as the *UCR* analysis has shown, they are driving girls' arrest trends for violence.

The findings from the Dickey-Fuller tests are shown in Panel B of Table 3.2. The results reveal that the gender gap in violence and assault among adolescent males and females has changed very little from 1980 to 2003. The findings are in sharp contrast to official statistics where the gender gap has narrowed significantly for both assault categories. Specifically, the gender gap is stable or trendless for *NCVS* robbery and rape, a pattern that is consistent with the *UCR* trends. However, the gender gap for both aggravated assault and simple assault is also stable, a pattern that is contrary to *UCR* arrest trends. Likewise, the gender gap is stable for the Violent Crime Index (sum of robbery, rape, and aggravated assault).[5]

Figure 3.2 further spells out these findings by displaying *NCVS* rates of violence for juvenile males and females, along with the relevant FPs. There are several key findings. First, *NCVS* plots show girls' assault and overall violence levels as being much lower than male levels, with wider gender differences for more serious forms of violence. For example, the FP for aggravated assault hovers around 10 percent to 15 percent compared with about 25 percent for simple assaults. Second, girls' rates of violence typically rise when male rates rise and decline when male rates decline, yielding a stable gender gap in overall violence. Partitioning the *NCVS* findings into two decades and calculating an average FP for each decade, the gender gap for the assault index is about 20 percent in both the 1980s and the 1990s, and the gender gap in the Violent Crime Index hovers close to 10 percent throughout both decades. These decade comparisons underscore the conclusion drawn using Dickey-Fuller methods—male and female rates move in tandem, yielding a stable or trendless gender gap in overall violence.

Viewing Figure 3.2 in combination with Figure 3.1 (arrest counts) elucidates the differing patterns in girls' and boys' violence across the two sources of national violence data. During the late 1980s through the early 1990s, both *NCVS* and *UCR* sources show girls' and boys' assault rates rising and then tapering off, but the rise is smaller and the decline is greater in the *NCVS* series. In recent years, the *NCVS* series shows *both* female and male rates of assault dropping considerably, as compared to the *UCR* series where only boys' arrest rates for assault have been declining. Similarly, the gender gap in violence is fairly comparable between *NCVS* and *UCR* figures in earlier years, but the two sources diverge in more recent years. There was no difference across the *NCVS* and *UCR* in the FP for the assault index in the early 1980s (about 18 percent to 20 percent), whereas by the late 1990s, the *UCR* jumps to roughly 30 percent but the *NCVS* holds at about 20 percent. This telling difference between the two reporting programs appears to document the greater impact of recent policy shifts on girls' more than boys' arrest proneness.

Conclusions Based on *NCVS* versus *UCR* Comparison
To the extent that the *NCVS* series provides reliable estimates, as many criminologists believe, we can draw several conclusions. First, there has been no meaningful change in the gender gap in juvenile violent offending, including for assault, despite marked female gains in assault arrests. The *NCVS* and the *UCR* agree in their depiction of stable female-to-male trends for the most serious violent crimes (homicide, rape, robbery) but differ sharply in their representation of gender gap trends for assault. Second, the *NCVS* series shows sharp declines in rates of assault among both female and male youths since about the mid-1990s, but the declines have been partly offset by the greater proneness of police to arrest youths—in effect sustaining high arrest levels of youths for assault crimes. Third, this greater proneness to arrest is particularly salient for female youths whose arrest figures have continued to rise (i.e., simple assault) or barely leveled off (i.e., aggravated assault) in sharp contrast to victim's reports that show sizable declines in girls' assaults since at least the mid-1990s. These findings support the policy change interpretation of the arrest data.

Trends in Girls' Self-Reported Violent Offending

Self-report surveys of crime and its correlates are a third major source of information and have most often been conducted with adolescents as respondents. Besides the detailed information that can be collected on the characteristics of the respondents, the main benefit of the self-report data is the information obtained on crimes committed by youths that were not discovered by the police. Most self-report delinquency surveys are cross-sectional (i.e., cover only one point in time) and localized (i.e., limited to a particular community or region). But two important surveys provide longitudinal or trend data on youth delinquency for the nation as a whole. One source is *MTF,* the only national youth survey from which trends in self-reported delinquency going back to the mid-1970s can be gauged. Another more recently available source is the *NYRBS*, which provides national estimates of youth trends in self-reported assault and weapons possession covering the period from 1991 to 2003. We later draw on the *NYRBS* to confirm the *MTF* findings on youth assault trends over the 1990s.

MTF asks a nationally representative sample of high school seniors and, since 1991, eighth and tenth graders, about violent behavior across all community

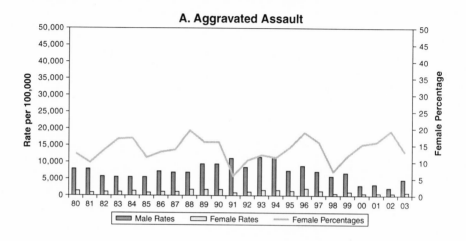

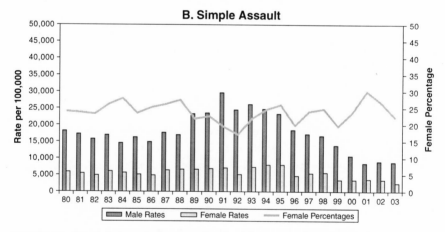

FIGURE 3.2 Trends in juvenile female and male violence rates (per 100,000) and female percentage of violent offending: National Crime Victimization Survey[a], 1980–2003. (*Continued on facing page.*)

a. Data are adjusted to take into account effects of the survey redesign in 1992. The multiplier is offense- and sex-specific and is calculated based only on juvenile data. The formula is: Multiplier = $(n_{92} + n_{93} + n_{94})/(n_{90} + n_{91} + n_{92})$.

b. The assault index includes aggravated and simple assaults.

c. The Violent Crime Index includes aggravated assault, robbery, and rape.

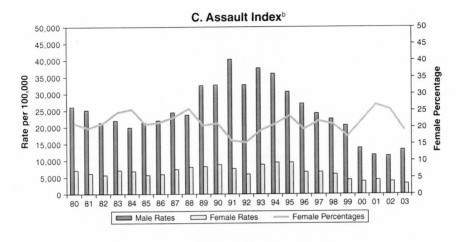

C. Assault Index[b]

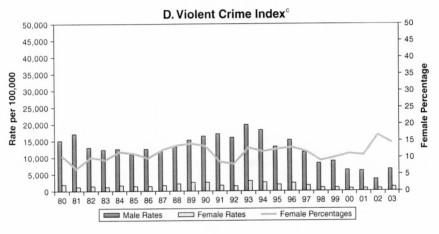

D. Violent Crime Index[c]

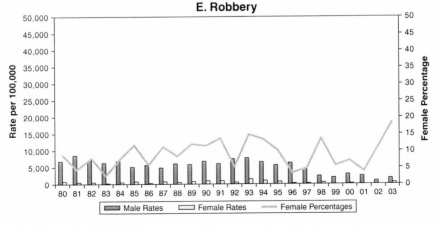

E. Robbery

FIGURE 3.2 *Continued*

settings. We calculate prevalence and high frequency estimates for robbery and for an assault index comprising three assault items for twelfth graders.[6] Because the trend patterns both overall and by gender are remarkably consistent across the assault items, our discussion targets the results for the assault index. Our analysis focuses on the findings for twelfth graders for reasons of parsimony since their time-series data extend backwards to the late 1970s. As we note in the following, the results are similar for the 1991 to 2003 period when all three grades were surveyed.

Table 3.2 (Panel C) displays results for the Dickey-Fuller method testing for statistically significant trends in the gender gap among seventeen- to eighteen-year-olds for prevalence (1+) as well as high-frequency (5+) measures for the time frame 1980 to 2003. Recall that a (significant) positive coefficient establishes a narrowing of the gender gap in adolescent violence. A visual representation of trends for the assault index and for robbery is provided in Figure 3.3.

Dickey-Fuller results indicate marked stability in the gender gap both for the composite assault index and for robbery over the 1980 to 2003 period, regardless of whether prevalence or high-frequency measures are used. These statistical patterns are underscored by the plots displayed in Figure 3.3, which show overall *constancy* in the gender gap over the past two decades (i.e., no movement or random fluctuations). Assault as well as robbery rates among both girls and boys are relatively unchanged over the 1980 to 2003 period (i.e., random or trendless fluctuations).

These figures also vividly demonstrate the gendered nature of interpersonal violence: (a) female assault levels are consistently lower than male levels across both prevalence and high-frequency measures and (b) the gender gap in repeat (high-frequency) assaultive violence is quite large—the FP averages only around 15 percent, as compared with about 35 percent for less frequent or minor involvement in violence. These findings are consistent with our earlier discussion and with prior delinquency research that shows that, as the delinquent behaviors or the violent offenses become more serious or chronic, the gender gap systematically widens (Steffensmeier and Allan 1996).

Last, the *MTF* findings contrast sharply with *UCR* arrest figures that show substantial gains in the female share of assaults. Instead, the *MTF* self-report data show that prevalence and high-frequency levels of assault for juvenile females and males have been fairly *constant* over the past two decades (including during the 1990s and early 2000) and that female involvement in violence has not increased relative to male violence.[7]

Summary of Gender Gap Trends in Violence across Data Sources, with Supplemental Self-Report Evidence

We summarize in Figure 3.4 the key results from the diverse data sources by comparing *UCR* arrest trends for assault with girls' violence trends as observed in victimization and self-report sources. To exhaust more fully the available time-

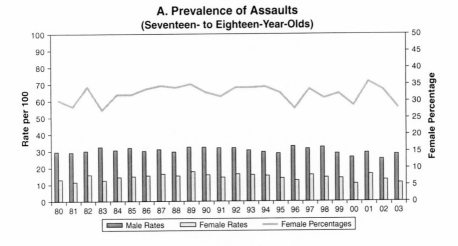

A. Prevalence of Assaults
(Seventeen- to Eighteen-Year-Olds)

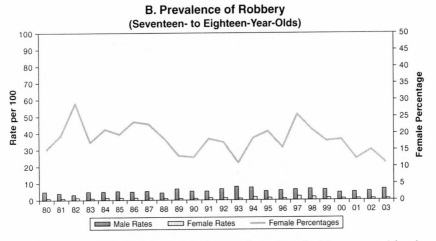

B. Prevalence of Robbery
(Seventeen- to Eighteen-Year-Olds)

FIGURE 3.3   Trends in female and male self-reported assault[a] and robbery rates and female percentage: MTF, 1980–2003 (seventeen- to eighteen-year-olds).

a. Assault index for seventeen- to eighteen-year-olds includes: during the last twelve months, how often have you (1) gotten into a serious fight in school or at work, (2) hurt someone badly enough to need bandages or a doctor, and (3) hit an instructor or supervisor. Assault index for all juveniles includes: during the last twelve months, how often have you (1) gotten into a serious fight in school or at work and (2) hurt someone badly enough to need bandages or a doctor.

series data from unofficial sources, Figure 3.4 also includes graphs depicting 1991 to 2003 assault trends from two self-report sources that capture more fully the ages in the juvenile population. One source is *MTF* data on eighth, tenth, and twelfth graders based on their responses to two assault items (school fight and injured someone). The other source is *NYRBS* of ninth to twelfth graders based on responses to physical fighting items.[8]

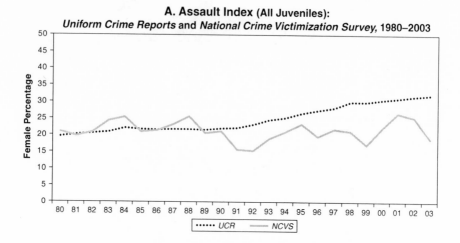

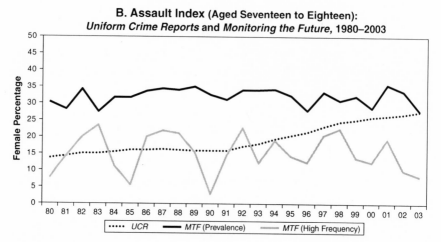

FIGURE 3.4 Summary of trends in juvenile gender gap for assault in arrest data compared with victimization and self-report sources: *Uniform Crime Reports, National Crime Victimization Survey, Monitoring the Future,* and *National Youth Risk Behavior Survey,* 1980[1991]–2003. *(Continued on facing page.)*

First, the analyses substantiate the axiom noted earlier about the gendered nature of interpersonal violence and its variation depending on behavioral item and measurement—the gender gap is small for minor kinds of violence (e.g., prevalence, misdemeanor assault) and very large for more serious forms (e.g., high-frequency, aggravated assault).

Second, in contrast to conclusions about rises in girls' violence based on arrest statistics, the results from sources independent of the criminal justice system (*NCVS, MTF,* and *NYRBS*) all show very little overall change both in girls'

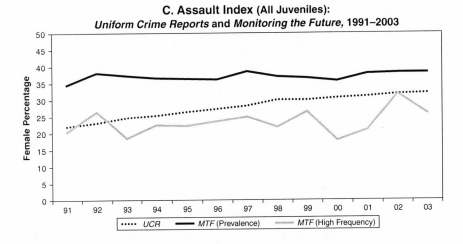

C. Assault Index (All Juveniles):
Uniform Crime Reports and *Monitoring the Future,* 1991–2003

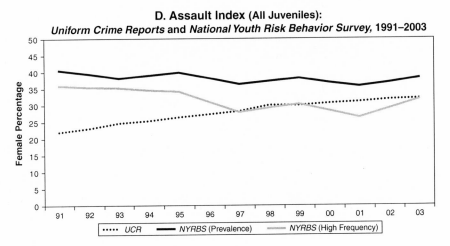

D. Assault Index (All Juveniles):
Uniform Crime Reports and *National Youth Risk Behavior Survey,* 1991–2003

FIGURE 3.4 *Continued*

assault levels and in the Violent Crime Index and, most notably, essentially no change in the gender gap or female-to-male percentage of violent offending (Canter 1982b).[9] These divergent findings across the *UCR* versus sources independent of the criminal justice system point to gender-specific effects of policy changes rather than shifts in girls' aggression.

Qualitative Observations

Qualitative evidence and anecdotal observations provide additional evidence in support of the policy change hypothesis that girls' arrest rates reflect shifts in law enforcement policies and practices rather than changes in girls' behavior. A recent study by the Children and Family Justice Center of Northwestern University

School of Law profiling violence and social control in several large urban school districts points to greater police involvement in events previously handled informally and finds that schools have "raised the stakes for certain adolescent behaviors" so that adolescents are being officially sanctioned for offenses that would not likely constitute a crime if an adult were involved (Children and Family Justice Center 2005).

For example, a girl in the eighth grade hit a boy for pulling up her skirt in the cafeteria during lunch. The police were called and the girl was charged with assault and disturbing the peace. In other schools, students were charged with "terroristic threatening" for playing cops and robbers or "assault" for throwing a snowball (Children and Family Justice Center, 2005, p. 7, 15). A fourteen-year-old girl poured a carton of chocolate milk on the head of a classmate for "talking about her." The local police stated they believed "the quickest way to resolve it was to charge her [with battery]" (p. 13). School discipline matters are being outsourced to or supplemented by the criminal justice system, leading to more student arrests than in the past. One juvenile court judge commented: "My court has become, in essence, the principal's office" (p. 43).

Girls' Arrest and Self-Report Trends for Nonviolent Types of Delinquency

Thus far, we have framed this discussion in terms of trends in girls' violence. The competing frameworks of behavior change and policy change are also applicable to girls' delinquency more generally. We briefly consider trends in nonviolent delinquency across several data sources to offer additional evidence regarding these two positions.

As is the case with violent crime, both popular and scientific writings often report rising levels of property crime and drug use among adolescent girls both relative to girls in previous decades and relative to boys. Thus, we compared girls' trends in arrests for nonviolent types of delinquency as compared with self-reports from *MTF*. Offense categories available in the self-report data that overlap with *UCR* categories include the minor property crimes of larceny-theft, motor vehicle theft, burglary,[10] vandalism, and arson. Both sources also include information on drug use. We only briefly recount specific findings because the main conclusion based on nonviolent crime parallels that for violence—*girls' relative share of arrest increases but self-reported involvement does not.* (Figures and Dickey-Fuller results are available from the coauthors.)

The findings for the property crimes are straightforward: The arrest statistics show the gender gap narrowing, whereas the self-report data show very little, if any, change in the gender gap. Similar trend patterns are found in both the longer and shorter *MTF* series and for both prevalence and high-frequency measures. The female share of *arrests* has increased fairly substantially and significantly for larceny, auto theft, vandalism, and burglary/trespass, although there is no significant change for arson. In contrast, the female share of *self-reported* involvement in theft crimes has held steady or is relatively unchanged over the 1980 to 2003 period across the property offenses. The narrowing gender gap in arrests results mainly from male declines matched with lesser female declines for burglary/trespass,[11] stability among females for theft, and small female increases for motor vehicle theft and vandalism in the post-1990s period. In the self-report data, both female and male rates are fairly stable across all the property-crime items for both prevalence and high-frequency measures. There is little in the way of any noticeable "crime wave" among teenagers—youths are about as delinquent today as a decade or two ago.

We also compared girls' and boys' arrest trends for drug violations relative to their self-reported substance use trends in *MTF*.[12] Key findings are as follows: First, the gender gap in arrests for drug abuse violations in 2000 is identical to the gap in 1980—about 16 percent (see Table 3.1), but with some fluctuation over this time frame. Although the gender gap is unchanged over this period, girls' rates of arrest for drugs have almost doubled over the past twenty years, but so have boys' rates. Both girls' and boys' rates declined from 1980 to the early 1990s, although female declines were more substantial. Since then, female and male youth arrests for drug offenses have continued to climb at a similar pace.

The gender gap in drug abuse over the past couple of decades as reflected in *MTF* self-report data is also fairly stable across most measures of drug offending. Shifts in usage patterns over time have been similar for boys and girls: Self-reported drug usage rates (e.g., for marijuana, cocaine, heroin) are at lower levels now than in the late 1970s and early 1980s, although recently they have rebounded some after the steady decline characterizing the mid-1980s through the early 1990s.

Thus, both official and unofficial sources depict a stable gender gap in drug offending over the past twenty or so years. However, girls' and boys' rates of arrest for drug offending have markedly increased since the early 1990s such that levels are twice what they were two decades ago. In contrast, self-report data show drug usage patterns being at much lower levels now compared with the 1980s.

Gender by Race Differences in Violence and Delinquency

Last, we examined gender-by-race trends for violent and nonviolent offenses because some analysts have proposed that violence trends of minority girls might differ from those reported for girls as a whole, for two reasons. One is that minority girls are more likely to have experienced increased stress and victimization in recent years that would lead to real increases in violent crime. The second argument is that the impact of recent policy changes in the juvenile justice system has been greatest on minority girls, thus leading to their higher arrest or referral rates and a narrowing gender gap (Holsinger and Holsinger 2005). For this portion of our analysis, we relied on three sources of data that provide a gender-by-race breakdown: juvenile court statistics covering the 1985 to 2000 period, 1980 to 2003 *NCVS*, and 1980 to 2003 *MTF*. (Note: the *UCR* arrest data do not provide a gender-by-race breakdown.)

First, notwithstanding some fluctuations and minor differences, the major finding is that trend patterns among white and black girls are basically the same as those reported earlier for girls as a whole (i.e., official or juvenile court data show a narrowing gender gap, whereas nonofficial sources show a stable gender gap).

Second, focusing on particular assault patterns, both court referral and *NCVS* data show large race differences in assault, with black male and black female youths having much higher rates of assault, respectively, than white male and white female youths (rates available from authors). But there are relatively small within-race gender differences, the gender gap or FP is similar across racial groups.

Third, regarding trends in the gender gap, the court data show the FP among whites rising from about 21 percent in 1985 to about 27 percent in 2000, as compared with a rise of about 20 percent to 30 percent among blacks. The slightly greater narrowing of the gender gap among blacks is due to a somewhat greater decline in black male rates in the late 1990s as compared with roughly stable rates for black female youths. By comparison, the trend in the FP of assaults in *NCVS* data is stable or slightly downward among whites (gender gap widens a bit), but slightly upward among blacks (gap narrows a bit). This narrowing of the gender gap among blacks is due to sharp declines in rates of assault among young black males since roughly 1994, a pattern that partly reflects the overall decline in gun and drug violence in inner-city neighborhoods during this time frame (Steffensmeier and Harer 1999). Black female rates also decline (beginning a few years later), but black male declines are more marked.

These findings are not supportive of the view that minority girls will be more greatly affected by stress- and violence-producing social changes in the lives of girls. Instead, the *NCVS* data, like the juvenile court data, portray generally parallel movement of white and black girls' rates of assaultive violence, yielding no evidence of a gender-by-race interaction and, instead, suggesting that similar factors underlie changes in the gender gap (or lack thereof) among whites and blacks.

Take-Home Points

In sum, this review and analysis of arrest trends highlights several important points.

1. The glaring differences between the official and nonofficial sources in their portrayals of changes in girls' delinquency, particularly their violence trends, are at *odds* with the behavior change hypothesis but *supportive* of the policy change position.

   a. The strongest evidence for the policy change argument concerns girls' violence trends where multiple types of unofficial sources of data (e.g., self-reports, victim accounts, and case studies) all show little or no change in girls' violence or in the gender gap. The lack of change portrayed by the unofficial sources is even more remarkable considering that changes in perceptions and expectations about girls' violence in society at large might itself have "self-fulfilling" effects leading to greater recognition and higher reported levels of girls' assaults in survey responses.

b. Although not the main focus of this chapter, patterns in nonviolent offending also offer support for the policy change position; the gender gap in minor property crime has narrowed according to official records, but self-report data show marked stability in the gender gap for these types of offenses.

2. The rise in girls' arrests for assault and the narrowing gender gap have less to do with differences in the underlying behavior of girls and more to do with (a) netwidening changes in law enforcement that have resulted in prosecuting less serious forms of physical attack or threat, especially those occurring in private settings and where there is less culpability, and (b) "less biased" or more efficient responses on the part of law enforcement, parents, teachers, and social workers to girls' physical or verbal aggression. The impact of these netwidening trends is manifested across offense types, including property crimes and drug violations; however, the effect on girls is most apparent in the arena of violence and aggression.

3. In light of recent media and scholarly interest in girls' violence, the apparently important role that recent shifts in penal philosophy and policing have had in escalating the arrest proneness of girls for criminal assault is particularly significant. As we have highlighted elsewhere (Steffensmeier et al. 2005), several key movements have played important roles in spawning and now embodying this new culture of crime control and juvenile justice policy, the collateral consequence of which is greater visibility of the delinquencies female youths commit. Because a full treatment is not possible here, we limit our discussion to significant aspects of these interrelated movements as they appear to bear on girls' arrest trends.

a. The major development in policing over the past one to two decades has been the movement toward situational crime prevention and the targeting of minor forms of crime as a strategy for controlling serious criminality (Garland 2001; Kelling and Coles 1996). The trend has been to lower the threshold of law enforcement, in effect to arrest or "charge up" and be less tolerant of low-level crime and misdemeanors, and to be more inclined to respond to them with maximum penalties. This shift has been especially marked in the area of youth "violence," where heightened citizen concern about personal safety has generated both more proactive reporting and pro-arrest policies by police and other authorities.

b. A coinciding trend both within academia and the prevention-security sector has been the movement—aimed primarily at children and youths—toward early and proactive intervention as a primary strategy for preventing escalation of minor conduct violations into more troublesome antisocial behavior, including chronic delinquency and perhaps an adult criminal career (see reviews in Beckett 1997 and Garland 2001). Spurred in particular by the increasing prominence of developmental perspectives in the social sciences and the growth in "psychological" criminology, the epistemologies shaping these strategies center around beliefs that less serious disruptive and delinquent behavior precedes more serious delinquency (Farrington and West 1993; Jenkins 1998; Wasserman et al. 2003b). The shift toward an interventionist ideology also corresponds to a sharp decline in the prominence of labeling theory within criminology and its attendant emphasis on judicious nonintervention as a viable prevention or treatment strategy (Lemert and Winter 2000).

The new ways of thinking about crime and delinquency (what Garland calls "new criminologies") are also important because (a) they tend to blur distinctions between delinquency and antisocial behavior more generally; (b) they lump together differing forms of physical aggression and verbal intimidation as manifesting interpersonal violence; and (c) they elevate interpersonal violence (defined broadly) as a high-profile social problem, particularly among youths. These beliefs have become core elements of popular thinking (e.g., among mass media, school officials, community leaders, the activist middle-class citizenry, medical and helping professions) about crime and violence.

c. These developments combine with and perhaps are co-opted by coinciding trends in society at large, such as (a) a more litigious society in which persons in positions of authority (including police, school officials, and social workers) have less leeway to sanction or "handle informally" wayward or defiant youth behavior but instead are inclined to resort to formal procedures to forestall legal reprisal or public criticism, (b) the expanded media role in shaping public and policy-maker views, and (c) "law and order" themes in the politics of crime control dating back to the late 1960s. The themes endorse stiffened criminal justice policies as the primary response to unacceptably high crime rates and an effective get-elected strategy by campaigning to crack down on crime by doing away with lenient justice-system practices (see reviews in Feld 1998 and Simon 1997). Notably, the effects of these political and policy changes toward greater punitiveness, while affecting all constituencies, have apparently been greatest on women and youths (Males 1996).

d. Finally, stakeholders or advocacy groups with special interests in girls' delinquency and youth violence have emerged to aid, repress, punish, rehabilitate, safeguard, or in other ways deal with both victims and offenders of violence (Feld 1998; Garland 2001). These private and public agencies and industries are prone to use official data as advocacy statistics to advance professional and economic interests (e.g., publications, grants, jobs in school security, media share, and other areas) and as proof of the correctness of their own actions as well as group or agency agendas (Fuentes 1998; Males 1996). These claims about the growing seriousness of the "social problem" (e.g., girls' violence, youth crime), buttressed with misinterpreted official data, heighten attention to the issue of female violence. The media's eagerness in reporting high-profile cases of girls' violence both creates and spreads conceptions of purported shifts in girls' violence and delinquency.

4. The practice of under- or overestimating girls' violence is far from a trivial matter. Resource allocation and public concern are stirred largely by reports of the magnitude of the problem, as are public policies that shape law enforcement practices.

   a. Understanding the collateral consequences of these developments is important not only because of past effects but also because this new culture of penal philosophy—with its emphasis on expressive and preventive punishment and with its economic underpinnings—continues to be at the core of juvenile justice policies today. By expressive punishment, we mean the use of formal punitive sanctions to express society's disapproval of a behavior, such as violence. Preventive punishment or risk management refers to the proactive strategy of attempting to identify or formally handle threats posed by offenders who may, but most often do not, become more serious (violent) offenders.

   b. While impacting all segments of society, targeting youth violence or aggression as a particularly serious social problem has promoted policies and agency involvements that have markedly expanded the reach of the criminal justice system into the lives of youths. Should these risk management and expressive-preventive punishment trends continue, they will result in arresting more adolescent females and in proportionately larger numbers than would be expected based on the typical sex ratio in violent offending. That is, future trends in girls' arrests for violence (and for delinquency more generally) are likely to depend less on what girls do than on whether the netwidening effects identified in this chapter as "causing" the rise in girls' arrests for violence continue to define public policies. Further, to the extent that the current inclination to stretch definitions of violence continues in the years ahead, we might expect girls' violence levels to also rise in the survey data—either because citizens more readily see girls as "violent" or because girls share in that view and more freely self-admit to committing minor acts of physical attack or threat.

Suggestions for Research

Future inquiry into girls' delinquency and the gender gap might focus on the following areas:

1. Localized studies of police and court records are needed to provide a contextual understanding of the organizational management of crime (including

changes in the law and in enforcement practices) and a detailed breakdown of the kinds of crime committed by girls and boys. At present, we have too little systematic, qualitative data on the nature of contemporary female offending, especially as it compares to contemporary male offending or to female offending in the past. Such studies not only would help overcome a lack of knowledge about which sorts of crimes might be subsumed under which FBI categories but also would provide a baseline for evaluating future trends in girls' delinquency.

2. Background profiles, interviews, and case studies of female offenders are needed to develop a portrait of juvenile female offenders and to describe the nature of their criminal roles and the circumstances leading to delinquent involvement. In particular, there is a need to examine whether girls and boys commit the same types of crime for similar reasons, and whether those reasons have changed over time. Moreover, instead of asking whether girls' delinquency has grown in a global sense, it might be more informative to ask whether specific kinds of crime have become more common among particular groups of girls and, if so, why. There is a need to think more concretely about girls' delinquency trends.

3. Trend analysis by race, ethnicity, social class, and rural/suburban/urban locality are needed because the effects of legal and social changes on girls' delinquency may vary by class or race-ethnicity or locality. Demographically disaggregated trend analyses are particularly needed today, in light of recent changes in the racial-ethnic composition of the U.S. population.

4. Declines in male delinquency and violence arrest rates require explanation as well. Juvenile male rates have declined over the past decade or so for some crimes such as burglary and assault, producing a higher share of female offending for those crimes. We need a more careful assessment of why male rates have declined for particular offenses. For a discussion of the crime drop, see Blumstein and Wallman (2005) and Zimring (2006).

Suggestions for Policy

In light of our key finding that—in sharp contrast to arrest reports—there has been *no* meaningful change in the gender gap or in girls' violence and delinquency, perhaps the most pressing policy issue is the unintended adverse consequence for girls of recent juvenile justice policies, including crime crackdowns on law-violating behaviors of marginal seriousness and on domestic/relational violence (including girl-on-girl fighting). Girls and boys commit similar types of minor offenses, as our analysis confirms. To the extent that juvenile justice policies and philosophies target minor sorts of violent and delinquent behaviors, girls' arrest trends will become more similar to boys'.

Modifying the disparate and possibly harmful effects of these netwidening policies will be difficult because they are nested in broader ideological and economic developments whose core beliefs and stakes are entangled in the expanded application of risk management and expressive-preventive punishment approaches. The immediate and long-term consequences of these perspectives' emphasis on early intervention and enhanced formal control of problem individuals or groups are unknown. But plausible harms include interrupted or skewed social development, separation from family, interrupted education, exposure to deviant peers, trauma, changed definition of self, and stigma, often lifelong. These and other social costs are likely to be greater when end-stage strategies (like arrest or residential placement) are used for minor behaviors that might be better addressed in other ways.

4

Biopsychological Factors, Gender, and Delinquency

Diana Fishbein, Shari Miller, Donna Marie Winn, and Gayle Dakof

The goal of this chapter is to highlight ways in which specific biopsychological vulnerability factors relate to girls' delinquency. Although the majority of these factors also influence delinquency proneness in boys, the factors considered particularly relevant to a chapter on girls' delinquency are those that either are more prevalent among girls than boys who are delinquent or relate to delinquency in distinctive ways among girls. Five general categories are thus considered salient:

1. Stress and adversity
2. Attention Deficit-Hyperactivity Disorder (ADHD) and Conduct Disorder (CD)
3. Intellectual deficits
4. Early pubertal maturation
5. Mental health issues

A host of additional biopsychological vulnerability factors (e.g., genetic liability, social-information processing, personality traits) might have been included, but there is insufficient research to show gender differences in their relationships with high-risk behaviors.

The conceptual basis for this chapter is derived from a developmental, multifactorial model of complex disorders (Tarter et al. 1999). Because no one theory attempts to understand the phenomenon of girls' delinquency, the specific vulnerability factors selected for our focus reflect an integration of new-generation etiological theories from cognitive neuroscience into developmental psychology and the social sciences. This interdisciplinary approach provides a foundation for future work to refine the model, with a goal of bridging the gap between existing theories and eventually informing gender-sensitive programming.

The chapter begins with an overview of gender differences, focusing on the individual-level influence of the extent of exposure and sensitivity to these factors on behavioral outcomes. We then review evidence for these five categories of factors and their association with risk for girls' delinquency. Within these sections, we discuss critical interactions between biological and psychological processes in order to understand the range of factors influencing girls' delinquency.[1]

Level of Exposure and Sensitivity to Prevailing Vulnerability Factors

Although an extensive literature outlines biopsychological factors in boys' delinquency (see reviews by Loeber et al. 2001 and Wasserman et al. 2003a), there is a dearth of empirical work on susceptibility for girls' delinquency. Currently, there is no consensus on whether vulnerability factors for boys' delinquency apply equally well to girls (Giordano and Cernkovich 1997). Some have espoused that these factors are essentially the same for both boys and girls (Fergusson and Horwood 2002; Moffitt et al. 2001). Either explicitly or implicitly, this viewpoint suggests that there is no need for sex-specific theories to explain vulnerability factors for girls' delinquency. Conversely, others have contended that the constellation of factors that confer susceptibility for girls is distinct from that of boys, or that girls need a different "push" to become delinquent, most often focusing on the centrality of relationships in girls' development and girls' experiences as victims of abuse (Bloom 2003; Chesney-Lind and Pasko 2004).

Notwithstanding the scarcity of research on girls, the question of vulnerability factors for delinquency is not a straightforward one. One issue to consider is that girls and boys may vary in their *exposure* to or experiences of different susceptibility processes. To illustrate, boys are more likely than girls to evidence underlying neuropsychological deficits and to be diagnosed with ADHD, a key vulnerability factor for antisocial behavior (Loeber and Farrington 2001; Moffitt 1993). However, the apparent fact that girls are less likely to be diagnosed with ADHD does not preclude this same process from being predictive of antisocial behavior for both genders. This question awaits empirical and longitudinal inquiry as we know very little about the developmental progression of girls with ADHD, although concurrent studies do indicate that ADHD girls manifest similar social, cognitive, and academic deficits as boys exhibit (Biederman et al. 1999, 2002; Hinshaw et al. 2002; M.T.A. Group Co-operative 1999). Thus, sex differences in the level of antisocial and delinquent behaviors may reflect differential rates of exposure to the same processes.

A second major issue is that the genders may vary in their *sensitivity* to the same process as a function of differences in underlying biological functions, psychological traits, and social interpretations of the experience. To illustrate, although similar sets of vulnerability factors (e.g., child abuse and other forms of adversity) may influence the behavior of both boys and girls, each gender may react internally to that stressor in different ways in terms of underlying biological responses and psychological perceptions and interpretations of the experience (Klein and Corwin 2002; Leve and Chamberlain 2004; Maccoby 1998; Moffitt et al. 2001). In such cases, subsequent behavioral manifestations would tend to differ between boys and girls even though they have been exposed to the same type or intensity of a potentially predisposing condition. In this example, both boys and girls who experience physical abuse are at high risk for delinquency; however, behavioral outcomes for girls tend to involve internalizing disorders (e.g., depression, anxiety, post-traumatic stress disorder [PTSD]), while boys tend to be more likely to engage in externalizing behaviors (Leve and Chamberlain 2004). Consequently, the question of whether vulnerability factors are the same for boys and girls is not simply a yes/no proposition. As is apparent throughout this book, many of the same factors appear to operate for both genders. However, girls and boys may vary in their exposure, as well as potentially differ in their sensitivity and reactions to the same factor. Accordingly, rather than using the term "gender-specific" (only early age of menarche applies specifically to girls), the term *gender-sensitive* is used throughout the remainder of this chapter to acknowledge that boys and girls may differ in sensitivity to and rates of exposure to various vulnerability factors.

Vulnerability Factor Category 1: Stress and Adversity

Studies clearly show that exposure to stress is a significant vulnerability factor for high-risk behavior in both genders (McBurnett et al. 2005; Sinha 2001). In fact, the expression of psychiatric disorders, as well as conduct problems in general, is influenced and often directly precipitated by exposure to uncontrollable stressors. However, not only are the genders prone to experiencing certain types of stress at differing rates (Ge et al. 1994), stress may also exert a somewhat different biological and psychological influence on girls versus boys. These underlying differences may be due to somewhat unique sensitivities or gendered responses to stress that, in turn, may produce somewhat differing effects on mental health and behavioral outcomes. In essence, early and severe stressful experiences are precursors to later concomitant behavioral disorders, the incidence of which appears to differ between sexes (Bays 1990; Teicher, Anderson, and Polcari 2003).

Recently discovered gender-related differences particularly in biological processes may account for many of the sex differences in stress reactivity (Rose et al. 2004). One primary example of tendencies for girls and boys to differ in stress responses pertain to "fight-or-flight" behaviors. Males more often actually engage in actual fight-or-flight behaviors than females; this tendency has been related to alterations in hormone levels that differ between the genders in terms of quality and quantity (Taylor et al. 2000). The behavioral response to stress among females is better characterized as "tend and befriend" (Klein and Corwin 2002; Taylor et al. 2000). This strategy involves the use of social interactions and supports to provide protection against the stressful agent or its detrimental consequences (Carter and Altemus 1997; Cho et al. 1999; Insel et al. 1998; McCarthy and Altemus 1997). Hormonal responses to stress underlying this tendency in females not only tend to suppress aggressive responses but also dampen the effects of stress, potentially protecting the brain to some extent from its damage. Another example of biological mechanisms that underlie gender differences in behavioral responses to stress involve females' somewhat advanced language and memory skills (Caplan et al. 1997; Collins and Kimura 1997; McGivern et al. 1997; Seidlitz and Diener 1998) and processing of emotional and social cues (Cozby 1973; Natale, Gur, and Gur 1983), which may operate to increase resiliency in the face of stressful experiences.

In other ways, however, females appear to be more sensitive to the effects of stress, thus leading to differences in sensitivity and ultimate behavioral outcomes. In response to stress, females appear to produce greater amounts of stress hormones from the pituitary gland and adrenal cortex, which can negatively alter mood (Kudielka et al. 2004; Roelfsema et al. 1993). In addition, although estrogens protect the brain under stressful circumstances to some extent, the cyclic fluctuations of the menstrual cycle may serve to amplify the response to stress, which confers susceptibility to depression and anxiety (Seeman 1997; Shansky et al. 2004). Additional reports show that females are more prone to negative affect in response to subjective perceptions of stress than males (Myin-Germeys et al. 2004). The extent to which symptoms of affective disorders (e.g., depression and anxiety) relate to delinquency proneness is discussed in the mental health section of this chapter.

Several reports suggest a heightened vulnerability to behavioral problems among females relative to males in response to traumatic events (Dornfield and Kruttschnitt 1992; Robertson, Bankier, and Schwartz 1987; Widom 1991). As mentioned earlier, girls' somewhat distinguishable susceptibility may be attributed to (a) an increased incidence of exposures to certain stressors, (b) increased sensitivity to similar stressors relative to boys, and (c) proneness to different types of behavioral outcomes (e.g., affective disorders, dysfunctional relationships) relative to boys that place them at risk for delinquency. In the first scenario, studies suggest that the incidence of physical and sexual abuse, as well as dysfunctional families and maltreatment, is pervasive among females who engage in antisocial behavior, particularly those responsible for violent crimes, relative to male offenders and even more so when compared with the general population (OJJDP 1996; Smith, Leve, and Chamberlain 2006; Snell 1994). Girls appear to experience not only a greater number of negative life events during adolescence than boys, but also are more likely to experience interpersonal stressors and be adversely affected by them (Ge et al. 1994). For example, a greater number of parenting disruptions are more predictive of delinquency and drug abuse among girls of substance-abusing parents than among boys (Keller et al. 2002). With respect to the second scenario, although both genders are subjected to stressors and are adversely affected, females may be more sensitive to their effects particularly in terms of susceptibility to mood disorders. Girls' sensitivity may be partially a function of their being more bound to the home and perhaps more directly influenced by family-centered and relational problems (Maccoby 1998; Pepler and Craig 1999). For example, Stroud, Salovey, and Epel (2002) reported that women were more physiologically reactive to social rejection challenges, while men reacted more to achievement challenges, which may contribute to women's increased rates of affective disorders. In the third scenario, stressful events may trigger different behavioral outcomes because of gender-related variations in predispositions and susceptibilities in processes such as coping, appraisals, social cognitive responses, mood vulnerabilities, and relationship orientations. Thus, differences in effects and outcomes may depend, at least in part, on the types of stressors experienced, setting, developmental age, propensity for mental problems, particular circumstances in the home environment, and other co-occurring conditions, as discussed in Chapter 5.

Vulnerability Factor Category 2: Attention Deficit-Hyperactivity and Conduct Disorders

ADHD is a persistent and clinically significant developmental disorder that affects 3 percent to 9 percent of children (Barkley 1998). The two core features of the disorder are symptoms of inattention and hyperactivity/impulsivity. Accordingly, the most current criteria include diagnoses of either inattentive only (IA), hyperactive/impulsive only (HI), or combined hyperactive/impulsive and inattentive (HIA) (American Psychiatric Association 1994). ADHD children also have difficulties in inhibiting impulses, self-regulating behavior and emotion, orienting to the future, and engaging in particular high-level cognitive functions, such as memory. As with most other developmental disorders, males outnumber females by a three-to-one ratio (Barbaresi et al. 2002; Lahey, Goodman, and Waldman 1999; Offord, Boyle, and Racine 1989). Consistent with these numbers, results from community-based samples suggest that girls with ADHD are less symptomatic and less impaired in terms of reading achievement, inattentive and hyperactive problems, internalization of symptoms, aggression, and peer status (Gaub and Carlson 1997; Gershon 2002). However, findings from clinic-based samples suggest the opposite, namely that girls evidence lower IQ, higher levels of inattentive symptoms (Gaub and Carlson 1997; Gershon 2002), and lower self-esteem than boys with ADHD (Quinn and Wigal 2004). Girls who are referred for ADHD problems may be the most seriously affected and more likely to exhibit co-occurring personality disorders, which exacerbate the outcome (Burket et al. 2005). Despite these sex differences in clinical features, results across three large-scale clinical samples are consistent in showing that girls with ADHD manifest similar social, cognitive, and academic deficits to boys (Biederman et al. 1999, 2002; Hinshaw et al. 2002; M.T.A. Group Co-operative 1999).

The ADHD–Delinquency Linkage in Girls

ADHD is a known risk factor for boys' conduct and delinquent problems (Loeber et al. 2001; Wasserman et al. 2003a). Because the study of ADHD has been male-dominated, much less is known about whether ADHD is a precursor to girls' delinquency. The few studies with girls that do exist are predominantly cross-sectional, with one exception. In a longitudinal study, Messer and others (2004) followed a sample of 183 females (eighty-six females raised in institutional care and ninety-seven in a comparison group) from young adulthood through ages thirty-four to forty to examine precursors of criminal behavior in women. They found that hyperactivity (based on retrospective reports) was significantly related to adult offending (other precursors included institutional rearing, childhood antisocial difficulties, and adolescent CD). Still, very little is known about the developmental progression of ADHD in girls. It is possible that the pathway to delinquency for girls with ADHD differs from boys on the basis of other influential factors that may moderate the relationship. For example, Becker and McCloskey (2002) provide support for the importance of an interaction with social factors, showing that family violence was related to ADHD and conduct problems in girls but not boys. On the other hand, the relationship between family violence and ADHD did not increase risk for later delinquency for girls, as it did for boys. Rather, family violence in childhood had a direct effect on delinquency in girls irrespective of the presence of ADHD.

Nevertheless, rates of ADHD are quite high for those youths in the justice system (Garland et al. 2001). In a study of 1,829 randomly selected delinquents in juvenile detention, 17 percent of boys and 21 percent of girls met diagnostic criteria for ADHD (Teplin et al. 2002). In another sample of 478 randomly selected juvenile justice youths who were "wards of the court," 15 percent of boys and 21 percent of girls were diagnosed with ADHD (McCabe et al. 2002). In both of these studies, statistical comparisons by sex were not significant. However, these results clearly point out that girls in the juvenile justice system are highly likely to have problems with ADHD. Also of relevance is that, for both genders, the presence of co-occurring Oppositional Defiant Disorder (ODD) or CD worsens the behavioral and emotional difficulties for children with ADHD. In fact, CD is not an uncommon diagnosis for girls and appears to be present in a sizable proportion of girls who are delinquent (Keenan, Loeber, and Green 1999).

Other distinctions between girls and boys with ADHD and their propensity for conduct problems have been reported. Girls with ADHD show more problems with anxiety, distress, depression, locus of control, and vocabulary scores (Rucklidge and Tannock 2001). Also, girls with ADHD were found to have greater developmental delays in brain function relative to boys; however, differences between girls with and without ADHD were not as pronounced as differences between boys with and without ADHD and improvement over time occurred faster in the girls (Clarke et al. 2001). Although many studies report greater behavioral and neurological impairment in girls with ADHD relative to boys (Ernst et al. 1994), findings from this study led the authors to suggest that the brain differences found may reflect sex-related referral biases. In other words, girls with fewer behavioral disturbances may have been diagnosed as a result of bias on the part of clinicians conducting the ratings. Interestingly, girls with ADHD themselves may have poorer self-perceptions than boys, irrespective of neuropsychological status (Arcia and Conners 1998).

In sum, the question of whether ADHD is a vulnerability factor for girls' delinquency cannot be answered definitively. Studies of ADHD in girls are sorely lacking, particularly in terms of prospective, longitudinal investigations. There is some suggestion across different lines of research that ADHD and conduct problems do co-occur for girls at rates greater than chance and that young girls with behavior problems do evidence signs of ADHD. Furthermore, considerable numbers of girls in the juvenile justice system meet diagnostic criteria for ADHD, CD, or both. These findings suggest the need for a greater sensitivity among professionals to the clinical features of ADHD and CD in girls. However, girls are less likely than boys to be referred clinically, particularly if their symptoms are primarily inattentive and not externalizing (Hinshaw et al. 2005). More concerning are results from a recent epidemiological study showing that, even when girls were diagnosed with ADHD, they were less likely to receive appropriate medication (Angold et al. 2000). As with delinquency in girls, there may be societal norms for perceiving girls as all "sugar and spice" that impact the underreferral and undertreament of ADHD (Wasserman et al. 2003a).

Vulnerability Factor Category 3: Intellectual Deficits

General intelligence, which includes basic, global cognitive functions often measured by IQ tests, has been shown to predict both delinquency and school achievement for girls and boys (Fergusson and Horwood 1995; Maguin and Loeber 1996). These global cognitive functions are thought to have an impact on language functioning and aggressive, oppositional, attentional, and hyperactive behaviors that, in turn, potentially mediate the effects of IQ on delinquency. Deficits in intellectual functioning may also be associated with impaired social cognitive processes, such as failure to attend to appropriate social cues (e.g., adults' instructions, peers' social initiations) (Loeber and Farrington 2001).

The IQ–Delinquency Linkage in Girls

In boys, lower IQs or discrepancies in verbal IQ (VIQ) and performance IQ (PIQ) are related to delinquency and recidivism for boys. Is this also true of girls?

Ouston (1984) found in her study of over 2,300 youths in London, England, that while, in general, girls had much lower rates of delinquency than boys (6 percent versus 29 percent, respectively) as measured by official police contact, lower IQ and low socioeconomic status were related to greater delinquency in both boys *and* girls. Moffit and Silva (1988) found similarly that both delinquent girls and boys had lower IQs than their nondelinquent peers. Similarly, Rohde, Noell, and Ochs (1999) found in their sample of fifty homeless adolescent males and females (aged sixteen to twenty-one) that higher IQ scores (WAIS-R) were correlated with lower self-reported delinquency. White, Moffitt, and Silva (1989) found additional evidence that delinquent girls and boys have lower IQs than their nondelinquent peers, although "it did not appear that the delinquency main effect was as marked in girls as in boys" (p. 723).

Numerous studies, dating back to the 1970s, document the association between recidivism and low IQ scores among boys and girls (Cymbalisty, Schuck, and Dubeck 1975; Ganzer and Sarason 1973; West and Farrington 1977). In an early study, Maskin (1974) found that first-time offender girls between the ages of ten and fourteen who successfully graduated from a residential treatment and aftercare program without recidivating had higher IQs (over eight IQ points higher) at the beginning of treatment than did girls who recidivated. More recently, Fendrich (1991) found that the types of programs adjudicated delinquents are placed in (alternative program versus training school), younger initial commitment age, lower IQ, and, most importantly, family problems as rated by the parole officer were associated with subsequent parole violations for boys and girls (only 11 percent of the sample).

Several studies examine the social contextual mechanisms through which low IQ or discrepancies between PIQs and VIQs may get translated into delinquent behavior, although there has been very little study of such mechanisms specifically in girls. Studies of factors that may moderate or mediate the impact of IQ on delinquency suggest numerous mechanisms to explain the relationship for both girls and boys, including less reliance on verbal skills and greater attributional biases in social problem-solving (Wong and Cornell 1999); school performance, curriculum tracking, self-esteem, attitude toward school, and peer influences that affect behavioral control (McGloin, Pratt, and Maahs 2004; Menard and Morse 1986; Ward and Tittle 1994); adverse family influences (Offord and Poushinsky 1981); a lower level of abstract thinking in interaction with early pubertal maturation (Orr and Ingersoll 1995); and disadvantaged neighborhood (McGloin and Pratt 2003). Still, with all of the research that has been conducted examining the link between IQ and delinquency, there are severe limitations when interpreting the significance of this link. Often researchers have measured IQ after arrest or after incarceration so that it is impossible to understand the temporal sequencing of the IQ–delinquency link. Lipsitt, Buka, and Lipsitt (1990) assessed the temporal link between IQ and delinquency, finding no significant differences between future offenders and nonoffenders (boys and girls, blacks and whites) when cognitive and motor development were measured at eight months of age, but by age four and then again at age seven, significant differences were evident. Further, those authors found that the majority of individuals with lower IQs did not engage in delinquent acts. Other limitations in interpreting the IQ–delinquency link are the lack of clarity about the influence of such factors as IQ measurement instability, test/tester bias, racial segregation, racial bias in processing juveniles, ingestion of substances (i.e., alcohol), and residence in high-unemployment/economically impoverished communities. Breslau and others (2001) and Brooks-Gunn, Klebanov, and Duncan (1996) reported that economic deprivation and home and community environments contributed to a decline in IQ scores across early childhood. Several studies provide evidence to support the importance of positive environmental influences on higher IQ scores (Daley et al. 2003; Dickens and Flynn 2001).

Vulnerability Factor Category 4: Early Pubertal Maturation

Puberty is a major developmental milestone in terms of the biological and social impact it has on the individual (Hayward 2003). Dramatic hormonal surges during puberty activate several processes involved in sexual maturation that present new social challenges. Complicating this already difficult adjustment, pubertal development occurs during adolescence, which constitutes a life-course stage that is coupled with an unprecedented level of social challenges and autonomy in decision-making and actions. Thus, puberty is a time of great vulnerability to high-risk behaviors including delinquency.

The focus in this section is on the effects of pubertal timing, which are typically categorized as early, on time, or late relative to a defined reference group. This measurement is distinct from pubertal status, which indicates the level or stage of pubertal development (e.g., age of menarche or Tanner stage ratings). On average, girls begin puberty about a year before boys (Sizonenko 1987). Data from a study of over seventeen thousand girls indicate that the age of pubertal onset (but not the age of menarche) has dropped in recent decades, with a decline of one year for white girls (mean age: ten years) and two years for African American girls (mean age: just under nine years) (Herman-Giddens and Slora 1997). These findings only serve to highlight research showing that the early occurrence of puberty may create a particular imbalance for girls between the development of observable physical signs of "maturity" relative to the maturity level of cognitive and emotional systems that are still largely underdeveloped (Graber, Brooks-Gunn, and Warren 1999).

The Puberty–Delinquency Linkage in Girls

Although there is substantial evidence that early pubertal maturation is related to greater susceptibility to delinquency in both boys and girls, the relationship appears to be stronger for girls (Brooks-Gunn, Graber, and Paikoff 1994; Graber et al. 1997; Laitinen-Krispijn et al. 1999; Magnusson 1988; Weichold, Silbereisen, and Schmitt-Rodermund 2003). For boys (but not for girls), late maturation is also associated with risk for behavioral disorders, poor adjustment, negative self-perception, and delinquency (Graber et al. 1997), although there is at least one discrepancy in the literature (Wichstrom 2000).

In one of the first studies of girls, Magnusson and Ohmen (1987) examined the relationship between biological maturity and norm-breaking behavior among 466 Swedish girls. Those girls who matured early were at increased risk for truancy and other norm-breaking behaviors. A more recent study of over thirty-eight thousand Finnish adolescents found that an early onset of puberty was linked to higher rates of bullying behaviors and truancy (Kaltiala-Heino et al. 2003). Graber and others (1997) found that the effects of pubertal onset were also linked to diagnosable levels of CD. This study found early maturing girls were at greater risk for a disruptive behavior disorder as compared with on-time or late-maturing girls. Particularly striking was that the rates of CD among early maturing girls were equivalent to the rates among boys.

The effects of early pubertal timing are not limited to delinquency. Numerous studies indicate that early maturing girls are at increased risk for a host of poor outcomes, including risky sexual behavior, intimate partner violence, adolescent pregnancy, internalization of problems, and comorbid psychiatric problems (Caspi and Moffitt 1991; Dick et al. 2000; Foster, Hagan, and Brooks-Gunn 2004; Ge et al. 2006; Ge, Conger, and Elder 2001; Graber, Brooks-Gunn, and Warren 1997, 2006; Hayward et al. 1997; Stice, Presnell, and Bearman 2001). Furthermore, the impact of early maturation does not appear to be transient. A recent study followed youths into young adulthood and examined the lifetime and current history of psychopathology. Young women who had been early maturers continued to be susceptible to psychiatric disturbance, including antisocial personality disorder. Clearly, the aforementioned research highlights the link between early pubertal timing and delinquency. What follows next is an examination of the research that seeks to discover the underlying mechanisms that drive the connection between pubertal timing and delinquency.

Possible Mechanisms Explaining the Puberty–Delinquency Linkage

Several factors potentially explaining both early pubertal maturation and its direct and indirect links to delinquency are important to consider given the significant influence of social factors on an essentially genetic and biological process (Kaprio et al. 1995; Treloar and Martin 1990). In other words, the psychosocial environment has a profound influence on the physiological mechanisms that initiate and control the timing of pubertal maturation (Ellis and Garber 2000; Ellis et al. 1999). Graber, Brooks-Gunn, and Warren (1995) reported the following antecedent factors as potentially important in the developmental timing of puberty: (a) hereditary transmission, (b) weight and weight for height, (c) stressful life events, (d) family relations, (e) absence or presence of an adult male in the household, and (f) psychological adjustment. In addition, prematurity, early malnutrition, smallness for gestational age, and excessive childhood weight gain during different critical developmental time windows have been implicated in early puberty and different long-lasting effects on pubertal development (Neville and Walker 2005; van Weissenbruch et al. 2005). Perhaps not coincidentally, many of these factors have been independently associated with risk for delinquency, including stress exposures, absence of the father in the home, and psychological adjustment (Lempers and Clark-Lempers 1990). Most studies suggest that the interaction between early puberty and the presence of these conditions increases the likelihood of problem behaviors, and there is further evidence that some of these factors may actually play a causal role in early puberty, which subsequently compounds vulnerability (Costello et al. 2007).

Numerous studies relate stressful experiences during childhood with early pubertal development (Caspi et al. 1993; Hulanicka, Gronkiewicz, and Koniarek 2001). In particular, the role of family dysfunction or distress has been emphasized as a primary stressor associated with early puberty for girls, including psychopathology in the mother, an absent father or father figure, rejection or emotional distancing of the child, and presence of a stepfather in the home (Ellis and Garber 2000; Moffit et al. 1992). Other stressors associated with early puberty include unstable parental bonds, insensitive rearing, insecurity within the family, familial mistrust, and scarce resources (Hulanicka et al. 2001; Kim and Smith 1998). Draper and Belsky (1990) and Belsky, Steinberg, and Draper (1991) suggest that the relationship between stress and the timing of puberty has evolutionary significance by accelerating sexual activity and, thus, reproduction. As a consequence, daughters of women who experience stress and consequently mature earlier may be more likely to travel down a similar developmental pathway because of both genetic (Leek 1991) and socializing influences (Hulanicka 1986, 1989; Kim and Smith 1998).

Although the causal mechanisms explaining the linkages between stress, pubertal development, and delinquency are not yet entirely understood, ways in which biological processes underlying stress responses and puberty overlap may provide some clues. It is possible that the risk for psychosocial problems may be related to early puberty with its commensurate early release of stress hormones (Rieder and Coupey 1999). Whether stress itself triggers early puberty, thereby leading to psychosocial problems or, conversely, the early increase in stress hormones directly causes psychosocial problems that compound the effects of early puberty on behavioral outcomes is unknown. The burgeoning literature on the relationship between stress, early puberty, and conduct problems, in either event, provides compelling evidence for the direct impact of stress on reproductive systems that, in turn, increases susceptibility to risky behavior, particularly in the presence of other conducive factors (e.g., disadvantaged neighborhoods, poor family relationships, etc., as described in the following chapters).

Genetic factors have also been implicated in susceptibility to rearing influences on both pubertal timing and CD, providing an example of how the biological and social environments intersect (see Ellis 2004). Comings and others (2002) reported that the metabolism of male hormones in both genders was partially genetic, and this effect mediated the association between father absence and daughters' conduct problems. An interpretation of this finding is that genes of this nature, which are shared by the father and daughter, would predispose the father to aggression, impulsivity, and disruptive interpersonal relationships and daughters to early puberty, early sexual behavior, and disruptive relationships.

Factors That May Explain and Moderate the Relationship Between Puberty and Delinquency

A number of psychological and social processes underlie the link between the early onset of puberty and subsequent negative outcomes. Moffitt (1993) contends that adolescents experience a "maturity gap" between their level of biological development and their desire to attain adult status. Delinquency is a way to achieve independence and autonomy from parental control and to evidence maturity in the social realm. For adolescents, delinquency becomes associated with power and prestige, and teens become increasingly exposed to peer models for which delinquency has become a desired social asset. In this way, peer and parent processes are important factors that may help explain links between puberty and subsequent delinquency. Girls may be attracted to the status of older, deviant males, and early maturing girls are more likely to date at younger ages and to affiliate with older male peers who are inclined toward delinquent activity and who will involve these girls in their antisocial behavior (Magnusson et al. 1990; Weichold, Silbereisen, and Schmitt-Rodermund 2003). The onset of puberty is also associated with increased conflict among parents and teens around issues such as dating, selection of friends, and shifting behavioral expectations (Paikoff and Brooks-Gunn 1991), particularly for those youths with an early onset of puberty (Ge, Conger, and Elder 1996; Kim and Smith 1998; Sagrestano et al. 1999). Haynie (2003), using data on 5,477 females from the National Study of Adolescent Health, found that earlier pubertal onset was associated with higher levels of delinquency, and that conflict with parents, exposure to peer deviance, and involvement in romantic relationships mediated the link between puberty and delinquent outcomes. Overall then, an early onset of puberty may lead to conflictual family relations and play a role in establishing a peer context with older, deviance-prone males in which antisocial behavior is promoted.

Other psychological characteristics may also help explain the relationship between pubertal maturation and various forms of delinquency for both males and females, including psychological distress such as depression (Ge, Conger, and

Elder 1996; Graber et al. 1997), internalizing and externalizing symptoms (Kaltiala-Heino et al. 2003), sensation seeking (Martin et al. 2002), conduct problems (Graber et al. 1997), and lower levels of cognitive functioning (Orr and Ingersoll 1995). In particular for girls, an early onset of internalizing symptoms appears to interact with the timing of pubertal maturation to increase risk for subsequent conduct problems (Hayward et al. 1997; Kaltiala-Heino et al. 2003).

Also important to consider are factors that may accentuate the association between pubertal onset and problem outcomes. Caspi and others (1993) took advantage of a naturally occurring experiment to examine the impact of mixed-sex versus same-sex schools and pubertal maturation on girls' delinquency. Early menarche was not linked with delinquency for girls attending same-sex schools. By comparison, early maturing girls who attended mixed-sex schools were involved in more delinquent activity. Furthermore, early maturing girls in mixed-sex schools, as compared to early maturing girls in all-girl schools, had greater familiarity with problem-prone peers. The authors suggested that puberty functions as a stimulus or signal to others in the peer social context and may generate a demand or a press for more mature behaviors. Using the same sample, Caspi and Moffitt (1991) also found that those early maturing girls with a history of behavior problems prior to puberty showed the most adverse outcomes.

In addition, girls with early onset puberty who live in disadvantaged neighborhoods appear to be at significantly greater risk for violent behaviors as compared to those with early onset puberty who live in less disadvantaged neighborhoods (Obeidallah et al. 2004). Early maturing children who live in disadvantaged neighborhoods may be particularly prone to affiliate with deviant peers (Ge et al. 2002). Such contextual differences may provide varying modeling, exposure, and reinforcement of delinquent activity. Thus, contextual variables such as school, parenting, and neighborhood context may accentuate the relations between pubertal timing and problem outcomes.

In sum, early pubertal maturation involves precocious body development with all of its consequences, including heightened risks in a variety of social contexts (e.g., with peers, in neighborhoods, and in terms of parental reactions that, in turn, can compromise self-image and self-esteem, academic achievement, impulse control, and adjustment and coping skills). These social contextual factors interact with hormonally influenced psychological processes, such as mood disturbance, and heightened sex drive that may further strengthen the link between pubertal maturation and high-risk behaviors. The confluence of these factors is experienced most profoundly during adolescence—a period characterized by an immature brain that cannot yet negotiate complex cognitive functions that regulate impulse and emotional control, goal-directed behaviors, decision-making, and social skills (Schaefer et al. 2003). As a result, the combination of early body development and underdevelopment of the brain can set the stage for heightened risk-taking behaviors.

Vulnerability Factor Category 5:
Mental Health Issues

Much like the literature that reveals gender differences in pubertal timing, a convincing body of literature highlights gender differences in rates of mental disorders that are, in turn, linked with delinquency proneness. On the other hand, however, studies are not indicative of any causal linkages (i.e., it remains unclear whether mental health issues precede, coincide with, or follow delinquent behaviors). Thus, this section focuses on differential prevalence rates between girls and boys rather than putative underlying mechanisms or pathways.

A large body of evidence from multiple disciplines suggests that following puberty, girls exhibit more internalizing disorders (e.g., depression and anxiety) (Angold, Costello, and Worthman 1998) and boys exhibit more externalizing symptoms (e.g., impulsivity, novelty seeking, risk-taking, aggression); before puberty, the rates of depression are equivalent for boys and girls. However, following the onset of puberty, girls who evidence affective disorders outnumber boys by a ratio of two to one (Born, Shea, and Steiner 2002). Both types of disorders are significantly associated with delinquency by early to mid-adolescence (Kellam, Brown, and Fleming 1983; Wiesner and Kim 2006), although externalizing behaviors are more strongly related to delinquency (Betz 1995; Farrington 1989; Moffitt 1993); hence, boys have much higher rates of delinquency than girls overall. Interestingly, girls with onset of behavioral problems in childhood are more likely to have externalizing disorders, similar to boys, and appear to be in higher numbers in a subgroup that continues to engage in antisocial behavior through adulthood (Dixon, Howie, and Starling 2004; Silverthorne and Frick 1999). Yet, overall, propensity toward affective or internalizing disorders is more characteristic of girls and may also play a role in their risk for delinquency (Davies and Windle 1997; Tarter et al. 1999). In general, although studies are not suggestive of causal relationships between depression and delinquency, the findings underscore the need for sensitivity to how girls' overall functioning may interact with the development of conduct problems.

The Mental Health–Delinquency Linkage for Girls

There is no doubt that an alarming proportion of girls in the juvenile justice system have a significantly high incidence of mental health disturbances that, in most cases, go untreated (Cocozza and Skowyra 2000; Robertson et al. 2004; Teplin et al. 2002). Although the rate of mental health problems among males involved in the juvenile justice system is far from minimal (estimates range from 50 percent to 75 percent), the data show that diagnostic rates are, on the whole, higher for girls (Cauffman 2004; Cocozza 1991; Grisso et al. 2001; Shelton 2001; Teplin et al. 2002; Timmons-Mitchell et al. 1997). Hence, the fact that girls' rates are even higher than the already high rates of problems among male juvenile offenders is indeed a cause for concern.

The vast majority of studies on females in the juvenile justice system have been conducted in short- or long-term detention facilities. That detained or incarcerated girls have psychological and substance abuse symptoms at extraordinarily high rates is arguably one of the most robust findings in the juvenile justice field (Acoca 1998a; Cauffman 2004; Dixon, Howie, and Starling 2004; Espelage et al. 2003; Kataoka et al. 2001; Lederman et al. 2004; Lenssen et al. 2000; McCabe et al. 2002; Myers et al. 1990; Robertson et al. 2004; Sanislow et al. 2003; Shelton 2001; Teplin et al. 2002). For example, several well-designed studies found that over two-thirds of detained females met diagnostic criteria for one or more disorders (Lederman et al. 2004; McCabe et al. 2002; Robertson et al. 2004; Timmons-Mitchell et al. 1997). One of the best designed studies was carried out by Teplin and others (2002) looking at the six-month prevalence of psychiatric conditions among 1,829 randomly selected youths in juvenile detention. Their results showed that 71.2 percent of females (and 66.3 percent of males) met diagnostic criteria for a psychiatric disorder, which is a rate three to four times higher than the incidence in the general population (Angold et al. 2002; Costello et al. 2003). Furthermore, the rates of disorder among girls dropped only slightly to 68 percent when looking at the six-month prevalence rates for a non-CD disorder.

Not surprisingly given the obvious diagnostic overlap with delinquency, girls in the juvenile justice system evidence high rates of externalizing disorders (Dixon, Howie, and Starling 2004; Silverthorn, Frick, and Reynolds 2001), including conduct, oppositional defiant, and substance abuse disorders (Dixon, Howie, and Starling 2004; Goldstein et al. 2003; Kim and Fendrich 2002; Lederman et al. 2004; Lenssen et al. 2000; Morris et al. 1998; Teplin et al. 2002). Notwithstanding, mental health problems are not limited to disruptive behavior disorders. Detained girls show high rates of internalizing disorders (Aalsma and Lapsley 2001; Dixon, Howie, and Starling 2004; Goldstein et al. 2003; Lederman et al. 2004; Robertson et al. 2004; Teplin et al. 2002), including suicidality (Corneau and Lanctot 2004; Farand et al. 2004; Walrath et al. 2003). Goldstein and others (2003) reported that 36 percent of girls in a pretrial detention facility had suicidal ideation. Several studies indicate that detained and incarcerated girls also experience significant amounts of trauma (Abram et al. 2004; Lederman et al. 2004; Wood et al. 2002), although rates of PTSD range widely from 15 percent to 49 percent (Abram et al. 2004; Cauffman et al. 1998; Robertson et al. 2004).

Girls in the juvenile justice system also show evidence of the co-occurrence of more than one psychological or psychiatric condition (Dixon, Howie, and Starling 2004; Lederman et al. 2004; Lenssen et al. 2000; Robertson et al. 2004; Timmons-Mitchell et al. 1997). To illustrate, Abram and others (2004) in the same study of 1,829 detained youths, found that 57 percent of females and 46 percent of males met criteria for at least two disorders. In addition, females were more likely than males to have two or more of the following psychiatric disorders: anxiety, affective, substance use, and ADHD.

In comparison to the numerous studies of detained and incarcerated youths, studies of mental health problems among youths at other points in the juvenile justice system (e.g., intake, diversion, or probationary status) are much fewer in number. Studies show that a large number of girls at intake show substance use problems, with estimates ranging from 25 percent to 70 percent (Funk 1999; Kim and Fendrich 2002). A recent study by Wasserman and others (2005) also found that 45.7 percent of youths at intake received a psychiatric diagnosis. Although the rate of overall disorder did not significantly differ between boys (45.7 percent) and girls (49.5 percent), girls did evidence significantly higher rates of anxiety (girls: 29 percent; boys: 17 percent) and depressive (girls: 13 percent; boys: 6 percent) disorders than boys. Furthermore, girls who were arrested for violent offenses were particularly likely to report anxiety disorders. Although this overall rate is lower than that seen in detained or incarcerated populations, this finding is not surprising since youths at intake have not penetrated the system as deeply and are therefore at much lower overall risk. These findings highlight the heterogeneity of youths in the juvenile justice system and that girls at different stages of the process may vary widely in their prevalence rates of mental health disorders. Nonetheless, that slightly less than one in two youths met criteria for a psychiatric diagnosis at intake is a cause for significant concern, particularly among delinquent girls.

Possible Mechanisms in the Mental Health–Delinquency Linkage

Given differences in the rates and types of mental health problems that appear to plague girls, an understanding of underlying mechanisms accounting for these differences may help to design and target more appropriate gender-sensitive interventions and policies. As mentioned earlier, puberty has been strongly associated with onset of depressed mood, particularly for white non-Hispanic girls relative to Hispanic and African American girls, and early maturing girls report the highest levels of depressed mood for all ethnicities (Siegel et al. 1998). Because of the timing of depression's onset for girls, the general consensus is that vulnerability to depression may be rooted in a combination of genetic traits, normal female hormonal maturational processes, and gender socialization (Charmandari et al. 2003). The same factors that may confer vulnerability to depression may aid in an understanding of mechanisms underlying the link between mental health disorders and risk for delinquency, particularly for girls who disproportionately experience internalizing symptoms.

Internalizing and externalizing disorders appear to share a link to delinquency in both sexes via several similar influences. For example, both disorders have been characterized by an inability to sufficiently regulate emotions, which has been consistently associated with neurological irregularities (Caetano et al. 2004; MacMaster and Kusumakar 2004; May et al. 2004; Rosso, Cintron, and Steingard 2005). These impairments may act to facilitate a pathway to delinquency

(Tarter et al. 1999). Development of both internalizing and externalizing disorders is also strongly predicted by stressful life events for both boys and girls (Wiesner and Kim 2006). Thus, not coincidentally, these disorders are associated with unusual physiological responses to stressful situations (e.g., large release of the stress hormone cortisol, high heart rate) (King 1998; Moss, Vanyukov, and Martin 1995; van Goozen et al. 1998; Vanyukov et al. 1993). Depression and anxiety are characterized by an abnormally high level of physiological responses to stress (Arborelius et al. 1999; Plotsky, Owens, and Nemeroff 1998; Raber 1998; Torpy and Chrousos 1996). Given the heightened sensitivity of the biological stress system among those predisposed to affective disorders, when exposed to chronic stressors, susceptible individuals are more likely to develop internalizing symptoms (McEwen 2003), which, in turn, increase risk for delinquency. In effect, stress may both explain and influence relations between these genetic, biologic, and social factors and vulnerability to internalizing disorders, which may influence propensity for delinquency.

Sex differences in physiological stress responses that are associated with externalizing and internalizing disorders may lead to different behavioral pathways for males and females. The internalizing disorders in particular are often precipitated by exposure to uncontrollable stress and frequently characterized by abnormal or impaired function of areas of the brain that are responsible for cognitive abilities, an effect mediated by estrogen. Also, glands that release stress hormones are also more sensitive to stressors in women, as mentioned earlier (Roelfsema et al. 1993). Relatedly, the menstrual cycle significantly influences the strength of stress responses in females (Jezova et al. 1996; Kirschbaum et al. 1999), which, together, play a large role in sex-related differences in cognitive functions that, when impaired, often underlie behavioral problems (Hampson 1990; Maki, Rich, and Rosenbaum 2002). Thus, in spite of the protection against stress-induced damage to the brain and behavioral orientations (e.g., "tend and befriend") conferred by female hormones, girls are more susceptible to the triggering effects of stress on affective disorders specifically (Shansky et al. 2004).

Given the relationship between stress and internalizing disorders, very high rates of family dysfunction, including physical, sexual, and emotional abuse, are likely factors in the high rates of mental health and substance abuse problems for both girls and boys (Acoca 1998a; Chamberlain 2003; Funk 1999; Henggeler, Edwards, and Borduin 1987; Lederman et al. 2004; Lenssen et al. 2000; Mason, Zimmerman, and Evans 1998; Shelton 2004; Wood et al. 2002). Females in general are also more likely to develop PTSD as a result of severe stressors (Cottler et al. 1992). PTSD is more frequent in conduct-disordered girls than in boys, and girls experience greater symptom intensity and anhedonia (inability to experience pleasure), difficulty feeling love or affection, and disturbance of sleep and concentration (Reebye et al. 2000). The development of CD may increase the likelihood of developing PTSD, particularly in girls, by exposing youths to situations in which they are traumatized (Reebye et al. 2000). PTSD often antedates drug abuse in girls but is preceded by drug abuse in boys, perhaps suggesting that females self-medicate their symptoms, whereas males are more likely to experience a trauma due to risky situations associated with drug abuse (Deykin and Buka 1997). Females are also at increased risk for substance abuse when exposed to the stressors of family violence and alcoholism (Chermack et al. 2000).

Epidemiological and Methodological Considerations

Additional epidemiological and methodological factors may also be important considerations in understanding the high rates of mental health and substance abuse problems among detained female juvenile offenders. First, although there has been a dramatic increase in female adolescent arrest and incarceration over the past twenty years, males still comprise over 70 percent of juvenile arrests (Snyder 2002). Arrest and incarceration are, thus, relatively rare occurrences among females. Hence, it is possible that arrested and especially incarcerated girls are by nature more likely to have mental health and substance abuse problems than their male counterparts because they deviate more from more typically developing adolescent females. It has been suggested that females tend to be treated more leniently by the juvenile justice system in comparison to males. By the time girls' misconduct has led to an arrest and detention, any underlying disturbance may be far advanced relative to those girls who do not attract the attention of the juvenile justice system (McCabe et al. 2002). Arrest and incarceration itself, then, might be an indicator of mental health problems in girls (Cauffman 2004).

It is also possible that the high rates of mental health and substance abuse problems among female offenders partially reflect methodological limitations. Research on female juvenile offenders is limited by the small number of girls included in many studies, low overall response rates, and the almost exclusive focus on detained and incarcerated girls or those referred for mental health services. The overall rates, then, of psychological symptoms and disorders could be artificially inflated by these methodological problems. For example, conclusions about the prevalence of mental health and substance abuse problems have been drawn from studies with females comprising less than one-third of the total sample (Funk 1999; Mason, Zimmerman, and Evans 1998; Shelton 2001; Timmons-Mitchell et al. 1997) or extremely small samples (Kataoka et al. 2001; Lenssen et al. 2000; Silverthorne, Frick, and Reynolds 2001; Timmons-Mitchell et al. 1997). Other studies have unacceptably low or no reported response rates (Acoca 1998a; Espelage et al. 2003; Farand et al. 2004; Goldstein et al. 2003; McCabe et al. 2002), or are based on youths referred for mental health services (Jasper, Smith, and Bailey 1998; Walrath et al. 2003). Finally, as mentioned before, the vast majority of studies, even the well-designed studies, have focused on detained or incarcerated samples (Goldstein et al. 2003; Lederman et al. 2004; Teplin et al. 2002). Other methodological problems that might bias the results include the use of unstandardized measures, the unavailability of parent reports, and the lack of appropriate comparison groups (Vermeiren 2003). Thus, it is important to not generalize findings from these juvenile justice samples to girls overall, or even to girls within the juvenile justice sample, as they comprise a heterogeneous group (Wasserman et al. 2005). Furthermore, girls in the juvenile justice system may be significantly different from those who are delinquent but not involved in the system due to actions on the part of social institutions (e.g., police, judges, attorneys) that may create a selection bias toward certain types of girls or girls' behavior, thus leading to arrest and possibly incarceration. Studies have yet to differentiate factors for juvenile justice involvement from vulnerability for delinquency.

Directions for Future Research

The purpose of this chapter was to address important definitional and methodological issues pertaining to biopsychological vulnerability factors and to highlight empirical evidence in gender-sensitive susceptibility processes; namely, stress and adversity, ADHD/CD, intellectual deficits, pubertal development, and mental health problems. It should now be clear to the reader that the question of vulnerability factors is not a simple one in terms of whether any particular variable is predictive of delinquency in one gender versus the other. Future research would benefit from moving beyond the question of whether vulnerability factors are the same for males and females, to the more complex question of how particular potentially detrimental conditions interact with normative development for each gender. For example, rates of depression are higher among girls following pubertal onset, so it should not be terribly surprising that girls in the juvenile justice system exhibit higher rates of affective disorders than boys. Furthermore, much of the literature has tended to examine factors in isolation from each other. However, empirical work presented here highlights the often interconnected nature of various susceptibility processes and their impact on delinquent activity. To illustrate, pubertal maturation in girls is linked with exposure to older, problem-prone males, thereby facilitating and promoting delinquent behaviors among girls. In addition, early maturing girls who live in highly disadvantaged neighborhoods appear to be at particularly high risk for increased delinquent activity. Indeed, identification of these critical mediating and moderating processes suggest important avenues for intervention. Thus, one conclusion is the need for future research to identify the interactive and dynamic nature of multiple potentially adverse conditions in order to better understand the development of girls' delinquency.

Additional research is also needed on the intersection of gender and ethnicity and how these issues impact delinquency among girls of color. It has been well established that ethnic disparities exist at virtually all points in the juvenile justice system for both girls and boys (Hawkins and Kempf-Leonard 2005; McCord, Widom, and Crowell 2001; National Council on Crime and Delinquency 2007). Youths of color are not only arrested at rates greater than their representation in the population, but they are also overrepresented in rates of secure detention, petitions to juvenile court, adjudication, and incarceration (Bishop 2005). Furthermore, although studies have generally found comparable rates of psychiatric diagnoses across ethnicity groups (Angold et al. 2002; Roberts, Roberts, and Xing 2006), children of color may disproportionately suffer from lower rates of mental health service use. In addition, despite their overrepresentation in the juvenile justice system, youths of color in the juvenile justice system are less likely than white youths to receive mental health services (Cauffman and Grisso 2005).

Although girls of color account for 34 percent of youths aged twelve to seventeen, they account for more than half (52 percent) of those detained for juvenile offenses. A recent report by the American Civil Liberties Union showed that girls of color were more likely to be placed in secure custody. Similarly, a report by the American Bar Association (American Bar Association and National Bar Association 2001) showed that African American girls comprised almost half of girls in secure detention, and the rate of detention for African American girls is three times that of white girls. Furthermore, more than two-thirds of delinquency cases involving white girls are dismissed, as compared to only 30 percent of cases involving African American girls (American Bar Association and National Bar Association 2001). Our theoretical models need to be sensitive to the intersection of ethnicity and gender and how these issues impact delinquency. Thus, identifying potential disparities that may occur specifically or disproportionately for girls of color within the system is a critical research agenda item.

We also call attention to the need for future research to integrate across social, psychological, and biological perspectives to improve our understanding of delinquency among girls. As scientists, we are often guilty of ignoring other perspectives (e.g., social sciences tend to discount biological perspectives and vice versa). And some of these barriers are quite practical—we talk different "languages," we have different definitions for the same terms; we are perhaps overly comfortable maintaining our own "silo" of research. Perhaps we are concerned about biology being "destiny" or deterministic, while we view our psychological variables as more amenable to change. However, studies have shown how interventions targeting highly vulnerable children can alter underlying biological response systems that are implicated in the development of problem outcomes (Fisher et al. 2000; Hermann and Parente 1996; Manchester, Hodgkinson, and Casey 1997; Rothwell, LaVigna, and Willis 1999; Wilson 1997). As outlined here, developmental processes leading to delinquent behavior involve a combination of interactive influences across both psychological and biological vulnerability factor domains (Fishbein 2000).

Implications for Practice

The work reviewed in this chapter has a number of direct implications for practice. First, there is now ample and convincing evidence showing that youths in the juvenile justice system, particularly girls, exhibit disproportionately high rates of mental health disorders (Cocozza and Skowyra 2000). A consensus panel of national experts outlined systematic guidelines for the screening and assessment of the mental health needs of juvenile justice youths, beginning with screening at the earliest point of contact (Wasserman et al. 2003a). Those youths with identified mental health needs should then be linked with appropriate, evidence-based services. Their report outlined the need for training and development of staff, standardization and implementation of procedures, instrument development, and sensitivity to legal protections.

A related issue is the need for greater integration across the mental health and juvenile justice systems. All too often, juvenile justice serves as the system of "last resort" as youths are shuffled from one service system to the next (Koppelman 2004). Practically speaking, juvenile justice personnel are typically not in a position to provide mental health services, in terms of the fiscal burden, high caseloads, and often a lack of relevant experience. Recent national efforts toward an expanded system of care have some promise in terms of linking mental health services to the juvenile justice system (Hornberger, Martin, and Collins 2006). Nevertheless, much work remains to be done both in terms of coordination and integration of services across the mental health and juvenile justice systems.

As previously noted, a particular area of concern for girls in the juvenile justice system pertains to trauma. It is well established that up to 70 percent of females in the juvenile justice system have a history of child sexual abuse (Hennessey et al. 2004). However, despite clear connections between delinquency and trauma, the literatures on interventions for abuse and delinquency have unfortunately tended to be quite disparate, and trauma-focused interventions are rarely used in juvenile justice settings. Such statistics underscore the need to assess exposure to child sexual abuse and other traumas among juvenile justice youths and to provide evidence-based interventions (Mahoney et al. 2004; Wolpaw and Ford 2004). Rigorous studies using random assignment to well-defined, manualized treatments have compared trauma-focused interventions to each other or waitlist control conditions. Trauma-focused cognitive behavioral therapy (TF-CBT) compared to supportive or child-centered therapy has been shown to be more effective in reducing symptoms of PTSD and depression as well as abuse-specific shame and distorted attributions (Cohen et al. 2004; Cohen and Mannarino 1998; Deblinger, Steer, and Lippmann 1999). Recent work has also considered how the components of TF-CBT are likely to decrease stigmatization (Deblinger and Runyon 2005), which appears to be an important mediating variable linking child sexual abuse and subsequent delinquency (Feiring, Miller, and Cleland 2007).

The work reviewed in this chapter also identifies pubertal maturation as a particular period of vulnerability for girls. Processes associated with this transition—cross-gender peer affiliations, early romantic affiliations, parent–daughter relations—may be of prime salience as a target for intervention. The ways in which girls learn to navigate cross-gender and romantic relationships are often based on their personal experiences and those of their peers. Clearly, there is a need to help these young girls, particularly those who have been exposed to trauma and poor role models or those with mental health concerns, better navigate these relationships successfully, thus avoiding further trauma and turmoil.

Take-Home Points

1. The only sex-specific vulnerability factor that differentiates girls from boys pertains to early menstruation. Rather, for the most part, vulnerability in girls relates to gender-linked differences in both levels of exposure to risk factors and girls' sensitivity to those factors once they have been exposed. Girls tend to be exposed more often, for example, to sexual trauma. And differences in their sensitivity and reactions to trauma are more often manifested as depression or other affective illness.

2. Gender-related differences in biological processes may account for many of the particular sensitivities that girls show in stress reactivity. Thus, while girls are more likely to be exposed to interpersonal trauma, their responses to that stress are commonly characterized by differing patterns of physiological stress responses. As a result, girls are more likely than boys to react "inward," expressing psychological distress as opposed to externalizing behaviors. Also, there is some evidence that girls may be more sensitive to stressors that occur within the home than boys.

3. Although ADHD, a developmental disorder, is more pervasive among boys and has a strong association with risk for externalizing behaviors and delinquency, it is also more prevalent in girls who engage in delinquent behavior. The expression of ADHD in girls, however, tends to be more of the inattentive type than the aggressive or hyperactive type. As a result, it more often remains undiagnosed. Moreover, girls with ADHD tend to have lower self-esteem and efficacy than boys with ADHD.

4. Low IQ is a risk factor for delinquency in both boys and girls. Nevertheless, the linkages are confounded by numerous shortcomings in the studies conducted to date and a lack of consistency. It does appear that several factors, such as violence in the home and early puberty, may moderate the relationship between IQ and delinquency for girls.

5. There is substantial evidence that early pubertal maturation is related to greater susceptibility to delinquency in girls. The incidence of CD in early maturing girls may be as high as it is for boys overall for whom it is much more prevalent. Several underlying mechanisms, both social and biological, may explain this association. In sum, the following antecedent factors are believed to explain the relationships that are considered potentially important in the developmental timing of puberty: (a) hereditary transmission, (b) weight and weight for height, (c) stressful life events, (d) family relations, (e) absence or presence of an adult male in the household, and (f) psychological adjustment. Studies consistently show that the absence of a biological father in the home and chronic stress in childhood, in particular, are related to early puberty and subsequent behavioral outcomes. Also, girls who mature early often capture the attention of older males who include them in their own criminal activities.

6. Girls, in general, exhibit more internalizing disorders such as depression and anxiety during and after puberty than boys. It is not clear whether this

disorder plays a causal role or whether it stems from delinquent activities. Nevertheless, the incidence of mental illness is remarkably high among girls in the juvenile justice system who, unfortunately, go untreated. Girls in the system also show significantly higher rates of externalizing behaviors than girls who are not in the system or who are not delinquent. And, finally, comorbidity (the existence of two or more psychiatric illnesses) is quite high in delinquent girls, often including substance abuse and PTSD.

7. Importantly, each of these conditions appears to interact to jointly exert an influence on the propensity for girls to engage in delinquency. Also, each is characterized by differences in biological, physiological, and, sometimes genetic, functions and processes.

8. The question of vulnerability factors is not a simple one in terms of whether any particular variable is predictive of delinquency in one gender versus the other. Future research would benefit from moving beyond the question of whether vulnerability factors are the same for males and females to the more complex question of how particular potentially detrimental conditions interact with normative development for each gender. In essence, future research is needed to identify the interactive and dynamic nature of multiple potentially adverse conditions to better understand the development of girls' delinquency.

5

Family Influences on Girls' Delinquency

CANDACE KRUTTSCHNITT AND PEGGY GIORDANO

The family has been one of the most heavily studied social domains linked to delinquency involvement, and virtually all theoretical frameworks incorporate family influences into their perspectives on these problem behaviors. Family processes also have been central to many analyses of the gender gap in rates of delinquency, as many literature traditions (delinquency, developmental and gender socialization) focus on girls' stronger connections to family throughout the life course (Gecas and Seff 1990; Gilligan 1982; Leonard 1982). Researchers have argued that this stronger relational orientation and bond to family generally operates as a protective factor. However, while girls' intimate connections to the family prefigure lower overall levels of delinquency involvement, it is also logical to expect that family deficits, disruptions, or stressors especially may be detrimental to girls' well-being. A complicating factor is that, even under high levels of family stress or dysfunction, girls generally are believed to cope by internalizing their problems (e.g., exhibiting depression or other "gendered" problem outcomes, such as anorexia) (Kavanagh and Hops 1994; Reynolds and Johnston 1994).

Nevertheless, in every jurisdiction, a subset of girls do externalize—that is, become involved in delinquent behavior. Using studies based on officially adjudicated and community samples, researchers have frequently documented that family influences are important to an understanding of girls' as well as boys' involvement in delinquency. In this chapter, we examine a range of family factors associated with girls' delinquency, with a special focus on whether research findings point to similar or distinctly gendered processes.

We review relevant research on family structure effects, family processes, and the role of parental criminality. The area of physical and sexual abuse is given special consideration here, because victimization experiences have been considered particularly influential precursors of girls' pathways into delinquency.

General Considerations in the Study of Family Effects

Although the research base on girls is not nearly as extensive as that focused on boys, the general notion that "bad families" figure into girls' delinquency has a long history (Thomas 1923b; Wattenberg and Saunders 1954). Some of this research emphasizes gendered processes (e.g., the emphasis on "wayward" girls' sexual behaviors). Nevertheless, in focusing on family dysfunction as a cause, this research parallels a much larger body of work showing significant effects of family discord and disruption as critical to an understanding of boys' delinquency (Glueck and Glueck 1950). Early research in this area often relied on captive populations drawn from juvenile court or institutional settings. Thus, a continuing criticism that applies across gender is that youths who do not reside in two-parent families may be subject differentially to official intervention because interventions conform to the stereotype of the typical delinquent (Wright and Wright 1994). Girls from problem families, particularly where supervision is low, often signal the need for official intervention given greater societal concerns about girls' morality (Schlossman and Cairns 1994). The issue of selection biases has led to the increased use of cohort, neighborhood, school, and community surveys, many relying on self-reported measures of delinquency involvement. These studies also generally provide support for the role of family processes, but establishing causal order has proven difficult in relation to some important areas of family functioning. For example, while studies often show links between family conflict and delinquency, it is not always clear whether conflict leads to delinquency or whether delinquent youths generate more conflict and discord within the home. These concerns, in turn, have led to an increased reliance on longitudinal designs, although some of the important early longitudinal research focused exclusively on boys (Farrington 1994; Loeber and Stouthamer-Loeber 1986). More recently, research designs have included adequate numbers of male and female respondents in surveys. Still, the low base rate of female delinquency in the general population remains a continuing challenge. Unselected cohort, neighborhood, or school designs typically do not capture a large number of male delinquents, but the problem is especially serious when the focus is on girls who exhibit violence or other law-violating behaviors (Cernkovich, Giordano, and Pugh 1985). Accordingly, these random surveys of youths have sometimes been supplemented with studies of adjudicated girls, as researchers have explored in more detail the family circumstances and backgrounds of girls who exhibit serious conduct problems. These issues also complicate the study of physical and sexual abuse, where research relying on adjudicated cases represents a similar mix of assets and limitations.

Family Structure Effects

Almost all studies show that youths living in two-parent biological families fare better on a range of developmental outcomes, including reduced delinquency involvement (Amato and Keith 1991). This research suggests that both girls and boys may be influenced negatively by nontraditional family structures. Nevertheless, this body of research typically finds that effects due to family structure type are not large (Hetherington and Kelly 2002), and often aggregate differences are explained largely by more tangible differences in family dynamics or processes. Longitudinal studies of children whose parents are divorced frequently suggest that boys experience more difficulties in adjustment, although some authors have posited a "sleeper" effect for girls—wherein the onset of puberty, a mother's remarriage, or the combination may place girls at special risk (Hetherington and Kelly 2002).

In a meta-analysis of fifty studies, Wells and Rankin (1991) documented that delinquency was, on average, 10 percent to 15 percent higher for youths living within nontraditional family circumstances compared with those residing in intact families. Wells and Rankin's analysis (consistent with the concerns raised earlier) also highlighted that studies relying on officially processed youths resulted in a higher estimate of influence than when focusing on studies based on self-reported delinquency involvement. Furthermore, the analysis showed that, in general, the larger and more representative the sample, the smaller the size of the family structure effect. It is also noteworthy that the effects appeared to be stronger for minor forms of delinquency (i.e., status offenses) than for more serious acts of law violation. Although some of the studies Wells and Rankin reviewed were single-gender studies, the authors found that six studies documented no gender differences in the effects of family background on delinquency, six studies showed a stronger effect for boys, and two studies showed a stronger effect for girls. As such, this analysis does not provide a clear foundation for positing uniquely gendered family structure effects.

A more recent meta-analysis by Price and Kunz (2003) focused on seventy-two studies. These researchers found that in 63 percent of the studies, effects of family structure (in this study defined as divorce) were negative. Price and Kunz found that studies employing mixed-gender samples showed stronger negative effects than either single-gender samples, but this observation does not itself specifically settle the question of whether nonintact family status influences the delinquency of girls more, similarly, or less than that of boys.

Researchers interested in effects of family structure have become increasingly more sophisticated in their categorization and analysis of household living arrangements other than the two-parent biological family. For example, in a recent analysis using the National Longitudinal Study of Adolescent Health (Add Health)—a large national probability sample of adolescents—Manning and Lamb (2003) found that, similar to many other studies, youths in two-parent biological families evidenced more favorable adolescent outcomes, including lower levels of reported delinquency involvement. However, these researchers also explored differences between youths residing in stepparent families and those who lived in homes in which a parent was cohabiting with an unmarried partner. Manning and Lamb (2003) found that the latter circumstance was associated with higher levels of reported delinquency, suggesting the need to continue to evaluate these different arrangements in more detail. The authors theorized that the lack of stability and clear boundaries or codified cultural meanings of cohabitation may be implicated in these results. It is possible that girls living in these less clearly defined family circumstances might be at particular risk, especially to the degree that such nontraditional arrangements are associated with increased risk for sexual or other abuse. Although the latter association has not been investigated extensively, in their analysis of the Add Health data, Demuth and Brown (2004) explored the role of the adolescent's gender and found similar effects of cohabitation on the likelihood of delinquency for both boys and girls. These researchers also documented that the highest delinquency rates were evidenced by youths living in father-only households, followed by father-stepmother and single-mother households. Within the context of this more refined analysis of family structure influences, most of these effects were attenuated once family process variables were taken into account. Specifically, Demuth and Brown (2004) found that weak direct and indirect controls mediated the family structure effects—suggesting, along with numerous other researchers, the importance of addressing the dynamic processes and qualities that characterize families as critical proximal links to delinquency involvement.

Family Processes

As suggested earlier, even where significant correlations between family structure and delinquency have been documented, researchers generally have endeavored to understand more about the ongoing family dynamics that may underlie any observed differences. A focus on dynamic processes also recognizes that many youths living in single-parent or other nontraditional family forms do not become delinquent. In short, family structure is understood generally as a limited, highly schematic marker of more complex family processes that themselves warrant direct and careful research scrutiny. In this tradition, researchers have explored the influence of general feelings of warmth and caring ("attachment"), supervision, and family conflict and instability as much more concrete or tangible factors that are frequently implicated in the onset of girls' and boys' delinquency.

Moffitt and others (2001) followed from early childhood to adulthood an entire cohort of one thousand male and female children born in Dunedin, New Zealand. Although Moffitt and colleagues' study involved assessment of many extrafamilial factors, including individual differences, these researchers also explored the role and impact of a range of family risks, moving well beyond the assessment of family structure effects. Another important consideration is that the investigators specifically were interested in questions of gender, and, thus, systematically evaluated the relative influence of family dynamics on male and female respondents. In their analysis, nine family factors (including harsh and inconsistent discipline and family conflict) were related to boys' antisocial behaviors, while eight family factors were correlated significantly with girls' delinquency involvement. Relying on multiple regression analyses, the authors concluded that most of these risk predictors had a stronger relationship to boys' delinquency. Moffitt and others (2001) theorized that males may experience a different type of reactivity to family stress; in addition, they noted that boys may be treated differently during times of family stress. The authors also underscored that the effect of gender on these processes was relatively small—interactions accounted for 1 percent of the variance in antisocial behavior. Moffitt and others thus incorporated family processes into their broader theoretical stance that, across multiple domains, similar factors are implicated in the delinquency of girls and boys.

Other researchers have carved out a more limited conceptual territory, examining one or more family processes in greater detail. Measured in a variety of different ways, basic feelings of attachment or caring generally are associated with a lower likelihood of delinquent involvement (Hirschi 1969), yet findings regarding differential effects of gender remain equivocal. For example, Anderson, Holmes, and Ostresh (1999) found that attachment to parents reduced boys' delinquency, while attachment to peers/school reduced girls' delinquency. Huebner and Betts (2002), in contrast, found that attachment to family variables was significant for both genders (relying on a general measure of "quality"), although the measure was more strongly related to girls' than boys' delinquency. One of the problems with measuring general warmth and caring is that, within the context of even the most dysfunctional and problematic families, parents generally indicate that they love their children. Thus, the range of parent-derived measures often is not extensive; youths' own reports vary somewhat more, but again these measures may not provide the most descriptive account of the distinctive family circumstances likely to be associated with youths' delinquency involvement.

Parental supervision thus emerges as a recurrent theme within the delinquency literature, as a particularly useful and important family process variable that has been linked reliably to delinquent behavior. In other words, consistent and effective monitoring of a youth's activities provides a more specific behavioral manifestation of a general sense of caring and is understood widely as an index of social control (Hirschi 1969). This variable is also a critically important factor implicated in girls' delinquency, as well as (a) higher supervision within the family explains at least part of the continuing gender gap in rates of delinquency involvement; (b) greater freedom of movement in contemporary as contrasted with earlier eras may be one factor that explains increases in girls' rates, especially where the opportunity for socializing is key (e.g., drug and alcohol use); and (c) lower and inconsistent supervision has also been found to be a significant predictor of variations within a number of specific sample groups.

Consistent monitoring has been inversely related to delinquency in numerous self-report studies, many of which include both genders in their study designs. For example, Cernkovich and Giordano (1987) explored family processes and delinquency using data from personal interviews with 942 youths, and found that parental supervision was negatively related to delinquency for both boys and girls. They also found that process variables, including supervision, fully mediated family structure differences (Broidy 1995). Patterson, Crosby, and Vuchinich (1992) studied family dynamics in much more detail and also document a strong effect of monitoring. They relied on direct observation and other methodological techniques to specify a range of ineffective parenting practices, including inconsistent discipline, and a pattern of nattering/nagging followed by explosive outbursts that characterized families of delinquents more than those of comparison families. While these studies initially focused on a sample of boys, research has subsequently documented that these negative family processes also are implicated in the family backgrounds of delinquent girls (Chamberlain 2003).

As studies of dynamic family processes have evolved, researchers increasingly have sought to move beyond the assessment of qualities of family life as a kind of unrelated "laundry list" of variables in order to explore ways in which parenting practices combine or coalesce in their effects. An especially influential typology, developed by Baumrind (1966, 1996), considered two dimensions of parenting: responsiveness or warmth and control/supervision. Research documented that the authoritative parenting style, characterized by high levels of warmth and responsiveness, as well as high control, is associated with lower levels of conduct and other developmental problems compared with authoritarian, permissive, or neglecting/rejecting parenting styles (Steinberg et al. 1991). Over time, researchers have elaborated more complex typologies, further distinguishing low-control parents who may simply be indulgent from those who are neglectful. Steinberg and others (1991), in a study of more than four thousand fourteen- to eighteen-year-olds, found that authoritative parenting was associated with the lowest levels of behavior problems, while adolescents in neglectful homes reported the most problem outcomes. In this study, gender did not interact with parenting style in its effect on problem behavior reports. More recently, Steinberg, Blatt-Eisengart, and Cauffman (2006) replicated these findings using a sample of serious juvenile offenders. In an examination of variations within this delinquent sample, the authors observed that those who described parents as authoritative reported the lowest levels of distress and problem behaviors, while the worst outcomes were associated with the neglect pattern. Authoritarian and indulgent parenting were associated with intermediate scores. Again, in this study, interactions with gender were not significant, suggesting a similar influence of parenting styles on boys' and girls' development.

Although a number of studies have documented similarity in such processes as attachment and supervision, some researchers have hypothesized that girls are likely to be more influenced by attachment (given the other-directed or relational orientation that is associated with female socialization) (Gilligan 1982), while boys are more influenced by physical controls (Hagan, Simpson, and Gillis 1998). Consistent with this notion, Seydlitz (1991) found that parental controls were more important for boys. Cookston (1999) distinguished groups reflecting low, medium, and high levels of parental supervision and found that only low supervision had a negative effect on girls' problem behavior; in contrast, both medium and low supervision were associated with greater problem behavior scores for boys in the sample.

More recently, Cota-Robles and Gamble (2006) investigated supervision and attachment dimensions of family life in a sample of Mexican American adolescents and found that the supervision–delinquency relationship not only was significant for this ethnic group, but that the influence of supervision was generally similar across genders. An exception was that mother–adolescent attachment had a stronger relationship to boys' than girls' delinquency.

Although the majority of studies reviewed earlier did not examine relationships with the child's mother and father separately, there has been an increased interest in distinguishing the mother's and father's influences individually; recent research especially has focused on father involvement (Amato and Gilbreth 1999; McClanahan 1999; Thomas, Farrell, and Barnes 1996). How parent gender influences girls' versus boys' delinquency is a complex issue requiring a large sample size and fine-grained measures of family dynamics. Liu (2004), for example, explicitly focused on gender of the parent in relation to child gender and developed three plausible arguments (Van Beest and Baerveldt 1999). First, because mothers remain close-in (primary) caregivers within a majority of families, it could be argued that relationships with mothers will remain a bottom line for children, regardless of gender. An alternative view is that because father involvement encompasses such a broad range (from families in which the father is completely absent to sporadically involved to a key parental figure), this range may be critical to understanding variations in child outcomes. A third dynamic suggested by Liu (2004) is that effects could be specific to the gender of the child, a hypothesis that flows from basic principles of identification. Liu (2004) found some evidence for a gendered identification effect: Conflict with fathers related to sons' school delinquency, while in Liu's study, conflict with mothers predicted daughters' school delinquency. Flouir and Buchanan (2002), focusing on a British sample, used a slightly different approach, examining father involvement effects after controlling for mothers' involvement and other risk and protective factors. The level of father involvement at age seven related to later delinquency for boys, but only nonintact family status and family size variables were significant for girls. Obviously, more research is needed on these complex family influence processes.

Gendered Family Dynamics

Most of the research reviewed earlier focuses on family variables, such as conflict or father involvement, and then explores the significance and magnitude of the effects for each gender. Heimer and De Coster's (1999) research offers a more

nuanced portrait of how gender influences family processes and, in turn, delinquency. These researchers found that emotional connections to the family were
inversely related to learning violent definitions for girls, but that coercive parenting practices influenced boys' learning of violent definitions. This suggests the
need in some instances to move beyond a common template when evaluating
how family (and other) domains influence boys' and girls' delinquent actions.

Another creative strategy was used by Bottcher (2001), who interviewed
male and female siblings of a sample of youths who were incarcerated under
the jurisdiction of the California Youth Authority. She interviewed fifteen brothers and twenty-five sisters of youths who were incarcerated, as a way of exploring gendered practices within families that might be expected to place youths
at generally high risk for delinquency (because one youth in the family had
already exhibited this behavior). Bottcher found that girls "spend more time
with mother and other female relatives" and that boys had much greater freedom of movement: "males spent more time in less traveled terrain and [were]
less monitored by their families" (p. 908). Bottcher also noted that "boys have
greater access to nighttime" (p. 909). Bottcher thus focused attention on how
some of the routine practices of gender (a sort of gendered "routine activities"
perspective) help explain the important condition wherein girls reared in high-
risk circumstances are nevertheless significantly less likely to take up delinquent
modes of action. Bottcher also noted that girls typically assume more childcare
duties, another gendered practice that tends to foster a closer-to-home orientation. These studies of within-family differences add significantly to our understanding of gender differences in delinquency, even under high-risk family circumstances. This work does, however, need to be supplemented by detailed
research on the everyday dynamics within families of delinquent girls, who
often have developed a "street" orientation and are less tied to home and family
concerns.

Another line of research that focuses on within-family differences derives
from Hagan's (1990) power-control theory. This research also focuses on gendered practices within the family, as Hagan argued that parents' own relationships with one another may vary as they mirror or depart from broader societal-
level gender arrangements. Hagan hypothesized that girls growing up in families
characterized by relatively traditional couple-level dynamics generally will exhibit
less delinquency when compared with girls living in households characterized
by a more egalitarian power balance. These power dynamics in turn are linked
to the relative occupational standing of mothers and fathers. Researchers have
found that girls in more egalitarian households may hold attitudes (including a
taste for risk) that are associated with delinquency, but others have produced a
mixed support for these associations (Singer and Levine 1988). Nevertheless,
Hagan's theory is important because it reflects a systematic attempt to understand how dynamics within the family may operate somewhat differently for sons
and daughters, depending on the characteristics of parental relationships.

Parental and Other Family Members' Criminality

Another way to conceptualize family effects is to focus on the criminality, drug and alcohol abuse, or other deviant behavior of parents and other family members. Parental crime has long been considered a risk factor for delinquency (Glueck and Glueck 1950; McCord 1991; Rowe and Farrington 1997), although this link has not been investigated as extensively in studies of girls. Miller's (1986) qualitative study of street women involved in prostitution and other illegal survival strategies documented that young women frequently were introduced to prostitution and a variety of other marginal and illegal activities by cousins, young aunts, and other relatives who were themselves heavily involved in the street life. This study provides a potentially important window into specific family precursors of girls' involvement in illegal behaviors. More quantitatively oriented research findings also suggest that children of drug-using parents are at high risk for antisocial behavior (Brown and Mills 1987). Many interrelated causal processes undoubtedly connect to this elevated risk, from direct observation of the parent's actions to specific socialization practices that have a criminogenic effect (e.g., teaching a child that fighting is an acceptable option in some circumstances). Family instability is also undoubtedly involved, as children born to criminal parents are more likely to experience multiple caretakers and residential moves. These shifting circumstances disrupt social ties and have a negative effect on academic achievement (Gabel and Johnston 1995). The child may experience a range of negative emotions as a consequence of a parent's actions, periods of incarceration, and erratic behavior and these may be implicated in cross-generational effects (Agnew 1997). Keller, Catalano, Haggerty, and Fleming (2002) disaggregated some of these influences, focusing on the number of parental figure transitions and delinquency over a period of two and a half years. These researchers found that, among children of drug-using parents, the number of parenting transitions was significantly associated with the child's own drug use, delinquency, or both. In this study, researchers did not find a differential effect of the child's gender on the likelihood of delinquency involvement, but the effect on drug use was found for girls only.

In a study of girls incarcerated in a state juvenile correctional facility, Giordano and Mohler-Rockwell (2001) examined the role of familial criminality, especially maternal deviance (e.g., violence, prostitution, drug and alcohol abuse) on girls' own delinquent involvement. These girls, originally interviewed in 1982, were followed up as they made the transition to adulthood. The majority of the girls who participated in the Ohio Longitudinal Study had been involved in a range of delinquent activities, many of them serious acts of law violation. During the adult interview conducted in 1995, the women (n = 109) provided detailed life history narratives that encompassed their childhood and adolescent years, as well as their current life circumstances. While these narrations of the "early years" documented extensive criminal behavior and drug use on the part of both parents, the narratives frequently contained especially graphic depictions of their mothers' criminal involvement and drug use. The narrative accounts also suggested that mothers, grandmothers, sisters, and aunts often were involved in socializing girls to defend themselves. Thus, aggression was learned within the familial context, and female relatives were often a source of these definitions. Some women learned to use drugs with their mothers or siblings and others were introduced to prostitution by these relatives. Such dynamics follow logically from basic principles of identification but are an understudied cause of girls' conduct problems. The women's life histories also document serious physical and sexual abuse, suggesting the need to explore ways in which particular constellations of family dynamics place girls at an especially high level of risk. Consistent with this notion of a "package" of risks, Gaarder and Belknap (2002) studied girls arrested for relatively serious offenses and found that, in addition to specifically gendered dynamics (e.g., sexual abuse, victimization by intimate partners), parental deviance and drug use were very common in the background circumstances of the girls they interviewed.

A number of longitudinal data sets permit a more systematic examination of the effects of parental criminality, as the generations of children born to original study respondents are now the subject of research attention. For example, Thornberry and others (2003) focused on the parenting experiences of young adults (n = 1,000) who participated in the Rochester Youth Development Study. Although the children born to this sample were relatively young at the time of assessment, researchers found a stronger overall correlation between fathers' (adolescent) delinquency and a child's antisocial outcomes a generation later. Mothers' delinquency was not related directly to a child's outcomes, except through an effect on parenting style. The researchers did not specifically explore the child's gender in their analysis, so there is a need to further explore the potentially important area of parental criminality as a precursor for both boys' and girls' delinquency.

Family Violence and Child Maltreatment

An area of family processes that has garnered much scholarly attention over the past two decades is family violence. Scholars have focused particularly on the developmental effects of maltreatment, broadly conceived, and especially child physical and sexual abuse and neglect. Nevertheless, a number of methodological problems that were initially noted in this body of scholarship remain. Critiques of this work frequently note the following limitations:

- The sample of maltreated youths studied is not representative of the general population of maltreated youths.
- The appropriate control groups are not included in the study design.
- The definitions of abuse and neglect vary across studies, and insufficient attention is given to examining the developmental effects of different kinds of maltreatment (e.g., child abuse and neglect) or the developmental effects of abuse at different ages.

- The use of retrospective study designs (particularly in the study of sexual abuse) introduces the possibility of recall bias.
- The studies fail to differentiate the effects of abuse from the effects of other family adversities that are commonly associated with maltreatment (e.g., poverty, parental instability, and substance abuse).
- There is a general inattention to gender effects and the interaction of race and gender (Howing et al. 1990; Lane and Davis 1987; National Research Council 1993; Rutter, Giller, and Hagell 1998; Weis 1989; Widom, Weiner, and Wolfgang 1989).

Remaining cognizant of these methodological weaknesses, the following review focuses on what is known about the effects of child maltreatment on the development of delinquency and drug use in girls. We include the following categories under the rubric of maltreatment: witnessing family violence, experiencing childhood physical abuse and neglect, and experiencing childhood sexual abuse. We also include studies that use both official and self-reported measures of delinquency and drug use. While most of this research relies on official records of delinquency, it is important to include self-reported measures to ensure that any noted associations are not simply due to "the tendency of some families to be dealt with by official agencies" (Smith and Thornberry 1995, p. 454). Finally, we give special attention to studies based on longitudinal prospective designs both because they provide the only way of accurately assessing the causal relationship between maltreatment and delinquency and drug use and because they provide an opportunity for determining the relative importance of mediating variables.[1]

Witnessing Marital Violence

Research on the developmental effects of witnessing partner violence emerged somewhat as an afterthought to the study of child abuse. Edleson (1999), in fact, suggested that these children have been referred to as the "silent," "forgotten," and "unintended victims of adult-to-adult domestic violence" (p. 839). Nevertheless, scholarly and policy interest in these "unintended victims" is growing, and the current literature on the problems associated with witnessing marital violence focuses on a wide range of outcomes: behavioral and emotional functioning (internalizing and externalizing behaviors, as well as anxiety and depression, trauma symptoms, and temperament problems), cognitive functioning (academic abilities), and attitudes toward conflict. The vast majority of studies, however, focus on very young children and often are restricted to shelter populations (Edleson 1999). Studies of shelter residents limit our understanding of the developmental effects of witnessing violence, because mental health measured while the child is residing in a shelter may have little bearing on the child's mental health in other contexts or at later developmental periods. One of the earliest reviews of this research suggested that girls exhibit more internalizing reactions (e.g., somatic complaints, withdrawal, dependent behavior), while boys exhibit more externalizing and aggressive reactions to witnessing domestic violence (Jaffe, Wolfe, and Wilson 1990). However, given study limitations, it is unclear whether these effects differ from those that would occur as a result of exposure to other stressors in the family (including the possibility of the child being a victim as well as a witness to the violence) and whether the effects ultimately translate into long-term differences in delinquent development.

Edleson (1999) identified eighty-four studies that report associations between witnessing domestic violence and children's developmental problems. However, many of these studies were methodologically weak. In fact, only thirty-one of the eighty-four studies controlled for child victimization when examining the effects of witnessing violence, included a control group, considered variation in outcome based on the child's demographics (e.g., age, race, sex), and applied and described appropriate measures and methodology. Furthermore, only one of the methodologically sound studies considered both gender as a moderating variable[2] and delinquency as an outcome; the results of this study suggest that witnessing violence is related to violence in girls but not boys (Song, Singer, and Anglin 1998).

Perhaps the most extensive studies of gender differences in the outcomes of witnessing violence were completed by Herrera and McCloskey (2001) and Becker and McCloskey (2002). Both studies used a prospective design. Mothers (n = 363) were interviewed about abuse in their families (i.e., marital violence and child abuse) when their children were between six and twelve years of age. Approximately five years later, these researchers examined the juvenile court records for the same children and interviewed the youths about their involvement in ten nonviolent behaviors and five violent behaviors. Herrera and McCloskey (2001) examined several interaction terms (sex × marital violence, sex × child abuse, and child abuse × marital violence) in a logistic regression predicting juvenile court referral. None of the interaction terms were significant except the sex × child abuse term in the model predicting court referral for a violent crime: Girls were at higher risk for an arrest for a violent crime if they had a history of physical abuse. As the authors noted, however, girls' referrals for violent crime typically followed an incidence of domestic violence or a parent–child altercation.

Becker and McCloskey (2002) used the same data to assess the pathways to self-reported delinquency for boys and girls. Specifically, they wanted to determine if different forms of family violence influence delinquency through attention and conduct problems. They found that, for boys, neither marital violence nor paternal abuse had direct or indirect effects on delinquency. For girls only, paternal abuse had a significant effect; paternal abuse was positively related to both conduct problems and violent and nonviolent delinquency. Although it may be tempting to conclude from these studies that girls are more vulnerable to physical abuse than boys, it also may be, as the authors suggest, that the higher rates of both attention and conduct problems in boys overshadow the effects of family violence on delinquent development.

Physical Abuse and Neglect

Attention to developmental effects of childhood physical abuse increased dramatically during the 1990s with the publication of findings from several prospective longitudinal studies. Here we draw attention to three of the most important studies in this field of research.

Widom (1989a) identified 908 substantiated abuse and neglect cases from 1967 to 1971 and a control cohort of 667 nonabused children matched on sex, race, age (six to eleven years of age), and approximate socioeconomic status. Official criminal records (juvenile and adult) were examined approximately twenty years later, when the average age of the subjects (both maltreated and control) was twenty-six years. Because the findings from this study focus on various outcomes (e.g., juvenile and adult arrests, specific offenses, and the prevalence and frequency of violence), they cannot be summarized readily. Nevertheless, in Table 5.1, we have tried to provide an overview of the significant findings pertaining to the effects of abuse and neglect on the offense records of the males and females in this study.

As can be seen in Table 5.1, initial findings from this study suggest that, for both males and females, a history of abuse/neglect significantly increases the chances of having both a juvenile and an adult criminal record (Widom 1989a, 1991). Notably, but not shown in this table, an examination of the interactions between race and sex revealed that this relationship is amplified for young blacks: Abused or neglected black males have more juvenile arrests than all other males, as do abused or neglected black females relative to all other groups of females

---

TABLE 5.1   FINDINGS FROM WIDOM'S PROSPECTIVE STUDY:
SIGNIFICANT RELATIONSHIPS BETWEEN ABUSE/NEGLECT AND ARRESTS[a]

Initial Arrest Record Follow-up ($\bar{X}$ age 26 years)		Subsequent Interview Follow-up ($\bar{X}$ age 32 years)[b]	
Females	Males	Females	Males
Juvenile[1,4]	Juvenile[1,4]		
Adult[1]	Adult[1]		
	Adult violence[1,2,3]	Prevalence of violence[5,6]	Frequency of violence[6]
Adult property[2]	Adult property[2]	Nonviolent[5]	Nonviolent[5,6]
	Adult sex[2]		
Adult drugs[2]		Drugs[6]	Drugs[6]
Adult order[c,2]			
	Juvenile property[4]		
Status[4]	Status[4]		

[a] Significant $p \le .05$ or less.
[b] Findings refer to both juvenile and adult arrest records.
[c] Order offenses include criminal mischief/vandalism, trespassing, disorderly conduct, vagrancy, and resisting arrest.

Sources: [1] Widom (1989b). [3] Rivera and Widom (1990). [5] Widom and White (1997).
[2] Widom (1989b). [4] Widom (1991). [6] Widom and Maxfield (2001).

(Widom 1991). However, when the focus shifts to what these males and females are being arrested for, there appear to be relatively few significant differences between the abused or neglected and the controls. For females, childhood victimization significantly increases the risk only for status offenses; victimized males have a higher risk of both property and status offenses relative to controls (Widom 1991). The effect of abuse or neglect on violent offending only appears for males and only in the case of adult arrests (Rivera and Widom 1990).

Two-hour follow-up interviews were conducted between 1989 and 1995, and additional arrest data were gathered on these subjects in 1994, when the average subject age was thirty-two. Notably, individuals who were located and interviewed (76 percent of the original sample) were significantly more likely to have an official arrest record than members of the initial sample (Widom and White 1997). Analyses of these data reveal somewhat different results from those initially reported (Widom 1989a, 1989b; Widom and White 1997). For both males and females, abuse/neglect significantly increases the likelihood of (juvenile/ adult) arrest for violent crime. However, for females, the significant effect of abuse/neglect on violent offending only appears when the prevalence of violent arrests is considered; for abused/neglected males, the comparable significant effect only appears when the frequency of violent arrests is examined (Widom and Maxfield 2001). While this may indicate that "childhood victimization increases arrests for violence among females and males . . . in different ways" (Widom and Maxfield 2001, p. 4), there is no test for sex-by-group (abused/ neglected versus control) interactions for these two measures of violent arrests that would permit us to determine whether this is the case. When such analyses were conducted (for both violent and nonviolent crimes), no significant sex-by-group interactions were detected (Widom and White 1997).[3]

From this research, it is also unclear which maltreatment experience (physical abuse, sexual abuse, neglect, or a combination) has the greatest impact on subsequent offending (Wolfe et al. 2001). Widom (1991) provides some evidence that, at least in the case of juvenile offending, physically abused girls have the highest rates of violence. But in a more thorough reanalysis of these data, Spohn (2000) found that all three forms of maltreatment were significant predictors of girls' juvenile and adult arrests. For males, only neglect had a significant effect on arrests and, in the case of adult arrests, this effect was mediated when juvenile delinquency was included in the model. However, because none of these gender differences were significant, there is little evidence that the relationship between specific types of victimization and offending are conditioned by gender (Bensley et al. 1999). Finally, although Widom and White (1997) controlled for several concurrent family problems (e.g., parental arrest and drug use) in their analyses of the co-occurrence of crime and drug use, none of this research considers how intervening life events may mediate the relationship between maltreatment and subsequent offending (Swinford et al. 2000).

Zingraff and others (1993, 1994) improved on Widom's research by examining the potential mediating effects of school performance on the maltreatment–

delinquency relationship and by taking substantiated (but not court) cases of maltreatment. That is, as Zingraff and others pointed out, Widom examined the most severe cases of maltreatment, making her study a "best-case" scenario for finding a relationship between maltreatment and delinquency.

Zingraff and colleagues used a random sample of children with substantiated reports of maltreatment (n = 655) and two control groups, one drawn from the general school population (n = 281) and the other from the Division of Social Services (n = 177). Their outcome variable—juvenile complaints taken from juvenile court records—is designed to tap problem behaviors that come to the attention of a variety of individuals (citizens, schools), not just the police. Initial findings from these data suggest that maltreatment significantly increases a child's risk of delinquency and that this increase is due to the greater involvement of maltreated children, relative to the school sample and the impoverished sample, in status offenses. In a subsequent set of analyses, Zingraff and colleagues (1994) considered whether school performance mediates the relationship between maltreatment and delinquency; in so doing, they also considered whether sex conditions this relationship. Focusing only on the maltreatment and school samples, and controlling for race, gender, age, and family structure, they found that neglected and physically abused children have a significantly greater risk of delinquent involvement than nonmaltreated school youths. However, when school outcome variables are controlled for, only neglect remains a significant predictor of delinquency and the magnitude of the neglect coefficient is reduced substantially. Using a number of multiplicative interactions terms to determine whether there are different school and delinquency outcomes for maltreated boys and girls, Zingraff and others (1994) found that good school performance protects physically abused girls, but not boys, from delinquent involvement.

The Rochester Youth Development Study sampled one thousand youths drawn from the seventh and eighth grades in public schools in 1988 (Kelley, Thornberry, and Smith 1997; Smith and Thornberry 1995). The youths and their caregivers were interviewed every six months for four and half years. Data also were collected from the Rochester public schools, police, and the department of social services. The researchers recorded any instance of maltreatment that occurred to these subjects from birth through 1992. Because the researchers used a stratified random sample, which yielded a representative study population, they had relatively fewer cases of maltreatment to examine than they would have had if they had sampled on the basis of maltreatment, especially for females (n = 74). Nevertheless, in one analysis that focused specifically on the "developmental consequences of maltreatment among young women," they found that when a variety of background experiences are controlled, maltreatment has no significant effect on self-reported general or violent offending (Smith and Ireland 2005).

Overall, these findings suggest that maltreatment increases the odds of criminal offending, but it remains unclear whether specific types of maltreatment place youths at a greater risk for offending than others and whether any of these relationships are conditioned by gender. Furthermore, because there is some evidence that both the timing and duration of maltreatment, as well as intervening life events, can either aggravate or mitigate the negative effects of maltreatment (Ireland, Smith, and Thornberry 2002; Leiter, Myers, and Zingraff 1994), it may be premature to conclude that the effects of maltreatment on the development of delinquency in girls is substantially greater than it is for boys or substantially greater than it would be for any other risk factor. A meta-analysis of the predictors of violent or serious delinquency in adolescence and early adulthood revealed that for six- to eleven-year-olds and twelve- to fourteen-year-olds, abusive parenting is one of the poorest predictors of subsequent violence for both age groups (Lipsey and Derzon 1998).

Sexual Abuse

Of all types of childhood maltreatment, the one that has been given the most attention for girls is sexual abuse. Most of the research on the developmental effects of childhood sexual abuse focuses on psychological outcomes such as post-traumatic stress disorder (PTSD), low self-esteem, depression, suicide, and gender behavior problems. Delinquency often is mentioned only in passing (Beitchman et al. 1992; Hotte and Rafman 1992; Kendall-Tackett, Williams, and Finkelhor 1993; Tyler 2002). Kendall-Tackett and colleagues' review of forty-five studies revealed that, while sexual abuse is strongly related to some symptoms, much of the symptomology is developmentally specific and one-third of the victims have no symptoms. Among the prospective longitudinal studies, most subjects are only followed for twelve to eighteen months, and about two-thirds of these subjects recovered over this period of time. These findings are bolstered by at least one other study, which showed that while sex abuse is a risk for delinquency, resiliency factors improved predictions of delinquency on girls at risk for this outcome (McKnight and Loper 2002).

Tyler (2002) updated Kendall-Tackett and colleagues' review of this research, focusing on forty-one studies of the emotional and social outcomes of child sexual abuse (suicide, substance use, gang involvement, risky sexual behavior and pregnancy, running away, PTSD, and behavioral problems). The research focused on the short-term effects of abuse and the degree to which the methodological concerns noted in previous research had been addressed. Most of the subjects of the reviewed studies ranged from twelve to eighteen years of age and, while the different outcomes exhibited by subjects varied with their developmental stage, three characteristics of the abuse incident(s) consistently were noted as being important: the severity of the abuse, the use of force, and the victim's relationship to the perpetrator.

Of greater concern, however, are the methodological problems that persist in these studies, which make it difficult to assess what the consequences of sexual abuse are for girls. Cross-sectional data are collected frequently from a variety of convenience samples (e.g., prenatal clinics, detention centers, chemical dependency treatment clinics), and few males and nonwhites are included, thereby precluding systematic gender and race comparisons. Only eight of the forty-one studies reviewed included a control group. Limitations in the measures also persist. There is no standardized measure of sexual abuse and researchers often let the respondent define abuse (e.g., "Have you ever been sexually abused?"). Who reports the abuse—victim, parent, official report—also varies across studies, as does evidence pertaining to the relative importance of other stressful life experiences and abuse characteristics.

Siegel and Williams (2003) addressed a number of these concerns. They prospectively followed 411 low-income, predominantly African American women who had been hospitalized in the 1970s; 206 of these women were reported to be victims of child sexual abuse. Controlling for race and family dysfunction, they found that sexual abuse victims had a significantly increased likelihood of both juvenile violent arrests and adult arrests.[4] The question of whether these effects are greater than those that would be observed for other types of maltreatment experiences is not known from this research, and the results from other studies are equally equivocal (Herrera and McCloskey 2003; Widom 1995). One notable exception to this generalization may be what is referred to as the "Sexual Abuse Plus group"—those who were sexually abused and additionally experienced either physical abuse or neglect (n = 28). Widom (1995) found that individuals in this group were more likely than individuals in other maltreatment groups and controls to be arrested for running away.

A number of studies report physical and sexual abuse in the backgrounds of shelter residents and street youths (Feitel et al. 1992; Janus, Burgess, and McCormack 1987; Stiffman 1989; Welsh et al. 1995), and it is well known that runaways are particularly vulnerable to delinquency and prostitution (Hagan and McCarthy 1997). However, prospective research linking abuse to delinquency through the experience of running away is extremely rare. Kaufman and Widom (1999) explored both the mediating effects of running away on the abuse–delinquency relationship and the potential way in which running away might moderate the abuse–delinquency relationship. They find that abused/neglected youths are more likely to run away than control children. Disaggregating these analyses into specific types of victimization, they found the same results for all types of maltreatment except physical abuse. Nevertheless, they aggregated all forms of maltreatment in subsequent analyses. These analyses revealed that being a runaway does not mediate the relationship between abuse and delinquency, but abuse does moderate the relationship between running away and delinquency and does so in an unexpected fashion. Running away has a stronger impact on the delinquency of control youths than the delinquency of maltreated youths (Siegel and Williams 2003).

Taken together, the findings of these studies suggest that (a) sexual abuse does appear to be related to delinquency; (b) relative to other forms of maltreatment, it is not clear whether sexual abuse has a greater or lesser impact on delinquency; and (c) there is little evidence that gender conditions this relationship (Curtis et al. 2001). Additionally, although maltreatment does increase the odds of running away, the relationship between maltreatment and delinquency does not hinge on this experience.

Finally, a number of studies have examined the relationship between sexual abuse and drug use. Most commonly, this association has been explored with clinical and cross-sectional data, which makes the generalizability of the findings and drawing inferences about the causal order problematic (Dembo et al. 1988; National Research Council 1993; Peters et al. 2003; Walrath et al. 2003; Watts and Ellis 1993).

Conclusions and Policy Implications

Are girls more vulnerable to the influences of family life than boys? We would suggest that this institution plays a critical role in the development of delinquency for both boys and girls. Yet we know that girls generally engage in less delinquency and less serious forms of delinquency than boys. Researchers frequently assume that girls have stronger connections to their families than boys and that problematic family life, accordingly, will be more detrimental for females than males. The research we have reviewed calls this assumption into question, as have other researchers before us (Cernkovich and Giordano 1987; Kruttschnitt 1996; Kruttschnitt, Gartner, and Ferraro 2002).

Take-Home Points

1. *Single-parent homes* and *divorce* have been found to have negative effects on both boys and girls, but effects are relatively weak on youths' respective involvement in delinquency, once other family processes are taken into account. Furthermore, what is known about the relationships among specific family processes (e.g., attachment and supervision) and female and male delinquency suggests that there are few, if any, consistent gender differences. Empirical literature suggests that negative family experiences and poor parenting have negative consequences for both boys and girls.

2. *Exposure to parental deviance* is another aspect of poor parenting with relevance to development of delinquency among girls and boys. Traditionally, scholars have operationalized the concept by examining the relationship between parental criminality and their children's delinquency and crime. Although studies of the "intergenerational transmission of criminality" have focused primarily on males, an increasing amount of qualitative research suggests that the effects of parental criminality on girls' delinquency may be comparable to what has been found for boys. Another way parental deviance has been operationalized is in the research that has examined the developmental effects of child maltreatment. While the extant research in this area

reveals little evidence of gender differences, attention to the question of whether the developmental effects of abuse and neglect are conditioned by gender has been sporadic.

3. *Emotional processes* that adhere to traditional gender roles, and the degree to which these processes create different levels of emotional control over and opportunities for crime, is another relatively unexplored area of family life that may help further our understanding of why girls engage in less delinquency and less serious delinquency than boys. Heimer and De Coster (1999; Heimer 1996) provided an important first step in mapping out how girls and boys may tend toward different internal constraints. Future research will need to further consider the degree to which gender roles shape internal and external barriers and avenues to crime and will need to do so in the context of considering other potential mediators of gender differences in delinquency.

Implications for Intervention and Research

1. This review of family influences on girls' delinquency also suggests that prevention and intervention efforts targeting girls will need to take the full range of family influences into account.

   Adding to early research that focused on relatively fixed areas such as family structure, empirical evidence increasingly points to the positive effects of consistent supervision and the deleterious consequences of various forms of abuse. These family influences are potentially more malleable than variables like family structure. However, early intervention is obviously needed to support positive family practices and to avoid the tendency for these negative family dynamics to become characteristic and entrenched.

   Some family problems are so all-encompassing (e.g., severe parental drug abuse) that alternative placements will likely be the most constructive option for some young women. Here, continuity and stability in alternative placements is particularly important, recognizing the centrality of social relationships to girls' development.

2. The current review also suggests areas for future investigation.
   - More research is needed on the connections between family dynamics and youths' involvement within other domains. For example, Zingraff and others' (1994) research finding that abuse experiences do not lead inexorably to delinquency under conditions of school success suggests additional avenues for successful intervention in the face of serious family problems.
   - Another research direction that holds promise for understanding the complex links between family processes and girls' delinquency is to investigate how processes such as sexual abuse may combine with other traditional predictors (e.g., familial criminality) to increase girls' own risk of involvement in delinquency. Here the notion of a nexus—or "package"—of risks may be an especially fruitful avenue for future investigation and intervention.

- Similarly, the research reviewed in this chapter provides little support for suggestions that, beyond genetics, the family has "little influence" on children's development (Harris 1998). Indeed, a recent study of practitioners such as juvenile probation, court, and detention personnel (Bloom et al. 2002b) highlighted that family factors represent the primary area of risk and protection for girls and should be a key emphasis of gender-specific programming. Nevertheless, peers and other extrafamilial influences (e.g., romantic partners) become increasingly important during the adolescent period and are the specific social context in which delinquency is frequently carried out. Thus, studies that actively connect family dynamics to these extrafamilial influences are also critical to a comprehensive understanding of girls' pathways to delinquent involvement.

6

Peer Influences on Girls' Delinquency

Peggy Giordano

R esearch has consistently shown strong support for the importance of friendship and peer processes in understanding adolescent delinquency involvement (Warr 2002). Peer processes have also been discussed in connection with the gender gap in delinquency. For example, some researchers have argued that girls' stronger connections to the family rather than friends generally inhibits their delinquency involvement (Leonard 1982). The assumption that girls are not as peer-oriented as boys is not, however, consistent with a large developmental literature that documents that, on average, girls are significantly influenced by peers and develop peer relationships characterized by intimacy, frequent contact, and mutual self-disclosure (Savin-Williams and Berndt 1990; Youniss and Smollar 1985). Thus, the connections between gender, peers, and delinquency (as well as conformity) are undoubtedly more complex than the notion that girls are family-oriented, while boys are more involved with their peers.

This chapter reviews research on several ways in which peers may influence delinquent behavior. We focus specific attention on whether these mechanisms appear to influence the delinquency of girls as well as boys, the extent to which such processes shed light on differential rates of involvement by gender, and the peer mechanisms that may be uniquely gendered. First, *unstructured socializing* increases the likelihood that various forms of delinquency will occur. Frequent unstructured socializing with one's peers results in more opportunities outside the purview of parents or other adults and may also decrease the adolescent's stake in conformity. A second pathway to delinquency involves the notion of *social skills deficits*. Some researchers have developed a peer deficit hypothesis, theorizing that young people who are unsuccessful within the peer arena early on are more likely to become antisocial and aggressive later in life (Coie, Dodge, and Kupersmidt 1990). This line of research fits well with early research suggesting that delinquent girls in particular are often lonely, rather asocial misfits (Konopka 1966). A third (and contrasting) mechanism involving peers focuses on the role of friends in providing *delinquent definitions* and an opportunity for modeling and reinforcement of delinquent conduct.

Another important area focuses on *group influence processes* themselves. Research suggests that the dynamics of interaction and communication within groups may amplify risk-taking beyond the general notion that friends may impart delinquent definitions. This is an important area of investigation in relation to issues of gender, because boys' and girls' styles of interaction within friendship and peer circles may be directly implicated in their differing levels of offense involvement. Finally, while less well developed than these other areas, research is beginning to link peer processes to influences within other social domains, including poor parenting practices and neighborhood disadvantage. In this way, peers can also be understood as an important factor that potentially *mediates family or community effects*.

Important also are a number of different types of peer affiliations, including same-gender peers, cross-gender friends, and romantic relationships. The latter type of liaison is especially important to consider, because relationships with males have been theoretically linked to girls' and women's more than boys' and men's delinquent conduct.

Mechanisms Underlying Peer-Delinquency Connections

Unstructured Socializing

Relying on a representative sample of 703 fourteen-year-olds, Mahoney and Stattin (2000) documented significant effects of unstructured socializing on antisocial behavior. These researchers found that participating in highly structured leisure activities was related to lower levels of antisocial behavior, and the converse was also observed. While this was the case for boys and girls alike, researchers found that the specific combination of being involved in less-structured activities, but no highly structured involvement was particularly productive of boys' antisocial behaviors. Research has also shown that involvement in structured activities decreases the chances of school dropout and, correspondingly, is linked to higher educational attainment in young adulthood; structured activities also lower levels of aggressive behavior (Eccles and Barber 1999; Mahoney and Cairns 1997; Mahoney, Cairns, and Farmer 2003). These findings suggest the importance of examining indirect as well as direct links (since school dropout and poor academic achievement generally are significant risk factors for delinquency involvement). Relying on indexes of participation developed from information contained in school yearbooks, Mahoney and colleagues found few gender differences in the effects of extracurricular activity participation in early adolescence on later educational status.

Researchers such as Eder, Evans, and Parker (1995) have also suggested that gendered socialization practices during preadolescence and adolescence (e.g., heavy emphasis on personal appearance and heterosexual relationship involvement) do not provide the optimal basis for enhancing girls' development and feelings of personal efficacy (Eder, Evans, and Parker 1995). Researchers have generally shown that girls involved in activities such as competitive athletics perform better academically, particularly in nontraditional arenas such as science (Hanson and Kraus 1998). Although these studies do not directly connect involvement in structured activities to delinquent behavior, it is reasonable to surmise from this extracurricular activities literature that structured involvement has a protective, prosocial effect on girls' development (Hansen, Larson, and Dworkin 2003). Conversely, simply "hanging out" with friends has long been considered a risk factor for delinquency involvement (Hirschi 1969).

The Peer Deficit Hypothesis

Another line of theorizing that has a significant empirical base focuses on the long-term effects of deficiencies or deficits in early childhood peer relations. Researchers have shown that children who are rejected by peers are more likely to fare poorly on a range of developmental outcomes, including a greater risk for antisocial and aggressive behavior (Asher and Coie 1990). It is argued that aggressive tendencies may make certain children less popular as playmates at the outset, but then a lack of success in the peer domain has further negative consequences, because such youths miss out on opportunities to build social competence and skills and to develop a more caring orientation toward others. Many of the most important studies in this tradition focus on peer processes during the grade school years and rely on indexes of sociometric status to measure peer rejection. Here children are given rosters of their fellow classmates and asked to indicate those that they would most and least like as friends. As Cairns and colleagues (1988) and others have noted, this provides a measure of popularity or status in the eyes of one's classmates but does not in itself document that such children are "loners" or friendless. Researchers such as Coie, Dodge, and Kupersmidt (1990) have examined association between peer status and behavior longitudinally and found links between these peer judgments and later conduct problems. Moffitt and others (2001) investigated a range of factors related to girls' and boys' delinquency in their New Zealand cohort study and found that boys and girls rejected by other children during the grade school years were more likely to be delinquent. These researchers also linked teacher reports of disliked youths to antisocial behavior as adolescents. In this study, a gender interaction was significant, indicating a stronger effect for boys. This study also found support for traditional peer variables, like associating with antisocial peers, although some of these associations were measured cross-sectionally.

The rejection findings fit well with Hirschi's (1969) control theory perspective on delinquency, which includes the notion that delinquents lack the capacity to develop intimate relationships with others, including peers. Early research on delinquent girls tended to echo these themes, as scholars such as Konopka (1966, p. 123) suggested that because of her basic "incapacity for friendship with contemporaries," the delinquent girl will often cope with her loneliness by temporarily "losing [herself] in the crowd" or moving into heterosexual relationships to fill a relationship void (see also Wattenberg 1956; who described delinquent girls as "lone wolves").

In contrast to this "deficit" view, Cairns and Cairns (1994) followed a sample of 475 youths who participated in the Carolina Longitudinal Study. These researchers asked youths directly about their own and other youths' peer affiliations and networks, rather than relying on the most liked/least liked strategy. The researchers found that aggressive boys and girls were generally solid members of peer clusters (rather than isolates), who had as many reciprocated friendship choices as nonaggressive youths (see also Cairns et al. 1988). However, their research did document the tendency of more aggressive youths to affiliate with other aggressive children, who likely provided further reinforcement for these attitudes and behaviors. This tendency was found for both male and female respondents (Cairns and Cairns 1994).

Studies focused on adolescent samples have also generally failed to support the idea that delinquents have inadequate or "cold and brittle" relationships with peers, as Hirschi (1969) suggested, and as is implied by the "peer rejection" hypothesis. For example, Giordano, Cernkovich, and Pugh (1986), in a study of interviews with 942 youths, found that delinquents reported levels of caring, trust, and intimate self-disclosure within their friendships that did not differ significantly from those reported by less-delinquent youths. In addition, girls, regardless of their levels of delinquency involvement, tended to report greater caring and intimacy within the friendship context. Thus, the findings do not support Wattenberg's early "lone wolf" hypothesis or the idea of a lack of social competence more generally. However, Giordano, Cernkovich, and Pugh's research did document that delinquent youths tended to report more conflict with friends, suggesting a more complex picture of relational dynamics within antisocial groups (see also Dishion, Andrews, and Crosby 1995). More recently, Pleydon and Schner (2001), in a study comparing young female offenders (n = 29) and high school students (n = 47), found that delinquent girls did not differ in reported levels of trust, alienation, and perceived intimacy with friends. However, delinquent youths perceived greater levels of peer pressure, findings that accord with the earlier Giordano, Cernkovich, and Pugh (1986) analysis (see also Claes and Simard 1992; and Kandel and Davies 1991; for a contrasting view see Marcus 1996).

Recently, Miller-Johnson and others (2003) examined peer status variables and links to problem behavior involvement in a sample of 657 urban, predominantly lower socioeconomic status African American seventh-grade students. In their analysis, the focus shifted to "controversial" rather than so-called "rejected" youths (controversial youths were frequently nominated by other students as both highly liked and highly disliked by other classmates). Miller-Johnson and others' theoretical discussion highlighted that, in disadvantaged settings, toughness, violence, and other risk-taking behaviors can be considered survival mechanisms and may even be accorded prestige (see also Burton, Allison, and Obeidallah 1995). Results suggested that youths identified as controversial on the basis of peer ratings evidenced the highest levels of involvement in risky behaviors. Gender was not a major focus of this study, but the findings suggest the importance of examining gender and peer status processes since these may be linked to the youth's race/ethnicity or social class position and the importance of broadening the focus beyond "rejected" youths to consider other peer-related social roles and identities.

Friends' Attitudes and Behaviors

Much research indicates that as children mature (and particularly during the adolescent years) it is highly normative to develop a greater interest in peers; to spend an increasing share of time with them; and, accordingly, to develop similar attitude and behavioral profiles (Collins and Laursen 1999; Csikszentmihalyi and Larson 1984). Most, if not all, cross-sectional studies find strong relationships between adolescent friends' prodelinquent attitudes and behavior and the adolescent's own delinquency (Warr 2002). These findings, in turn, accord with research on other domains such as smoking and sexual behavior, where behavioral concordance has also repeatedly been documented (Miller et al. 1997; Urberg, Shyu, and Liang 1990). Researchers have also found that differential exposure to delinquent peers is an important mediator of the gender–delinquency relationship. For example, Morash (1986) studied the peers–delinquency relationship within a sample that included adjudicated delinquents as well as school youths and found that variation in peer support for delinquency was a factor that significantly mediated the positive association between gender and delinquency within this sample group (see also Jensen 2003; Simons, Miller, and Aigner 1980).

Most of the early studies examining the attitudinal and behavioral influence of peers relied on cross-sectional data, thus limiting researchers' abilities to establish clearly that this high level of "concordance" within friendships reflected a process of influence. Researchers such as Hirschi (1969) argued that most of the observed similarity found within cross-sectional studies was due to initial preferences in making friendship alliances, rather than to an influence process. Longitudinal approaches add significantly to this picture: Most studies find evidence of selection as well as socialization using a longitudinal design (Matsueda and Anderson 1998; Thornberry et al. 1994). Thus, it is rather well documented that both male and female youths and their friends share some initial similarities in terms of prosocial or antisocial tendencies, but frequent interaction and communication amplify risk beyond these initial proclivities (Warr 2002).

Initially, research on peer effects relied on reports of friends' behavior provided by the respondent. This is potentially limiting, since youths may be imperfect reporters of friends' attitudes and behavioral profiles. Kandel's (1978) research represented an important advance. Kandel studied best friend dyads, collecting data directly from friends as well as from focal respondents. Kandel's longitudinal study of male and female adolescents provided support for the notion that the concordance typically observed in friends' behaviors reflects an approximately equal measure of selection (initial similarity of friends) and socialization (the tendency to become more similar over time, presumably as a result of social influence processes). Haynie (2001) recently relied on a large national probability sample of male and female youths (The National Longitudinal Study of Adolescent Health [Add Health]) to study connections between friends' behaviors and adolescents' own delinquency involvement. The Add Health design also allows researchers to link respondents' data with that of nominated friends, provided the latter attended schools that also participated in this survey. Haynie also examined the total set of friends nominated by the respondent, not only the best friend nomination. Her results indicated a significant effect of peer delinquency on the respondent's own delinquency. Further, Haynie found that characteristics of the network such as its cohesiveness and density influence these effects. This research is important because it shows that the well-documented peer effect is not entirely due to the adolescent's own potentially "distorted" view of friends' behaviors (Haynie 2001). There is, however, some indication that the peer effects, while significant, are not as strong as shown in studies relying on respondents' reports about their friends alone (Aseltine 1995). And, while the sample contains adequate representation of female respondents, the possibility of gendered effects of friendship influences was not explored in this analysis.

In another analysis that also relied on the Add Health data, Haynie (2002) explored variations in the character of adolescents' friendship networks and the effects of these variations. She found that a majority of adolescents (56 percent) actually reported friendships with others who represented a mix in terms of delinquency involvement and conforming behavior. Their reported friends represented both the prosocial and antisocial friends. This finding is also important because it has been more typical to conceptualize delinquent or prosocial friends in rather monolithic terms. Haynie's analyses did document that those instances in which virtually all of the adolescent's friends were delinquent also were related to the highest levels of reported delinquency involvement, which suggests a kind of "encapsulation" effect. This observation is potentially useful because it may help explain some of the complexities underlying peers, gender, and delinquency connections. Although Haynie did not focus separately on girls and boys in her analysis, it is likely that girls' networks are more often composed of entirely prosocial or mixed (some delinquent, some not) associations (Morash 1986). Even in the latter instance, individuals may be differentially influenced by particular individuals within the friend network. The broader developmental literature highlights much shifting of alliances and levels of closeness/contact during the adolescent period (Bowker 2004). For example, researchers have documented that close dyadic friendships have a salience/meaning for adolescent girls that frequently do not have an exact counterpart within adolescent male friendship circles (Berndt 1982). Thus, even under conditions of some exposure to delinquent definitions, girls may be more likely to avoid delinquency, because of the availability of alternative definitions provided by other friends. The generally pervasive societal-level norms also do not provide support for girls to engage in various forms of antisocial behavior (Harris 1977).

Conversely, girls who do engage in delinquent behavior may be affected by an encapsulation process in which they have been exposed to definitions across a large proportion of their social network affiliations. Giordano and Mohler-Rockwell (2001) previously developed an encapsulation argument with reference to gender and family influences. The argument is based on the observation that delinquent girls in their longitudinal study frequently reported that a rather large number of family members had been involved in crime, violence, or drug abuse (see Chapter 5 in this book). This idea could also be extended to the characteristics and composition of delinquent girls' peer networks.

Although the aforementioned studies focused primarily on friends' delinquent behaviors, some studies have attempted to disentangle and assess the relative effect of friends' attitudes compared with their behaviors. In a study relying on National Youth Survey data, Warr and Stafford (1991) found a stronger effect of peer behaviors—a consistent pattern of both prodelinquent friends who enact delinquent behaviors was, perhaps not surprisingly, most productive of delinquency. But in those cases where attitudes and behaviors were discordant, peer behavior was more predictive of the adolescent's own involvement.

In general, the study of peer attitudes deserves much more research scrutiny, especially with regard to understanding girls' involvement. It is likely that, in most situations, friends communicate a range of attitudes and definitions that coalesce with their behavioral choices. Given the importance of these definitions to an understanding of delinquent conduct, research on such attitudes remains surprisingly limited and sketchy. Often the assessment of attitudes involves little more than a tautological restatement about the outcome of interest (e.g., individuals who use marijuana have friends who hold relatively positive attitudes about marijuana use). Future research needs to be much more specific about the full range of everyday or routine attitudes/beliefs that foster delinquency, in general, or in relation to specific outcomes such as fighting/aggression or drug use. In this work, understanding the normative climates within which girls develop and mutually reinforce actions that are subject to sanction across the wider society, particularly when engaged in by girls and women, is important (Schur 1984). Thus, where such cognitive and attitudinal processes are concerned, including but moving beyond a common measurement template for boys and girls will be useful. Qualitative methods could be especially important in connection with this line of inquiry.

Heimer and colleagues have relied on quantitative approaches to highlight additional areas of complexity in the way attitudes influence girls' delinquency and the gender gap (Heimer 1996; Heimer and De Coster 1999). These researchers suggest that, while learning deviant and delinquent definitions is important to an understanding of girls' violent or other delinquent actions, the learning of *traditional gender definitions* transcends and contributes independently to the likelihood that girls will exhibit physical aggression or other types of delinquent acts. Through strong emotional ties to family and their more general socialization as young women, girls often develop views of self and other attitudes that are essentially incompatible with violence and other acts of risk-taking. Conversely, those with weaker emotional ties to family who develop less-traditional gender attitudes are more likely to become involved in delinquent acts. One study relying on National Youth Survey data (Heimer and De Coster 1999) found that, while girls who had learned violent definitions were more violent than other girls (and traditional gender definitions limited girls' involvement), association with aggressive friends did not explain additional variance. In contrast, having aggressive friends did explain additional variance in boys' delinquency. However, another analysis documented that anticipated *disapproval* for delinquency from friends influenced girls more than boys (Heimer 1996). These intriguing findings suggest the need for additional study of the ways in which gendered and more generic attitudes favor or alternatively discourage delinquent involvement, including research on how peers influence the development of a range of prosocial and antisocial attitudes.

Group Dynamics

Most of the literature reviewed earlier highlights that, for both male and female adolescents, friends influence or at least provide the social connections that make delinquent behavior much more likely. As Demuth (2004) found, in a study relying on National Youth Survey data, youths who did not report having one or more friends (youths defined in the study as "loners") tended to score low on delinquency involvement (see also Tolone and Tieman 1990). Further, numerous studies have shown that delinquency actually occurs most often within a group context—whether gauged by self-reports or the presence of codefendants (for those who have entered the official justice system (Reiss 1986). Indeed, Emler, Reicher, and Ross (1987) showed that girls were actually more likely to report being with companions than males when committing a delinquent act. Given the solid body of research on behavioral concordance as well as the group character of adolescent delinquency, research on the nature of group dynamics that serve to amplify delinquent tendencies is not particularly well developed.

Warr's (2002) recent theoretical treatment of the peers–delinquency relationship provides one of the most nuanced discussions of these group dynamics, that is, of specific mechanisms that serve as underpinnings of observed peer effects. Warr focused on processes such as fear of ridicule, loyalty concerns, status enhancement processes, feelings of anonymity the group provides, and diffusion of responsibility. In addition, he noted that delinquency needs to be conceptualized as a kind of "collective behavior," an observation that focuses squarely on the group's unfolding dynamics, rather than character flaws of the individuals who comprise various friendship networks. In line with this emphasis, researchers such as Katz (1988) have highlighted that criminal and other antisocial behaviors do have positive meanings for the individual. The positive emotional connections to crime not only refer to elements of the criminal activity itself (e.g., the "sneaky thrill" of shoplifting), but also to the perceived fun of discussing, carrying out, and reliving these shared situations with one's friends.

In life history accounts narrated by female offenders who participated in the Ohio Longitudinal Study, we found that women as well as men often focused on these positive meanings as important to their early involvement in crime and drug/alcohol abuse (Erez 1987; Giordano, Cernkovich, and Holland 2003). Respondents often mentioned the thrill of the street life, or the fun of their early escapades with friends—"it was like a rush you know, let's see what we can do today and get away with" (Giordano, Schroeder, and Cernkovich 2007, p. 1624). Rhonda, for example, actively cultivated a friendship with a delinquent companion she described as more exciting than her square friend Jackie: "Sunshine seemed more exciting than Jackie. She always had new clothes, money, boys around her . . . It was the thrill to be with Sunshine because she received more attention from other people" (p. 1625). Although these life histories also frequently revealed evidence of sexual abuse and other highly negative family circumstances, these references to peer dynamics suggest that through their peer interactions and relationships these young women were able to carve out a more positive, active sense of self as a "partier" or "risk-taker" type (Matsueda 1992). A focus on victimization experiences alone leads to the construction of an image of girls as rather hapless demoralized victims, one that does not reliably accord with such girls' own self-portraits and perspectives (Gaarder and Belknap 2002).

The adolescent's social connections, then, provide general support for antisocial behavior (as reflected in delinquent definitions and modeling of friends' behavior), amplify risk-taking in specific situations, and foster and reinforce a delinquent view of self (Matsueda 1992). Friends also provide numerous intrinsic and extrinsic rewards (social support, opportunities for intimate self-disclosure, tangible aid) that have long been understood as more universal benefits of intimate interactions. This powerful constellation of influences needs to be taken into account in any comprehensive perspective on girls' involvement in delinquent behavior. However, more research on specific dynamics within peer networks is needed. For example, fear of ridicule, a dynamic that Warr (2002) emphasized in his analysis of group effects may be particularly important in relation to boys' groups, while issues of loyalty (as an example) might prove to be more salient for understanding girls' friendship influences.

This line of research could be more effectively integrated with research in the developmental tradition, because such studies have shown that girls frequently offer more supportive communications within friendships, while boys more often develop a competitive mode of discourse, emphasize themes of toughness, and negatively sanction displays of positive, caring, or other presumably "softer" emotions (Eder, Evans, and Parker 1995). These norms about appropriate comportment within the peer context may help explain observed gender differences in delinquency, beyond the general provision of "delinquent definitions" within boys' and girls' peer circles. However, what is less clear is whether girls who have delinquency experience have developed friendship and communication styles that are more consonant with styles observed within male groups, or whether delinquent solutions are generated via a distinctive set of (gendered) group dynamics.

Research on bullying and relational aggression provides another caution to the idea that an "ethic of care" and concern for others is generally protective for girls. This research examines direct and indirect acts that are perceived as mean, harmful, or otherwise negative by others, but that are not necessarily physically aggressive (Crick and Grotpeter 1995). Bullying specifically evokes a power advantage over victims and also may include social exclusion, gossip, the silent treatment, and other acts that are not physically harmful but are relationally harmful (Pepler et al. 2004; Underwood 2003b). This research has generally documented that, when these broader definitions are employed, rates of aggression against others are not as strongly gendered as when physical acts alone are considered. Additional research on causes and consequences of these behaviors is important, because victims often experience significant distress, and because perpetrators may have problems in relationship building within the context of concurrent and later relationships. For example, Pepler and others (2004) found that girls who bullied reported higher levels of aggression in connection with romantic relationships, and that those who reported being both bullies and victims had especially problematic peer relations (see also Xie et al. 2002). In addition, research has generally shown significant correlations between more overt and indirect forms of aggression (Crick et al. 1999; Tomada and Schneider 1997).

Another area that warrants additional study is the role of race/ethnicity in understanding peer effects. Some early research suggested that African American youths may be even more peer-oriented than their white counterparts because of (presumed) deficits within the family arena (Silverstein and Krate 1975). This compensation argument has not received strong empirical support, however. For example, early studies documented that African American youths were less likely than whites to respond to peer pressure within an experimental setting (Iscoe, Williams, and Harvey 1964), and Billy and Udry (1985) found that among whites there was a more direct relationship between the sexual behavior of same-sex friends and respondents than for the African American youths in their sample. A greater homogeneity of peer behavior was evidenced in the friendship pairs of whites, especially white females. Consistent with this portrait, Giordano, Cernkovich, and DeMaris (1993), relying on an eight-item "peer pressure" index, found that African American youths perceived significantly lower levels of peer pressure than white youths. Larson and others' (2001) study of how adolescents spend their time is generally consistent in finding that African American urban seventh and eighth graders, compared with similarly aged white youths, spent significantly more time with family members and significantly less time talking with their friends. Certainly friends are important to all youths during the adolescent period, but these findings suggest the need to further refine our understanding of the unique confluence of race/ethnicity, gender, and social class as influences on peers–delinquency relationships.

Effects of the Gender Composition of Friendship Networks

Most of the group dynamics studies focus either implicitly or explicitly on effects of same-gender peers; the literature contains volumes of research on all-male groups and gangs (Cohen 1955; Thrasher 1927), and basic principles of identification lead to the expectation that adolescents are likely to be most influenced by "similar" others (Savin-Williams and Berndt 1990). Scholars have appropriately emphasized the role of same-gender peers in social development processes, because the strong similarities within such friendships create feelings of comfort and rapport that are reciprocally related to high levels of interaction and communication. These dynamic processes, in turn, maximize the likelihood that influence will occur. However, social psychologists have also underscored that the self frequently develops around elements of discontinuity or contrast within the social environment (Cooley 1902/1992; Mead 1934). Thus, we previously argued that relationships based in elements of distance or difference can also be quite important to the developing child and influential from a developmental standpoint. As Simmel (1950) noted, "For the actions of the individual, his difference from others is of far greater interest than is his similarity with them. If something is objectively of equal importance in terms of both similarity with a type and differentiation from it, we will be more conscious of the differentiation" (pp. 30–31) (see also Giordano 1995; Giordano, Longmore, and Manning 2001).

Further adding to the complexity of these social processes, other basic principles often highlighted within the social influence literature might lead us to expect that the effect of dissimilar others (notably cross-gender friends) would itself tend to be gendered. First, it is important to focus attention on the overall base rates of involvement in delinquency by gender. Because boys on average are likely to be more delinquent than similarly situated girls, it is intuitive to expect that girls will sometimes learn about delinquent modes of behavior from male rather than female companions. A second consideration follows directly from feminist perspectives and findings based on studies of influence within mixed-gender experimental "task" groups. It has frequently been noted that males not only hold more power societally, but within micro-level interactive contexts as well (Komter 1989). Indeed, experimental studies of mixed-gender groups show that men initiate more talk and actually have more influence within these settings (Crawford 1995). This asymmetry in men's power leads to the hypothesis that male friends will be most important as models for adolescent males' own delinquency, but are also likely to be implicated in girls' delinquency involvement. This notion has also been a core theme within the adult female crime literature, as scholars such as Richie (1996) have found that many women's crimes relate either directly (committing crimes at the behest of a man) or indirectly (arrests for domestic violence stemming from prior victimization experiences) to association with males. Although the research on peer effects is compelling, providing consistent evidence of same-gender influences on girls' as well as boys' delinquency, we need to examine cross-gender influences as another important peer dynamic that may influence girls' delinquency.

In a study relying on school and homeless youth samples, McCarthy, Felmlee, and Hagan (2004) found that female friendships within social networks generally decrease delinquency involvement of boys and girls. The authors found that female friendships did not inhibit offending among street (homeless) males but did among three other categories of youth: school males, school females, and homeless females. These authors argued that the dynamics of female friendship bonds—closeness, greater likelihood of connecting to conventional institutions, less preference for risk-taking, less physical in ways of relating to one another—are generally "protective" in terms of delinquency. Focusing specifically on girls, Giordano (1978) in an early study found that mixed-gender peer groups were the most common context in which girls actually reported committing delinquent acts. In a study of forty-nine girls held in detention facilities, and a comparison group of forty-three nondelinquent females, Johnson (2002) found that the delinquent girls were significantly more likely than their nondelinquent counterparts to identify males as a best friend. Caspi and others (1993) also documented that early maturing girls who attended mixed-gender schools were more likely to be delinquent than girls attending all-girl schools, a finding that also suggests, at least in a general fashion, an effect of exposure to male influence.

Using National Youth Survey data, Warr (1996) found that girls, relative to boys, reported that delinquent offenses were more likely to occur within a mixed-gender group. This extends Giordano's early findings based on a small convenience sample to a nationally representative sample of adolescents. Warr also found that male instigation of a delinquent act was more likely to occur in these mixed-gender groups (see Heinze, Toro, and Urberg 2004; who found that the number of delinquent peers increases delinquency regardless of the number of males in the group).

Romantic Partner Effects

Studies that have examined cross-gender peer effects have generally left unclear the question of whether these are actually friendships with males or romantic liaisons. Some of the findings about males exerting a negative influence strongly suggest that romantic relationships are involved, and association with older males, in particular, has been implicated as a causal path to girls' delinquency involvement. For example, Stattin and Magnusson (1990) document an effect of girls' early maturation on delinquency but suggest that this is largely due to their increased likelihood of associating with older males. Giordano (1978) asked respondents directly about whether romantic partners were involved in the delinquent acts girls committed and found that approximately 35 percent indicated the presence of a romantic partner when committing delinquent acts. This suggests an important, but not ubiquitous role for the romantic partner, but again these results were based on a small nonrepresentative sample.

Haynie and others (2005) recently examined the impact of romantic partner involvement directly, using the large, national probability sample of youths selected for participation in the National Longitudinal Study of Add Health. Restricting the sample to those adolescents who reported about a romantic relationship, the authors linked the focal respondent's own self-reported delinquency involvement to that reported by the romantic partner, provided that the partner attended a school that also participated in the Add Health study. The authors found that romantic partners' delinquency influenced respondent delinquency, net of the well-documented peer effect. The analysis relied on direct measures of peer delinquency (that is, self-reports provided by the peers themselves) and direct partner measures. The analyses suggested a gendered effect for minor delinquency (partner's delinquency was a significant predictor for both male and female respondents, but a gender-by-partner's delinquency interaction was significant, suggesting a stronger influence of the partner for girls relative to boys, where the outcome was minor delinquency). For serious delinquency, no significant gender interactions were found, indicating that a romantic partner's delinquency had a similar effect on male as well as female serious delinquency. The effect was not as large as the relationship to peers' delinquency but was nevertheless significant in a multivariate model that included other relevant controls. Consistent with social learning theories (Sutherland 1934), these findings highlight that romantic partners may have a prosocial or antisocial influence, depending on the normative orientation of the romantic partner. In this study, this was measured by the partner's level of self-reported delinquency behavior. Since these findings are cross-sectional, the limitations described in prior research on peer effects also apply here (i.e., some selection is undoubtedly involved in the behavioral concordance observed within the sample). Nevertheless, the romantic partner's delinquency level explained additional variance in delinquency, even after peer behavior had been taken into account (and the findings are significant for male as well as female respondents), and suggests the need for additional research on romantic partners as potentially consequential reference others.

In another analysis specifically focused on girls, Haynie (2003) revisited the issue of pubertal timing, again relying on the assets of the Add Health sample. She found an effect of early maturation on the "partying" type of delinquency and minor delinquency primarily due to the increased likelihood that the early maturing girl had become romantically involved. Haynie did not, in this analysis, find an effect of male delinquency.

The findings about romantic partner influences provide a point of connection between the adolescence research and research focused on offenders' later life-course circumstances and criminal trajectories. The "desistance" literature, for example, has documented that a high-quality marriage frequently has a significant influence on criminal career paths later in life; Sampson and Laub (1993) refer to this as "the good marriage effect." In this literature focused on adult crimes, wives have generally been theorized as having a relatively prosocial effect, while male romantic partners have generally been considered to have a negative influence on the likelihood and course of women's criminal involvement (Richie 1996). Some research qualifies these associations, suggesting a more conditional relationship that depends on the behavioral profile of the focal spouse (Giordano, Cernkovich, and Holland 2003; Moffitt et al. 2001; Simons et al. 2002). Future research also usefully might explore instances in which a romantic partner merely reinforces existing peer attitudes or, alternatively, represents a departure from them. Under what conditions does the romantic partner influence a significant shift, either in a prosocial or antisocial direction?

In a related vein, we also have recently suggested that the specific dynamics underlying romantic partner influence may be similar in some respects to peer group influence but may also involve distinctive mechanisms. Feminist perspectives focused on gendered imbalances of power suggest one important dynamic, but others may be involved as well. It is important to avoid an adult perspective on these early romantic relationships. For example, in a four-wave longitudinal study of over 1,100 adolescents' romantic and sexual lives, we found that boys, on average, report more influence attempts on the part of their romantic partners, score higher on a scale measuring "actual" partner influence (as perceived by the respondents), and describe either egalitarian dynamics or a tilt favoring girls' greater power within these relationships. Girls' reports and the content of one hundred in-depth qualitative interviews with a subset of these respondents provide additional support for this pattern of results. We also found that boys, relative to girls the same age, perceive significantly less confidence navigating various aspects of their romantic relationships but scored similarly on a scale measuring levels of "heightened emotionality" or love (Giordano, Longmore, and Manning 2006). Although these findings reference general processes of influence, rather than the dynamics of romantic interactions that lead to delinquent outcomes, they do serve to complicate the assumption that girls' delinquency routinely emerges from asymmetrical and traditionally gendered power/dependence relations within the romantic context.

Our own hypothesis is that the less serious girls' involvement in crime or drug abuse, the more efficient or powerful the "bad boyfriend" explanation—a view that is generally consistent with the findings of Haynie and others (2005), reviewed earlier concerning minor versus serious delinquency. Where girls have shown a rather consistent pattern of involvement in serious crime, violence, or drug use, it is likely that cross-gender influences, including romantic partner effects, will need to be theorized as occurring within a constellation of other social dynamics. Delinquent definitions and support from same-gender peers unfold against a backdrop of serious family-related risk (abuse, parental criminality, and the like—see Chapter 5 on family influences). Nevertheless, romantic relationships become increasingly salient as respondents mature into adulthood, and partners may begin to replace peers and family as a source of reference and influence. Research has shown a strong tendency toward assortative mating (Caspi and Herbener 1990; Quinton et al. 1993). Delinquent or even moderately aggressive girls may partner with men who may represent a more serious level of aggression or drug involvement and, in turn, amplify girls' own delinquency or tendencies toward interpersonal conflict (Capaldi, Kim, and Shortt 2004). Drug and alcohol use may also be a coping strategy for dealing with partner abuse or other romantic difficulties (Giordano, Schroeder, and Cernkovich 2007), and violence stemming from gendered patterns of behavior and relational concerns (e.g., jealousy and cheating may contribute to girls' problem behaviors and, in some cases, juvenile justice system contact; Miller and White 2003). Clearly, more research is needed on romantic partner choices and influences to explicate fully the role of heterosexual relationships as either inhibiting or exacerbating girls' delinquency.

Links between Individual, Family, or Community Dynamics and Peer Effects

Although statistical analyses in this area typically explore the role of peers or partners, controlling for other potentially important influences, or analyses that specifically compare the relative explanatory power of, for example, family versus peers variables, newer research is beginning to more systematically investigate the interconnected nature of family, community, individual, and peer effects. Scaramella and others (2002) found that poor parenting influenced male and female delinquency indirectly via an increased likelihood that children will affiliate with delinquent peers, and other researchers have examined similar terrain. Svensson (2003) documented a significant gender effect—although girls in the Swedish sample were, on average, subject to higher levels of monitoring—peer deviance exerted a stronger influence under conditions of low supervision. In these analyses, control theory's emphasis on a breakdown of familial bonds has been effectively integrated with learning theory's focus on delinquent peers (Elliott, Huizinga, and Ageton 1985). Less often, researchers have explored community and peer linkages. For example, Simons and others (1996) found that community context influenced the delinquency of girls and boys in a somewhat distinct fashion. A general measure of community disadvantage influenced the likelihood of boys affiliating with delinquent peers, while the proportion of single-parent households in the community was linked to girls' affiliation with delinquent peers (and in turn higher delinquency). Aside from these traditional "community" variables, additional research is needed on the adolescent's wider circle of friends and other peer contacts. This recognizes that the adolescent's immediate friendship network is necessarily "nested" within a larger peer context (friends of friends, reputational groups within/outside school) that must also be navigated by the adolescent and may influence boys' and girls' perceptions of what constitutes the normative climate they inhabit. For example, fights between girls are extremely rare within affluent suburban school settings but are more common in disadvantaged school contexts. This reality reflects a nexus of community and family disadvantages that foster unique cultural (peer) worlds for adolescents. A focus on this broader ecology is important, because single-factor explanations (e.g., sexual abuse) set up conditions favorable to, but do not on their own, fully explain girls' movement into delinquent or aggressive actions. In short, girls in an affluent school, even if they have been subjected to a victimization experience, such as sexual abuse, typically do not begin to deal drugs or join a delinquent gang. Conducting research on these broader normative climates also will require moving outside the confines of school settings (since the research reviewed earlier suggests that unstructured socializing, rather than involvement in [school-based] structured activities, is most productive of delinquent behavior). It is also well documented that being absent from school and dropping out are very significant correlates of delinquency involvement (see Chapter 7 on school effects), suggesting the general importance of designing studies that incorporate peer contexts that flourish outside of school and, in effect, compete with school for youths' attention.

Another potentially fruitful line of inquiry links factors typically constructed as "individual differences" to social dynamics and, in turn, delinquency. For example, feelings of empathy and a more overarching "ethic of care" are associated with girls' development (Gilligan 1982), and such orientations toward others are also associated with a lower likelihood of aggressing against others. In line with this general notion, but extending these observations to a focus on variations in involvement, Broidy and others (2003a) found that girls who do become delinquent are less empathic, on average, than their nondelinquent counterparts. Relying on Ohio Longitudinal Study follow-up data on serious offenders, Giordano and others (2007) recently documented that the respondent's "anger identity" was a significant predictor of women's and men's continued participation in crime. Anger identity not only predicted violence and criminal activity, but it also predicted problem use of alcohol and drugs. Although this could be theorized as an individual difference (i.e., the idea of a latent trait that negatively influences individuals throughout the life course), drawing on the core assumptions of the "sociology of emotions" tradition, we emphasize that many of these feelings of anger have a social origin, and so can be conceptualized as potentially malleable in light of subsequent positive social experiences (see also Agnew 1992).

A recent study by Piquero and others (2005) provides another example of a more complex analysis that connects individual and social levels. These researchers investigated the strength of girls' and boys' own moral beliefs/prohibitions against engaging in particular delinquent acts in concert with peer influence and found that where girls' moral beliefs were strong, delinquent peers had a greater effect (presumably as a social force that helped girls "overcome their inhibitions"), which, in turn, fosters delinquency (see also Mears, Ploeger, and Warr 1998).

Conclusions

Youniss and Smollar (1985) noted that within adolescent friendship, reality is often "co-constructed." This suggests a relatively egalitarian process of mutual influence, rather than the image of a one-directional or coercive dynamic (i.e., the idea of peer "pressure"). The research reviewed here is generally consistent with Youniss and Smollar's general description of close friend relationships: Youths with relatively similar attitudes and identities undoubtedly feel comfortable forming friendships with one another, but over time, interaction and communication result in even more behavioral "concordance." Research reveals that these age-related social dynamics appear to significantly influence girls' as well as boys' delinquency. Indeed, in a recent meta-analysis of factors associated with girls' delinquency across a range of different studies, peers' delinquency emerged as one of the strongest predictors (Hubbard and Pratt 2002).

Some treatments of female delinquency have ignored the important role of same-gender peers, as the idea of a relatively egalitarian process of influence does not immediately and directly link to considerations of patriarchy and attendant asymmetries of power. Yet the broader developmental literature continually highlights that girls care about their friends and about how others view or judge them. It is thus unlikely that girls will move into delinquent behavior absent perceived support from these important and "like-me" others. More time spent in unstructured peer activities and prodelinquent attitudes/behaviors on the part of friends are reliably linked to girls' as well as boys' delinquency; viewed from a different vantage point, peer variables have also been shown to partially mediate the gender–delinquency relationship observed in most sample groups. These findings regarding peer dynamics call for further integration of key insights of feminist perspectives with insights originally developed with reference to boys' behavior (notably, principles of social learning). Sexual abuse and other victimization experiences are significantly associated with girls' delinquency, but, as suggested earlier, this association may be conditional, that is, dependent on peer involvement providing support for and the specific context within which delinquent behavior actually occurs. Without this peer connection, many girls who would qualify in terms of family-related risk will not turn to delinquent modes of expression. In such cases, depression, eating disorders, and other traditionally gendered responses are a more likely developmental outcome.

In turn, these family and peer dynamics take place within the wider arenas of the neighborhood and school. Thus, a lack of social and cultural capital influences the likelihood that peer support for delinquency will be found within the immediate environment—a dynamic that influences the network characteristics and behaviors of girls as well as boys. This is a generic, rather than a gendered, pattern of influences. Yet, in most instances, girls find comfort and safety within the home and in connection with their interactions with relatively prosocial friends. Sexual abuse and other negative family experiences may significantly compromise girls' well-being but may not result in delinquent solutions—without considering poverty, lack of school success, parental criminality, and the like, factors that increase the likelihood of affiliating with "delinquent" others and, in turn, amplify the risk of sustained involvement. In short, both gendered and generic processes are needed to adequately explain girls' delinquency.

This review does, however, suggest that the mixed-gender peer group is more productive of delinquency for girls, findings that point to another specifically "gendered" social dynamic. The research on romantic partners is also intriguing; however, it would be premature to conclude from these studies that the boyfriend or male friends push girls into crime, any more than we can surmise that peer "pressure" is the sole dynamic that underlies the correspondence in friends' attitudes and behaviors. We should explore in more detail the specific relationships that develop to constitute these mixed-gender groups and the conditions under which influence derives from a relatively egalitarian influence process, or alternatively from inequalities of power, or even an element of coercion. It may be that subtypes of girls need to be identified, and longitudinal data sets would be important in connection with this line of research. A subgroup may be "compelled to crime" (Richie 1996) by a boyfriend's negative influence, but other girls' antisocial tendencies may be found to predate their romantic involvements and may be sustained over the long haul by their (on average longer lasting) peer associations, as well as familial influences (e.g., parental criminality, neglect, and abuse). As suggested earlier, our view is that the "bad boyfriend" explanation is more adequate for explaining the conduct of girls who can be found on the margins of criminality; this relationship does not in isolation provide a comprehensive understanding of paths to more serious levels of involvement. For some girls, however, cross-gender associations could provide an initial "gateway" or entrée to the "street life" or other deviant associations, and this broader set of shifting network affiliations may subsequently exert a longer-term deleterious effect. Still other girls' circumstances may well accord with Konopka's (1966) original notion that girls are engaging in delinquency as a way to fill a "relationship void." More research is needed on the connections between peers and romantic partners and also on some of the more tangible or utilitarian aspects of romantic partner involvement, particularly within disadvantaged contexts. In some poverty areas, the partner, especially older partners, may provide not only social but monetary or other useful benefits that are part of a larger arsenal of survival strategies that bring young women closer to the world of drugs and other types of criminal activities (Miller 1986). Such social dynamics also reflect the play of gendered and more generic (i.e., poverty) processes.

Policy Implications

The single most important way in which research and policy relating to girls' delinquency has been distinguished from efforts targeting boys is the focus on girls' victimization experiences—recognizing the key insight that these experiences are central to an understanding of girls' involvement. The research reviewed here suggests that while practitioners and policy makers should continue to focus on preventing or ameliorating effects of victimization experiences (see also Chapter 5), we should recognize that girls' delinquency occurs within a peer context, is fostered by peers' attitudes and behaviors, and undoubtedly is amplified by group dynamics that unfold within the adolescent girl's circle of friends. While most girls do not develop delinquent associations, some do, and delinquent companions have a significant effect on girls' behavioral choices. It is important for practitioners to fully recognize the developmentally appropriate benefits friendships provide adolescent girls, including highly valued opportunities for socializing and "fun" and social and tangible support (including the comfort of affiliating with others whose family circumstances may be similar to one's own). Over time, delinquent identities and the "escapades" that solidify them also take on positive meanings for the individual and become a further source of social bonding and connection. During adolescence, many of the highly negative consequences of long-term involvement in crime, drug abuse, or both have not yet fully materialized. Service providers will need to work to provide alternative sources of positive meanings to replace the associations/lifestyle features that girls themselves define in relatively positive or at least comfortable/familiar ways. Providing structured social activities that permit affiliation with more prosocial others may be helpful, and Haynie's (2002) finding that most youths' networks do contain some prosocial friends is also potentially important. This suggests that girls in general count some as friends who are relatively more prosocial— it may be more realistic and palatable to ask girls to move closer to these familiar prosocial others than to attempt to develop an entirely new network of same-aged companions. This will prove more difficult if the young women appear to be encapsulated within a highly deviant network that includes parents, siblings, and peers.

Given the significant effects of romantic partners on girls' and boys' delinquency involvement, prevention and intervention efforts would also benefit from increased attention to these cross-gender relationships. Relationship-focused curricula could be developed that cut across specific topics such as pregnancy prevention, relationship violence, and conflicts with peers that involve issues of romance, as well as the role of partners in delinquency involvement or drug use. Researchers such as Eyre, Hoffman, and Millstein (1998) have previously noted that relationship issues are likely to be of greater interest to teens than many of the knowledge- and health-based programs currently in wide use that have been shown to be rather limited in their effectiveness.

7

Girls, Schooling, and Delinquency

ALLISON ANN PAYNE, DENISE C. GOTTFREDSON,
AND CANDACE KRUTTSCHNITT

Although school-related deaths, violent victimizations in school, and overall school crime have declined over the past decade (Kaufman et al. 2001), public concern about school safety has increased, especially in the wake of several highly publicized school shootings between 1992 and 1999 (Anderson et al. 2001). Although infrequent, violence in schools is a problem. The Youth Risk Behavior Surveillance Surveys (YRBSS), a survey conducted biannually in schools in thirty-two states and certain localities by the Centers for Disease Control and Prevention, provides statistics regarding violent youth behavior. The 2003 survey shows that fighting is common among high school students: 33 percent of students (40.5 percent of males and 25.1 percent of females) surveyed had been in a physical fight in the last year. In fact, students experience more victimization in school or on their way to and from school than out of school. In the 2001 National Crime Victimization Survey (NCVS),[1] 36 percent of all serious, violent crimes against twelve- to eighteen-year-olds (e.g., rape, sexual assault, robbery, or aggravated assault) occurred during school or on the way to and from school. Girls' violent delinquency is greater in middle schools than in high schools (Payne and Gottfredson 2005).

Research has identified several characteristics of students and schools that might be manipulated in efforts to reduce these problems (Gottfredson 2001). Much of a substantial body of research on the effects of school and school-related factors on delinquency is framed in social control, strain and social disorganization theories (Battistich and Hom 1997; Biglan et al. 2004; Bryk and Driscoll 1988; Felson et al. 1994; Galloway, Martin, and Wilcox 1985; G. D. Gottfredson 1981; D. C. Gottfredson 2001; Gottfredson and Gottfredson 1985; Hawkins et al. 1995; Hawkins and Lishner 1987; Hellman and Beaton 1986; Howell 2003; Maguin and Loeber 1996; Ostroff 1992; Payne, Gottfredson, and Gottfredson 2003). However, the majority of this research fails to address whether gender moderates these relationships (Brier 1995; Carr and Vandiver 2001; Gil, Vega, and Turner 2002; Lipsey and Derzon 1998; Lynam, Moffitt, and Stouthamer-Loeber 1993; Thornberry, Moore, and Christenson 1985). A few studies specifically test for group differences in the influence of school-related risk factors on delinquency or drug use (Gottfredson and Koper 1996; Payne and Gottfredson 2005; Rosay et al. 2000), and Howell (2003) summarizes other pertinent literature about gender differences and risks for problem behavior. However, the majority of the studies do not distinguish between the effect of school-related factors on boys' delinquency and girls' delinquency; firm evidence regarding gender-based effects is lacking.

In this chapter, we examine the relationships between risk and protective factors found in the school domain and female delinquency and drug use. We divide this chapter into two sections. In the first section, we examine research on the most frequently studied individual-level factors related to school, such as school performance or academic success and failure, and school bonding factors such as attachment and commitment to school. In the second section, we focus on the school level, examining both school context factors (such as grade level, size of student enrollment, class size, racial and ethnic composition, and school location) and school climate factors (such as the social organization of the school, the cultural system of norms and values in the school, and the discipline management of the school). We begin the discussion of each factor by presenting evidence regarding the general relationship between that factor and delinquent behavior, without regard to subgroup differences. We then discuss whether the relationship differs for males and females—first in cross-sectional studies, then in longitudinal studies. Finally, we summarize evidence (when it is available) about the extent to which extraneous variables account for the relationship. When a study examines race/ethnicity differences, these findings are included.

Individual-Level Factors

In this section, we discuss the relationship between delinquency or substance use and academic performance, including dropping out of school, and school bonding, representing attachment and commitment to school and aspirations for future educational pursuits (Gottfredson 2001). While other school-related factors, such as school transitions,[2] may have an effect on delinquency, the research is scant; we focus on relationships between school factors and delinquency that are well documented by research.

Academic Performance

General Relationship

Much research supports the general relationship between academic performance and various forms of deviant behavior (Gottfredson 1981; Maguin and Loeber 1996). In general, "consistent evidence supports an association between poor school performance and drug use and other adolescent problem behaviors" (Gottfredson 2001, p. 32).

The most thorough review of the relationship between academic performance and delinquency to date is a meta-analysis conducted by Maguin and Loeber (1996). They first examine forty-two cross-sectional studies and find a small negative relationship (−.149) between academic performance and delinquency: Lower academic performance is related to greater delinquency. A major problem with cross-sectional studies, of course, is that conclusions about temporal orderings are impossible. While the relationship could act in the hypothesized direction, such that poor school performance leads to involvement in delinquency, it could also act in the reverse direction, such that involvement in delinquency leads to poor academic performance. To address this problem, Maguin and Loeber (1996) also examine twenty-six longitudinal studies. Results from these studies suggest that, independent of the time period between the measurement of the two variables, poor academic performance is related to greater involvement in delinquency.

Maguin and Loeber (1996) also point out that the relationship between academic performance and delinquency may be spurious, suggesting that both might be explained by intelligence, socioeconomic status, attention problems, or earlier problem behavior. To investigate this possibility, they first examine seventeen cross-sectional studies that include possible common causes of both academic performance and delinquency. Results from the thirteen studies that examine socioeconomic status provide no support for the common cause possibility. Conversely, results from the five studies that examine intelligence and the two studies that examine attention problems show that both variables are common causes; that is, inclusion of these two variables reduces the relationship between academic performance and delinquency to close to zero. Five longitudinal studies also include socioeconomic status and conduct disorder as covariates of academic performance and delinquency, but results from these studies reveal that neither variable is a common cause of the association between academic performance and delinquency. While such analyses of potential spurious relationships are important, suggesting the necessity of early interventions to alter the common causes of academic performance and delinquency, gender differences are seldom examined.

Academic Performance and Female Delinquency

Attention to gender differences in the relationship between academic performance and delinquency can be found, however, in several cross-sectional studies.

Paulson, Coombs, and Richardson (1990) examine a sample of 446 white and Hispanic boys and girls, aged nine to seventeen, in which 46 percent of the sample had used illegal substances and 54 percent had not. They found that abstainers performed better than users regardless of gender and ethnicity. In a multigroup comparison, Rosay and others (2000) examined the correlation of academic performance and drug use in the National Education Longitudinal Study, which contains large samples of blacks, Hispanics, Asian Americans, Native Americans, and whites. The negative relationship between academic performance and substance use is equal across race and gender groups.

Examining correlates of delinquency as opposed to substance use, Junger-Tas, Ribeaud, and Cruyff (2004) studied a sample of forty-five hundred European students and found that the relationship between school achievement and delinquency is stronger for boys than girls. Similarly, in the aforementioned meta-analysis, Maguin and Loeber (1996) found that the association between academic performance and delinquency in cross-sectional studies is significantly stronger for boys than for girls (mean ES = −.15 for males and −.09 for females). In addition, the association is larger for whites than blacks, although this difference is not statistically significant. Hence, the majority of cross-sectional studies examining gender and race differences between academic performance and delinquency found a lack of differences when studying drug use but found stronger relationships for boys than for girls, and when studying delinquency, researchers found stronger relationships for whites than for blacks.

Several longitudinal studies also examine gender differences in the relationship between academic performance and delinquency. In a sample of 806 boys and 721 girls in Denver, Colorado, Huizinga, Loeber, and Thornberry (2000) found that academic failure (grades of Ds and Fs) is significantly associated with later delinquency for boys only. Maguin and Loeber's (1996) meta-analysis of longitudinal studies found comparable results, suggesting that the association between academic performance and later delinquency is stronger for boys than for girls (mean ES = −.17 for males and −.09 for females). However, the difference in effect sizes for males and females is only .08. Although this is a statistically significant difference, one questions whether such a small difference is practically significant.

Some longitudinal studies compare the effects of academic performance on a variety of substance use outcomes, and others examine the extent to which academic performance moderates the relationship between other risk factors and delinquency. For example, in a study of 1,332 boys and 1,714 girls in nine high schools in California and Wisconsin, Crosnoe, Erickson, and Dornbusch (2002) found that the influence of academic performance differs for girls and boys, depending on the type of deviant behavior. Better school performance predicts lower levels of delinquency for both genders. However, academic performance is related to lower levels of alcohol use for boys only and lower levels of tobacco, marijuana, and other illegal drug use for girls only. In addition, Crosnoe, Erickson, and Dornbusch (2002) examined the moderating effects of academic performance in the relationship between delinquent peers and delinquency. They found an interactive effect of academic performance and delinquent peers only for girls, such that better school performance protects girls from delinquency when they had delinquent friends. Zingraff and others (1994) found similar effects by examining the relationships among child abuse, school performance, and delinquency: Academic performance serves as a buffer against the negative effects of abuse, more so for girls than for boys.

As previously mentioned, it is possible that the relationship between academic performance and delinquency is spurious; other factors may affect both academic performance and delinquency and make it appear as if the two are causally related. Only a few studies examine this possibility separately for girls and boys. Tremblay and others (1992) found that academic performance in grades one and four does not predict delinquency at age fourteen, once early disruptive behavior is included in the model. However, academic performance *at age ten* significantly predicts personality traits at age fourteen that are predictive of delinquency (e.g., aggression and antisocial values). These findings, which appear for both boys and girls, suggest that later academic performance may have a stronger causal effect on delinquency than earlier academic performance. Additionally, as discussed earlier, Maguin and Loeber (1996) examined possible common causes in both cross-sectional and longitudinal studies, but both sets of studies were largely confined to males. The cross-sectional results show that intelligence and attention problems do act as common causes for academic performance and delinquency, while socioeconomic status does not. The longitudinal analysis offers no support for socioeconomic status being a common cause. Finally, in the case of conduct disorder, which includes a small number of studies that permit gender comparisons, there are no significant differences between boys and girls: Conduct disorder is not a common cause for poor academic performance and delinquency for either gender.

In summary, there seems to be slightly more support for a stronger effect for boys than girls in the relationship between academic performance and delinquency (Huizinga, Loeber, and Thornberry 2000; Junger-Tas, Ribeaud, and Cruyff 2004; Maguin and Loeber 1996). There appear to be differences, however, based on the type of behavior studied: Some studies found that the relationship between academic performance and *drug use* is equal for the genders (Paulson, Coombs, and Richardson 1990; Rosay et al. 2000).

Dropping Out of School

Research on the influence of dropping out of school on delinquency for both boys and girls is mixed. Some studies have found that delinquency increases after dropping out (Farrington et al. 1986; Thornberry, Moore, and Christenson 1985), while others have found that, for some students, dropping out has no influence on future delinquency (Jarjoura 1993, 1996). Jarjoura (1993) examined the issue further by (a) controlling for factors that would likely predict both dropping out and delinquency and (b) differentiating among the reasons for dropping out. After controlling for prior factors, he found that those who drop out of school are *not* more likely to engage in delinquency. However, the reason for dropping out also has an effect on this relationship. Youths who drop out because they do not like school or for unspecified reasons are more likely to engage in delinquency than high school graduates, while those who drop out because of problems at home do not have higher levels of future delinquency. Dropping out because of financial reasons or poor grades does not increase future crime; however, these youths already engage in more crime than their peers before they drop out, and they continue to do so after leaving school. Finally, and especially relevant for research on female delinquency, students who drop out for personal reasons, such as marriage, pregnancy, or both, are not more likely to engage in theft or sell drugs, but they are more likely to engage in future violence (Jarjoura 1993).

None of this research specifically differentiates the effect of dropping out on delinquency by gender; the specific effect of dropping out of school on female delinquency is unknown. However, there is some indirect evidence of the effects of leaving school on girls' delinquency. Pregnancy as a precursor to dropping out (or the reverse, dropping out preceding pregnancy) is related to significantly lower levels of schooling, which, given the results discussed previously, could lead to greater involvement in delinquency. These results hold for white females, black females, and Hispanic females; that is, the impact of pregnancy and dropping out of school does not differ for white, black, or Hispanic females (Hofferth, Reid, and Mott 2001; Klepinger, Lundberg, and Plotnick 1995; Manlove 1998).

Attachment to School

General Relationship
Attachment to school is shown by the extent to which students care about the school and the teachers and the extent to which they care about the teachers' opinions. The more students feel as though they belong in their school, the less likely they are to engage in delinquent behavior. The negative relationship between school attachment and delinquency is well documented by cross-sectional and longitudinal research (Cernkovich and Giordano 1992; Gottfredson, Wilson, and Najaka 2002; Jenkins 1997; Liska and Reed 1985; Welsh et al. 1999). Cross-sectional studies also link weak school attachment to smoking cigarettes, higher rates of emotional distress, suicidal behavior, violence, substance use, and early sexual activity (Bonny et al. 2000; Resnick, Harris, and Blum 1993). In fact, some scholars maintain that school attachment has a stronger association with absenteeism, delinquency, polydrug use, and pregnancy than other factors, including attachment to family (Resnick et al. 1997; Resnick, Harris, and Bloom 1993).

In contrast to the questions regarding the spuriousness and causal direction of the relationship between academic performance and delinquency, longitudinal studies support the causal effect of attachment to school on delinquency and drug use, but mainly in studies of males. For example, Sampson and Laub (1993) found that attachment to school is a large predictor of subsequent male delinquency and continues to predict delinquency even when earlier antisocial behavior is included in the model (Liska and Reed 1985). However, it is also possible that the relationship between academic performance and delinquency is indirect via its relationship to school attachment (Ward and Tittle 1994).

Attachment to School and Female Delinquency

Some studies examine gender-based differences in the relationship between attachment to school and delinquency. Cernkovich and Giordano (1992) separated a cross-sectional sample of 942 twelve- to nineteen-year-olds into four race-sex subgroups and find that the relationship between school attachment and delinquency does not significantly vary across the groups; school attachment plays the same role in delinquency for girls and boys, for blacks as for whites. Similarly, in a cross-sectional study using the Add Health data, Zweig and others (2002) examined the association between attachment to school and delinquency by determining the risk profiles of 12,578 male and female students. Low-risk females and low-risk males both report more school connectedness than other males and females who had higher risk profiles (Zweig et al. 2002). In a multigroup comparison, Rosay and others (2000) examined the correlations between attachment to school and delinquency and drug use in two large national data sets. Attachment to school displays a negative relationship with substance use for both males and females of black, white, and Hispanic origins. For delinquency, however, the results are not as straightforward. The relationship is similar across race and gender groups in one of the data sets, but in the other, the correlations tend to be higher for males than for females and for whites than for ethnic minority groups. In a sample of forty-five hundred European students, Junger-Tas, Ribeaud, and Cruyff (2004) found that school attachment has a stronger association with both delinquency and drug use for boys than girls. Similarly, Payne and Gottfredson (2005) found significant gender and racial differences in the relationship between school attachment and various forms of delinquency. This study examined over thirteen thousand white and nonwhite students in over 250 schools with the specific intent of investigating gender and racial differences in the relationships between a variety of school factors and delinquency. In this study, the mean level of attachment to school is higher for girls than boys. Controlling for student age, attachment to school is related to lower levels of overall delinquency and violent delinquency for all groups, but this association is larger for boys than girls and for nonwhites than whites. Similarly, attachment to school is related to lower levels of property delinquency for all groups, but the effect is larger for boys than girls. However, the negative relationship between school attachment and drug use is equal across all groups.

Longitudinal studies provide a sounder basis for causal interpretation on gender differences in the relationship between school attachment and delinquency, with attachment seemingly having a stronger influence for girls than boys. In the Crosnoe, Erickson, and Dornbusch (2002) study, higher levels of teacher bonding are associated with lower levels of illegal drug use for girls only. In addition, an interactive effect between teacher bonding and delinquent peers is found only for girls, such that girls who are more bonded to their teachers are protected from delinquency, even when they have delinquent friends (Crosnoe, Erickson, and Dornbusch 2002). However, Gottfredson and Koper (1996) examined risk factors for drug use for whites and blacks in a sample of 981 male and female students and found that most factors, including attachment to school, do not differ in their predictive ability across groups.

As with academic performance, some longitudinal studies compare the effects of school attachment on substance use using a more complex model that includes other risk factors. In a study of 10,473 youths between the ages of nine and eighteen in forty-eight high-risk communities, Sale and others (2003) found that attachment to school has a significant association with academic performance, which, in turn, is significantly associated with peer substance use; peer substance use, in turn, significantly predicts individual substance use. Thus, students who are more attached to school are more likely to perform better in school; these students are then less likely to have friends who use drugs, which leads them to use drugs less frequently themselves. Although this model is significant for both boys and girls, there are gender differences in the magnitude of the effects. The paths from school attachment to academic performance and from academic performance to peer substance use are stronger for girls than boys. However, the path from peer substance use to one's own substance use is stronger for boys, leading the researchers to conclude that school factors are more influential for girls, while peer factors are more influential for boys (Sale et al. 2003).

Essentially, the findings for gender differences in the effects of school attachment are mixed, and we are unable to settle on any firm conclusions. Many studies demonstrate that the protective effect of attachment to school on delinquency is equal for males and females (Cernkovich and Giordano 1992; Gottfredson and Koper 1996; Payne and Gottfredson 2005; Rosay et al. 2000; Zweig et al. 2002), while others note that it depends on the type of delinquency examined (Junger-Tas, Ribeaud, and Cruyff 2004; Payne and Gottfredson 2005). Finally, two studies found that school attachment has a protective effect on girls only (Crosnoe, Erickson, and Dornbusch 2002; Sale et al. 2003).

Commitment to School

General Relationship
Commitment to school is generally defined as time and energy invested by students in the pursuit of educational goals. Students who invest considerable effort in school are more likely to be concerned about losing their investments if they are deviant. Conversely, students who invest little in school will not have anything to lose; therefore, they are more likely to be delinquent. As with attachment to

school, the negative relationship between commitment to school and delinquency is well supported by cross-sectional and longitudinal research (Cernkovich and Giordano 1992; Gottfredson, Wilson, and Najaka 2002; Jenkins 1997; Thornberry et al. 1991; Thornberry, Esbensen, and Van Kammen 1993; Welsh, Greene, and Jenkins 1999) (see Gottfredson 2001 for more detail). Cross-sectional studies also find that low school commitment or educational aspiration is associated with early sexual debut and promiscuity (Coker et al. 1994; Luster and Small 1997; Resnick et al. 1997). As with school attachment, longitudinal studies also support the causal path from low commitment to school to later delinquency (Thornberry, Esbensen, and Van Kammen 1993; Thornberry et al. 1991).

Commitment to School and Female Delinquency

The gender-specific results of cross-sectional studies of commitment to school and delinquency and related outcomes are mixed. Some studies find stronger relationships for girls than boys. For example, lower levels of school commitment are significantly related to gang involvement for eighth grade girls but not boys (Esbensen and Deschenes 1998). Additionally, academic motivation is associated with reduced drug use for girls but not boys (Razzino et al. 2004). More generally, academic motivation is reported to have stronger effects on drug use for girls than boys (Paulson, Coombs, and Richardson 1990).

By contrast, in the large, multigroup comparison study by Rosay and others (2000), the negative relationship between commitment to school and substance use is similar across race and gender groups. However, the correlations with *delinquency* vary across groups. The gender differences seem to vary by ethnic group, with black males displaying the lowest correlations. For whites, the correlations are somewhat larger for males than females; for other races, the correlations are somewhat larger for females than males (Rosay et al. 2000). In the Payne and Gottfredson (2005) study, in which whites are the predominant ethnic group and age was controlled, the negative relationships between school commitment and overall delinquency, property offenses, and violent offenses are significantly larger for boys than girls and for nonwhites than for whites. In this study, the mean level of commitment to school is higher for girls than boys. However, the negative relationship between drug use and commitment to school does not differ between the genders. Finally, one study found no gender differences in the relationship between commitment to school and delinquency: As with school attachment, Cernkovich and Giordano (1992) found that the relationship between investment in academics and school activities and involvement in delinquency does not vary significantly across groups. School commitment plays the same role in delinquency for girls and boys and for blacks and whites.

Findings from longitudinal data are scant. Some find that commitment to school is more strongly related to subsequent drug use for whites than blacks and for girls than boys (Gottfredson and Koper 1996), while others find that school commitment influences only boys' use of alcohol (Crosnoe, Erickson, and Dornbusch 2002).

In summary, as with attachment, we are unable to settle on any firm conclusions regarding the findings for gender differences in the effects of school commitment on delinquency. Many studies found that commitment to school has a stronger protective effect for girls' drug use than boys' drug use (Paulson, Coombs, and Richardson 1990; Payne and Gottfredson 2005; Razzino et al. 2004; Rosay et al. 2000). Other studies, however, found that the relationship between commitment to school and delinquency is the same for boys and girls (Cernkovich and Giordano 1992), or that the protective effect is larger for boys' than girls' delinquency (Payne and Gottfredson 2005).

School-Level Factors

In this section, we discuss school-level factors that are related to delinquency and investigate whether these effects differ for males and females. We first examine school contextual factors, or predetermined characteristics of a school, such as grade level, size of student enrollment, class size, racial and ethnic composition, and school location. We then examine school climate, or the "inner workings of the school" (Ma, Stewin, and Mah 2001, p. 256). By inner workings of the school, we mean the social organization of the school, the system of social relations between and among teachers and students, the cultural system of norms and values in the school, and the management of school discipline, such as the clarity of rules and fairness of rule enforcement. Much of the research that examines school-level factors does not examine the differentiating effect on boys and girls; thus, greater emphasis will be placed on the relationship between these factors and overall delinquency. We highlight the findings of the Payne and Gottfredson (2005) study that investigates gender-based differences in delinquency outcomes. However, firm conclusions regarding gender differences in the effects of school-level factors on delinquency are just not possible.

School Context

General Relationship
One of the earliest examinations of the effects of school characteristics on school disorder is Gottfredson and Gottfredson's (1985) reanalysis of the Safe School Study data for a 1976 national sample of more than six hundred U.S. secondary schools. Although this study focuses on victimization, it establishes that school characteristics, such as student–teacher ratio and resources, do predict problem behavior at the school level.

Subsequent studies also found that school context influences delinquency. Two studies based on the National Study of Delinquency Prevention in Schools (Gottfredson et al. 2005; Payne, Gottfredson, and Gottfredson 2003) found that schools with a greater percentage of male students and a greater percentage of black students and teachers have higher levels of delinquency (see also Felson et al. 1994; these findings held true regardless of the socioeconomic status, size, and urbanicity of the schools). Wilcox and Clayton (2001) found that school-level socioeconomic status significantly affects weapon carrying, such that students are more likely to carry weapons in schools that have a higher percentage of students receiving free or reduced lunches. Finally, using hierarchical linear modeling in order to study students nested within schools, Bryk and Driscoll (1988) demonstrated that individual-level problem behavior is more prevalent in larger schools and in ethnically diverse schools.

School Contextual Factors and Female Delinquency

While none of the studies discussed earlier address gender-based differences in outcomes, Payne and Gottfredson (2005) used hierarchical linear modeling to examine gender differences in the association of school contextual factors and various forms of deviance in a nationally representative study of over thirteen thousand students in over 250 schools. Hierarchical linear modeling is preferable for this type of study because it allows the researcher to include both student-level and school-level characteristics in one model, thus allowing the examination of the effect of school-level contextual factors on student-level delinquency. This study examined the association of school-level factors on individual delinquency, controlling for the gender, race, and age of each student. The following findings are excerpted from that work.

Student compositional variables, such as the age and racial makeup of the student body, were examined, and no gender differences were found. While having a larger percentage of students who were overage for their grades is related to greater amounts of overall delinquency, violent delinquency, and drug use, there were no significant gender or racial differences. Following the findings of Payne, Gottfredson, and Gottfredson (2003) and Gottfredson and others (2005), this study also found that having a larger percentage of black students in the school is related to more involvement in overall delinquency, violent delinquency, and drug use; as with overage students, there were no significant gender differences in this relationship.

The percentage of black students in the school does, however, display significant racial differences. This variable has a small but significant negative relationship with overall delinquency, property delinquency, and drug use of nonwhite students: Nonwhite students engage in less delinquency and drug use when they are in schools with a greater percentage of black students. This contrasts with the small but significant positive relationship with the drug use of white students and nonsignificant relationship with the overall delinquency and property delinquency of white students: White students use drugs more often when they are in schools with a greater percentage of black students.

Teacher compositional variables, such as the racial and gender makeup of the faculty, were also examined. Having more black teachers is associated with greater involvement in overall delinquency and violent offending, but this relationship is the same for all students regardless of their gender. Having more female teachers is related to less student involvement in property offenses and drug use, again regardless of the student's gender.

No gender differences in the relationships between school-size variables and delinquency are found. Student enrollment is significantly related to delinquency and violent delinquency. Similarly, having a greater number of students per teacher is associated with slightly higher student involvement in all forms of delinquency for both boys and girls.

Significant gender differences *are* found for school level (e.g., middle/junior versus high school). School level is not significantly related to girls' overall delinquency and property offending, but it has a significant positive relationship with boys' overall delinquency and property crimes: Boys' delinquency is greater in high school than middle or junior high school. School level is associated with lower levels of violent delinquency for girls only: Girls' violent delinquency is greater in middle school than in high school. Finally, school level is related to drug use for both genders. High school students use drugs more than middle school students, but the association is stronger for boys than girls.

In summary, most school contextual factors, such as student and teacher composition and school size, affect the genders equally. One exception to this is school level: Boys' delinquency is greater in high school than middle or junior high school.

School Climate

General Relationship

Research demonstrates a strong relationship between school climate and general school disorder. Gottfredson and Gottfredson (1985) found that schools with low levels of cooperation between teachers and administrators, schools in which teachers have punitive attitudes, schools in which the rules are not perceived by students as fair and firmly enforced, and schools in which students had low levels of belief in conventional rules and laws governing behavior experience higher levels of teacher victimization, net of community and student demographic characteristics.[3] Results from other school-level studies on the importance of school organization and climate on misbehavior are mixed. Galloway, Martin, and Wilcox (1985) and Hellman and Beaton (1986) found no evidence for school effects on student absenteeism or suspension once community characteristics were controlled. In both of these studies, however, the measures of school characteristics are limited to what we would consider more contextual factors, such as features of the school building (e.g., age of building), and aspects of formal school organization (e.g., school size, use of ability grouping, staff turnover) commonly found in archival records.

Studies demonstrating more substantial school effects measure aspects of the school social organization as well and include more schools. In a more recent study employing a larger sample of schools, Ostroff (1992) showed that teacher satisfaction and commitment predict lower student dropout rates, fewer disciplinary problems, and higher attendance rates.

In addition, studies examining a specific form of school social organization, communal school organization, found a negative relationship with school disorder. Bryk and Driscoll (1988) found that communally organized schools have lower levels of student misbehavior and dropouts and higher levels of academic interest and math achievement. Similarly, Battistich and Hom (1997) found that higher levels of student sense of school community are associated with lower levels of drug use and delinquency. Finally, Payne, Gottfredson, and Gottfredson (2003) found that communally organized schools experience less disorder, while Gottfredson and others (2005) found that schools with a positive psychosocial climate experience less disorder.

The discipline management of a school also influences school disorder. Gottfredson and others (2005) found that schools with clear and fair rules and rule enforcement experience less disorder. Overly punitive responses to misbehavior appear to increase delinquency: Peterson, Larson, and Skiba (2001) discussed this possibility with zero-tolerance policies that respond to even minor infractions with immediate, certain, and severe punishments.

Essentially, prior research shows that school organizational characteristics predict the level of school disorder beyond the effects of the externally determined factors such as school size and racial heterogeneity. More specifically, discipline management and psychosocial climate are related to levels of student delinquency and victimization. Schools that establish and maintain rules, effectively communicate clear expectations for behavior, consistently enforce rules, and provide rewards for rule compliance and punishments for rule infractions experience lower levels of crime and victimization.

School Climate Factors and Female Delinquency
As with school context, none of the previous studies address the gender composition of the schools or whether there are gender-based differences in outcomes. However, Payne and Gottfredson (2005) used hierarchical linear modeling to examine gender differences in the influence of school climate factors on various forms of deviance. Their study examined the association of school-level factors on individual delinquency, controlling for the gender, race, and age of each student. The following findings are excerpted from that work.

They examined the school psychosocial climate that includes concepts such as the commonality of direction and organizational focus of the faculty and staff and the level of morale of the faculty. They found the psychosocial climate is significantly related to property delinquency. This effect does not differ by gender.

Another area within school climate that Payne and Gottfredson examined is the management of discipline in the school. This includes student perceptions of the clarity of the rules and the fairness of rule enforcement, as well as principal reports of appropriate responses to misbehavior and unusual or punitive responses to misbehavior. In this study, the mean level of clarity of rules and fairness of rule enforcement is higher for girls than boys. Student involvement in delinquency and drug use is lower in schools in which students perceive rules and rule enforcement as clear and fair. In addition, there are significant gender differences for all forms of deviance: The relationship with boys' delinquency and drug use is larger than the relationship with girls' delinquency and drug use. There is also a significant racial difference in the association between student perceptions of clarity and fairness of rules and violent delinquency, such that the negative relationship is greater for nonwhites than for whites.

Principal reports of discipline management also yield interesting findings. The use of punitive responses to misbehavior, such as removing the student from school, is significantly related to more involvement in all forms of delinquency, but this association does not differ by gender. However, the relationship does differ by race for overall delinquency, property delinquency, and drug use: Punitive responses to misbehavior are related to greater delinquency for white students but not for nonwhite students. In contrast, the relationship between the use of less punitive responses to misbehavior and delinquency does differ by gender. Sending the student to the school counselor, notifying the parent, or briefly excluding the student from the classroom is considered less punitive. For all forms of delinquency except drug use, this type of discipline management is not significantly associated with girls' delinquency but is associated with slightly more boys' delinquency.

In summary, most school climate factors have an equal effect on boys' and girls' delinquency. One difference is found in student reports of the management of school discipline: How the students perceive the clarity of rules and the fairness of rule enforcement has a protective effect for both genders, but this effect is larger for boys than girls.

Victimization as an Element of School Climate

Although victimization is often studied as an outcome of school climate, it is also possible to consider victimization as an element of school climate and, thus, as a predictor of delinquency. Some studies examine gender differences in school victimization. For example, Olweus (1993) found that, while 15 percent of students are involved in bullying as either the bully or the victim at some point in their elementary or middle school careers, there are significant differences between the genders. Boys are more likely to be both perpetrators and victims of direct bullying, either with physical actions, words, or gestures. Girls, in contrast, are more likely to be the perpetrators and victims of indirect bullying, or relational aggression, such as spreading rumors. In addition, boys are more often the perpetrators in bullying incidents in which girls are the victims (Olweus 1993).

Other research examines sexual harassment and sexual or dating violence as negative school climate factors (Stein 1999). Bennett and Fineran (1998) found that, while boys are more likely to be both perpetrators and victims of physical violence, girls are more likely to be victims of dating and sexual violence perpetrated by boys. Molidor and Tolman (1998) found similar results. They also documented that the worst incidents of dating violence tend to occur on school grounds or in the school building.

None of these studies examine gender-based outcomes of the effect of sexual harassment or dating violence victimization on delinquency. Although specific investigation of sexual victimization or relational aggression is not possible, Payne and Gottfredson (2005) examined the relationship between overall victimization and delinquency. Not surprisingly, victimization is strongly related to all forms of deviance, such that higher levels of victimization in schools are associated with more student involvement in delinquency and drug use. Additionally, gender differences are seen for violent delinquency, such that victimization is more strongly related to greater involvement in violence for boys than girls. Payne and Gottfredson (2005) also find that, while victimization is related to greater involvement in delinquency and property offending for all races, this association is substantially larger for nonwhites than for whites. Similarly, victimization is related to greater drug use by nonwhites but is nonsignificant for whites.

Conclusions

Although criminological research has firmly established that certain school-related factors influence delinquency and substance use for both males and females, very few firm conclusions can be drawn from this literature regarding gender differences in the magnitude of these effects. The individual-level school-related factors most often studied include academic performance or school success and failure and the social bonding elements of attachment and commitment to school; studies indicate that poor school performance and low attachment and commitment to school are related to subsequent delinquency for both girls and boys. Studies are less clear, however, on whether the strength of these relationships differs between the genders. The results appear to depend on the form of delinquency (e.g., delinquency versus substance use), the ethnic mixture of the sample included in the study, and perhaps the age of the sample. The strength of the relationship between academic performance and delinquency seems to be slightly stronger for boys than girls (Huizinga, Loeber, and Thornberry 2000; Junger-Tas, Ribeaud, and Cruyff 2004; Maguin and Loeber 1996). There appear to be differences, however, based on the type of deviance studied (Paulson, Coombs, and Richardson 1990; Rosay et al. 2000). When looking at school attachment, most studies demonstrate that the protective effect on delinquency is equal for males and females (Cernkovich and Giordano 1992; Gottfredson and Koper 1996; Payne and Gottfredson 2005; Rosay et al. 2000; Zweig et al. 2002), although others note that it depends on the type of delinquency examined (Junger-Tas, Ribeaud, and Cruyff 2004; Payne and Gottfredson 2005) and the ethnic composition of the study sample (Gottfredson and Koper 1996; Payne and Gottfredson 2005; Rosay et al. 2000). Finally, most researchers who look at the effects of school commitment on delinquency find that commitment has a stronger protective effect for girls' drug use than boys' drug use (Paulson, Coombs, and Richardson 1990; Payne and Gottfredson 2005; Razzino et al. 2004; Rosay et al. 2000), while a few find that the relationship is equal for boys and girls (Cernkovich and Giordano 1992), or that the protective effect is larger for boys' than girls' delinquency (Payne and Gottfredson 2005).

Most school contextual factors, such as student and teacher composition and school size, affect the genders equally (Payne and Gottfredson 2005). One exception is school level: Boys' delinquency is greater in high school than middle or junior high school. Similarly, most school climate factors have an equal effect on boys' and girls' delinquency (Payne and Gottfredson 2005). One difference is found in student reports of the management of school discipline: How the students perceive the clarity of rules and the fairness of rule enforcement has a protective effect for both genders, but this effect is larger for boys than girls (Payne and Gottfredson 2005).

Firm conclusions regarding gender differences in the causal processes linking risk factors to delinquency and substance use are not possible. The studies discussed in this chapter seem to indicate that academic performance and clarity and fairness of rules and rule enforcement are stronger protective factors for boys, while student-bonding elements are stronger protective factors for girls. Is it the case that girls are more influenced by interpersonal social controls, such as bonding to teachers, while boys are more influenced by instrumental restraints, such as clear consequences of rule violations? This is possible, but more basic research is needed on the possibility of gender differences in school-related risk factors for delinquency, especially given the relatively small number of studies that have examined gender differences in these processes.

The studies also seem to indicate that the existence of a gender difference is related to the type of deviance studied. When delinquency is considered, risk factors seem to have a stronger influence for boys, but when drug use is considered, risk factors seem to have an equal influence for the genders. However, the gender gap in substance use is much smaller than the gender gap in delinquency—especially forms of delinquency involving interpersonal aggression. The greater variability in delinquency for boys than for girls, therefore, is a likely explanation of at least some of the observed gender differences in the correlations of risk factors with delinquency. Again, this is possible, but more basic research is clearly needed.

Even without considering gender differences, the school-related factors discussed in this chapter are related to deviance and problem behavior, indicating the usefulness of certain school-based prevention programs and practices. Studies show that interventions that increase school-bonding elements such as attachment and commitment to school reduce later delinquency and problem behavior (Najaka, Gottfredson, and Wilson 2001). Interventions that increase academic performance also reduce problem behavior (Maguin and Loeber 1996), but the influence is much smaller than that of the bonding interventions (Najaka, Gottfredson, and Wilson 2001). School-level prevention strategies are also promising; such strategies include interventions that clarify and communicate norms for behavior, that increase the participatory governance structure of the school, and that guide schools in planning and implementing improvements through a structured organizational change process. Studies show that these interventions improve the climate of the school, the clarity and fairness of rules and rule enforcement, and student bonding to the school and, importantly, reduce delinquency and problem behavior (Gottfredson, Wilson, and Najaka 2002).

Although questions related to the mechanism through which these interventions achieve their results remain (Hirschi 1969; Maguin and Loeber 1996; Najaka, Gottfredson, and Wilson 2001; Sale et al. 2003), studies demonstrate positive outcomes. Thus, interventions that target the factors discussed earlier hold promise for reducing delinquency and drug use for females as well as males. It is possible that interventions focused on school bonding, such as schools-within-a-school organizational changes or individual-level mentoring programs, will have more of an impact on girls' delinquency, while those focused on academic performance or the clarity and fairness of rules and rule enforcement will have more of an impact on boys' delinquency. However, given the scant gender distinctions observed, we cannot conclude that gender differences in the outcome of these interventions exist. What can be said is that these interventions are likely to reduce delinquency and problem behavior regardless of the gender of the participants.

Future research should include a more thorough examination of large, longitudinal data sets to establish temporal ordering, as well as the inclusion of possible common causes to control for spuriousness. Further, data sets must include sufficient numbers of different ethnic groups to facilitate comparison of gender differences within ethnicity. Attention must be paid to the dependent variable as well. Gender differences in the relationship between risk factors and delinquency appear to differ for different forms of delinquency. Future research should also examine more complex causal processes, such as the interaction between academic performance, delinquent peers, and delinquency examined by Crosnoe, Erickson, and Dornbusch (2002) or the causal links between academic performance, school bonding, and delinquency discussed by Hirschi (1969), Najaka, Gottfredson, and Wilson (2001), and Sale and others (2003). These complex processes should also include relationships between individual-level and school-level characteristics, as presented in Payne, Gottfredson, and Gottfredson (2003). Only with more in-depth research can we truly come to firm conclusions regarding the differences or similarities experienced by girls and boys in the link between school factors and delinquency.

Take-Home Points

1. Very few firm conclusions can be drawn regarding gender differences in the magnitude of the effects that certain school-related factors have on delinquency and substance use.

2. In terms of individual-level characteristics, poor academic performance, low attachment to school, and low commitment to school are related to subsequent delinquency for girls and boys. However, studies are unclear on whether the strength of these relationships differs by gender. The results appear to depend on the form of deviance (e.g., delinquency versus substance use), the ethnic mixture of the sample included in the study, and perhaps the age of the sample.

3. Far less research has studied school-level characteristics. The research that has been conducted suggests that most school contextual and climate factors affect the genders equally. Two exceptions are school level (boys' delinquency is greater in high school than middle or junior high school) and student reports of the management of school discipline (how the students perceive the clarity of rules and the fairness of rule enforcement has a protective effect for both genders, but this effect is larger for boys than girls).

4. Firm conclusions regarding gender differences in the causal processes linking risk factors to delinquency and substance use are not possible. The studies discussed in this chapter seem to indicate that academic performance and clarity and fairness of rules and rule enforcement are stronger protective factors for boys, while student-bonding elements are stronger protective factors for girls. More basic research is needed on the possibility of gender differences in school-related risk factors for delinquency, especially given the relatively small number of studies that have examined gender differences in these processes.

5. The studies also seem to indicate that the existence of a gender difference is related to the type of deviance studied. When delinquency is considered, risk factors seem to have a stronger influence for boys, but when drug use is considered, risk factors seem to have an equal influence for the genders. However, the gender gap in substance use is much smaller than the gender gap in delinquency, especially forms of delinquency involving interpersonal aggression. The greater variability in delinquency for boys than for girls, therefore, is a likely explanation of at least some of the observed gender differences in the correlations of risk factors with delinquency. Again, this is possible, but more basic research is clearly needed.

6. Future research should include a more thorough examination of large, longitudinal data sets to establish temporal ordering, as well as the inclusion of possible common causes to control for spuriousness. Further, data sets must include sufficient numbers of different ethnic groups to facilitate comparison of gender differences within ethnicity. Attention must be paid to the dependent variable as well. Gender differences in the relationship between risk factors and delinquency appear to differ for different forms of delinquency. Only with more in-depth research can we truly come to firm conclusions regarding the differences or similarities experienced by girls and boys in the link between school factors and delinquency.

8

Gender Differences in Neighborhood Effects and Delinquency

Margaret A. Zahn and Angela Browne

There is a disparate and growing literature on the effects of communities—or more specifically, neighborhoods—on behavioral outcomes of residents (Buka et al. 2001; Margolin and Gordis 2000); see Kroneman, Loeber, and Hipwell (2004) for a review of neighborhood context, delinquency, and gender. This literature stems from a long history of sociological work, embodied primarily in the social disorganization tradition (Bursik and Grasmick 1993a; Sampson and Groves 1989; Sampson, Morenoff, and Gannon-Rowley 2002), developmental psychology (Brooks-Gunn, Duncan, and Aber 1997a, 1997b; Brooks-Gunn, et al. 1993; Jencks and Mayer 1990; Leventhal and Brooks-Gunn 2000) and, more recently, economics (Durlauf 2004). Literature reviews have been done in each of these areas (Durlauf 2004; Jencks and Mayer 1990; Leventhal and Brooks-Gunn 2000; Salzinger et al. 2002b; Sampson, Morenoff, and Gannon-Rowley 2002).

Unlike theories focused on individual characteristics, theories emphasizing neighborhood context include an emphasis on the place where individuals live and events transpire. Variables examined include household structure, residential mobility, population density, cultural disadvantage, poverty, concentrated disadvantage, social cohesion or disorganization, and social capital. Dependent variables are highly variable, making comparisons between studies more difficult. They include risky behaviors, school dropout or truancy, physical and emotional health, exposure to and use of violence, victimization, and crime and delinquency.

In general, studies find that urban neighborhoods with concentrated poverty have higher rates of juvenile violence (Lauritsen and White 2001; McNulty and Bellair 2003a, 2003b; Messner, Raffalovich, and McMillan 2001), violent victimization, exposure to violence (Farrell and Bruce 1997; Margolin and Gordis 2000; Molnar et al. 2005), and juvenile and adult arrests for property and personal crime (Krivo and Peterson 1996; Schuck and Widom 2005; Steffensmeier and Haynie 2000a) than rural poor neighborhoods or neighborhoods without this concentration. They are also associated with earlier teen pregnancy, earlier school leaving, and a host of other negative effects. How specifically neighborhoods impact girls versus boys, and whether the effects vary for girls, is not well researched (Jacob 2006; Steffensmeier and Haynie 2000b, 2002b).

Theoretical Underpinnings

The importance of community context for antisocial and delinquent behavior among youths, and the association with impoverished urban communities, has been acknowledged for more than fifty years (Brooks-Gunn, Duncan, and Aber 1997a, 1997b; Kroneman, Loeber, and Hipwell 2004; Sampson and Groves 1989). Social disorganization theory has long been the underpinning for the study of neighborhood effects. Conceptualized as the inability of a community to realize common goals and solve chronic problems, social disorganization theory was developed by Shaw and McKay (1942a), and revised and extended by many others, including Bursik and Grasmick (1993a), Sampson and Groves (1989), and Sampson and Wilson (1995). According to the theory, poverty, residential mobility, ethnic heterogeneity, and weak social networks decrease a community's capacity to control the behavior of people in public and hence increase the likelihood of crime (Kubrin and Weitzer 2003). Social disorganization theorists argue that crime rates are higher in deprived communities because the residents of such communities are less likely to exercise effective control over one another (Bursik and Grasmick 1993a; Morenoff, Sampson, and Raudenbush 2001).

Of course, effects of strong networks and social control may be positive or negative, depending on the type of network or control exercised (Kubrin and Weitzer 2003). Some communities have a strong sense of neighborhood and intense informal control via gangs, drug markets, and other antisocial entities, who then recruit youths into criminal activity and suppress reporting by residents through fear or retaliation (e.g., MacDonald 1999; Pattillo-McCoy 1999; Pattillo 1998). Kubrin and Weitzer (2003) note that effects of informal social control depend in part on "the ratio of persons who hold conventional versus street values, and . . . the degree to which those who live by the street code are able to dominate others" (p. 381). Markowitz (2001) proposes a cycle theory of reciprocity, where decreases in positive neighborhood cohesion lead to increases in disorder and crime, heightening fear among residents and further decreasing cohesion. Prosocial residents withdraw and those who are able may leave the community.

Since the 1940s, researchers have employed theories of community-level social disorganization as an explanatory model for youth problem behaviors, including delinquency, crime, and carrying weapons (Sampson and Groves 1989; Sampson and Morenoff 1997; Shaw and McKay 1942a). Sampson, Morenoff, and Gannon-Rowley (2002) note that structural factors in neighborhoods such as concentration of poverty, racial isolation, and instability are powerful explanatory factors for variations in delinquency among youths. Communities struggling with social disorganization are less likely to monitor juveniles and sanction them when they engage in deviance (external control) and less likely to teach juveniles to condemn crime and exercise self-control. Residents of economically disadvantaged communities are less able to exert these controls for several reasons: They are struggling with a range of economic and family problems that limit their ability to control. They have weaker ties to their neighbors—since people are frequently moving into and out of the community—and are less able to form or support community organizations that often assist and guide youths, although new means of doing this via community–police partnerships may temper negative effects (Carr 2003).

Neighborhoods with concentrated disadvantage have fewer resources for protecting youths from involvement in illegal and dangerous activities, preventing the proliferation of gangs, or halting illegal drug markets (Pattillo 1998; Reiboldt 2001). Lacking opportunities for quality education, safety, and work, adolescents may turn to illegal acts or alternative lifestyles to attain safety, possessions, and status (Anderson 1999; Champion and Durant 2001) and may respond to atmospheres of threat by using violence, affiliating with delinquent peers, and arming themselves (Anderson 1999; DuRant et al. 1994; Stewart, Simons, and Conger 2002).

In their classic review, developmental psychologists Jencks and Mayer (1990) developed a theoretical framework for linking neighborhood effects with individual behavior, including (a) Neighborhood Institutional Resource Models, (b) Collective Socialization Models, (c) Contagion or Epidemic Models, (d) Models of Competition, and (e) Relative Deprivation Models. A decade later, Leventhal and Brooks-Gunn (2000) reformulated that framework into three distinct but related mechanisms by which neighborhood effects may be transmitted to youths: (a) The Institutional Resources Model, (b) The Relationship Model, and (c) the Norms Collective Efficacy Model (p. 322). They note, however, that at that time research findings were too scant to draw firm conclusions in most of these areas.

Leventhal and Brooks-Gunn (2000) also identified key levels at which mechanisms of influence may occur, including parent/family, peer group, school, and community. In a more recent review, Salzinger and others (2002b) posit a similar developmental–ecological framework, taking into account the domains of family and household context, parent–child relationship, peer relationships, and neighborhood and community context. None of these conceptual or theoretical approaches specifically posit differential impacts of communities on boys and girls, although there are easily deduced possibilities. For example, since girls tend to be at home more, they may be less affected by community street life than boys, who tend to be external to the home with more frequency. This chapter attempts to summarize evidence on the differences in impact of neighborhoods on adolescent girls as distinct from boys, with particular attention to the effects of violence and delinquency.

Methodological Issues

Before reviewing studies, it is worth noting that there are a number of methodological limitations to many studies in this area. Good methodological summaries include Kubrin and Weitzer (2003), Leventhal and Brooks-Gunn (2000) and Sampson, Morenoff, and Gannon-Rowley (2002). Sampson, Morenoff, and Gannon-Rowley (2002), based on a review of forty studies, found very little consistency across studies in the way neighborhood was operationalized or theoretically situated. The concept and measurement, for example, of social capital or of social ties varies from study to study. Thus, it is difficult to determine consistency of results across studies.

Selection bias also remains one of the biggest difficulties facing work in this area (i.e., the difficulty of distinguishing whether results emanate from neighborhood factors or from differential selection of adolescents or their families into certain neighborhoods). Defining neighborhoods remains problematic as well. Much of the research is based on census geography as a definition, which is problematic for studying social processes, since the relationship of Census tract boundaries to various social processes may not be either theoretically or empirically relevant to outcome variables. As Durlauf (2004) indicates, the definition of neighborhood is determined by the information available in the data set and not by any substantive criteria. The need to determine an appropriate social notion of a neighborhood has yet to be adequately addressed. There is also the simultaneity bias (what is causing what?) since many aspects of communities (e.g., poverty, few institutional resources, and mobility) may operate at the same time. Omitted variable bias—whether effects are a result of unmeasured characteristics associated with individuals, families, or neighborhoods actually account for a proportion of such effects—is an issue as well (Leventhal and Brooks-Gunn 2000).

While there are some longitudinal studies (e.g., the Project on Human Development in Chicago Neighborhoods [PHDCN]), many studies do not take into account the dynamics of neighborhood change, and cross-sectional studies cannot capture the dynamic processes that may change the social control mix. The influx of immigrant groups or the gentrification of a neighborhood, for example, may change the crime-inducing pattern dramatically, but are not captured by static methods and designs. Further, some recent critics (Kubrin and Weitzer 2003) suggest that the extensive contemporary literature on neighborhood effects focuses almost exclusively on structural variables, without including information on cultural or subcultural responses, thus hindering a full explanation. Recent work by Elliott and others (2006) demonstrates how focusing on "good kids from bad neighborhoods" requires looking at positive outcomes from presumed less-than-optimal conditions. Many authors also suggest the importance of establishing the relationship among family level, peer, and community variables, as they intersect and interact (Margolin and Gordis 2000; Salzinger et al. 2002b; Schuck and Widom 2005). Neighborhood effects are at a minimum bidirectional, affecting families and peers as much as the family structure and peer groups affect neighborhoods.

Adding to this, there are more specific problems when attempting to determine if there are neighborhood contextual effects on girls' compared to boys' delinquent behavior. Few theorists have postulated the linkages and there are few empirical studies dealing with the issue. Figueira-McDonough (1992) is one of the few theorists who suggests that certain community characteristics may affect the sex ratio, which in turn affects gender ideologies, and thus delinquent behavior of girls. Kroneman, Loeber, and Hipwell (2004) do review the existent knowledge of how neighborhood context affects conduct problems and delinquency, with somewhat more emphasis on conduct problems. Our review updates and expands this earlier one, and focuses on delinquent and violent behavior specifically. Given the lack of literature specific to girls, we begin each section with an overview of evidence on general relationships noted in the literature on youths. We then present cross-sectional and longitudinal studies with findings specific to girls.

Effects of Neighborhood Context: General Findings

In this section, we discuss the relationship between neighborhood and community context and youth delinquency and violence, including the domains of race/ethnicity, exposure to criminogenic neighborhoods, witnessing or experiencing violence, and cumulative effects. Neighborhoods are a prime context for socialization of youths, with differing impacts, depending on children's developmental stage (Ingoldsby and Shaw 2002). While still mediated through parents and families, as children grow into adolescence, effects of neighborhoods become more direct (Elliott et al. 1996; Leventhal and Brooks-Gunn 2000; Wikstrom and Loeber 2000). Urban neighborhoods with concentrated poverty have higher rates of juvenile violence (Lauritsen and White 2001; McNulty and Bellair 2003a, 2003b; Messner, Raffalovich, and McMillan 2001), violent victimization, exposure to violence (Farrell and Bruce 1997; Margolin and Gordis 2000; Molnar et al. 2005), and juvenile and adult arrests (Krivo and Peterson 1996; Schuck and Widom 2005; Steffensmeier and Haynie 2000a). Conversely, affluent neighborhoods seem to protect youths from involvement in violence and delinquency and encourage more positive development (Leventhal and Brooks-Gunn 2000; Molnar et al. forthcoming; Sampson and Morenoff 1997; Sampson, Morenoff, and Gannon-Rowley 2002).

Race/Ethnicity

Effects of concentrated disadvantage and social disorder fall particularly heavily on families and youths of color. Mobility into and out of poverty in the United States has decreased over time, with higher exit rates for households headed by white males and very low exit rates for households headed by black women. Urban communities with concentrations of black residents have become increasingly structurally disadvantaged, differentially exposing youths in these communities to elements highly associated with perpetration of violence and criminogenic activities (Massey and Denton 1993; Sampson 1987; Sampson and Wilson 1995). In their multilevel longitudinal analyses of 2,974 youths aged eighteen to twenty-five, based on three waves of PHDCN data from 180 Chicago neighborhoods, Sampson, Morenoff, and Raudenbush (2005) found that the odds of perpetrating violence were 85 percent higher for black than for white youths, with Latinos 10 percent lower. However, the total Latino–white gap and over 60 percent of the black–white gap was explained by the marital status of parents, immigration generation, and neighborhood social context. Similarly, in their prospective study (n = 11,207) combining Census data on community context with panel data from the National Longitudinal Study of Adolescent Health (Add Health, a nationally representative, probability-based survey of U.S. adolescents in grades seven through twelve), De Coster, Heimer, and Wittrock (2006) found that the black versus nonblack differences in youth violence were largely a function of residence in disadvantaged communities and noted that knowledge of the structural characteristics of neighborhoods is central to understanding why individuals become involved in violence and offending (see also Jargowsky 1997; South and Crowder 1997).

Exposure to Criminogenic Neighborhoods

A consistent finding across studies is that exposure to social disorder, illegal activities, and violence has strong impacts on adolescents during the transition to adulthood, when they may have greater independence, more unsupervised time with peers, and are especially prone to experimenting with alternate lifestyles or identities (De Coster, Heimer, and Wittrock 2006; Kubrin and Weitzer 2003; Sampson, Morenoff, and Gannon-Rowley 2002). Given the lack of temporal ordering in cross-sectional studies, in the section that follows we will emphasize evidence from longitudinal research on the effects of neighborhoods on youths.

Herrenkohl and colleagues (2000), using four waves of panel data from the city-based Seattle Social Development Project's prospective study (n = 808), analyzed factors of youths aged ten, fourteen, and sixteen predictive of violence at age eighteen. Half of the sample were female; 46 percent of the sample were white, 24 percent were black, 21 percent were Asian, and half (52 percent) came from low-income families. This ethnically and economically diverse study found that neighborhood factors were key predictors in the development of later aggression.

Risk-taking, drug selling, gang membership, and the presence of neighborhood adults involved in crime at age fourteen, and community disorganization, availability of drugs, and the presence of neighborhood adults involved in crime at age sixteen, *tripled* the odds for perpetration of violence by youths at age eighteen (Herrenkohl et al. 2000). One gender difference was reported; as with other studies, male gender was more strongly associated with perpetration of violence than was female gender.

Using the first two waves of Add Health data (n = 11,207) for seventh to twelfth graders, combining individual-level with neighborhood measures, De Coster, Heimer, and Wittrock (2006) note that criminogenic street contexts were more important in explaining mechanisms by which residence in disadvantaged communities leads youths to violence than social capital variables such as parents' participation in organizations, collective neighborhood supervision, and family cohesiveness, suggesting this as a critical dimension for study and intervention (see also Leventhal and Brooks-Gunn 2000).

Witnessing or Experiencing Violence

Within communities, cross-sectional and longitudinal studies consistently identify witnessing or experiencing violence as one of the most potent factors differentiating youths involved in delinquency and violence from youths who are not involved (Buka et al. 2001; Champion and Durant 2001; DuRant et al. 1994; Margolin and Gordis 2000; Molnar et al. 2005; Patchin et al. 2006; Scarpa 2003). DuRant and others (1994), analyzing cross-sectional data on a sample of 225 black male and female eleven- to nineteen-year-old adolescents in nine high-crime housing projects in Georgia, found that levels of violence and victimization in the community were the strongest predictors of use of violence for both boys and girls and were also highly associated with weapon carrying. National longitudinal data support these findings. Shaffer and Ruback (2002), in their analysis of Add Health data over two time points for an ethnically diverse sample of five thousand youths aged eleven to seventeen, reported a strong positive association between exposure to and perpetration of violence among adolescents from Time 1 to Time 2. Similarly, in their study of the effects of criminogenic street scenes using data on community context combined with individual-level panel data from the national Add Health sample of seventh through twelfth graders, De Coster, Heimer, and Wittrock (2006) reported that youths who had witnessed serious violence by Wave 1 were more likely to be involved in a range of violent acts one year later, even after previous violence and other variables were controlled.

Cumulative Effects

Finally, empirical evidence demonstrates that youths with multiple experiences, or youths who are at risk both inside and outside their homes, seem particularly vulnerable to the development of delinquent and violent behaviors (Fagan 2003;

Garbarino 2000; Herrenkohl et al. 2000; Kroneman, Loeber, and Hipwell 2004; Lynch and Cicchetti 1998; Osofsky 1995; Stouthamer-Loeber et al. 2002). Using official data from a prospective cohort design study of 908 maltreated children and 667 matched controls in the Midwest (followed into young adulthood), combined with Census and arrest data, Schuck and Widom (2005) explored how neighborhood conditions influenced the relationship between maltreatment as a child and later involvement in criminal behavior, based on a multiyear prospective cohort design. In this carefully controlled study, the effect of early child maltreatment was strongest on individuals from the most disadvantaged neighborhoods. This association of neighborhood conditions with offending held even when individual and family factors were taken into account.

In the Seattle Social Development Project's city-based study of elementary, middle, and high school-aged youths, assessing potential risk factors for the development of violence across five domains of youths' lives (individual, family, peer, school, and community), the odds for violence by youths exposed to more than five risk factors, versus those for youths exposed to fewer than two risk factors, were ten times greater at age fourteen and nearly eleven times greater at age sixteen. Youths exposed to multiple risks at each development point were much more likely to perpetrate violence in the future (Herrenkohl et al. 2000). These findings on youths in general highlight the importance of placing violence by teenagers in a community context.

Neighborhoods in Relationship to Girls' Delinquency and Violence

Most studies on how interactions between individual- and neighborhood-level characteristics influence delinquency among youths focus on males or do not disaggregate findings by gender, leaving the impact of community factors specifically on girls largely unstudied (Kroneman, Loeber, and Hipwell 2004; Stouthamer-Loeber et al. 2002; Wikstrom and Loeber 2000). Empirical research does indicate differences in girls' and boys' involvement in delinquency and crime. Girls are less likely to be involved in antisocial and deviant activities than boys; onset tends to be later for girls and they desist from delinquency more quickly; girls demonstrate less overt physical aggression, and overall their violence is less frequent and less severe in terms of types of acts, injuries to victims, weapon carrying, or weapon use; they are less likely to become involved with gangs; and they are less likely to victimize strangers (Farrell and Bruce 1997; Kroneman, Loeber, and Hipwell 2004; Liu and Kaplan 1999; McGee 2003; Snyder and Sickmund 1999; Steffensmeier and Allan 1996; Steffensmeier and Haynie 2000b).

Despite much lower rates of delinquency and offending by girls, however, male and female crime trends seem to run in parallel over time and most predictive factors are similar for males and females (e.g., see reviews by Daly 1994; Kroneman, Loeber, and Hipwell 2004; Rosenbaum and Lasley 1990; and Steffensmeier and Allan 1996). This suggests that structural forces affect both boys and girls similarly, but at different levels of intensity (Steffensmeier and Haynie 2000a). Two studies based on national-level data attempted to address this issue by assessing the intersection of structural disadvantage, urbanicity, and crime perpetration by gender.

In the first study to specifically focus on the link between female offending rates and structural characteristics of U.S. cities, Steffensmeier and Haynie (2000a) assessed the effects of structural disadvantage on *Uniform Crime Report* (*UCR*) Index offending arrest rates, comparing effects of structural variables on female rates with effects of those variables on male rates. Data were drawn from the 1990 Bureau of Census and the *UCR* for the 178 U.S. cities with one hundred thousand or more residents. The dependent variable was sex-specific rates for the Federal Bureau of Investigation's (FBI's) Index offenses (homicide, robbery, aggravated assault, burglary, and larceny); structural measures of disadvantage included female and male poverty and joblessness, female-headed households, income inequality, distribution of family income, and percent black. As in other studies, males had much higher perpetration rates than females, especially for the more serious offenses. Index offending rates were higher in all cities with high levels of structural disadvantage for both genders; effects of structural concentrated disadvantage were greater for violent than nonviolent offenses. City-based measures of disadvantage were robust predictors of female as well as male arrest rates, although the disadvantage index was more strongly associated with male than with female rates. The primary gender difference found was for homicide, where structural disadvantage measures were predictive for males but much less so for female rates.

In a later analysis of data on Canadian youths arrested for crimes (delinquency and offending known to the police), Jacob (2006) combined data from the 1996 Canadian Census and the Canadian Uniform Crime Reporting Survey (UCR) to examine the relationship between community characteristics and delinquent activities for female and male youths. As with Steffensmeier and Haynie's U.S. findings, Jacob found a predominant main effect for community characteristics with few differences by gender. Social conditions of communities that related to boys' arrest rates were related to girls' arrest rates as well. Socioeconomic status and residential instability were the primary predictors of arrest rates for both girls and boys, although residential instability was not associated with adolescent arrests for violence. Ethnic heterogeneity was correlated only with male arrests (although its impact was weak) and had no impact on female arrests. Conversely, population density was related only to female arrests for property offenses—again a weak association. Communities with a higher proportion of two-parent families had lower rates of juvenile arrests for both genders.

Exposure to Criminogenic Neighborhoods

Empirical literature investigating gender typically suggests that girls are exposed to less street violence and deviant peers and activities than are boys (Bottcher

2001; Farrell and Bruce 1997; Kim, Hetherington, and Reiss 1999; Margolin and Gordis 2000; Rosario et al. 2003). City-based studies sometimes differ, however. In a cross-sectional stratified sample of five hundred inner-city high school–aged black youths in a high-crime Census tract in the Hampton Roads area of Virginia, males were more likely to report victimization overall; however, girls were more likely to report having been mugged or attacked with a gun and having witnessed someone else being chased by gangs, beaten, or mugged (McGee 2003). In this study, for both boys and girls, direct victimization in the community best predicted problem behaviors such as delinquency.

Although they may be exposed less directly to community disorder and violence, empirical evidence from cross-sectional and longitudinal studies indicates that girls who live in disadvantaged or violent communities are more likely to perpetrate violence or other delinquent behavior compared to their female counterparts who live in more advantaged circumstances (Brooks-Gunn et al. 1993; Ingoldsby and Shaw 2002; Molnar et al. 2005). For example, DuRant and others' (1994) cross-sectional study found that eleven- to nineteen-year-old black girls living in housing projects in highly disadvantaged neighborhoods with high levels of violence were much more likely to attack someone out of anger, carry a hidden weapon, and be involved in a gang fight than girls not exposed to this severity of neighborhood disorder. In Song, Singer, and Anglin's (1998) cross-sectional study of 3,735 fourteen- to nineteen-year-old high school students in six public high schools in Cleveland, Ohio, exposure to a shooting or a knife attack had the strongest association with violent behavior for boys. However, for girls, exposure to a knife attack or a shooting, becoming the victim of violence at school, and witnessing parental violence at home were equally associated with violent behavior. Findings from some longitudinal studies support a more negative impact of exposure for girls as well. Farrell and Bruce (1997) examined witnessing community violence across three time points with a sample of 436 mostly black youths from urban public schools in a large Southeastern city. Witnessing violence in the community was positively associated with frequency of violent behavior for both genders. However, a positive association between witnessing violence and frequency of violence perpetration over time was found only for girls.

In a more focused investigation, Obeidallah and others (2004) analyzed longitudinal data from the PHDCN to assess links between girls' pubertal timing, violent behavior, and neighborhood characteristics. The sample of 501 Hispanic, black, and white adolescents and their parents were interviewed over a three-year period and U.S. Census data were mapped onto each neighborhood cluster. Obeidallah and colleagues found that girls who experienced early onset puberty and lived in highly disadvantaged neighborhoods were at significantly greater risk for perpetration of violence than girls in less disadvantaged neighborhoods. Although pubertal timing was not associated with violence in *itself,* early maturing girls were more likely to be violent if they lived in neighborhoods of higher concentrated disadvantage. This relationship between early maturation and perpetration of violence only became significant if girls lived in highly disadvantaged neighborhoods. The authors hypothesized that disadvantaged and violent neighborhoods offer girls an increased risk of encountering negative role models, especially among older youths, which in turn may heighten the likelihood that girls will become involved with delinquency and violence. Early maturing girls also are more likely to date at younger ages and to experience pressure from older males, who involve them in antisocial activities (Caspi et al. 1993; Stattin and Magnusson 1990).

Witnessing or Experiencing Violence

As noted, one of the most robust findings in the literature is the association between victimization and subsequent youth violence (Champion and Durant 2001; De Coster, Heimer, and Wittrock 2006; DuRant et al. 1994; Margolin and Gordis 2000; Shaffer and Ruback 2002). In analyses of Wave 1 of the Add Health data, based on in-home interviews with 17,036 youths (8,836 girls, 8,290 boys), Blum, Ireland, and Blum (2003) examined environmental factors (school connectedness, friend's suicide, urbanicity, and family income), family factors (family size, presence of guns in the home), and individual factors (grade point average, learning problems, skipping school, carrying a weapon to school, use of alcohol or illicit drugs, and history of victimization). Among these factors, victimization had the strongest association with juvenile violence regardless of gender. The authors note that, similar to boys, experiences with victimization "overrode every other factor for adolescent girls' involvement with violence" ($p <$ .0001; p. 237).

A recent study from the PHDCN combined information on neighborhood context and victimization histories in prospective analyses of girls' violence, based on three waves of data on 635 girls (aged nine to fifteen at baseline) from a representative sample of over eighty Chicago neighborhoods (Molnar et al. 2005). As in other studies, concentrated poverty was independently associated with a higher probability of girls perpetrating violence. However, adolescent girls were more likely to act violently if they had previously experienced physical or sexual victimization *and* lived in impoverished or severely violent communities. Girls who had been violently victimized also were more likely to report associations with deviant peers and use of illegal substances. Physical or sexual victimization remained an important predictor of subsequent violence by girls even when factors such as socioeconomic status, illegal substance use, previous violence perpetration, deviant peer behavior, and other family and individual characteristics were controlled. Overall, girls were 2.4 times more likely to perpetrate violent behavior if they had a *victimization history* of prior physical or sexual molestation/assault or other violent victimization. Victimized girls in *violent poor neighborhoods* were twice as likely to behave violently than their nonvictimized peers. Girls in *disadvantaged neighborhoods* were 1.5 times more likely to behave violently than girls in more advantaged neighborhoods.

Moderating Factors

Since living in economically disadvantaged neighborhoods has deleterious effects for some adolescents, it would appear that moving to more affluent circumstances would improve outcomes. Several Moving-to-Opportunity studies directly tested that possibility.

Moving-to-Opportunity: General Findings

In response to empirical findings on the negative impacts of community-concentrated disadvantage on youths, the effects of moving from disadvantaged to more advantaged neighborhoods have recently been studied. In a two-year follow-up study designed to evaluate the outcomes of a court-order neighborhood desegregation effort in Yonkers, New York, Fauth, Leventhal, and Brooks-Gunn (2005) analyzed whether moving from high- to low-poverty neighborhoods would reduce victimization and involvement in violence and delinquency among mostly minority youths. In this project, low-income black and Latino residents residing in segregated neighborhoods of concentrated disadvantage in South Yonkers were relocated via lottery to predominantly middle-class white neighborhoods elsewhere in Yonkers. Almost all (95 percent) of the families randomly selected to relocate moved to the new housing. Youths in the study who moved (n = 147) were eight to eighteen years of age and were compared to demographically similar youths who remained in their original neighborhoods (n = 114). The average age of youths in the study was thirteen; 54 percent were female.

At the end of two years, youths who moved experienced significantly less physical assault, neighborhood disorder, and access to illegal substances than nonmoving youths. Younger children, who were aged eight to nine at the time of the move, had fewer reported behavioral, family, and delinquency problems than their peers who did not move. However, for adolescents sixteen to eighteen years old, both boys and girls who moved experienced *more* behavior problems (getting into trouble, problems with behavior at home, problems with behavior at school) and more delinquency (stealing, hitting someone with the idea of hurting them, damaging or destroying property) than their counterparts who did not move. Youths who were thirteen to fifteen years old reported slightly more problems than youths who did not move, although differences were not statistically significant. In this project, minority families from poor neighborhoods were moved to newly built, publicly funded, fourteen- to forty-eight-unit row houses in predominantly white neighborhoods consisting mostly of single-family dwellings. Moves were preceded by nearly a decade of high-level media attention and negative publicity. Families who moved were easily identifiable both by race/ethnicity and dwelling type and faced neighborhood resistance to their presence. Fauth, Leventhal, and Brooks-Gunn (2005) speculate that older youths may have been more affected by stigma, racism, and negative visibility than younger children, as well as by separation from familiar neighborhoods and friends, thus explaining these effects.

Moving to Opportunity: Relationship to Girls' Delinquency and Violence

A multisite demonstration project also was sponsored by the U.S. Department of Housing and Urban Development. In this project, housing vouchers were assigned via random lottery to low-income, predominantly minority, public housing residents in five cities: Baltimore, Boston, Chicago, Los Angeles, and New York City (Kling, Ludwig, and Katz 2005). The "Moving to Opportunity" (MTO) program randomly assigned community households to one of three conditions: (a) an experimental, or treatment, group in which families were offered the opportunity to relocate using a housing voucher to lease a unit in a neighborhood where 10 percent or less of the residents were poor; (b) a control group who received Section 8 housing vouchers—families could relocate wherever the vouchers could be redeemed, but received no other support or assistance; and (c) an in-place control group who received no services through MTO and thus did not move. Families were eligible if they had children in the household and lived in public housing or in a Census tract with greater than a 40 percent poverty rate. Families moved to racially diverse neighborhoods with relatively little publicity.

As reported in Kling, Ludwig, and Katz (2005), after random assignment, both girls and boys in the experimental group experienced fewer violent crime arrests compared to their counterparts in the control group (see also Orr et al. 2003). Youths in the experimental group were arrested less for other crimes as well. However, several years after the move, effects for nonviolent crimes changed for males. Although arrests for violence remained low for both genders, property crime arrests became more common for boys who had moved to more advantaged neighborhoods than for their male counterparts who had not moved from disadvantaged neighborhoods. In contrast to boys, the positive effects for girls' arrests for property crime remained over time. Moving to a better neighborhood not only reduced arrests for all forms of crime for girls, it also improved girls' expectations for completing college and their participation in sports and was associated with a reduction in school absences and an increase in associations with peers who engaged in school activities (Kling, Ludwig, and Katz 2005).

Interpreting MTO study findings can be complicated. Overall program "take-up rates" (families offered vouchers who actually used them to move) was approximately 50 percent. Some reported effects were found only for the "Intent-to-Treat" groups (families eligible for the opportunity, whether or not they moved), rather than for the "Treatment-on-Treated" group (youths and families offered vouchers who actually moved) (Katz, Kling, and Liebman 2001; Kling, Ludwig, and Katz 2005; Sampson, Morenoff, and Gannon-Rowley 2002; see Goering and Fiens 2003 for a review). The finding that boys' rates of property crime and self-reported problem behaviors began to increase several years after moving has been interpreted as an opportunistic response by males to the "economic advantages" of property crime in more advantaged surroundings (Kling, Ludwig, and Katz 2005). However, it may reflect a gradual sinking process based on MTO findings that boys who moved did more poorly in their new schools than their sisters or other female participants, began to skip school, and became involved with delinquent peers and illegal substances. Differential responses by community members and local police to potential misdeeds by male youths versus female youths may contribute to these findings by gender as well. And, as recently found, MTO girls reported more adult role models with whom they could discuss their problems than did boys. Adult contact may thus also help explain MTO gender differences (Kling, Liebman, and Katz, forthcoming). In sum, the MTO study finds positive outcomes for girls for both violence and property crime, and for boys for violent crime. Additional analyses on specific processes surrounding respondents, support for youth, and other explanatory mechanisms remain to be completed (Sampson, Morenoff, and Gannon-Rowley 2002).

While living in highly disadvantaged neighborhoods has documented negative effects, it is also true that many "good kids come from bad neighborhoods" (Elliott et al. 2006). This means that other factors are important in generating behavior. In the next section, we briefly review evidence on moderating factors related to neighborhood effects. Borrowing from Salzinger and colleagues' (2002b) framework, we discuss findings across the contextual domains of family and household, parent–child relationships, and peer relationships. For each domain, we first note findings for youths in general and then present the few findings specific to girls.

Family and Household

Most studies of effects of family on youth delinquency have focused on single-parent versus two-parent/marriage family structures, finding correlations between concentrations of single-parent households and delinquency or criminal involvement by youths (Bell and Jenkins 1993; Esbensen and Huizinga 1991; Sampson, Morenoff, and Raudenbush 2005). In an important break from tradition, Forehand and Jones (2003) explored a family structure unanalyzed in the literature but often used by black families in impoverished neighborhoods: coparenting, in which parental responsibilities are shared between a single parent (usually a mother) and a relative. Data from a sample of 141 inner-city single-mother-headed black families and one referent child in inner-city families in New Orleans were analyzed cross-sectionally and longitudinally. Most participants lived in federally funded or low-income housing in neighborhoods characterized by poverty and crime. Coparents included grandmothers (35 percent), grandfathers (24 percent), biological fathers (12 percent), and other family members. Neighborhoods were analyzed based on physical fighting, shootings or knifings, and people being killed. In addition to coparent conflict, maternal monitoring, supervision, warmth, and support were assessed at baseline and fifteen months later. In this study, when controlling for maternal parental style, low levels of conflict between coparents moderated the association between neighborhood violence and youths' aggressive behaviors (as measured by the Child Behavior Checklist; Achenbach 1991). For girls—although not for boys—the interaction between neighborhood violence and coparent conflict was significant at both time points, even when positive maternal parenting was controlled. Even in contexts of high neighborhood violence, when coparent conflict was low, the level of aggressive behavior by girls was significantly lower than when coparent conflict was high.

Studies of youths typically find that family conflict, parental involvement in violent behavior, and exposure to family violence increase risk for adolescents' victimization, exposure to community violence, and involvement in delinquent or violent behavior (e.g., reviews by Margolin and Gordis 2000; Salzinger et al. 2002b). Accumulating evidence (see Chapter 5 of this book) now suggests that families of delinquent girls are characterized by more conflict and overt deviance than the families of their male counterparts (see review by Kroneman, Loeber, and Hipwell 2004). Characteristics of dysfunctional family settings among girls involved in delinquency and violence include heavy alcohol or other drug use in the family, physical and sexual abuse, lack of supervision or outright neglect, criminal involvement among parental caretakers or siblings, and predatory or aggressive relatives and associates of the family (Champion and Durant 2001; Molidar 1996). As with all studies involving disaggregation by gender or a focus on girls, more research is needed before firm conclusions can be drawn.

Parent–Child Relationships

Parenting is a particularly important moderator of neighborhood disadvantage on adolescents' risk for delinquency and violence (Kroneman, Loeber, and Hipwell 2004; Leventhal and Brooks-Gunn 2000). Positive parent–child relationships may buffer the impact of neighborhood disadvantage or violence on children, while negative relationships may exacerbate it (Garbarino 2000; Margolin and Gordis 2000). Children in female-headed families may be especially likely to suffer economic deprivation (O'Brien, Stockard, and Isaacson 1999) and to lack adult monitoring and supervision if the head of household is working and there is no other parent available. Supervision and monitoring can be particularly challenging for parents living in poverty, when families need to devote long hours to work and may lack resources to provide alternate care, particularly during after-school hours (Reese et al. 2000; Salzinger et al. 2002b). Sampson and Groves (1989) argue that single parents also experience greater strains in terms of time, money, and energy, hindering their ability to supervise children and communicate with other adults in the neighborhood. In discussing similar supervision findings, Margolin and Gordis (2000) note that, in the face of community violence, parents' caretaking abilities may be "negatively affected by their own feelings of helplessness, fear, and grief" (p. 452).

In their study using longitudinal data from the National Longitudinal Survey of Youth to examine community-level influences (n = 463), Pratt, Turner, and Piquero (2004) indeed found that neighborhood conditions were significantly related to parental supervision, with parents in neighborhoods experiencing adverse conditions less likely to supervise their children. The few studies assessing this by gender suggest that girls tend to be supervised more closely by their parents and are kept closer to the home than boys (Pratt, Turner, and Piquero 2004). Thus, girls may be less exposed than boys to the street violence and deviant peers and activities found in some disadvantaged neighborhoods (Bottcher 2001; Farrell and Bruce 1997; Kim, Hetherington, and Reiss 1999; Kroneman, Loeber, and Hipwell 2004; Margolin and Gordis 2000; Rosario et al. 2003).

Family connectedness and positive family expectations (e.g., expecting that a girl will do well in school or will finish school) also seem to be a significant moderator for girls. For example, in their analyses of Add Health data based on a sample of 20,704 youth, Blum, Ireland, and Blum (2003) found that affective dimensions of families (e.g., family caring/connectedness, parental expectations) appeared to be much more critical for adolescent girls in terms of involvement in violence than for adolescent boys. In a more specialized cross-sectional study of 667 predominantly Hispanic (65 percent) or black (32 percent) eleven- to fourteen-year-old inner-city students in Bronx Public Schools, Rosario and others (2003) found that attachment to parents/guardians buffered the relationship between victimization by community violence and delinquency for girls, but did not moderate that relationship for boys.

Conversely, even relatively normative corporal punishment of children has been found to have negative effects on later outcomes, including behavior (Bell and Jenkins 1993; Gershoff 2002; Margolin and Gordis 2000). In their cross-sectional study of black male and female eleven- to nineteen-year-old urban adolescents in nine high-crime housing projects, DuRant and others (1995) reported that higher scores on a corporal punishment measure were associated with frequency of fighting by these children as teenagers. Empirical literature consistently indicates that girls are at greatest risk of physical victimization from family members and other intimates and are more affected by family dynamics such as harsh parenting and maltreatment than are boys (Caspi and Moffitt 1991; see Garbarino 2000; Margolin and Gordis 2000; and Chapter 5 of this volume for reviews).

Peer Relationships

Finally, literature from across disciplines indicates that peers may play a significant role in moderating the impact of disorganized or violent communities on delinquent and violent behavior for both girls and boys (Leventhal and Brooks-Gunn 2000). For example, McNulty and Bellair (2003a, 2003b), in their study of data on 10,131 youths (7,310 white; 2,821 black) from the National Longitudinal Survey of Adolescent Health (Add Health) over a two-year period, found that deviant peers were *more* influential than family bonds in understanding associations between community characteristics and individual crime. In De Coster, Heimer, and Wittrock's (2006) prospective study combining community data with panel data from Add Health 2006, youths who were more involved with deviant peers had a strongly elevated risk of violent delinquency. This was true even though their measure captured use of illegal substances in peers rather than violence. In examining moderating factors, in a city-based study using multilevel, longitudinal data from the PHDCN across eighty Chicago neighborhoods and a sample of 2,226 youths, having prosocial peers, supportive friends, or both was significantly associated with lower levels of delinquent behavior for both girls and boys (Molnar et al. forthcoming). Rosario and others' (2003) within-city cross-sectional study of eleven- to fourteen-year-old black and Hispanic students in Bronx Public Schools did find differences in effects of peer relationships by gender. Support from peers buffered the effect of witnessing community violence for boys, but not for girls. However, peer support amplified negative effects of being victimized by community violence in terms of delinquent behavior for both boys and girls.

Conclusions

Research investigating effects of neighborhoods on the behavior of residents provides an enhanced understanding of the genesis and maintenance of delinquency and violence by youths. Despite differences in methodologies, the importance of neighborhood context to analyses of girls' and boys' delinquency is consistently demonstrated by cross-sectional and longitudinal studies across types of samples and disciplines, with important implications for prevention and social policy. Since the early 1980s, responses to offending in the United States have centered on law enforcement, sentencing, and incarceration (Browne and Lichter 2001). Yet a growing body of criminal justice literature suggests that these investments may have disappointing results unless preconditions of community-concentrated disadvantage are addressed (MacDonald and Gover 2005; Ousey and Lee 2002). Herrenkohl and colleagues (2000), Steffensmeier and Haynie (2000a), and others argue that identifying and modifying conditions of structural disadvantage and community risk offers our most promising option for producing social changes that reduce youth offending.

Take-Home Points

1. This review of extant literature found compelling evidence for differences *between girls* who are exposed and not exposed to structural disadvantage and violence in communities (e.g., PHDCN studies). There are less dramatic differences *between genders,* however, at least where overall patterns are concerned. For example, national-level examinations of associations between youth offending rates and the structural characteristics of cities—Steffens-

meier and Haynie (2006a) in the United States and Jacob (2006) in Canada—found strong similarities by gender in links between structural disadvantage and arrest rates. Social conditions affecting boys appeared to affect girls as well, although measures of disadvantage were more strongly associated with the arrest of boys than of girls (Steffensmeier and Haynie 2000a). Similarly, the majority of studies that differentiate detailed findings by gender find that exposure to criminogenic neighborhoods and witnessing or experiencing violence are strongly related to delinquency and offending for *both* boys and girls.

2. Some gender differences are suggested by the literature, however. Girls seem to be (a) less exposed to street violence than boys, (b) more positively affected by family connectedness and positive parental expectations, (c) more negatively affected by discord and abuse at home, and (d) more negatively affected by community violence when exposure does occur than are boys. Similarly, studies of moves from structurally disadvantaged to non-disadvantaged neighborhoods in five U.S. cities demonstrated suppression effects for both girls and boys in perpetration of violence over time. However, suppression of property offenses over time occurred only among girls (Kling, Ludwig, and Katz 2005). Other positive effects of these moves (e.g., better performance in school and subsequent college attendance) were found among girls but not among boys. The lack of neighborhood-based studies with a focus on girls leaves more far-reaching conclusions untenable without additional empirical evidence.

3. *Critical gaps* in the literature on gender differences in neighborhood effects and delinquency include the following:
   • Study of mechanisms underlying differential impacts of neighborhoods and moderating factors for girls and boys.
   • Study of differential outcomes of neighborhood conditions among girls.
   • Investigation of whether the impact of structural concentrated disadvantage on delinquency and violence differs for white girls compared to girls of other racial/ethnic backgrounds—a focus missing from empirical studies to date.

4. *Methodological challenges* noted at the beginning of this chapter also need to be resolved. As progress is made on these issues, researchers must expand their focus on the differential impacts of community structures on adolescent girls and boys. For example, the role of women in the institution of social control in neighborhoods needs elaboration. As recent studies suggest (Carr 2003), women often play substantial roles in this regard. How the modeling of this affects daughters and sons in low-income, structurally disadvantaged neighborhoods presents a new frontier in the study of gender differences in neighborhood effects on delinquency and violence.

9

The Context of Girls' Violence

Peer Groups, Families, Schools, and Communities

MERRY MORASH AND MEDA CHESNEY-LIND

Since girls' violence has long been either ignored or demonized, it is important to avoid either of these extremes in any discussion of this phenomenon. It is far more useful to consider girls' aggression and violence in its context, which requires a discussion of the role of not only social class (and poverty), but also of geography, culture/race, and finally the sex/gender system. This chapter demonstrates how each of these factors affects the production, shape, and dynamics of girls' violence.

The role of economic marginalization in girls' (and boys') violence is hard to overstate. Because of economic and social forces in the United States, the broad socioeconomic context is characterized by concentrations of poor families in under-resourced and disorganized communities. Mother-headed households and their children are disproportionately represented in both poor urban and poor rural areas. Poverty as manifested in disorganized communities, racial and ethnic differences within communities and schools, the social status and the psychobiology of girls, and their exercise of agency combine to explain girls' violence (Hawkins and Catalano 1993; Tolan, Guerra, and Kendall 1995). For some groups, immigration creates a new pool of girls at risk for being in a disorganized community or having outsider status among peers and in schools, and who may react to their circumstances with violence.

This chapter begins with an examination of the types and levels of girls' aggression. It then considers their aggression in the contexts of peer groups, families, and communities. These are the places where girls most often act violently. Also discussed are schools and drug markets, which provide specific settings for violence in some communities, particularly the economically marginalized ones that produce high levels of youth violence. Throughout this chapter, insofar as the existing research makes it possible, girls' perspectives on their violence are presented. Research that considers the perspective of girls and examines the context of girls' use of violence is often qualitative. There is a dearth of information on girls' perspectives in the United States; thus, it is problematic to answer the most fundamental questions. How do girls view their own use of violence? How do they explain it? What sequence of events leads to girls' violent acts? How is girls' violence affected by the interaction of their own identity and psychology and their environment? Examination of pertinent findings from other countries with demographic mixes and societies similar to the United States supplements the limited available information.

Nature and Amount of Violence

In both the United States and other countries, there has been concern that girls have become increasingly violent (Alder 1996; Batchelor and Burman 2001; Chesney-Lind 1997, 2001; Chesney-Lind and Shelden 1997). Yet numerous studies have shown that girls break the law less often than boys, and when they do break the law, they are generally less violent (Elliott, Huizinga, and Menard 1989; Maguire and Pastore 1997; Osgood et al. 1988; Wolfgang, Thornberry, and Figlio 1987). In schools, boys are more likely to be both the perpetrators and the targets of aggression and violence between schoolmates (Attar, Guerra, and Tolan 1995). When girls carry a weapon to school, it is usually a knife, not a gun, the weapon of choice for boys (Flannery 1997; Webster, Gainer, and Champion 1993). In families, boys are more likely to be physically abusive toward their parents (World Health Organization 2000). At least in some gangs, girl members are less likely to be involved in fighting than are boy members (Joe and Chesney-Lind 1995). Overall, fewer girls than boys are in physical fights and carry weapons (Girls Inc. 1996).

Arrest statistics fuel concern with girls' increasing violence. In 2002, arrest rates for aggravated and simple assault remained near their highest levels, but for boys these rates fell between the mid-1990s through 2002 (Snyder 2004). Still, in 2002, girls accounted for relatively small proportions of violent crime arrests of juveniles: 10 percent of arrests for murders or negligent manslaughter, 3 percent for forcible rapes, 9 percent for robberies, and 24 percent for aggravated assaults (Snyder 2004). Data from the Federal Bureau of Investigation's National Incident-Based Reporting System confirm the low level of girls' violence compared with boys'; relatively few (26 percent) victims who reported violent crimes by juveniles said that the offender was a female (McCurley and Snyder 2004). Girls were responsible for just 8 percent of sexual assault victimizations, 6 percent of robberies, 22 percent of aggravated assaults, and 30 percent of simple assaults committed by a juvenile. In no category did they account for close to half of the victimizations.

In some situations and contexts, girls come closer but do not surpass boys in their levels of violence. In large cities, significant numbers of girls are beaten by their peers, in most cases by other girls (Singer et al. 1995). Also, probably because of their involvement in childcare, for children younger than two who were victimized by a juvenile, 34 percent were victimized by a girl. National surveys of U.S. schools reveal that boys are three times more likely than girls to carry weapons (Odgers and Moretti 2002), but in selected inner-city schools, there is no gender difference (Webster, Gainer, and Champion 1993).

There is distrust of police and court statistics showing that, although girls are maintaining or increasing their use of violence, boys are decreasing their use. Some evidence suggests that police and courts treat girls more harshly than boys (Horowitz and Pottieger 1991). In recent years, zero-tolerance policies in public schools and increased arrests for domestic violence may have led to more arrests of girls for acts that previously would have been considered either family matters, school matters, or for some other reason outside of the purview of the police and the courts (Bartollas 1993; Russ 2004). Also, because assaultive behavior, even if minor, is highly inconsistent with stereotypical female behavior, police and court officials may intervene with girls involved in minor fighting because violence by girls is viewed as particularly unacceptable, even outrageous (Chesney-Lind 1999; Chesney-Lind and Shelden 1997). Research suggests that girls may not be becoming more violent, but they may be officially labeled as more violent than in the past (see Chapter 3).

Relational Aggression

When girls talk about violence, they include not only threats and physical violence, but also indirect or social aggression, including relational aggression.[1] Relational aggression includes episodes during which youths try to damage the social standing or self-esteem of peers by using verbal rejection, gossip, rumor spreading, and social ostracism (Cairns et al. 1989; Galen and Underwood 1997). A study of Scottish girls is unique because it examined how girls in urban, small-town, and rural settings defined violence (Burman, Brown, and Batchelor 2003). The girls described violence as including verbal abuse; self-mutilation; personalized, sexualized, and racialized name-calling; insulting remarks about families, especially mothers; and ongoing, repeated negative comments, slights, and insults. Some of these acts are classic covert aggression techniques and others, like name-calling and insults, are "direct" aggression. Following is an excerpt from a discussion with thirteen- and fourteen-year-old girls who were asked to define violence:

> KIKI: [Gossip and bad-mouthing] can break up friendships and that, those that have been together for ages.
> ANNE: And that hurts more than getting a punch in the face or something . . .

Jo: ... and I can tell you a lot about that! [All laugh]

Kiki: It depends who is punching.

Jenna: I think that verbal stuff hurts you longer. Physical violence, well, that is going to go away ...

Anne: Yeah.

Jo: Verbal violence is really gonna, it's really gonna be there for ever. I think verbal abuse is actually worse than physical abuse. (Burman, Brown and Batchelor, 2003, p. 79)

Research also showed that Canadian girls define violence as including emotional, mental, and verbal acts; threatening; uncontrollable anger; put-downs; screaming; and swearing (Cummings and Leschied 2002). Many girls view relational aggression as more harmful than physical violence, and more than boys, they see it as damaging (Galen and Underwood 1997). Negative effects of relational aggression on girls may result from the value they place on intimate relationships with same-sex friends (Gilligan 1982; Griffiths 1995; Hey 1997) and the tendency for their friendships to emphasize expression of emotions, reciprocity, mutual support, intimacy, and the disclosure of information (Martin 1997). Such relationships can make girls vulnerable to having their confidences disclosed or experiencing group rejection.

Using the expanded definition that includes covert, indirect, or relational aggression, several researchers found that girls are as aggressive as or more aggressive than boys (Crick and Grotpeter 1995; Everett and Price 1995; Paquette and Underwood 1999; Rys and Bear 1997; Xie et al. 2002). The research findings have been reinforced in a number of journalistic accounts that emphasize that girls are extremely mean and hurtful toward each other (Simmons 2002). Social science research has not been fully supportive of the popular view. Some studies show no gender differences in the reported use of relational aggression (Hart et al. 1998; Rys and Bear 1997; Tomada and Schneider 1997) or in peers' perceptions of boys' and girls' use of it (Putallaz et al. 1999). In some settings, boys use more relational aggression than girls do (Craig 1998; Hennington et al. 1998). Also, as youths near the end of adolescence, boys catch up to girls in the use of relational aggression (Bjorkvist 1994; Chessler 2001). It may be that the use of physical versus relational aggression depends on age, context, and the way that aggression is measured. Physical and relational aggression do not share a similar metric, so it is difficult to compare gender groups on some combination of both types of aggression (Maccoby, Putallaz, and Bierman 2004).[2] Overall, no clear research support exists for the "mean girls" portrayal.

The Targets and Location of Girls' Violence

In a nationally representative sample, for both girls and boys, relational and physical aggression is most common among same-sex peers and account for about 50 percent of incidents (Franke, Huynh-Hohnbaum, and Chung 2002).

For girls who are physically assaultive, a family member is the next most common target of violence (20.2 percent of girls' versus 5.7 percent of boys' fights). Boys' assaults are next most often committed against a stranger. Consistent with this pattern, girls' violence more often occurs at home, while boys' violence occurs away from home. To consider the contexts of girls' violence, we begin by discussing peer violence, including violence within schools. We then provide information on girls' violence in their families and focus on girls' violence in disorganized communities. This last context for violence includes girls assaulting peers and being involved in gangs and drug markets.

Aggression toward Peers

A study of 250 physically violent incidents reported by forty girls and seventy boys in schools with a large proportion of at-risk youths showed that, regardless of gender, youths' most common goals were to punish a peer for some action, to get a peer to back down from offensive action, and to defend themselves (Lockwood 1997). Physical touching was the most frequent precipitator of a violent incident. One girl gave an example:

> Well, we was in this science class and my science teacher had asked me to take names on the board and I took the names, I had his [a male student's] name on the board ... Then another girl took names and the teacher told her to keep the names that I had took on the board, and she forgot one name, so I told her and he told me not to say anything. Then I had said it, and he slapped me. Then I got up and then I just started fighting ... I got mad and then everything did break loose and I just started fighting ... I got up and I hit him. Then he hit me. Then I started punching him and he started punching me, and then my friend jumped in. A girl ... She jumped on his desk and started punching him in his head. (Lockwood, 1996, p. 18)

This incident involves a girl's defending herself against a boy's aggression. Girls in violent schools turn to self-defense when the schools they attend fail to protect them, or, as explained later in this chapter, the school personnel exacerbate peer conflict.

Another girl said,

> We were in the classroom and we was talking, and being I had said something, and then this other girl, I had been talking to this other girl, she went back and told her. And then the same girl who told her went on and told a story about what I had said. And then my friend wanted to fight, and then I told her, "Come on, then." (Lockwood, 1996, p. 18)

Other fights are of the "she-said-then-another-said" variety, which was the second major class of fighting after those that started with one student touching another. Note that relational aggression issues are prominent in these sorts of events, which are common in girls' aggression, but relational issues are not as central to boys' aggression, which is often instrumental in nature.

Another precursor of fights is *the look* that conveys dislike or contempt or draws attention to oneself as "special" (Ness 2004, p. 40). Girls who were repeatedly violent and who responded to *the look* described their relationships with peers and friends as characterized by constant competition. One girl explained,

> Personally, like I can't say that I like everybody, right? So I have my share
> of girls that I totally hate . . . My share of girls that I victimize . . . I victim-
> ize a girl because she pissed me off, or she did something . . . that I want
> to get her for . . . Like she looks at me the wrong way . . . [or like the girl
> I assaulted] she told a lie about my boyfriend. . . . (Artz 2000, p. 48)

Gang and racial tensions, boyfriend and girlfriend issues, rumors, or a prior look can be a motivation for giving *the look*. *The look* is usually exchanged between boys or between girls, not between girls and boys.

Regardless of gender, relational aggression, like gossiping, spreading rumors, and *the look*, can lead to a physical fight. Research is inconsistent regarding the degree to which *the look* is a catalyst. Focus groups with girls in one high school suggested that *the look* may more often evolve into a fight if the youths involved were males (Worcel, Shields, and Paterson 1999). However, a greater proportion of girls' physical violence can be connected to relational aggression because so much of boys' physical aggression is for other purposes, for example, for committing a robbery (Burman, Brown, and Batchelor 2003; Cairns and Cairns 1994; Cairns et al. 1995; Talbott et al. 2002). In some social and cultural groups, the influences against fighting weaken the connection between relational and physical violence. Goodwin (1990) found that among middle-class African American youths, relational aggression was followed by nonphysical confrontations and ostracism, not by physical fighting. In the United States, lower-class youths emphasize toughness and independence, and lower-class girls place less emphasis on niceness than do middle-class girls (Corsaro and Eder 1990). Whether gossip and rumors lead to physical fighting is therefore tempered by expectations for each gender group in combination with ethnicity, social class, and local community and peer group norms (Crick, Bigbee, and Howes 1996, p. 1012 on peer group norms).

In many cases, the dynamics leading to girls' violence are regulated by the sex/gender system by which they live (as is true for adult women), a system that both sexualizes them and rewards them for being "nice," seeking male approval, being "pretty," and dressing "right" (Adler and Adler 1998; Simmons 2002). The role of the sex/gender system in producing girls' violence is clear. From interviews and observations with Canadian girls who were repeatedly violent toward peers, Artz (1997, 1998a, 1998b) discovered that girls' standards for what other girls should be like—standards maintained by gender arrangements—influenced them to fight. Lamb (2001) and Brown (2003) similarly documented that much relational violence is based on rigid social norms that dictate which girls are "good" and which types of aggression are acceptable. Relational and other aggression of one girl against another is often about whether the target fits a social script for femininity that requires little or no display of power, refraining from messing with other girls' boyfriends, no sexual activity, considerable attractiveness to males, and niceness to all (Hadley 2004).

The well-documented role of girls enforcing the sexual double standard is a particularly significant influence on their violence. Artz (1997) found that, because girls accepted a double standard for the sexual behavior of boys and girls, they closely monitored each other's sexual activity and harshly judged other girls who flirted with or in other ways expressed interest in boys, especially those who had girlfriends. Girls labeled flirting by other girls as "acting like a slut," and being seen as or called "a slut" were common provocations for violence (Artz 1997, p. 17). Girls in gangs similarly sanction each other for being too sexually active (Campbell 1990; Miller 2001).

Aside for these reasons for beating another girl, one of Artz's informants fought to stop other youths from pushing her around and calling her fat. Another resented her father's delegation of household chores to just herself and her mother and fought to prove she was equal in worth to her brothers. Each reason for fighting tells us about unique experiences of girls. Being called fat or ugly plays on the extremely limited vision of females' desirability and worth. Feeling that one has to fight like a man (or boy) to establish one's power is a reaction against limited gender roles considered acceptable for girls. The motivations for fighting are resistance to the suggestion that one does not live up to the image of an idealized (virginal and slim) female and the struggle to escape from the limitations of patriarchal gender roles. Both of these sorts of gender-related motivations result in girls beating each other up.

Outsiders in School Settings

When teachers mark students as troublemakers, outsiders, and academic non-achievers, they stimulate girls' use violence to maintain status. In a school with Hispanic, African American, and Asian students, teachers created a hostile environment that fed antagonisms among youths (Rosenbloom and Way 2004). Many teachers favored Asian youths because they accepted the model minority myth that all Asians value education and hard work. Resenting the favoritism, Latino and African American youths verbally and physically harassed Asian American students. The result was fighting among the different groups.

A different dynamic of bias and exclusion led to violence in a deindustrialized small town in Michigan. Teachers pointed to girls' academic inadequacies in front of other students, with the result that the girls (and boys) looked for status through fighting. The girls saw themselves as marked by minority racial and lower-class status, and they maintained their status by not backing down when they were threatened by peers and were angry with teachers (Brown 1998; Grant 1984; Leitz 2003).[3]

Girls also may be violent in schools to protect themselves. Sexual harassment and objectification are pervasive in some schools. One researcher observed a group of girls who tried to express their concerns about harassment by writing a speech for a schoolwide competition to be given at the school assembly (Brown 1998). Teachers told them that these topics were not appropriate for a school assembly, but that school officials would address their problems. Feeling that they had been silenced and needed to take things into their own hands to stop the abuse, the girls continued to fight to stop their own continued victimization and in response to having this victimization ignored by teachers.

A focus group with delinquent girls in Ohio found an extreme example of girls' preparation for being violent to prevent violence against themselves (Belknap, Dunn, and Holsinger 1997). Asked why she was incarcerated, one girl told a story of her otherwise "clean" delinquent record until she carried a knife to school. She had repeatedly told school authorities that she feared an older male student who followed her to and from school. The school refused to look into it, but when the girl put a knife in her sock to protect herself, the school's "no tolerance" code for weapons kicked in. This girl reported extreme frustration. The school tolerated a boy's stalking and sexually harassing her, but not her attempts to protect herself when they would not.

Fighting for Enjoyment or to Fill the Time

Some girls say they fight for enjoyment or because they are bored (Burman 2003; Ness 2004). A Samoan girl in Hawaii explained how she and her friends would get involved in beating up people to alleviate boredom after school:

> [E]verybody would meet at Brother Brian's Bar, drink, dance, talk story, then when the sun was going down that's when all the drug dealing started. And then [later] couple times we would go out and look for trouble. Some of us just felt hyped and would go out and beat people up. We went up to the park and had this one couple, and so for nothing we just went and beat 'em up. (Joe and Chesney-Lind 1999, p. 223)

Chicanas in California similarly told a researcher that they sometimes beat people up just for something to do. "Somedays it's like, you know, we're bored. So we jump people for fun" (Dietrich 1998, p. 130). Another researcher in inner-city Philadelphia neighborhoods was surprised when she observed the enjoyment that girls got out of beating each other up and causing physical injury (Ness 2004).

Interpreting girls' accounts of their enjoyment of fighting requires careful consideration of context. Low-income neighborhoods are woefully short on recreational options, particularly for teens. Added to that, common forms of youthful female "recreation" like going to the mall are frustrating for youths with no access to transportation and no money to spend once they get there. Documentation across multiple settings reveals that some girls do look for a fight to fill their time and provide excitement. However, we should pay greater attention to the possible inadequacies of community resources contributing to girls' individual characteristics and choices that result in fighting as a preferred pastime.

Girls' Violence against Family Members

A discussion of girls' violence against their parents requires recognition of an important feature of the family context. Parents are much more physically violent toward adolescents than adolescents are toward parents (Straus and Gelles 1990). A survey in the 1980s showed that 34 percent of teenagers aged fifteen to seventeen had been physically assaulted by a parent, and 7 percent had experienced severe violence. In contrast, 10 percent of teenagers were violent toward their parents, and 3.5 percent had been severely violent. More recently, Browne and Hamilton (1998) found from a survey that college students were twice as likely to have experienced violence from their parents as they were to be violent toward their parents.[4] For 80 percent of the youths who were violent toward parents, their parents were also violent toward them. In contrast, 41 percent of mothers' violence and 29 percent of fathers' violence were not met or precipitated by violence from the youths. In a Canadian sample, youths who were most aggressive had most often been physically punished and continued to be punished physically at ages fifteen and sixteen (Pagani et al. 2004). Youths were violent in a cycle of interactions during which they were hit by and then they hit their mothers. The youths were aggressive early in childhood, and the cycle of aggression continued over time. All of the families of a Canadian sample of violent girls were characterized by battles for control and dominance (Artz 2004). Fathers fought with mothers. Some mothers fought back. Parents fought with children. Siblings fought with each other. Verbal fights would turn into physical fights. Adolescent violence toward one or more parents is very much of a reciprocal fight that has in some cases gone on for years.

Some girls are at particularly high risk of violence in their families. If their culture is very patriarchal and devalues females, immigrant youths may be more at risk for abuse, neglect, and sexual assault (Jiwani et al. 2002). No research adequately examines whether this greater abuse of immigrant girls translates into their greater use of violence. It is plausible that in very patriarchal families the gender-related restrictions on girls block their use of violence and expressions of anger.

Although there is some general understanding that many girls who attack a parent were attacked by that parent, very little research explains the more specific circumstances or the youths' characteristics that result in an instance of aggression against a family member. Girls and boys in Nova Scotia and British Columbia were physically violent toward a parent, most often a mother or stepmother, for a very wide variety of reasons (Cottrell and Monk 2004). Some boys had developed masculine identities that supported abuse and intimidation of women. Alternatively, girls who hit parents rejected the view of themselves as stereotypically feminine. One girl said,

> Well, everyone thinks that I am supposed to be so perfect and nice, and I don't want to be like that so I'm going to go totally opposite. (Cottrell and Monk 2004, p. 1081)

In a strategy to distance and distinguish themselves from an undesirable image of females, some girls were abusive toward mothers who were perceived as weak and powerless.

Many girls react with violence to sexual and physical victimization by their fathers or to their fathers' abuse of a sibling. A girl who had been repeatedly physically abused said,

> I wanted to get out of the abuse and stuff ... so I raged out on my dad when he tried to touch me.... I laid boundaries, as [to] what I knew boundaries were. (Cottrell and Monk 2004, p. 1083)

Ryder's (2005) research on girls in custody for violent offenses in New York reported extremely violent family lives. Listen to this account from eleven-year-old Marcella, who violently attacked a man who was abusing another girl in the family:

> I went to sleep, and I wake up and she's screaming, "get away from me, get off me." My instinct was to beat him off—that's what I did. She was calling me and I came and I fought the guy off with a broomstick. (Ryder 2005, p. 15)

One girl explained how abuse by her father resulted in her hitting her mother:

> I started beating my mom up when I was 8.... So I think [the violence] came from that, like through the sexual abuse and stuff.... I was trying to let her know maybe that I needed her to listen to me ... that I was being hurt by my dad. (Cottrell and Monk 2004, p. 1083)

Some girls also deal with their own victimization and the victimization of others by using violence to either stop it or to express their anger about it.

Lockwood's (1997) study revealed that when girls fought at home, it was often with a brother (also see Batchelor and Burman 2001). One girl described a situation when her brother tried to take her new shoes and wear them to school:

> Then, next thing I know he had hit me, and then I say, "You still ain't wearing my shoes. I don't care if you do hit me." Then we got in a fight. I pushed him off the bed. He tried to throw them on top of the house.

He hit me in the mouth. We got in a fight . . . I had picked up the broom and I hit him. (Lockwood 1996, p. 16)

Asked about the counterattack, the girl responded, "Now I won't be hit" (Lockwood 1996, p. 16). Boys' greater privilege in some families by virtue of being male is a plausible explanation for some girls' violence.

When girls describe their own violence in the family, they talk about offensive acts or reactions related to victimization by stronger and older family members. We see this in the case of the domineering brother and the girls who are trying to ward off sexual attacks. The documented high levels of girls' sexual and other physical abuse within the family exemplify gender inequities in the home that are relevant to understanding girls' violence against family members.

Violence in Disorganized Communities

As fully reviewed in Chapter 8, there is a clear connection between exposure to high levels of violence in disorganized communities and youths' use of violence (Burman 2003; DuRant et al. 1994; Fitzpatrick 1997). As stated earlier, at least three possible reasons may explain why living in a disorganized neighborhood would result in a girl's use of violence (Leventhal and Brooks-Gunn 2000). First, there is a high risk of victimization in communities where no informal institutions monitor and supervise youths' behavior, and girls may be violent to prevent or stop attacks on themselves (Leitz 2003). Second, parents who are themselves coping with bad neighborhoods and poverty may lack the capacity to buffer the negative results of the area, for example, by providing close monitoring or safe places for recreation and socializing. Finally, in disorganized communities, schools and recreational activities often do not provide safe places for youths, again leaving girls to their own devices to establish status among peers and to counteract violence.

A girls' physical maturity can place her at special risk in bad neighborhoods, with the result that she acts with violence. Again, as reviewed in Chapter 8, only in communities that were most disorganized did girls who reached menarche early engage in notably high levels of violence (Obeidallah et al. 2004).

Although there are examples of each of these ways that the disorganized community places girls at risk, there remains a need for systematic assessment of the threats that girls feel in disorganized communities and the ways they cope with these threats and actual attacks. When girls feel threatened and suffer attack, and there are no safe places in a community, some will use violence for self-protection.

Out on the Streets—Joining Fighting Gangs to Cope with Neighborhood and Family

Girls who are most involved in physical violence spend a large amount of time away from their homes (Burman 2003). Most of the research on girls who spend time on the streets has focused on girl gang members in urban, disorganized communities. Thus, we concentrate on this group. However, it should be noted that nongang girls who are disenfranchised from their families also use violence when they find themselves "on the streets" (Batchelor and Burman 2001).

Some girls become involved in gangs as a way to deal with violence or restriction to narrow gender roles at home. A Hawaiian-Samoan girl explained how the gang was a solution to her victimization through family violence (Joe and Chesney-Lind 1999). The gang taught her ways to defend herself physically and emotionally, and she was able to protect herself from her father, who had beaten her repeatedly. In Phoenix, girls openly rebelled against parents who severely restricted and closely monitored their activities in an effort to restrict their activities to narrow gender roles (Portillos 1999). One girl explained,

> I went to the forty gangsters with two big tote bags and went to where everyone was kickin' it and I said, "I'm here," and moved in. They fed me, they gave me clothes, they gave me beer, they gave me drugs, they gave me fights, they gave me power that I never had. At home, I was always the mother, always taking care of the kids. Getting no respect, never going anywhere because I was too young, this and that. (Portillos 1999, p. 235)

Latinas in Phoenix, Arizona, said they joined gangs to escape patriarchal family practices that emphasized girls' taking care of the household or siblings and that afforded them little personal freedom or independence (Portillos 1999). Milwaukee girls, who were members of both mixed-sex and all-girl gangs, were proud of their fighting ability (Hagedorn and Devitt 1999). Their fighting was "mainly tied to adolescent rebellion from home, school, and traditional gender roles" (Hagedorn and Devitt 1999, p. 275).

Aside from reactions against the family, there are myriad gang membership–related reasons that girls join gangs and become involved in fighting. Social scientist Miranda (Miranda 2003, p. 29) explained that, before she undertook a study of girls in gangs, she herself had been a "situational" gang member who claimed "gang identity with the kids on my street to prevent threat, harassment, and assault from bullies from other neighborhoods." An African American teenager whose family moved to Los Angeles found herself in a crowded classroom in a school district that served over half a million children (Sikes 1997). To protect herself from other youths, she became a bully and joined a gang. A girl in Hawaii summed it up, "You gotta be part of the gang or else you're the one who's gonna get beat up" (Joe and Chesney-Lind 1999; also see Campbell 1991).

Like boys, once a girl is in a gang, she might fight to defend the group's honor or avenge an insult to the group (Dietrich 1998; Portillos 1999). Usually fights are with girls from other gangs, but this is not always the case (Dietrich 1998). Girl gang members also fight for many of the reasons that other girls fight, including conflicts over boyfriends and derogatory comments about reputation (Dietrich 1998; Hunt and Joe Laidler 2001; Moore 1991). For San Francisco Bay area girls, the context of street life made it unrealistic for the girls to completely refrain from violence. Respectability required not just adhering to traditional notions of femininity, but also being able to stand up for oneself. In a hostile street environment, the girls aggressively postured and engaged in violence with each other in an attempt to *look bad* and to protect themselves (Joe Laidler and Hunt 2001; also see Maher 1997). Given the constraints of their social location, both on the streets, which were dominated by powerful males, and as lower-class girls of color within the larger society, fighting brought status and honor and made it possible for girls to confirm they were "decent" and "nobody's fool" (Joe Laidler and Hunt 2001, p. 675).

In some ways, the motivations of girls are similar to those of U.S. inner-city men who engage in violence. They fight to gain respect and status and to keep from being victimized (Anderson 1999; Bourgois 1995). However, for girls, the immediate issues leading up to a fight may be different from the issues that lead to boys' fighting. For girls in gangs, the sequence of events leading up to a fight often begins with accusations of sexual activity, breaking of confidences, and rejection by the group (Baskin and Sommers 1998). Again, notice that particularly for girls, even girls in gangs, relationship/relational aggression issues prompt direct physical aggression. Boys and boyfriends are often the cause of girls' violence, and not infrequently, they are also the audience for girls' violence (Artz 1998a). Additionally, girls do fight for some of the same reasons that boys fight—for self-protection and to send a message, "don't mess with me." For a full review of young women and street gangs see Chapter 10.

Girls Who Deal Drugs

It has been widely recognized that there is a certain easy entry into the manufacture and distribution of both methamphetamine and crack cocaine, because no large start-up costs are involved. Thus, girls and women may have new opportunities to become involved in selling drugs. Some theorists and researchers have noted that it is not unexpected that drug-dealing girls would commit violent acts to survive on the streets when they are attacked by robbers or business competitors or other violent actors involved in dealing drugs (Baskin and Sommers 1998; Kruttschnitt 2001). A study of many gangs and members drawn from several ethnic groups in the San Francisco area revealed that members of all-girl gangs who dealt in drugs and sold stolen goods routinely carried knives and guns for protection (Hunt and Joe Laidler 2001). But, are girls similarly violent as young men who deal drugs? And how widespread is the movement of girls into drug manufacture, marketing, and distribution?

Maher (1997) observed a very active drug market in Brooklyn, New York City. She found that males heavily dominated the managerial and supervisory activities in the network that distributed drugs. They were the ones who carried guns and engaged in regular violence to protect their money, their drugs, and their markets. Women's opportunities for higher-level involvement in the drug market depended on support from a male partner (Koester and Schwartz 1993).

However, drug markets of the sort that Maher observed have declined in recent years; indeed, the decline of the crack cocaine market is credited with the drop in the male juvenile arrest rate. Whether the emerging crystal methamphetamine market will offer girls and women an increased role in distribution is uncertain, despite the undeniable appeal of the drug for girls and women (because of its unique mix of effects including increased energy and weight loss) (Chesney-Lind and Pasko 2004). Research on drug markets so far suggests that girls and women are often low-level drug sellers who sell small amounts of drugs and execute more sales than their male counterparts (English 1993).

Identity, Anger, and Rage

Girls' violence is not just the product of their context and their history. It is also affected by their identity, their feelings, and other aspects of their personal makeup. Girls have agency—within constraints—to act out in a violent way or not to do so.

School curriculum, extracurricular activities, interactions with teachers, and the media contain mixed messages about appropriate behaviors and attributes of girls and boys, but ideas consistent with what is called *emphasized femininity* are readily available. Emphasized femininity idealizes passivity, subordination to males, and other stereotypical characteristics for girls and women. Many girls who fight, however, do not see physical and verbal violence as inconsistent with being feminine. As one girl saw it, "I can be cute and still mess some girl up if that's what I have to do" (Ness 2004, p. 44). Girls can conform to traditional ideas about femininity with boyfriends or parents but exhibit violence toward their peers and people they view as antagonists (e.g., members of gangs). The view of femininity as inconsistent with aggression is tempered by ethnicity, social class, and one's immediate situation (Bettie 2000).

In contrast to girls who wholeheartedly accept and enact emphasized femininity (a group that may be dwindling), some speak of fighting as an integral part of their identities, referring to themselves as bullies or bitches with pride (Batchelor and Burman 2001; Ness 2004). Although, on average, girls see their aggression in a negative light and boys are proud of their aggression (Tapper and Boulton 2000), many girls who use violence justify it as necessary and acceptable for defending themselves, maintaining status, and stopping rumors about their sexual activity.

Families often support girls' violence (Tapper and Boulton 2000). In one community in Maine, working-class girls who were violent had mothers who were known in the school for supporting their daughters' right to protect themselves physically or to fight for a just cause (Brown 1998). In inner-city Philadelphia neighborhoods, girls had been socialized from childhood to stand up to people who disrespected them and to "hold their own" (Ness 2004, p. 37). In a deindustrialized Michigan town, mothers of girls who would not fight their own battles decried this as a weakness (Leitz 2003).

Some researchers have concluded that girls' proclivity toward assault is most often found in inner-city neighborhoods, but research has identified a wide variety of settings where girls feel that fighting is necessary to maintain status and safety (Batchelor and Burman 2001; Ness 2004). Girls are often supported in this perception by parents, especially mothers, who themselves found that physical aggression was effective in taking care of themselves and their children.

Anger about long-standing family problems can trigger physical violence that is directed at peers. This happens as a result of the girl's (or boy's) approach to dealing with feelings combined with the opportunities and acceptance for peer fighting in a particular school or neighborhood. An inner-city Philadelphia girl explained,

> Sometimes things feel like they get too much for me and I just need to let off steam. My mom used to beat me and she even burned me with cigarette butts a couple of times. I can't take it out on her so sometimes I get my anger out on the street. (Ness 2004, p. 41)

A girl in San Francisco similarly explained her violence:

> I would get hate for my dad, 'cause he didn't take care, he left me alone when he was supposed to take care of me and his best friend raped me when I was 7.... That's why I got so violent, you know, where I could just kill somebody ... 'cause that anger that was inside of me.... I feel a lot of frustration, you know, those people hurt me, man, they hurt me ... (Hunt and Joe Laidler 2001, p. 378)

Based on analysis of the case histories of women before the court, Daly (1992) identified a group that she called *harmed and harming*. In Artz's research (1998a), the key informants, who were very violent girls, had experienced tremendous harm through exposure to violence in their families, and they felt they could not trust even the people who were closest to them, they were devalued (for example, by their fathers) because they were female, and they were seen as marred in character and appearance. When girls are exposed to all sorts of repeated harm in their homes, schools, and neighborhoods, it is not unexpected that they have little efficacy, control, or power, except as they build status by fighting or they express their anger and rage with violence. In extreme cases of physical and sexual abuse, some girls have responded with murder as a way to express anger and escape continuous rape and battering (Heide 1992).

Predicting Girls' Violence

Existing explorations of the context in which girls act with violence show that acting with violence is not a unitary concept. Girls may be physically violent in self-defense or in an effort to prevent their future victimization. Their violence may be a signal that others should not "mess with me." They may be violent because of bonds to and expectations of their friends, who may be in gangs. They may be violent because of rage about abuses in their past and present. Alternatively, in communities where violence is endemic or girls' backgrounds can lead to violence, many girls cope without using violence. Thus, it is not surprising that predictive models do not fully answer the question of why some girls are violent. Violence includes a host of reactive and proactive behaviors, and girls vary in the degree to which context promotes their violence.

In fact, quantitative research has shown that the weights of various risk factors for youth violence depend on the context and the developmental stage of the youth (Odgers and Moretti 2002). As an example of changes due to developmental stage, by late adolescence, many violent inner-city Philadelphia girls that Ness (2004) studied abstained from fighting. They reasoned that they could walk away from youths who looked at or spoke to them the wrong way. Status no longer depended on fighting.

Interaction between multiple risk factors seems to be especially important for explaining girls' violence (Odgers and Moretti 2002). The qualitative research we have reviewed provides many examples of how abuse in the family, threats in the community, a girl's drive to survive in schools and on the streets, and her psychological makeup and exercise of agency come together to explain instances or patterns of violence. A quantitative study (Saner and Ellickson 1996) confirmed that the combination of influences on violence had a pronounced effect. When forty-five hundred high school seniors and dropouts were followed over time, boys and girls with five or more environmental risk factors (e.g., poverty, single-parent household) were four to six times more likely to be seriously violent or to engage in persistent hitting. For girls more than for boys, the following predicted violence: selling drugs; impaired relationships with parents; low academic orientation; parental drug use; and separation, divorce, or the death of a parent.

Findings about quantitative predictors of girls' violence have important implications. Girls who are violent are especially likely to have multiple problems. Also, their family and community context magnify the effects of other influences on violence. Quantitative research to develop further predictive models of girls' violence must consider measures of contextual influences, including the probability and the reality of violence by family and peers within the school, community, and family. Threats and instances of sexual harassment and assault/abuse must be considered. Researchers need to conduct multilevel analyses to understand the role of both contextual and individual factors in supporting girls' violence.

What Is to Be Done?

Girls' violence makes sense when it is placed in context. The research certainly does not lead to the conclusion that girls' current levels and patterns of violence are inexplicable or the result of perverse and shocking individual characteristics.

It is clear that there is no one explanation for why girls are violent, and as Miller (1986) showed many years ago, and others have shown more recently (Sampson and Laub 1993), for both females and males, violence (or any illegal behavior) can be the result of different explanations or a combination of influences that come to bear over the life course. However, the constraints on girls' agency are most apparent in the families, schools, and communities where they are most often violent. We would not deny that girls do exercise some agency, but we do emphasize the importance of context in explaining their violence. They are violent in the very places where they are threatened, abused, and denigrated.

In the literature that is reviewed in this chapter, some general themes cut across geographic place and social context. These themes are presented in Table 9.1, which summarizes the ways that context affects youths' violence and highlights the gender-related ways in which context matters uniquely for girls. Table 9.1 can be used as a heuristic to suggest the range of contextual explanations of violence, especially the violence of girls. In practice settings, the table suggests the starting point for exploring why a particular girl has acted with violence once or repeatedly. The qualitative research we have reviewed provides many examples of how combinations of abuse in the family, threats in the community, a girl's drive to survive in schools and on the streets, and her psychological makeup come together to explain instances or patterns of violence. To reduce girls' violence, negative contexts must be addressed; they need to be eliminated, changed, or coped with.

TABLE 9.1   CONTEXTUAL EXPLANATIONS OF VIOLENCE

Context	For Girls and Boys	Uniquely for Girls
In groups of peers	Violence in response to physical touching, "he-said-she-said," and the look.	Violence between peers to enforce stringent standards for being a respectable girl (not "a slut"), a girl that males value.
		Girls attack each other for being too sexually open and active, for not fitting an idealized picture of attractiveness. Girls respond back with violence.
		More than the members of independent all-girl gangs, girls in gangs that are affiliated with boys' gangs are in more situations that are conducive to them being violent, for example, in response to a male gang member's trying to rape them, when male gang members encourage them to fight girls affiliated with other gangs, and when other gangs attack them in the course of confronting the boy gang members.

(Continued on facing page)

TABLE 9.1 *Continued*

Context	For Girls and Boys	Uniquely for Girls
Within the family	Violence in response to oppression or abuse by siblings. Violence to stop sexual and other physical abuse. Joining gangs to learn emotional and physical defense against abusive family members; gangs provide new reasons to be violent.	Violence against brothers enforcing ideas that they, by virtue of their gender, have control and power. Violence to stop a sexually or otherwise physically abusive member from hurting her or another family member. Violence to signal to a family member that she is being sexually abused by another family member. Violence to distance oneself from weak and ineffective images of femininity. Violence against peers to escape from constricting gender roles in the family. Joining a gang to escape from constricting gender roles and devaluation of females in the family.
Community Around the neighborhood	Violence in self-protection or to signal capacity and willingness to self-protect because: • Adults in low-resource households in disorganized communities may not be able to monitor and protect youth. • Neighborhood streets, schools, and recreational settings are not safe places. Joining gangs to acquire a protective group, but gangs provide new reasons for violence.	Violent when threatened by sexual harassment and attacks in school and in the neighborhood. Girls who are physically mature at a young age and who live in disorganized communities may be at special risk.
In school	Fighting when stereotyped as academically unsuccessful to maintain status. Carrying weapons and acts of self-protection in response to unsafe school environments.	Violence to maintain status in the face of assumed lack of academic ability and motivation for girls who do not fit images of femininity that emphasize passivity and quietness. Violence by girls who feel unprotected from stalking, harassment, and other gender-related threats from other students.

Intervention into Escalating Incidents

Based on his research into the sequence of events just before a youth is violent, Lockwood (1997) recommended that school personnel recognize and intervene aggressively in the precursors to the youth's use of violence. He also provided some evidence of the effectiveness of this approach in reducing violence in schools. Youths who were posturing aggressively toward each other, who were giving each other *the look*, or who engaged in name-calling were spotted and interrupted. No doubt, this approach could make some places more peaceful and immediately safer for both girls and boys. Intervention into the events just before a violent act is intended to eliminate the contextual triggers for violent acts. This is a worthwhile aim for school personnel and other people who work with youths in a group context. However, for much change in girls' violence, interventions that directly address dangerous and damaging contexts in the family, neighborhood, or schools are also essential.

Individual-Level Interventions

A theme in Table 9.1 is that girls' violence is often a response, and sometimes an effective one, to threatened or actual victimization. Girls are violent against fathers who sexually abuse them or other children in the family, brothers who push them around, schoolmates who threaten or attack them, and more generally people of all ages who threaten them with physical harm. Across multiple contexts, girls have the special problems of sexual harassment and sexual attack. Intervention programs cannot begin to address violence by girls without knowing about past victimizations and the potential for new victimization across the multiple settings, and providing a substitute for violence as a way to be safe.

Another crosscutting theme that is relevant to intervention is that oppressive gender arrangements and expectations promote girls' violence, not the reverse, as much of the popular culture discourse about girls' violence seems to suggest. Not only do these gender constraints put girls at risk for sexual and other sorts of physical abuse, but they also result in girls using violence to resist stereotypes and traditions that encourage them to be weak, passive, restricted to the home, and anything but strong and self-directed. Girls do not want to be like mothers or other women who have these characteristics and who may themselves be victimized. They sometimes join gangs in an effort to learn to be active and to be fighters. Effective intervention programs need to provide girls with a variety of ways of being an empowered girl. While strong female role models can help, it is no simple task to empower girls, particularly those in low-resource neighborhoods and schools or in outcast ethnic and racial groups. Also, many girls have been socialized to direct their energies at maintaining rigid definitions of appropriate "girl" behavior among their peers and for themselves. Sometimes their enforcement of traditional standards for femininity results in violence toward other girls and then violence in retaliation. Prevention and intervention programs need to work with girls to untangle the contradictory images of "girl" and "women" and to see the damaging effects of both highly restrictive and violence-promoting versions of femininity. Girls need help identifying the structures that, and the people who, put them in situations where they feel angry and in accessing the resources to moderate those structures.

A third theme in the research on girls' violence is that girls strike out at other girls who share similar disadvantages of social class, racial or ethnic bias, sexual harassment and objectification, and impoverished and dangerous community. Much of girls' fighting occurs in contexts where girls compete for males, in part because of the status and material goods that males can bring them. The flip side of the importance of boys to girls is that girls lack ways to gain their own status and material goods. Cummings and Leschied (2002) made a case that girls need to understand that, by striking out at each other, they are not addressing the sources of their disadvantage and anger. Girls need help in analyzing their relationships with each other, and they particularly need help understanding that anger at other girls can be resolved in ways that avoid both relational and physical aggression (Brown 2003). Artz (2004) made the similar recommendation that, to promote healthy psychological development and functioning, programs for girls should create opportunities through inclusion, relationship building, community partnerships, collaboration, and communication. She points out that in contrast many delinquency interventions are founded on competition-based external reward systems that do not respond to girls' needs and do not respond to their strengths in building relationships with each other. Programming that builds relationships among girls can enhance peer support, self-confidence, empowerment, trust, and understanding (Pollack 1993; Batchelor et al. 2003), at the same time that it reduces peer violence.

Should There Be Increased Intervention to Stop Girls' Relational Aggression?

Girls' violence is most commonly directed at peers, and in many cases it is expressed through relational aggression against other girls, primarily friends and ex-friends. Relational aggression is damaging to victims, but depending on the girls involved and their norms and ideas regarding appropriate behavior, relational aggression may or may not have a connection to physical violence. The judgment of inappropriate relational aggression is complicated by the recognition that it exists along a continuum from minor to extreme.

There are reasons for being cautious about imposing either formal or informal sanctions for girls' covert aggressive behavior. Many girls are socialized to be conciliatory and to avoid conflict so that they are included in relationships and liked by others (Brown and Gilligan 1993; Underwood 2003a; Zahn-Waxler and Davidson 2000). Indirect acts are sometimes girls' only way to express anger or even their preferences for friends. Covert aggressions are, fundamentally, weapons of the weak, and as such, they are as reflective of girls' powerlessness as they are of girls' "meanness." Girls, women, and others in relatively powerless groups have not, historically, been permitted direct aggression (without terrible consequences). As a result, in certain contexts and against certain individuals, relational aggressions were ways the powerless punished the bad behavior of the powerful. This was, after all, how slaves and indentured servants—female and male—got back at abusive masters, how women before legal divorce dealt with violent husbands, and how working women today get back at abusive bosses.

As one psychologist put it, "There is reason to question any approach that potentially serves to discourage females from expressing anger and aggression and reminds them of their subordinate positions in society" (Zahn-Waxler 1993, p. 81). Additionally, there is evidence that relational aggression does not predict developmental maladjustment and may indeed be normative and desirable for youths (Underwood, Galen, and Paquette 2001; Xie et al. 2002). Aggression makes separation from others, individualization, competition, achievement, and the initiation of new relationships possible (Hadley 2003). Also it is debatable that girls are particularly inclined to use or approve of relational aggression, and if there are gender differences in these forms of aggression, they seem to end by late adolescence.

Probably everybody needs to know about behaviors that are included in alternative aggression, if only to recognize when they are being targeted. The myopic focus of a recent popular book on mean girls (Simmons 2002) tends to blur the fact that girls exist in a world that often ignores them and marginalizes them—all the while empowering young boys (whose physical and relational aggression against girls is rarely regulated in schools). Certainly, we want to change much about girlhood, and we do want to stop girls from hurting other weaker girls, but to survive, perhaps girls will need to know something about how to "do" relational aggression.

Any intervention should focus on the extreme forms of relational aggression (i.e., forms that seriously harm other people or that lead to physical aggression). For girls, much relational aggression grows out of interpersonal relationships and an emphasis on being a "good girl," "not a slut," and generally conforming to the notion that girls' worth lies in being successful with boys and conforming to traditional gender-role expectations. Interventions could help girls sort out why and whether they accept traditional expectations. Because girls do very much value relationships with each other (Xie, Cairns, and Cairns 2005), it is possible to capitalize on those relationships and help girls develop them to enhance peer support, self-confidence, empowerment, trust, and understanding (Batchelor and Burman 2001; Pollack 1993).

Individual- and Family-Level Interventions for Physically Violent Girls

When an intervention that had been designed for violent young boys was ineffective for young girls, the Earlscourt Child and Family Center in Toronto developed a program targeted to girls' needs (Levene, Walsh, and Augimeri 2004). Considering the many times that girls' violence resulted from relational aggression toward them, the therapeutic team developed cases of triggering events for discussion. Girls met in a club to talk about how to handle being teased or called names by other girls, brainstormed about alternative reactions, and practiced reactions. Parenting groups taught effective strategies that mothers could use to respond when their daughters were victimized or were aggressive and discouraged mothers from also using relational aggression, for example, being sarcastic with daughters. In recognition of the pervasive violence that females experience, a mother–daughter group considered how women and girls portrayed in the media could recognize and handle sexual aggression. Programming like that offered by Earlscourt can be effective if the triggers for girls' violence are not ongoing and from multiple sources. It is important to recognize that many girls who are physically violent also experience clinical depression (Leschied et al. 2000). The percentage of violent boys reporting some internalizing disorder (like depression or anxiety) ranges between 8 percent and 12 percent in various studies; for girls, most studies find a rate of 40 percent, and some even higher (Leschied et al. 2000). In Chicago, regardless of race, ethnicity, or social class, 57 percent of mildly to moderately depressed girls engaged in aggressive behaviors, but just 13 percent of girls who were not depressed did (Obeidallah and Earls 1999). Positive intervention for violent girls requires concomitant assessment and treatment for depression and anxiety and for related problems of substance abuse and suicide risk.[5]

The Relevance of Context to Intervention

When the context of girls' violence is an abusive family, a school where sexual harassment and put-downs (even by teachers) are pervasive, or a dangerous community, the focus cannot be solely on girls' reasoning and coping strategies and minor adjustments within the family. Girls in these situations need a safe place to live, learn, and socialize.

Creating safe places in families, schools, and neighborhoods where girls feel empowered and worthwhile would go a long way in preventing and stopping their violence. Artz (1998b) summed up the themes that reoccurred in her notes on the lives, experiences, and viewpoints of violent girls:

> [F]amily violence, sexual harassment and abuse, power imbalances based in narrowly traditional understandings of gender, anger, rage and emotional abandonment, identities premised on self-descriptions that included

negative self-concepts, tenuous friendships and social activities that involved risks, and approaches to violence grounded in victim blaming and self-justification. (p. 84)

The many studies reviewed in this chapter reinforce the themes that Artz identified. Gender has its impact on the complex and unique nature of girls' environment and experiences; thus, it runs through the explanation of girls' violence. For an intervention to be effective, it needs to consider the broader gender-based constraints on girls, whether these manifest themselves in disempowering restrictions to narrowly defined "feminine roles," disorganized communities, or exposure to violence and abuse at home or in school. Interventions must go beyond a focus on cognitions and coping to include full attention to violence and threats that girls face in various, often multiple contexts (Reitsma-Street, Artz, and Winterdyk 2000).

Much of girls' aggression with peers involves striking out at girls who share similar disadvantages of social class, racial or ethnic bias, sexual harassment and objectification, and impoverished and dangerous community. Cummings and Leschied (2002) made a case that girls need to understand that by striking out at each other they are not addressing the sources of their disadvantage and anger. Much of girls' fighting must be understood as part of a context in which girls compete for males who are often a source of status and material goods. The flip side is that girls lack ways to gain their own status and material goods.

Safe places for girls can capitalize on the benefits of close relationships among them. The Valentine Foundation (1990) worked in a disorganized and dangerous community to establish physically and emotionally safe space away from males. The space provided a place for girls to talk and support each other, opportunities for girls to develop trusting relationships with women in their lives, programs that tap cultural strengths, and mentors who have survival and growth skills and share experiences.

Conclusions

When considering girls' violence, consider the context. For many girls, violence is an attempt to survive in extraordinary circumstances (Odgers, Schmidt, and Reppucci 2004). Interventions must address these circumstances, related depression and anger, and girls' capacity and resources to cope or to get out. Also needed is the reduction of girls' victimization in families and schools, where girls use violence often as a cry for help or in response to abuse that others have normalized.

Girls' aggression against their peers is often colored by a sex/gender system that discourages girls from expressing their real feelings, including anger, and that confines them to excessively limited notions of what girls can and should do. In many settings, girls are encouraged to cultivate male approval while viewing other girls as competition. Like the boys whose approval they seek, girls are growing up in a world that celebrates boys and men and trivializes and sexualizes girls. For this reason, many advocate media literacy as part of any program of girl empowerment (Brown 2003; Wiseman 2002).

Finally, when considering girls' aggression in disorganized and economically marginalized communities, we stress the need to address the economic and political structures that produce these sorts of damaged and damaging communities. If not, we cannot be surprised if girls use violence to survive on the streets of these neighborhoods (Jones 2004).

Take-Home Points

1. Most of girls' violence is directed toward other girls. Sometimes girls and boys explain their violence in similar ways, attributing it to efforts to maintain status, needs for self-protection, and enjoyment of fighting. However, for girls, violence also may come about when they try to affirm that they are decent in their sexual behavior, in contests to keep boyfriends, and in efforts to express a generalized rage that comes from being sexually victimized or stereotyped and restricted by expectations for female behavior.
2. School settings can promote girls' use of fighting and carrying weapons for protection and to establish status. They do this by ignoring sexual harassment and stalking of girls and by assuming that, because of gender, race, or ethnicity, girls are not academically able.
3. Girls' violence toward family members is often rooted in their rejection of sexual and physical abuse or other exploitation due to their lack of power. It is very much a part of a reciprocal fight that in some cases has gone on for years. Violence may be directed toward the exploitative family member, family members who fail to provide protection, or family members who are used as targets for expression of anger.
4. Programs to help violent girls need to provide them with alternative avenues for identity, protection, and empowerment. They need to shed light on how one can be female and empowered in a society in which many elements limit the roles available to girls and where many places are not safe for girls.
5. Programs for violent girls must operate on multiple levels, not only helping girls set priorities and cope with difficulties, but also creating safe places for them in their families, alternative living situations, schools, and neighborhoods.

Unanswered Questions

- When does relational aggression move beyond being normative to being seriously harmful? Are some girls more likely than others to use seriously harmful relational aggression?
- Are police and court statistics indicators of increased social control of girls, increased violence by girls, or both? Racial and ethnic differences need to be considered separately in answering this question.

- What is the role of boys in the production of female violence, particularly in peer and gang settings? Do boys prompt this behavior? Provide an audience for it?
- What media, family, and peer messages do girls hear about how to "be girls"? What bearing do these messages have on girls' use of violence to express their anger, protect themselves from exploitation and harm, and form an identity?
- How can explanations that focus on peer group, family, community, and school contexts be integrated with those that consider girls' individual differences in explanations of violence?
- Do various immigrant groups of girls disproportionately experience abuse within the family, rejection in schools, and danger in communities that can account for their violence or other negative outcomes?

10

Young Women and Street Gangs

JODY MILLER

Numerous gang scholars have become attentive to the importance of examining gender in the context of gangs (Bjerregaard and Smith 1993; Curry 1998; Curry and Decker 1998; Deschenes and Esbensen 1999a, 1999b; Esbensen and Deschenes 1998; Esbensen, Deschenes, and Winfree 1999; Esbensen and Winfree 1998; Fagan 1990; Hagedorn 1998), and a core group of researchers have dedicated themselves to understanding the lives of young women in gangs (Chesney-Lind and Hagedorn 1999; Fleisher 1998; Hunt, Joe Laidler, and MacKenzie 2000; Miller 2001; Moore 1991; Nurge 1998; Portillos 1999). In fact, contemporary research on girls in gangs has its roots in earlier foundational work; see Curry (1999) for an overview; see also Bowker, Gross, and Klein (1980); Bowker and Klein (1983); Brown (1978); Fishman (1995); Miller (1973); Moore (1991); and Quicker (1983).

This early research is especially important to highlight because it tempers popular claims of "new violent female offenders" routinely depicted as young women in gangs (see Chesney-Lind 1993; Chesney-Lind, Shelden, and Joe 1996 for a discussion). From the available information, it appears that there has been both continuity and change in young women's participation in gangs. However, overall, the proportion of gang members who are girls and the nature of girls' gang involvement do not appear to have shifted substantially over the years (Klein 2001; Moore 1991). Research from this earlier era shows that while there was variation in young women's gang involvement, girls were actively involved in violence, most often fighting. In addition, their place in gangs was never as mere "tomboys" or "sex objects." Instead, girls' roles and activities in gangs were negotiated, with varying results, in the context of male-dominated settings.

In the contemporary era, scholarly concern with young women's gang involvement has grown substantially. In part this is because of the growth in gangs in the 1980s and early 1990s and the tremendous growth in gang research during this period. Recent estimates suggest that there are now more than twenty-three hundred cities and towns across the United States reporting gangs—more than five times the number that existed as recently as 1980 (Egley and Major 2004; see also Klein 1995). The good news is that the number of jurisdictions reporting gang problems has declined 32 percent since 1996, although this decline appears to be concentrated among smaller cities and rural counties. Larger cities and suburban counties consistently account for the largest proportion (around 85 percent) of reported gang members, and these numbers have not declined appreciably (Egley and Major 2004).

The growth in gangs and gang research, however, does not account entirely for the scholarship research on girls in gangs. Instead, the move away from a primarily androcentric approach to the study of gangs is in large part because of the expansion of feminist criminology and its requisite attention to the experiences of women. Just as gang research has increased considerably in the last several decades, so has the number of feminist scholars within the discipline of criminology. As a consequence, young women's gang involvement is just one area of research on offending and victimization that has benefited from attention to the importance of understanding gender.

So then, what have we learned in the last two decades? For starters, we have come to recognize that young women's involvement in youth gangs is a varied phenomenon. Girls' experiences in gangs and the consequences of their gang involvement vary by—among other things—their ethnicity, the gender composition of their gangs, and the community contexts in which their gangs emerge. This chapter provides an update of our knowledge about girls in gangs, particularly focusing on four issues:

1. The level of female gang involvement
2. The risk factors for gang membership and girls' pathways into gangs
3. The level and character of gang girls' delinquency and its context in gang life for girls
4. The consequences of gang involvement for girls, including both victimization risks within gangs and long-term costs associated with gang involvement

This discussion draws from a wide range of studies to emphasize the comparisons that can be drawn across research methodologies, study sites, ethnicities, and gang structures.

Levels of Female Gang Involvement

Recent estimates suggest that female participation in gangs is more widespread than typically has been believed. Data from official sources continue to underestimate the extent of girls' gang membership. For instance, Curry, Ball, and Fox (1994) found that some law enforcement policies officially exclude female gang members from their counts. Controlling for data from these cities, Curry and colleagues still found that females comprised only 5.7 percent of the gang members known to law enforcement agencies. Part of law enforcement's underestimation of girls' gang involvement is attributable to male gang members' greater likelihood of being involved in serious crime, as well as average age differences between males and females in gangs (Bjerregaard and Smith 1993; Fagan 1990). While young men are more likely to remain involved in gangs into young adulthood, gang membership for girls is much more likely to remain a primarily adolescent undertaking (Hunt, Joe Laidler, and MacKenzie 2005; Miller 2001; Moore and Hagedorn 1996).

On the other hand, results from survey research with youths indicate that young women's gang involvement is relatively extensive and at levels only slightly below that of young men, particularly in early adolescence. For instance, findings from the Rochester Youth Development Study (RYDS), based on a stratified sample of youths in high-risk, high-crime neighborhoods, actually found that a slightly larger percentage of females (22 percent) than males (18 percent) claimed gang membership when self-definition was used as a measure (Bjerregaard and Smith 1993). Later evidence from this longitudinal study suggests that girls' gang involvement tends to be of a shorter duration than boys', with girls' peak gang involvement around eighth and ninth grades (Esbensen and Deschenes 1998; Thornberrry 1999).

In addition to prevalence rates, two additional issues are important in considering the level of girls' participation in gangs. One is the proportion of gang members that are female versus male, and the other is the distribution of female gang involvement across various gang types. Estimates of the ratio of female to male members suggest that young women approximate between 20 percent and 46 percent of gang members (Esbensen and Huizinga 1993; Esbensen and Winfree 1998; Fagan 1990; Moore 1991; Winfree et al. 1992). There is wide variation, however, across gangs. In Miller's (2001) comparative study of female gang involvement in Columbus, Ohio, and St. Louis, Missouri, girls in mixed-gender gangs (i.e., gangs with both male and female members) reported being as few as 7 percent or as many as 75 percent of the total gang membership of a given group, with the vast majority in predominantly male gangs.

Although standard approaches for categorizing (presumably or implicitly) male gangs continue to focus on a broad range of issues exclusive of gender (see, for example, Maxson and Klein 1995; Spergel and Curry 1993), studies of female gang types focus specifically on gender organization, most often drawing from

Miller's (1975) tripartite classification: (a) mixed-gender gangs with both female and male members; (b) female gangs that are affiliated with male gangs, which he refers to as "auxiliary" gangs; and (c) independent female gangs. Several scholars have noted that this tripartite division misses the complexity of gang formation, and that it is androcentric to focus on gender organization when examining female but not male gang involvement (Hagedorn and Devitt 1999; Nurge 1998). Nonetheless, research on the gendered organization and gender ratio of girls' gangs has yielded important information.

There are several case studies of the various gang types Miller describes (Fleisher 1998; Lauderback, Hansen, and Waldorf 1992; Quicker 1983; Venkatesh 1998), but less evidence of their prevalence. Curry's (1997) study of female gang members in three cities found that only 6.4 percent of girls described being in autonomous female gangs, while 57.3 percent described their gangs as mixed gender, and another 36.4 percent said they were in female gangs affiliated with male gangs. Several ethnographic studies also suggest that mixed-gender gangs are a predominant type (Miller 2001; Nurge 1998). However, there appears to be variation across ethnicity. For example, Chicana/Latina gang members are those most likely to describe their gangs as female groups affiliated with male gangs, while young African American women are more likely to describe their gangs as mixed gender. The handful of all-female gangs documented by scholars has largely been African American as well (Curry 1997; Joe Laidler and Hunt 1997; Lauderback, Hansen, and Waldorf 1992; Miller 2001; Venkatesh 1998).

A recent analysis of the Gang Resistance Education and Training (G.R.E.A.T.) data (Peterson, Miller, and Esbensen 2001) supports the finding that most youth gangs are composed of both male and female members. Of the 366 gang members reporting, 84 percent of male gang members and 93 percent of female gang members described their gangs as having both female and male members. In terms of the ratio of males to females in their groups, approximately 45 percent of male gang members and 30 percent of female gang members described their gangs as having a majority of male members; 38 percent and 64 percent, respectively, said their gangs had fairly equal numbers of males and females. This and several additional studies suggest that the gender composition of gangs has a significant effect on the nature of gang members' activities, including their participation in delinquency (Joe Laidler and Hunt 1997; Miller 2001; Miller and Brunson 2000; Peterson, Miller, and Esbensen 2001).

Finally, several scholars have suggested the need for a broader conceptualization of gang involvement to fully understand the effect of gangs on young women. For example, Cepeda and Valdez (2003) examined the effect of gangs on young women who associated with neighborhood gangs but did not self-identify as gang members. Their results suggest that risks for young women—including substance use, crime, and early and sometimes exploitative sexual relations—are also faced by young women who affiliate but do not join gangs. Likewise, Fleisher and Krienert (2004) focused on the size and gender composition of social networks among both active and inactive female gang members and highlighted that youths' definitions of gang membership are often more fluid than those employed by scholars (Fleisher 1998).

Girls' Risk Factors for Gang Membership and Pathways into Gangs

Research shows that youths typically spend some time with gang members—often as much as a year—before making a commitment to join (Decker and Van Winkle 1996). The young women in Miller's (2001) study began spending time with gang members when they were around age twelve, and joined at an average age of thirteen. This finding is quite similar to other research and appears to be relatively consistent across ethnic groups. Joe and Chesney-Lind's (1995) study of Samoan and Filipino gang youths in Hawaii reported an average age of entrée of twelve for girls and fourteen for boys. Portillos (1999) reported that most of the Chicana girls in his study joined a gang between the ages of twelve and thirteen. Recall that the RYDS also found the highest prevalence rates of female gang participation in the early waves of their study, again suggesting that girls' gang membership starts at a young age (Maxson and Whitlock 2001).

Research on why girls join gangs generally has included two approaches. The first approach uses survey research to analyze the etiological risk factors for gang membership; the second approach qualitatively analyzes girls' accounts of why they join gangs, what they gain from their gang participation, and how their lives are both prior to and at the time of joining. Both types of study focus on two or more of five sets of issues: structural and neighborhood conditions, family factors, school factors, peer influence, and individual factors.

Many scholars have found evidence that the recent proliferation of American gangs has been spurred by the deterioration in living conditions brought about by deindustrialization (Hagedorn 1998; Huff 1989; Klein 1995). The resulting lack of alternatives and sense of hopelessness are believed to have contributed to the growth of gangs in many cities; scholars point to the gang as a means for inner-city youths—male and female—to adapt to oppressive living conditions imposed by their environments. For example, findings from RYDS suggest that growing up in disorganized, violent neighborhoods is a risk factor for gang involvement for young women[1] (Thornberry 1997).

Qualitative research highlights the importance of this link even further. Campbell (1990) noted that, in addition to the limited opportunities and powerlessness of underclass membership shared with their male counterparts, young women in these communities also face the burdens of childcare responsibilities and subordination to men. For example, in their study of youths from distressed poor communities, Joe and Chesney-Lind (1995) argue that "the gang assists young women and men in coping with their lives in chaotic, violent and economically marginalized communities" (p. 411) (see also Fleisher and Krienert 2004; Moore 1991). Moreover, because these neighborhoods are often dangerous, gangs may assist young women by providing opportunities to learn street and fighting skills (Fishman 1995) and by offering protection and retaliation against victimization in high-crime communities (Miller 2001).

In addition to structural conditions such as racial and economic segregation and community isolation, neighborhood exposure to gangs increases the likelihood that young women will join. For example, Miller's (2001) comparison of gang and nongang girls from the same communities found that one factor distinguishing young women who joined gangs from those who did not was the extent of gang activities in their neighborhoods. Gang members were significantly more likely to report that there was a lot of gang activity in their neighborhoods and that there were other gang members living on their street. Thus, coupled with other risk factors, living in neighborhoods with gangs in close proximity increases the likelihood that girls will join gangs. These findings suggest the importance of developing a better understanding of the role of a social network in shaping both girls' decisions to join gangs and the consequences of gang involvement for young women (Fleisher and Krienert 2004).

Impoverished and dangerous neighborhood conditions only partly explain why girls join gangs. Research shows that fewer than one-quarter of youths living in high-risk neighborhoods claim gang membership (Bjerregaard and Smith 1993; Winfree et al. 1992), and researchers have not found differences in perceived limited opportunities between gang and nongang youths in these communities (Esbensen, Huizinga, and Weiher 1993). Another factor that has received quite a bit of attention is the family, which has long been considered crucial for understanding delinquency and gang behavior among girls.

Findings from survey research have been somewhat inconsistent with regard to the family. Esbensen and Deschenes (1998), in a multisite study of risk factors for delinquency and gang behavior, found that weak supervision and low parental involvement were significant risk factors, although they suggest that lack of maternal attachment was more predictive of gang membership for males than females. Bjerregaard and Smith (1993) measured both parental supervision and parental attachment within the family and found neither to be significantly related to gang membership for girls. However, Thornberry's (1997) analysis of later waves of the RYDS project found that low parental involvement was a significant risk factor for girls.

Qualitative studies, such as those reviewed in Chapter 9, are much more likely to find an association between serious family problems and girls' gang involvement. Joe and Chesney-Lind (1995) observed that the girls in their study had parents who worked long hours or who were un- or underemployed—circumstances they suggested affected girls' supervision and the quality of family relationships. Fleisher (1998) documented intergenerational patterns of abuse and neglect, exacerbated by poverty and abject neighborhood conditions. Likewise, Moore (1991) documented a myriad of family problems that contribute to the likelihood of gang involvement for young women: experiencing childhood abuse and neglect, witnessing wife abuse, having alcohol and drug addiction in the family, witnessing the arrest of family members, having a family member who is chronically ill, and experiencing a death in the family during childhood. Comparing males and females, Moore (1991) found that young women were especially likely to come from troubled families (see also Thornberry 1997).

Portillos's (1999) study of Chicana gang members suggests that girls also are drawn to gang involvement as a means of escaping oppressive patriarchal conditions in the home. Likewise, Miller's (2001) comparison of gang and nongang girls found that gang members were significantly more likely than girls who were not in gangs to come from homes with numerous problems, including physical violence between adults, childhood sexual and physical abuse, and drug use among adult family members. Most important, gang members were significantly more likely to describe experiencing multiple family problems.

In Miller's (2001) study, the ways in which family problems facilitated girls' gang involvement were varied but shared a common thread—young women began spending time away from home as a result of difficulties or dangers there and sought to meet their social and emotional needs elsewhere. Researchers suggest that "the gang can serve as a surrogate extended family for adolescents who do not see their own families as meeting their needs for belonging, nurturance, and acceptance" (Huff 1993, p. 6; see also Campbell 1990; Joe and Chesney-Lind 1995; cf. Decker and Van Winkle 1996; Hunt, Joe Laidler, and MacKenzie 2000). Gangs may offer a network of friends for girls whose parents are unable to provide stable family relations; moreover, girls' friendships with other gang members may provide a support system for coping with family problems, abuse, and other life problems (Fleisher and Krienert 2004; Joe and Chesney-Lind 1995). Regardless of whether gangs actually fulfill these roles in young women's lives,[2] it is clear that many girls join gangs believing these needs will be met.

Some girls who lack close relationships with their primary caregivers can turn to siblings or extended family members to maintain a sense of belonging and attachment. However, if these family members are involved in gangs, it is likely that the girls also will choose to join a gang. Moreover, even when relationships with parents or other adults are strong, having adolescent or young adult gang members in the family often heightens the appeal of gangs (Hunt, Joe Laidler, and MacKenzie 2000; Joe and Chesney-Lind 1995; Moore 1991). In fact, Miller (2001) found that the themes just reviewed—neighborhood exposure to gangs, family problems, and gang-involved family members—were overlapping in most gang girls' accounts, further distinguishing them from nongang girls in the sample.

While qualitative studies are most likely to find family problems and community conditions at the heart of girls' gang involvement, a number of studies based on surveys of juvenile populations note school-based problems (see Thornberry 1997 for an overview). Bjerregaard and Smith (1993) found that low expectations for completing school were a significant predictor of gang membership for young women. Likewise, Bowker and Klein (1983) reported that female gang members were less likely than nonmembers to intend to finish high school or go to college. More recently, Esbensen and Deschenes (1998) reported that school commitment and expectations are associated with gang involvement for girls, and Thornberry (1997) described negative attitudes toward school as a risk factor for girls.

Survey research also has examined individual characteristics and behaviors as risk factors for gang membership, as well as relationships with delinquent peers. Esbensen, Deschenes, and Winfree (1999) reported that gang girls were more socially isolated and had lower self-esteem than their male gang peers. Their findings also suggested that risk-seeking was a predictor of female, but not male, gang membership (Esbensen and Deschenes 1998). On the other hand, Bjerregaard and Smith (1993) did not find self-esteem predictive of gang membership for girls. With regard to values, activities, and exposure to antisocial peers and situations, Esbensen and Deschenes (1998) reported that commitment to negative peers was associated with gang membership for girls; Thornberry (1997) reported that delinquency, drug use, and positive values about drugs were risk factors for girls; and Bjerregaard and Smith (1993) reported that both delinquent peers and early onset of sexual activity were associated with gang membership for girls. As Maxson and Whitlock (2001) argued, these survey results suggest a "lack of stable, unique predictors" of gang membership for young women (p. 23). Combined, however, survey and qualitative research highlight many of the salient issues researchers are continuing to examine.

Gang Life, Delinquency, and Violence among Girls

One reason criminologists have studied gangs so extensively is that young people in gangs—male and female—are substantially more involved in delinquency than their nongang counterparts. Research comparing gang and nongang youths consistently has found that serious criminal involvement distinguishes gangs from other groups of youths (Battin et al. 1998; Esbensen and Huizinga 1993; Fagan 1990; Klein 1995; Thornberry 1997; Thornberry, Esbensen, and Van Kammen 1993). This pattern holds for female gang members as well as their male counterparts (Bjerregaard and Smith 1993; Deschenes and Esbensen 1999a, 1999b; Esbensen and Winfree 1998; Miller 2001). The enhancement effect of gang membership is most noticeable for serious delinquency and marijuana use (Thornberry, Esbensen, and Van Kammen 1993). Bjerregaard and Smith (1993) summarized, "our study suggests that for females, gangs are consistently associated with a greater prevalence and with higher rates of delinquency and substance abuse. Furthermore, the results suggest that for both sexes, gang membership has an approximately equal impact on a variety of measures of delinquent behavior" (p. 346).

Perhaps most significant is evidence that female gang members are more delinquent than their female nongang counterparts, but also more so than their male nongang counterparts. Fagan (1990) (see also Esbensen and Winfree 1998) reported that "prevalence rates for female gang members exceeded the rates for non-gang males" for all the categories of delinquency he measured:

More than 40% of the female gang members were classified in the least serious category, a substantial difference from their male counterparts. Among female gang members, there was a bimodal distribution, with nearly as many multiple index offenders as petty delinquents. Evidently, female gang members avoid more serious delinquent involvement than their male counterparts. Yet their extensive involvement in serious delinquent behaviors well exceeds that of non-gang males or females. (p. 201)

There is also evidence of gender differences within gangs with regard to criminal involvement. Fagan (1990) reported greater gender differences in delinquency between gang members than between nongang youth. Male gang members were significantly more involved in the most serious forms of delinquency, while for alcohol use, drug sales, extortion, and property damage, gender differences were not significant. Specifically, he reported a bimodal distribution among young women in gangs: Approximately 40 percent of the gang girls in his study were only involved in petty delinquency, while one-third were involved in multiple index offending, compared with 15 percent and 56 percent, respectively, for young men (Miller 2001).

Moreover, evidence from a number of studies suggests that gun use is much more prevalent among male than female gang members (Decker, Pennell, and Caldwell 1996; Fleisher 1998; Hagedorn and Devitt 1999; Miller and Brunson 2000; Miller and Decker 2001). For example, Miller and Decker (2001) drew from police data in St. Louis to examine young women's roles in gang homicides in the city. During the peak years of gang homicide in the city (1990 to 1996) not one of the 229 gang homicides was committed by a female gang member. Only nineteen of these incidents involved a female victim, most often when the perpetrator opened fire on a group. In contrast, the majority of male victims were specifically targeted. Thus, while lethal violence is a serious problem for gang members, it is primarily a male-on-male activity.

Several explanations have been offered for these gender differences. In keeping with a large body of literature showing that gender stratification is a key organizational element of delinquent and criminal street networks (Maher 1997; Miller 1998), there is evidence of the "structural exclusion of young women from male delinquent activities" within mixed-gender gangs (Bowker, Gross, and Klein 1980, p. 516; Miller 2001; Miller and Brunson 2000). Bowker, Gross, and Klein's (1980) male respondents suggested that not only were girls excluded from the planning of delinquent acts, but when girls inadvertently showed up at the location of a planned incident, it was frequently postponed or terminated. Likewise, the majority of young women in Miller's (2001) study did not participate routinely in the most serious forms of gang crime, such as gun use, drive-by shootings, and (to a lesser extent) drug sales. This was, in part, a result of exclusionary practices by male gang members, although in addition, many young women purposively chose not to be involved in what they considered dangerous or morally troubling activities (Miller 2001).

Other researchers suggest that gender differences in norms supportive of violence and delinquency account for differences in gang girls' and gang boys' delinquency. Joe and Chesney-Lind (1995) (see also Campbell 1993) suggested that participation in violence is a stronger normative feature of male gang involvement than it is for young women in gangs. They argued that for girls, "violence (gang and otherwise) is not celebrated and normative; it is instead more directly a consequence of and a response to the abuse, both physical and sexual, that characterizes their lives at home" (Joe and Chesney-Lind 1995, p. 428). Other research has found that even when young women describe violence as a normative activity for girls, it is rarely at extreme levels such as gun use or homicide (Hagedorn and Devitt 1999; Miller 2001).

There is growing evidence that part of the answer to these competing explanations for between-gender differences and within-gender variations in gang delinquency and violence can be found by examining the gender organization and composition of gangs (Joe Laidler and Hunt 1997; Miller and Brunson 2000; Peterson, Miller, and Esbensen 2001). Ethnic differences also may account for variations. Moore and Hagedorn (1996) suggested that Latina gang members are more bound by "traditional" community patriarchal norms than African American gang girls (Portillos 1999). Likewise, girls in Joe and Chesney-Lind's (1995) study were from Samoan and Filipino communities, which have strong patriarchal norms for girls.

Miller (2001) did not find strong supportive relationships among most gang girls in her study; instead, many girls identified with masculine status norms in the gang and desired acceptance as "one of the guys." This finding contradicts other research on girls in gangs (Campbell 1984; Joe and Chesney-Lind 1995; Lauderback, Hansen, and Waldorf 1992; Miranda 2003) and is likely the result of variations in gang structures across these studies. Kanter (1977) noted that often conclusions drawn about differences between males and females, and attributed to gender roles or cultural differences between women and men, are in fact more appropriately attributable to situational or structural factors such as the gender composition of groups. The vast majority of girls in Miller's (2001) study were in mixed-gender gangs that were numerically male-dominated. In contrast, the handful of girls in female-only gangs or gangs with a substantial representation of female members were more likely to emphasize the social and relational aspects of their gangs, particularly their friendships with other girls.

In fact, research suggests that differences in girls' levels of participation in violence, and the normative salience of violence for girls, might be influenced by the gender organization of their gangs. Fleisher and Krienert (2004) suggested that having a sizable proportion of males in their social networks increases young women's participation in delinquency and violence (see also Miller and Brunson 2000). Peterson, Miller, and Esbensen's (2001) analysis of G.R.E.A.T. data classified youths' gangs according to four types of gender composition: all male, majority male but with female membership, gender balanced, and majority or all female. Comparing youths' descriptions of their gangs' activities, as well as individual delinquency rates for males and females across these groups, Peterson, Miller, and Esbensen's (2001) research offers support for the importance of gender composition in shaping both the nature of gang activities and individual gang members' delinquency. Based on member characterizations of their gangs, majority/all-female gangs were the least delinquent groups, followed by all-male gangs. Both gender-balanced and majority-male gangs were similar with regard to the gangs' involvement in delinquent activities. These differences suggest that delinquency, particularly of a serious nature, is a less normative feature of primarily female gangs than of other gangs.

On the other hand, Peterson, Miller, and Esbensen's (2001) findings are not fully supportive of the notion of "gender differences" in normative acceptance of violence and delinquency.[3] Instead, they found significant within-gender differences in rates of delinquency for both girls and boys across gang types (Peterson, Miller, and Esbensen 2001). For example, they found that girls in majority/all-female gangs had the lowest rates of delinquency, but that girls in majority-male gangs reported higher rates of delinquency than boys in all-male gangs. Thus, girls' (and boys') gang-related delinquency appears to be strongly associated with the gender organization of their groups.

Other research offers additional support for the importance of examining the types of gangs girls are involved in. Lauderback, Hansen, and Waldorf (1992) provided one of the few thorough descriptions of an autonomous female gang (Venkatesh 1998), the Potrero Hill Posse (PHP), a group that was heavily involved in drug sales in San Francisco. The authors suggested that PHP actually came about because these young women were dissatisfied with a "less than equitable . . . distribution of the labor and wealth" that had been part and parcel of their previous involvement selling drugs with males (Lauderback, Hansen, and Waldorf 1992, p. 62). Moreover, this was a gang characterized by close, familial-like relationships between its female members. Joe Laidler and Hunt (1997) extended Lauderback, Hansen, and Waldorf's (1992) analysis of PHP, comparing the social contexts of violence for young women in PHP with the social contexts facilitating violence among female gang members in other gangs in San Francisco. While members of PHP were African American, the vast majority of other young female gang members were Latina (with a small number of Samoans) and were in female groups affiliated with male gangs.

Joe Laidler and Hunt (1997; see also Hunt and Joe Laidler 2001) found important differences in young women's exposure to violence across gang types and reported that girls in "auxiliary" gangs were exposed to a greater variety of violence-prone situations, many of which were tied to their associations with young men. The young women in PHP described violence occurring in three types of situations: violence associated with the drug trade, fights with girls in other gangs, and intimate partner violence at the hands of their male partners. In contrast, young women in auxiliary gangs were subject to more violence-prone situations: violence in the context of gang initiations, conflicts with rival gang members, conflicts among "homegirls" in the same gang, and intimate partner violence at the hands of boyfriends. These findings offer further evidence that dynamics resulting from the gendered social organization of gangs shape young women's exposure to and participation in violence.

Although additional research is needed on the role of ethnicity in shaping girls' gang experiences, there appears to be a relationship between the ethnic composition of gangs and their gender organization, as well as young women's experiences in gangs (Moore and Hagedorn 1996). Contemporary research on African American gang girls has not found evidence of a strongly sexualized component of their gang activities (Miller 2001). However, Portillos (1999) reported that Chicana gang girls' sexuality was often used to set up rival gang males. Portillos (1999) described Chicana gang girls constructing an oppositional femininity that is clearly differentiated from (and subordinate to) male gang members' gang masculinity. Likewise, Hunt and Joe Laidler's research (2001; Hunt, Joe Laidler, and Evans 2002; Hunt, Joe Laidler, and MacKenzie 2005; Joe Laidler and Hunt 2001; Schalet, Hunt, and Joe Laidler 2003), which includes sizable numbers of African Americans and Latinas, has consistently found variations across race/ethnicity in young women's experiences within gangs and found that these variations are tied to the gender composition and organization of these groups.

Thus, gender plays a complicated role in girls' gang participation and gang delinquency. Gender intersects with ethnicity and culture and is a structural determinant of girls' experiences rather than simply a result of individual differences between young women and young men. For some girls, and in some contexts, delinquency is part of the allure of gang life. However, evidence suggests that some girls are ambivalent about criminal involvement, even though they report finding it fun or exciting at times. On one hand, delinquency brings gang girls status and recognition within the group, as well as economic remuneration; on the other hand, it can get the girls into trouble with the law or put them at greater risk for being victimized by rival gang members or others on the streets. But for girls in particular, many aspects of gang involvement, including delinquency, go against dominant notions of appropriate femininity. This shapes girls' experiences within and outside of their gangs, often locking them into what Swart (1991) described as a series of double binds.

Consequences of Gang Involvement for Girls

Research examining the consequences of gang involvement for girls has focused on two issues: First, what are the consequences of gang involvement for girls while they are active in gangs? Second, what evidence do we have about the long-term consequences of gang involvement for young women? Although young people often turn to gangs as a means of meeting a variety of needs within their lives, frequently their gang affiliation does more harm than good, increasing their likelihood of victimization and decreasing their opportunities and life chances.

Girls' gang participation can be viewed as transgressing social norms concerning appropriate feminine behavior; thus, a number of scholars have discussed gang girls as constructing an "oppositional" or "bad girl" femininity (Hagedorn and Devitt 1999; Messerschmidt 1995; Portillos 1999). However, research has consistently shown that youth gangs—with the exception of autonomous female gangs—are male-dominated in structure, status hierarchies, and activities, even as young women are able to carve meaningful niches for themselves (Campbell 1984; Fleisher 1998; Hagedorn 1998; Joe Laidler and Hunt 1997; Miller 2001; Moore 1991). Even young women in all-female gangs must operate within male-dominated street networks (Lauderback, Hansen, and Waldorf 1992; Taylor 1993). As a consequence, during the course of their gang involvement, girls face a number of risks and disadvantages associated with gender inequality. Moreover, there is some evidence of long-term detrimental consequences for gang-involved young women (Moore 1991; Moore and Hagedorn 1996).

Research has shown that girls in gangs face social sanctions for not behaving in "gender-appropriate" ways. Swart (1991) suggested that girls' experiences are complicated by the contradictions they face as they balance deviant and gender norm expectations. On the one hand, "the female gang member's behavior must be 'deviant' to those outside of the gang in order to ensure her place within the gang itself" (Swart 1991, p. 45). On the other hand, if a girl's behavior is too deviant, she risks the danger of offending other gang members by violating norms about appropriate female conduct in matters of sexual activity, alcohol and drug use, violence, and motherhood (Hunt, Joe Laidler, and Evans 2000; Hunt, Joe Laidler, and MacKenzie 2002; Joe Laidler and Hunt 2001; Miller 2001; Schalet, Hunt, and Joe Laidler 2003).

Despite these gender-based tensions, a "social injury" approach is incomplete and complicated by evidence suggesting that young women's gang involvement provides a means of overcoming limitations placed on them by narrow social definitions of femininity, which can further reduce their options in an environment where they are already quite restricted (Curry 1998; Hunt and Joe Laidler 2001; Miller 2001). For example, Campbell (1987) found that "gang girls see themselves as different from their [female] peers. Their association with the gang is a public proclamation of their rejection of the lifestyle which the community expects from them" (pp. 463–464). Likewise, Taylor's (1993) study of female gang members in Detroit found young women highly critical of the entrenched misogyny on the streets and the difficulties females often face interacting in these environments.

Regardless of girls' awareness of gender inequality, it remains an inescapable element of their experiences within gangs and brings with it particular consequences. For instance, there is a clear sexual double standard in operation within gangs (Campbell 1990; Fleisher 1998; Miller 2001; Portillos 1999; Swart 1991). Moore (1991) suggested that some young men viewed young women as sexual objects, "a piece of ass," or "possessions" (pp. 52–53). In addition, gang girls' dating options were narrowed, because gang participation was stigmatizing for girls, making them less attractive to boys outside the gang. On the other hand, male gang members frequently had girlfriends outside the gang who were "square."

These "respectable" girls were looked to by the boys as their future (Moore 1991, pp. 74–76; see also Fishman 1995).

Moreover, research suggests that rather than challenging this sexual double standard, young women often reinforce it in their interactions with one another. Several studies revealed that gang girls create hierarchies among themselves, sanctioning other girls, both for being too "square" and for being too promiscuous. Schalet, Hunt, and Joe Laidler (2003) emphasized the importance young women place not just on maintaining a "respectable" sexual reputation (and policing the sexual behavior of other girls), but also in establishing their independence, including independence from men. Despite their emphasis on the importance of being independent, by sanctioning those they perceive as too sexually active, young women routinely reinforce the sexual double standard. Girls have not been found to gain status among their peers for sexual promiscuity (Campbell 1990; Miller 2001; Swart 1991). Rather, they are expected to engage in serial monogamy. On the whole, the sexual double standard disadvantages young women in their relationships with young men, but also interferes with the strength of their own friendship groups (Campbell 1987).

Attention to the association between gang membership and delinquency has overlooked an equally important relationship: that between gang membership and victimization. For example, Miller (2001) found that gang girls were significantly more likely than nongang girls to have been sexually assaulted, threatened with a weapon, or stabbed, and to have witnessed stabbings, shootings, drive-by shootings, or homicides. However, gender inequality in gangs, and young men's greater participation in serious gang crime, suggests that victimization risks within gangs are shaped by gender, sometimes to girls' advantage. Because they are less likely than their male counterparts to engage in serious gang crime, gang girls face less victimization risk at the hands of rival gang males. This is bolstered to the extent that rules exist against male gang members' targeting rival females (Joe Laidler and Hunt 1997; Miller 2001). Girls' lesser risks are most notable for lethal violence, particularly because young women themselves rarely engage in gun use (Hagedorn and Devitt 1999; Miller 2001; Miller and Decker 2001).

However, because leadership and status hierarchies in mixed-gender gangs are typically male-dominated, and because girls are less likely to engage in those activities that confer status within the gang, they are often viewed as lesser members within their gangs. This devaluation of young women can lead to girls' mistreatment and victimization, especially by members of their own gang, because they are not seen as deserving of the same respect as male members (Hunt and Joe Laidler 2001; Joe Laidler and Hunt 1997; Miller 2001). These problems are further exacerbated by the sexual double standard described earlier, as well as by high rates of intimate partner violence among gang youths as documented by Hunt and Joe Laidler (2001) (see also Joe Laidler and Hunt 1997; Fleisher 1998). One particularly troubling issue for some gang girls is the use of sexual initiations for entrée into the gang. Both Miller (2001) and Portillos (1999) uncovered the use of this practice—having sexual relations with multiple male gang members—although in neither instance was it found to be the primary initiation pattern for girls. Nonetheless, when a sexual initiation occurs, girls are highly stigmatized and disrespected by other gang members, both male and female. They are viewed as promiscuous and sexually available, thus increasing their subsequent mistreatment. In addition, they are viewed as taking the "easy" way in and are not seen as valuable members of the gang (Miller 2001; Portillos 1999). Miller (2001) found that the stigma could create a sexual devaluation that all girls in the gang had to contend with. In addition, Cepeda and Valdez (2003) suggested that young women who associate with gangs but do not join them also face risks for exploitative sexual practices at the hands of male gang members.

Nonetheless, there appears to be tremendous variation in girls' experiences within gangs. Among the girls in Miller's (2001) study, some were able to carve a niche for themselves that put them, if not exactly in the same standing as young men, at least on par in terms of much of their treatment. Other young women were severely mistreated, and there was a range of experiences in between. Ironically, those young women most respected within the gang were more likely to face gang-related victimization at the hands of rivals. Those young women defined as "weak" because of their lack of participation in gang-related fighting and delinquency were more likely to face abuses at the hands of their gang peers (Miller 2001).

Thus, gang involvement has serious consequences for girls while they are in their gangs. What about after they leave? As noted earlier, research has consistently shown that young women's gang involvement is typically of shorter duration than young men's involvement, and tends to remain an adolescent phenomenon. Several studies suggest that pregnancy and motherhood often facilitate young women's exit from gangs or at least significantly curtail their participation in gang activities (Fleisher and Krienert 2004; Hunt, Joe Laidler, and MacKenzie 2005; Miller 2001). However, research has not examined specifically whether gang-involved young women are more likely to become adolescent mothers than their nongang peers.

Few studies offer evidence of the long-term consequences of gang involvement for girls (Miller 2001; Moore and Hagedorn 1996). Available evidence suggests that young women in gangs are at greater risk than others for a number of problems into and during their adult lives. Whereas many opportunities for legitimate success are gravely limited for young women living in impoverished communities, the negative consequences associated with gang membership can prove crippling. Moore's (1991) research on Chicano and Chicana gang members in Los Angeles found that ex–gang members could be divided into three categories: *tecatos, cholos,* and *squares.* Moore (1991) reported that approximately one-quarter of the males in her study and "a much smaller proportion of the female sample" (p. 125) were *tecatos*—heroin addicts involved in street life; about one-third of the men but more of the women were *cholos*—persisting in gang and criminal involvement into adulthood. Women and men in this category typically had not held down regular jobs and had unstable marriage patterns, often characterized by early marriage and childbearing, followed by early divorce (Moore

1991). Finally, she reported that while around 40 percent of males went on to lead conventional lives (i.e., become "squares"), fewer women did so[4] (Moore 1991).

While Moore's Los Angeles research was about individuals who had been in gangs in the 1950s and 1970s, her more recent work (Moore and Hagedorn 1996) compared these gang members with contemporary African American and Latina gang members in Milwaukee, Wisconsin. In this study, Moore and Hagedorn (1996, p. 209) reported that substantially fewer female gang members continued their gang involvement into adulthood, concluding that "for women—but not for men—the gang was almost completely an adolescent experience." However, Latinas were more likely to be involved in drug sales and use into adulthood compared with African American women. The authors concluded:

> For Latinas in both cities, gang membership tended to have a significant influence on their later lives, but for African American women in Milwaukee, the gang tended to be an episode. There is much less sense in Milwaukee that gang girls of any ethnicity were as heavily labeled in their communities as were Chicana gang girls in Los Angeles. (Moore and Hagedorn 1996, p. 210)

It seems reasonable to suggest that the earlier a girl exits the gang, the greater her chances for a better life. As noted, some evidence suggests that childbearing and the childcare responsibilities that result often facilitate young women's maturation out of gangs (Miller 2001; Moore and Hagedorn 1996). However, although having children may expedite girls' exit from gangs, doing so does not necessarily increase their chances for successful lives. This consequence is partly because stable marriages and jobs are less available in the current socioeconomic climate in urban communities in the United States than in the past. Communities where many gangs are located have dwindling numbers of males in the marriage pool; moreover, skyrocketing rates of incarceration and lethal violence have greatly contributed to this shortage (Moore and Hagedorn 1996; Wilson 1996). Considering the high unemployment rates in most gang neighborhoods, many young men have few conventional opportunities and are increasingly likely to continue their gang and criminal involvement into adulthood (Klein 1995). The bleak futures that await the men in their communities often mean marriage is less desirable among gang-involved women (Moore and Hagedorn 1996). The attacks on many social programs have also negatively affected women's lives after gang membership. Moore and Hagedorn (1996) observed:

> Ironically, the most important influence on gang women's future may be the dismantling of the nation's welfare system in the 1990s. This system has supported women with children who want to stay out of the drug marketing system and in addition has provided a significant amount of cash to their communities. Its disappearance will deepen poverty and make the fate of gang women ever more problematic. (p. 217)

These issues are of vital importance for gang-involved young women and represent an area strongly in need of further research.

Conclusions

This chapter has addressed a number of issues concerning young women's involvement in gangs—the extent of their gang involvement; their reasons for becoming involved; and their experiences in gangs, including their participation in delinquency and exposure to violence. Young women join gangs in response to a myriad of problems in their lives; however, gang involvement only exacerbates rather than improves these problems. Gang involvement increases the likelihood that young women will engage in delinquency and exposes them to risks of victimization, both at the hands of rival gangs and of gang peers. Although young women are not as involved in the most serious forms of gang violence as young men and although gangs are less likely to be life threatening for their female than their male members, gang involvement still often narrows young women's life options (Moore 1991).

There are four primary areas in which our understanding of young women's gang involvement can be strengthened: (a) research on organizational structure, social networks, and peer effects; (b) research on the role of race/ethnicity in shaping young women's risks for gang involvement and their experiences within gangs; (c) systematic attention to the long-term consequences for young women that result from gang involvement; and (d) research that contributes to the development and evaluation of programmatic interventions for young women in gangs. Attention to the first issue has provided a promising area for future research because of its explanatory utility in recent studies. Research on race/ethnicity and the life consequences of gang involvement has received considerably less attention, although several studies have suggested their importance as topics that we need to better understand. Finally, as Moore and Hagedorn (2001) pointed out, young women in gangs have received little attention when it comes to developing and evaluating prevention and intervention programs.

Nonetheless, a number of suggestions for policy and practice emerge from this overview. With regard to prevention, the research highlights several notable issues. Girls begin spending time with gang members quite early and often join gangs in their early teens. Thus, prevention efforts must begin quite early. In addition, a series of risk factors appear to increase the likelihood that gangs become an alluring option. These risk factors include living in neighborhoods where gangs are in close proximity, having multiple problems in the family including violence and drug abuse, and having siblings or multiple family members in gangs. Most significantly, it appears to be the convergence of such risk factors that particularly heighten girls' risk for gang involvement. Prevention efforts should target girls exposed to these problems. However, as Maxson and Whitlock (2001) suggested, etiological research on female gang involvement has not identified clear risk factors for girls above and beyond those identified for girls' risks for delinquency.

Their suggestions regarding gender-specific prevention approaches appear prudent given the state of our knowledge about these issues.

Findings presented in this chapter also have implications for gang intervention with young women. Most notable is the need to recognize variations in young women's experiences and activities within and across gangs. Research suggests that, while in some instances gender-specific interventions may be useful (particularly in dealing with sexual assault and abuse), some features of gang programming for young men are likely to be important for girls as well. For example, while girls are rarely as involved in serious violence as boys, group processes, conflicts, and rivalries provoke girls' participation in confrontations with rival gang members in ways similar to that of young men. Thus, interventions for girls need to take such issues into account (Klein 1995).

Intervention strategies also should be tailored to meet the diverse needs of female gang members, with sensitivity to ethnic and cultural differences. In addition, given variations across gangs, specific knowledge about girls' gangs can provide suggestions for effective intervention approaches. Specifically, attention to the gender composition and organization of girls' groups is likely to provide important information about girls' victimization risks and their exposure to violence-prone situations (Hunt and Joe Laidler 2001; Joe Laidler and Hunt 1997). In particular, the level and nature of young women's participation in gang crime may be an indicator of the particular types of victimization risks these young women face: Girls who are heavily involved in street crime are at heightened risk for physical violence such as assaults and stabbings; other young women are at greater risk for ongoing physical and sexual mistreatment by male gang members (Miller 2001; Miller and Brunson 2000). Most important is the need to recognize that young women in gangs are not a monolithic group and should be approached accordingly.

Unfortunately, responses to gangs and gang members are often primarily punitive in nature, disregarding the social, economic, and personal contexts that cause gang participation. This punitive orientation toward gang members means that gang-involved youths are not seen as in need of assistance and protection, and this—coupled with the problems they face in their daily lives—has further detrimental effects (Fleisher 1998; Moore and Hagedorn 1996). Moreover, programming and policies targeted specifically to the needs of female gang members have been scant (Curry 1999). When solicited, however, female gang members themselves have been articulate voices in public policy debates (Miranda 2003). Given the findings detailed in this chapter, the best course of action with regard to young women's gang involvement should involve policies that consider the social, economic, and personal contexts that influence gang participation, gang crime, and young women's victimization within gangs. Initiatives that actually consider the best interest of youths are needed in order to rationally respond to gangs and young women's gang involvement.

11

Girls in the Juvenile Justice System

BARRY C. FELD

Introduction

The Progressive reformers who created the juvenile court in 1899 envisioned a specialized agency to separate children from adult offenders and to treat them rather than to punish them for their crimes (Platt 1977; Rothman 1980; Ryerson 1978). Initially, juvenile courts' delinquency jurisdiction encompassed only youths charged with crimes, but within a few years reformers added status offenses—noncriminal misconduct prohibited for juveniles that would not be criminal if engaged in by adults, such as "incorrigibility," runaway, and "indecent and lascivious conduct" (Feld 2004)—to its jurisdiction. Historically, juvenile courts responded to boys primarily for criminal misconduct and to girls mainly for status offenses (Schlossman 1977; Sutton 1988). The status jurisdiction reflected Progressives' cultural construction of childhood dependency as well as their sexual sensibilities. From the beginning, juvenile courts focused on controlling female sexuality (Schlossman and Wallach 1978; Sutton 1988; Tanenhause 2004). Judges detained and incarcerated females for minor and status offenses at higher rates than they did boys (Platt 1977; Schlossman 1977). A century later, the issues posed by status offenders remain unanswered. How should the juvenile justice system respond to youths who disobey parents, truant from school, run away from home, or engage in misconduct that places them in dangerous and vulnerable circumstances (Maxson and Klein 1997)?

The Supreme Court's *In re Gault* (387 U.S. 1, 1967) decision precipitated a critical reexamination of juvenile court procedure, jurisdiction, and practice

(Feld 1999). *Gault* granted procedural rights to delinquents—youths charged with criminal behavior whom the state could confine—but had no immediate applicability to status offenders. Juvenile courts' greater formality provided some impetus to divert status offenders at the jurisdictional "soft" end, to transfer serious offenders for adult criminal prosecution at the "hard" end, and to punish more severely the delinquents who remained within the "tougher" juvenile justice system (Feld 1999).

Although the courts' status jurisdiction potentially encompassed nearly all misbehaving youths, by the early 1970s critics objected that it allowed judges to incarcerate noncriminal offenders with delinquents in detention facilities and institutions, that it stigmatized them with delinquency labels, discriminated against females, and provided few beneficial services. Judicial intervention at the behest of parents provided some access to state power to control children, but exacerbated intrafamilial conflicts and enabled some caretakers to avoid their responsibilities. Status offenses overloaded juvenile courts with domestic disputes, diverted scarce resources from more serious offenders, and raised troublesome legal issues about vague jurisdictional definitions and procedural deficiencies. In the early 1970s, states charged about three-quarters of the girls with whom juvenile courts dealt as status offenders (National Council on Crime and Delinquency 1975; Schwartz, Steketee, and Schneider 1990).

Supreme Court decisions, state law reforms, and the federal Juvenile Justice and Delinquency Prevention Act of 1974 (JJDPA) provided the impetus for three types of reforms of jurisdiction over status offenders—diversion, deinstitutionalization, and decriminalization. Increased procedural formality and administrative costs provided impetus to divert many troublesome juveniles' cases and to handle them informally and outside of the juvenile justice system. Federal prohibitions on confining noncriminal status offenders with delinquents in secure detention facilities and training schools spurred efforts to deinstitutionalize status offenders and greatly benefited girls. States redefined status offenses to remove them from the generic definition of delinquency, relabeled them as Persons or Children in Need of Supervision (PINS or CHINS) or other euphemism, or shifted them into juvenile courts' dependency or neglect jurisdiction.

The JJDPA limited judges' authority to confine status offenders in secure public facilities. However, it did not adequately fund resources for community-based alternatives or provide effective interventions to address the inevitable conflicts that arise between children and their parents, schools, and other agencies (Maxson and Klein 1997). After three decades of juvenile justice reforms, states' failure to create and fund services on a voluntary basis—family counseling, shelter care, crisis centers, work programs, and the like—provides a continuing impetus to intervene coercively because the social problems posed by status offenders remain unaddressed. The lack of alternatives creates systemic pressures to circumvent the federal deinstitutionalization mandate, "where there's a will, there's a way to detain legally undetainable youth" (Maxson and Klein 1997, p. 20).

Status offenders are not a discrete or unique category of miscreants, but rather share many of the characteristics and behavioral versatility of delinquent offenders and lend themselves to reclassification as delinquents. Juvenile courts have adopted three subversion strategies to evade the obligation to deinstitutionalize status offenders. One strategy is to relabel status offenders involved in domestic disputes as delinquents by charging them with minor criminal violations, such as simple assault. A second is to impose conditions of probation that youths will fail to meet and then to incarcerate them for contempt of court. A third strategy is to transfer them into private mental health and chemical dependency facilities for treatment and confinement (Costello and Worthington 1981; Federle and Chesney-Lind 1992; Kempf-Leonard and Sample 2000).

Coinciding with federal deinstitutionalization policies, macrostructural economic and racial demographic changes during the 1970s and 1980s led to the emergence of an urban black underclass and increased the punitiveness of juvenile justice policies in ways that indirectly affect girls. In the late 1980s and early 1990s, the epidemic of crack cocaine, increased gun violence, and homicide committed by young black males spurred states to "get tough" and "crack down" on youth crime (Blumstein 1996; Feld 1999; Zimring 1998). Over the past two decades, legal changes transferred more juveniles to criminal courts for prosecution as adults and endorsed punishment as appropriate responses for those delinquents who remain in juvenile courts. Waiver of juvenile court jurisdiction involves the transfer of chronological juveniles to criminal court for prosecution as adults. Recent reforms have expanded categories of youths eligible for transfer, reduced the age of criminal responsibility, shifted discretion from judges to prosecutors, and reflected a broader cultural and jurisprudential shift from rehabilitative to retributive penal policies (Feld 2003; Garland 2001; Tonry 2004). Similar legal changes authorized juvenile court judges to punish delinquents more severely (Feld 1998; Torbet et al. 1996). Although the punitive legal changes primarily targeted and affected boys, especially black youths (Feld 1999), the shift in juvenile justice responses to youth violence adversely affected girls charged with assault, even though they were not the intended object (Chesney-Lind and Belknap 2004; Poulin 1996).

This chapter focuses on justice system responses to girls in light of contradictory policies to deinstitutionalize status offenders and to get tough with violent offenders. It assesses the offenses for which police arrest girls, how juvenile courts process them, what dispositions they receive, and what collateral consequences they experience as a result of legal intervention. It analyzes comparatively how juvenile courts process girls and boys charged with similar offenses. It examines how juvenile courts handle cases of white girls and those of other racial groups to assess disproportionate minority confinement. Finally, because of the "crackdown" on youth violence, it focuses on how juvenile courts handle girls' assaults as an indicator of their changing mission and an example of an adaptive strategy to relabel girls' misconduct to circumvent federal policies. The chapter argues that at least some of the perceived increase in girls' violence of the past decades is an artifact of justice system responses. The deinstitutionalization of status offenders provided impetus to relabel status offenders to allow coercive intervention. The crackdown on youth violence and the separate emphasis on combating domestic violence exacerbated the relabeling of status offenders by lowering the threshold for conduct defined as an assault, especially within the family context.

This review summarizes many studies conducted in different jurisdictions and at different times. Juvenile courts vary substantially from state to state and by geographic locale within states, and organizational diversity limits somewhat the generalizability of research findings (Feld 1991). The National Center for Juvenile Justice (NCJJ) and Office of Juvenile Justice and Delinquency Prevention (OJJDP) maintain a number of analytical data sets accessible on the Internet—the Statistical Briefing Book, Easy Access to Juvenile Court Statistics (EZAJCS) (Snyder, Puzzanchera, and Kang 2005), the Census of Juveniles in Residential Placements (Sickmund, Sladky, and Kang 2004), national population estimates derived from census data (Puzzanchera, Finnegan, and Kang 2005), and juvenile crime statistics derived from the FBI's Uniform Crime Reports (Federal Bureau of Investigation 2003). The NCJJ and OJJDP also provide analyses of numerous topics in juvenile justice administration (Snyder 2002, 2004; Snyder and Sickmund 1999). These resources provide a wealth of valuable data and the bases for these analyses.[1]

Girls in the Juvenile Justice System[2]

About 33.5 million juveniles are between ten and seventeen years of age, the age of juvenile court delinquency jurisdiction in most states (Puzzanchera, Finnegan, and Kang 2005). Slightly fewer than half (49 percent) of those age-eligible youths are girls. The juvenile population is 78 percent white, 17 percent black, 1 percent American Indian, and 4 percent Asian/Pacific Islanders (Puzzanchera, Finnegan, and Kang 2005). The rate at which police arrest and refer youths to juvenile court and the ways in which the justice system processes them vary by gender and by race. Police arrest and juvenile courts handle proportionally fewer females than their makeup of the population. By contrast, police arrest proportionally more black juveniles than they do white youths or those of other races, especially for Violent Crime Index offenses. Despite some real differences in rates of offending by race, the successive discretionary decisions made by juvenile justice officials produce cumulative racial disparities in the treatment of minority youths (McCord, Widom, and Crowell 2001).

Arrests of Girls

In 2003, police arrested an estimated 13.6 million offenders, and juveniles comprised about 16 percent of arrestees for all offenses, about 16 percent of those arrested for Violent Crime Index offenses, and about 29 percent of those arrested for Property Crime Index offenses (Federal Bureau of Investigation 2003, table 38). Girls comprised nearly one-third (29 percent) of juveniles arrested (378,895), about one-third (32 percent) of youths arrested for Property Crime Index offenses, and less than one-fifth (18 percent) of those arrested for Violent Crime

Index offenses (Federal Bureau of Investigation 2003). While serious and violent crimes capture media and public attention, police arrested three-quarters (75 percent) of all juveniles for nonindex and status offenses (Federal Bureau of Investigation 2003).

Police arrested only about 4 percent of juveniles for Violent Crime Index offenses, and they arrested about two-thirds (67 percent) of those youths for aggravated assaults (Federal Bureau of Investigation 2003). Girls comprised about one-quarter (24 percent) of all the juveniles arrested for aggravated assaults (Federal Bureau of Investigation 2003). By contrast, police arrested 11 percent of *all* juveniles for simple assaults (135,908), the largest number and proportion of arrests for any crimes other than larceny-theft and "all other offenses." Significantly, girls accounted for about one-third (32 percent) of juveniles arrested for simple assault, the largest female proportion of arrests for any violent crime. Girls made up large proportions of youths arrested for larceny-theft (40 percent), prostitution (71 percent), and runaways (59 percent).

Patterns and Changes in Boys' and Girl's Arrests

Changes in boys' and girls' arrests may reflect real differences in rates of offending, or they reflect gendered differences in the ways that police and courts respond to them (Girls Inc. 1996). Although girls comprise a smaller portion of juvenile arrestees than do boys, their arrest patterns have diverged over the past decade. This divergence distinguishes recent female delinquency from earlier decades in which males and females followed roughly similar patterns and in which female increases occurred primarily in minor property crimes rather than violent crimes (Steffensmeier 1993).

As Table 11.1 indicates, the percentage of arrests of female juveniles for various offenses either have increased more or decreased less than those of their male

TABLE 11.1 PERCENTAGE CHANGE IN MALE AND FEMALE JUVENILE ARRESTS, 1994–2003

	Female	Male
Total Crime	−3.0	−22.4
Violent Crime Index	−9.9	−36.1
Property Crime Index	−21.1	−43.7
Aggravated Assault	−1.9	−31.0
Simple Assault	35.9	1.2
Larceny-Theft	−18.6	−42.8
Vandalism	−10.9	−35.7
Drug Abuse	56.3	13.0
DUI	83.5	24.9
Liquor	25.6	−5.2
Curfew-Loitering	5.3	−3.1
Runaway	−40.2	−44.3

Source: FBI, *Uniform Crime Report* (2003), table 33.

counterparts. Between the peak of most juvenile criminality in 1994 and 2003, the overall totals of juveniles arrested have dropped about 18 percent, primarily because arrests of boys decreased by 22 percent, while those of girls decreased only 3 percent. Arrests of boys decreased more substantially than did those of female offenders for Violent Crime Index and for Property Crime Index offenses. Over this past decade, arrests of boys for Violent Crime Index offenses declined 36 percent while those of girls decreased only 10 percent. The decrease in Property Crime Index offenses was even more dramatic, as boys' arrests declined 44 percent, while girls' arrests decreased 21 percent. Boys' arrests for aggravated assaults decreased by nearly one-third (−31 percent), while girls' arrests remained almost unchanged (−2 percent). By contrast, girls' arrests for simple assaults increased by more than one-third (36 percent), while boys' arrests remained essentially flat (+1 percent). In the categories in which the number of arrests of juveniles of both genders increased over the past decade, the proportional increase for girls was larger than that for boys (e.g., simple assault, drugs, DUI, liquor offenses, and curfew violations).

Figure 11.1 shows the arrest rate per one hundred thousand juveniles aged ten to seventeen of boys and girls for all offenses between 1980 and 2003. Figures 11.2 and 11.3 display the arrest rates per one hundred thousand juveniles aged ten to seventeen of boys and girls for Violent Crime Index offenses and for Property Crime Index offenses over the same period. Figures 11.1, 11.2, and 11.3 reveal a similar pattern. Police arrested boys at substantially higher rates than

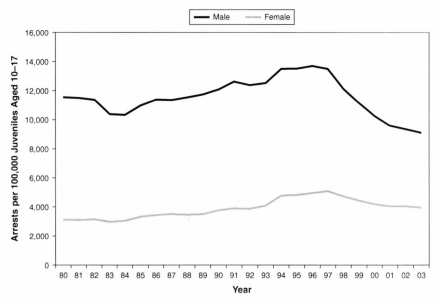

FIGURE 11.1   Male and female arrest rates, 1980–2003—total offenses. (*Source:* National Center for Juvenile Justice 2005.)

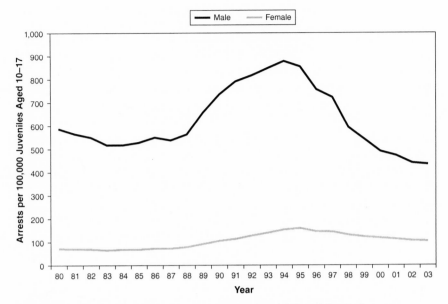

FIGURE 11.2 Male and female arrest rates, 1980–2003—Violent Crime Index. (*Source:* National Center for Juvenile Justice 2005.)

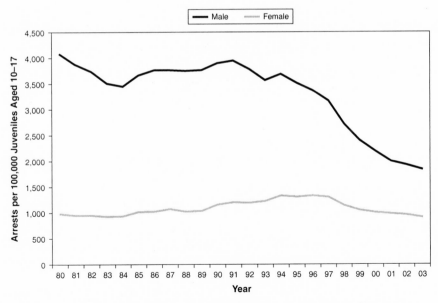

FIGURE 11.3 Male and female arrest rates, 1980–2003—Property Crime Index. (*Source:* National Center for Juvenile Justice 2005.)

they arrested girls. Arrest rates for both groups peaked in the mid-1990s, and then boys' rates exhibited a much sharper drop-off than girls' rates. The boys' arrest rates in 2003 were lower than they were in 1980 for total offenses, for Violent Crime Index offenses, and especially for Property Crime Index offenses. By contrast, the girls' arrest rates in all three categories were either higher or virtually unchanged. Female arrest rates for all crime increased from 3,104 per one hundred thousand in 1980 to 3,926.5 in 2003, a 27 percent increase. Girls' arrest rates for Violent Index Offenses rose from 70.4 to 103.1 per one hundred thousand over the same period, a 46 percent increase. Girls' arrest rates for Property Index offenses declined modestly from 975.7 to 903.6 per one hundred thousand, a 9 percent decrease, while boys' arrest rates plummeted precipitously from 4,081.9 to 1,833.8, a 123 percent decrease. Thus, the juvenile "crime drop" of the past decade primarily reflects changes in arrest rates of boys.

Aggravated assaults comprise the largest single component of the Violent Crime Index, and simple assaults constitute the largest component of nonindex violent arrests. Over the past two decades, clear changes have occurred in girls' arrests and between boys' and girls' patterns of arrests in these two categories. As Figure 11.4 indicates, boys' and girls' arrests for aggravated assault diverged conspicuously—the female arrest rate in 2003 was nearly double (96 percent) the arrest rate in 1980 (88.3 versus forty-five girls per one hundred thousand). Although police arrested males for aggravated assault at a rate five times higher than

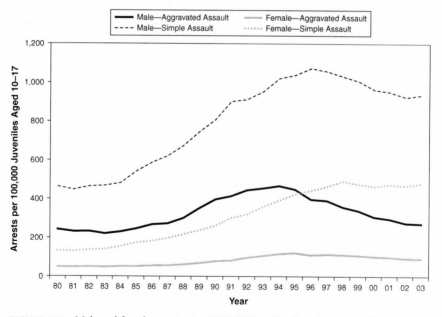

FIGURE 11.4 Male and female arrest rates, 1980–2003—simple and aggravated assaults. (*Source:* National Center for Juvenile Justice 2005.)

girls, boys' proportional increase (12.5 percent) was much more modest than girls' over the same period (269.5 versus 239.4 boys per one hundred thousand).

Police arrest juveniles for simple assaults more than three times as often as they do for aggravated assaults. Again, changes in arrest rates of females for simple assaults over the past two decades greatly outstripped those of their male counterparts. The arrest rate of girls for simple assault in 2003 was more than triple (3.5) the rate at which police arrested girls in 1980 (478.3 versus 129.7 per one hundred thousand). Although male arrests for simple assaults started from a higher base rate, it barely doubled (2.02) over the same period (934.4 versus 462.7 per one hundred thousand).

Figure 11.5 compares ratios of arrest rates of simple assault and aggravated assaults over two decades for boys and girls. In 1980, police arrested girls for simple assaults about three times (2.9) as often as they did for aggravated assaults. They arrested boys for simple assaults about twice (1.9) as often as they did for aggravated assaults. By 2003, police arrested girls more than five times (5.4) as often for simple assaults as for aggravated assaults. By contrast, the ratio of boys' arrests for simple to aggravated assaults *only* trebled (3.5). Police arrest boys more frequently for aggravated assaults because they more frequently use weapons and inflict more injury on their victims than girls do. However, boys' arrest rate for aggravated assaults declined nearly one-third (31 percent) over the past decade, which raised their ratio of simple to aggravated assaults. By contrast,

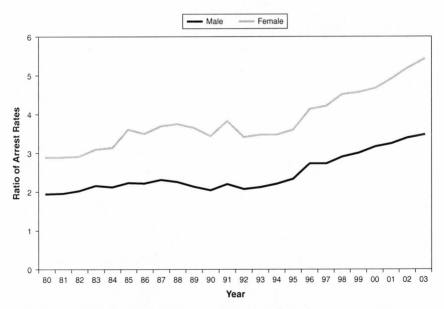

FIGURE 11.5 Ratio of male and female simple/aggravated assault rates, 1980–2003. (*Source:* National Center for Juvenile Justice 2005.)

girls' one-third (36 percent) increase in arrests for simple assaults over the same period raised their ratio even more so.

Despite increases in arrests, arrest rates, and simple/aggravated assault ratios, do they signify real changes in girls' violent behavior or rather a police reclassification of assault offenses? Chapter 3 of this volume strongly suggests the latter. Police discretion affects both arrest decisions and classification of behavior as simple or aggravated assaults, and some analysts attribute increased assault arrest rates of juveniles to "a greater police willingness to report and upwardly classify assault crimes and a greater willingness to arrest those who commit assaults" (Zimring 1998, p. 42). Criminologists have analyzed the changing nature of assaults over the past decades by comparing ratios of aggravated assaults to homicide (Zimring 1998) or of assaults to robbery (Snyder and Sickmund 2000; Zimring and Hawkins 1997). Because arrests for assaults increased *without* corresponding increases in arrests for homicides or for robbery, they attribute the rise to changes in law enforcement policies, such as responses to domestic violence, rather than to real increases in assaults *per se*.

The demarcation between status offenses and delinquency is as imprecise and malleable as the definitions of assault, and the heterogeneity and elasticity of "violent" behavior affects girls' likelihood of arrest (Steffensmeier et al. 2005). Girls' changing ratio of simple to aggravated assaults (Figure 11.5) suggests that many of their arrests for "violence" involve relatively trivial offenses. Police policies (e.g., "zero-tolerance," "quality of life," "broken windows," and mandatory domestic violence arrests) that lower the threshold to arrest for an assault or to aggravate it may create an artificial appearance of a crime wave when the underlying behavior remains more stable.

Heightened sensitivity to domestic violence combined with prohibitions on incarcerating status offenders may encourage police to arrest girls for trivial domestic disturbances. Charging them with simple assaults rather than with status offenses (e.g., incorrigibility or unruliness) enables families, police, and juvenile courts to relabel the same behavior as delinquency and thereby evade the prohibitions of the JJDPA (Chesney-Lind and Belknap 2004; Girls Inc. 1996; Mahoney and Fenster 1982; Schneider 1984).[3] Parents may attribute different meanings to similar behavior by their sons and daughters (Chesney-Lind 1988a), and these differences in expectations affect how the justice system responds to girls when they "act out" within the home (Krause and McShane 1994). Girls fight with family members or siblings more frequently than do boys, who fight more often with friends or strangers (Bloom et al. 2002a). Some research suggests that girls are three times as likely to assault a family member as are boys (Franke, Huynh-Hohnbaum, and Chung 2002). Parents who, in the past, charged their daughter as "incorrigible" or as a "person in need of supervision" now may request that police arrest her for domestic violence arising out of the same family scuffle (Russ 2004). Analysts attribute growth in girls' assault arrests "to the relabeling of girls' family conflicts as violent offenses, the changes in police practices regarding domestic violence and aggressive behavior, [and] the gender bias in the processing of misdemeanor cases ..." (American Bar Association and National Bar Association 2001, p. 3).

Policies of mandatory arrest for domestic violence, initially adopted to restrain abusive males from attacking their partners, provide parents with another tool with which to control their "unruly" daughters. Regardless of who actually initiates a violent domestic incident, police find it easier to identify the youth as the offender, because the parent takes care of other children in the home (Gaarder, Rodriguez, and Zatz 2004).[4] Analyses of girls' assault cases referred to juvenile court report that about half were "family centered" and involved conduct that parents and courts previously addressed as "incorrigibility" cases (Chesney-Lind and Pasko 2004). Police charge many girls with assault for a minor altercation with a parent who oftentimes initiated the conflict (Acoca 1999; Acoca and Dedel 1998). Probation officers describe most girls' assault cases as a fight with a parent at home or as between girls at school or elsewhere over a boy (Artz 1998b; Bond-Maupin, Maupin, and Leisenring 2002; Gaarder, Rodriguez, and Zatz 2004). "Zero-tolerance" policies at schools toward violence further increase the numbers of youths referred to juvenile courts for quarrels previously handled internally. Policies to reduce discretion and get tough with youth violence disproportionately affect minority females whom police arrest at rates higher than their white counterparts (Chesney-Lind 2002; McCluskey et al. 2004).

Figure 11.6 examines the offender–victim relationship of youths involved in violent offenses and further suggests a relabeling of domestic disputes. The National Incident-Based Reporting System (NIBRS) collects information about

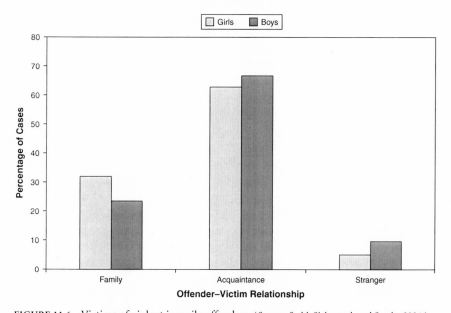

FIGURE 11.6   Victims of violent juvenile offenders. (*Source:* Stahl, Sickmund, and Snyder 2004.)

offenders, victims, and their relationships. Nearly one-third of girls (32 percent), as contrasted with less than one-quarter (24 percent) of boys, perpetrated violence against their family members. Although both boys and girls primarily assaulted acquaintances, boys did so more frequently than did girls and they were twice as likely as girls to assault strangers. Increase in girls' arrests for simple assault and their greater likelihood than boys to victimize family members supports an inference that some of these incidents involve a relabeling of "incorrigibility" as "domestic violence."

Other studies also find evidence of a relabeling of status offenders as delinquents in order to incarcerate them. A comparison of juvenile court petitions filed against girls before and after Pennsylvania repealed its status jurisdiction in the mid-1970s reported that the proportion of girls charged with assaults more than doubled (from 14 percent to 29 percent) (Curran 1984). Although the proportion of girls confined in training schools for status offenses declined from 71 percent in 1971 to 11 percent in 1987, the proportion confined for minor delinquencies rose dramatically during the same period (Schwartz, Steketee, and Schneider 1990). Moreover, states confine girls for less serious offenses than they do boys. In 1987, juvenile courts confined over half (56 percent) of girls for misdemeanor offenses, compared with only 43 percent of boys (Schwartz, Steketee, and Schneider 1990).

In contrast with assaults, runaways represent the prototypical juvenile status offense and the one that produces the largest gender disparity. In 2003, police arrested about 6 percent of all juveniles for runaways, and girls comprised more than half (59 percent) of those arrested (Federal Bureau of Investigation 2003). Figure 11.7 reports changes in male and female juvenile arrest rates for runaways between 1980 and 2003. Police arrest girls as runaways at substantially higher rates than they do boys; both genders have followed similar trajectories with significant increases in the mid-1990s, followed by a very sharp decline. As Table 11.1 reports and Figure 11.7 illustrates, between 1994 and 2003, arrests of boys for running away declined by 44 percent and arrests of girls declined by 40 percent. Girls' increase in arrests for simple assault coincides with restrictions on confining status offenders and the corresponding decline in arrests of boys and girls for running away. The next section examines how changes in juvenile courts' handling of status offenders have provided impetus for the justice system to develop alternative methods to control girls.

The Front End of the Juvenile Justice System: Jurisdiction, Deinstitutionalization, and Diversion

The 1974 federal JJDPA (42 U.S. C. § 223 (a)(12)) prohibited states from confining status offenders with delinquents in secure detention facilities and training schools and threatened to withhold federal funds if states failed to develop programs to remove them (Schwartz 1989b). The JJDPA provided impetus to deinstitutionalize status offenders (DSO) and to relocate them to community-based

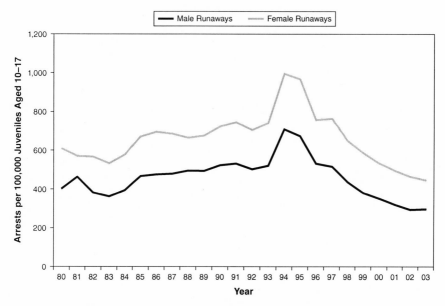

FIGURE 11.7   Male and female arrest rates, 1980–2003—runaways. (*Source:* National Center for Juvenile Justice 2005.)

facilities. A 1980 amendment to the JJDPA, adopted at the behest of the National Council of Juvenile and Family Court Judges, allowed states to continue to receive federal funds even if status offenders remained in institutions if states demonstrated "substantial compliance" with OJJDP guidelines, if OJJDP deemed noncompliance *de minimis,* or if juvenile court judges committed noncriminal youths to institutions for violating a "valid court order." The valid court order exception allows judges to "bootstrap" status offenders into delinquents and to incarcerate them by finding them in contempt of court—a misdemeanor—for violating a court-ordered condition of probation. The 1992 reauthorization of the JJDPA included a requirement that states provide "an analysis of gender-specific services for the prevention and treatment of juvenile delinquency . . . and a plan for providing needed gender-specific services for the prevention and treatment of juvenile delinquency." Most states used funds received under the 1992 "gender-specific" amendment to collect data on girls in the juvenile justice system, rather than to develop new programs (Bloom et al. 2002a; Community Research Associates 1998; Kempf-Leonard and Sample 2000; MacDonald and Chesney-Lind 2001).

The 1974 JJDPA initiative to remove status offenders from secure detention facilities and institutions produced dramatic decreases in confinement by the early 1980s, and girls disproportionately benefited (Chesney-Lind 1988b; Handler and Zatz 1982; Krisberg et al. 1986; Maxson and Klein 1997). By 1988, the number of status offenders detained declined 95 percent from the numbers detained prior to adoption of the Act (U.S. General Accounting Office 1991). The National Academy of Sciences evaluated the impact of the JJDPA mandate and concluded that "[t]he placement of adjudicated status offenders in secure public institutional facilities has been virtually eliminated. . . . There has been a substantial reduction in the use of detention for preadjudicated status offenders" (Handler and Zatz 1982, pp. 88–89).

While the JJDPA encouraged states to DSO, it could not compel them to appropriate funds or to develop community-based programs to meet their needs. Controlling status offenders remains a problem, even if the law bars confinement as a solution. As policy makers struggled for decades to find noncoercive options for status offenders, analysts warned that states could evade deinstitutionalization by relabeling or bootstrapping them as delinquents or by confining them in private facilities. A state may relabel a youth as a delinquent in order to incarcerate her by charging her with assault rather than incorrigibility (Handler and Zatz 1982). A juvenile court judge may bootstrap a youth to incarcerate her by finding her in criminal contempt of court for violating a valid court order, even if the underlying conduct was a status offense (e.g., absconding from a court-ordered community placement) (Costello 2003; Costello and Worthington 1981; Federle 1990; Schwartz 1989b). Judges detain and confine many youths charged with public order offenses or "technical violations" for violating court orders and this power remains a continuing source of gender bias (Bishop and Frazier 1992). The juvenile justice, child welfare, and mental health systems deal with children with many similar characteristics. Because of this overlap, a parent or court may place or transinstitutionalize a troublesome youth in a mental health or chemical dependency facility rather than in a delinquency institution (Weithorn 1988).

The original JJDPA encouraged states to remove status offenses from delinquency codes and to place them in other jurisdictional categories such as PINS or CHINS, or Children in Need of Protection and Services (CHIPS) (Rubin 1985; Sutton 1988). Some states repealed jurisdiction over generic "incorrigibility" or "stubbornness," but retained jurisdiction over age-specific misconduct such as running away, violating curfew, or consuming alcohol. Other states expanded their juvenile courts' dependency or neglect jurisdiction (Bishop and Frazier 1992; Sutton 1988). These changes make it difficult to obtain reliable data about how states handle former status offenders because they employ different labels, relegate them to other parts of the juvenile or family court systems, and deal with them informally on the periphery of the system (Steinhart 1996).

A few jurisdictions restricted judges' authority to intervene in the lives of status offenders. Maine repealed its status offense statute in 1977 and enacted an "interim care" law to provide temporary services for abandoned, runaway, or seriously endangered children (Me. Rev. Stat. Ann. Tit. 15 §§ 3103, 3501 [West 1980]). The legislative policy dealt with status offenders as normal adolescents who need housing, social welfare, and community tolerance rather than deterrence or treatment (Maxson and Klein 1997). In 1978, Washington only allowed police to hold runaway or endangered children in nonsecure custody for brief periods of time and restricted juvenile courts' power over "families in conflict" (Wash. Rev. Code Ann. § 13.32A.050 [West 1982]). However, in 1993, after the murder of a chronic runaway girl, Rebecca "Becca" Hedman, Washington reinstated police and court authority to hold noncriminal youths in secure "Crisis Residential Centers" for up to five days (Wash. Rev. Code Ann. § 13.40.050 [West 1995]; Eggers 1998). Following passage of "Becca's Bill," detention of status offenders increased eight-fold, the majority of whom were girls (MacDonald and Chesney-Lind 2001).

Diversion constitutes another strategy to minimize court intervention. It reserves judicial resources for serious cases, provides informal supervision to respond to minor misbehavior, and allows flexible access to community resources and services. Critics of diversion programs contend that most youths do not participate voluntarily and that most service providers are extensions of the justice system (Klein 1979; Polk 1984). Moreover, diversion may have a "netwidening" that extends controls further into the normal population (Decker 1985; Klein 1979). It shifts discretion from juvenile court judges to the periphery of the system and enables police, prosecutors, and intake workers to make low-visibility decisions without any accountability. It provides a means to deal with minor offenders without any formal finding of guilt and disproportionately includes girls (e.g., Alder 1984; Miller 1996).

Referrals

Police, victims, schools, social service agencies, parents, and probation officers refer delinquency and status offense cases to juvenile courts. In some states, juvenile court intake personnel screen cases to determine whether to handle them informally (i.e., dismissal, diversion, or informal probation) or formally (i.e., by filing a delinquency or status offense petition). In other jurisdictions, a prosecutor's office screens cases and decides whether to process them informally or formally. States handle most status offense cases informally and by nonjudicial agencies, and these analyses are limited to those cases in which they file a formal petition in juvenile court (Puzzanchera et al. 2004). An early evaluation of DSO presciently warned that "[i]t is unclear what is happening to youth who commit status offenses but do not enter the juvenile justice system or its closely related diversion programs . . ." (Handler and Zatz 1982, p. 89).

Police refer a vast majority of delinquents to juvenile courts for youths' violations of criminal laws. As Table 11.2 indicates, police referred 84 percent of all delinquency cases with minor variation based on the type of violations. This predominance had not changed over the past decade (Puzzanchera et al. 2004). Significantly, police referred less than two-thirds (63 percent) of youths for public order offense. Public order referrals include weapons, liquor, and disorderly conduct offenses. In addition, public order also includes "technical violations" and obstruction of justice (e.g., probation and parole violations, contempt of court cases, violating a valid court order, and escape from confinement) for

TABLE 11.2   SOURCE OF REFERRAL TO JUVENILE COURT

Delinquency Cases Referred by Law Enforcement, 2000		Status Offenses Referred by Law Enforcement, 1990–1999	
Offense	Percentage	Offense	Percentage
Delinquency	84	Runaway	40
Person	89	Truancy	10
Property	92	Ungovernability	11
Drugs	89	Liquor	92
Public Order	63		

Sources: Delinquency cases: Puzzanchera et al. (2004). Status offenses: Puzzanchera et al. (2003).

which probation officers frequently refer juveniles and that provide the bases for bootstrapping status offenders.

The source of referral of petitioned status offenders exhibits a different pattern. Between 1990 and 1999, police referred the vast majority (92 percent) of underage drinkers for liquor violations. However, for other types of status offenses, the agencies responsible for controlling youths dominated referrals (e.g., schools referred most truants, parents referred most runaway and ungovernable children, and the like). One study reports that parents refer girls to juvenile court more frequently than boys (31 percent versus 7 percent), especially when they refer their child for a status offense (45 percent girls versus 13 percent boys) (Minor, Hartmann, and Terry 1997).

Intake Screening and Diversion

The juvenile justice system entails a multistage sequence of decisions: Police arrest and refer; intake screens, disposes informally, or files a formal petition; judges detain, adjudicate, and sentence youths. Discretionary decisions at each step differentially affect the processing of boys and girls and of youths of different racial groups (McCord, Widom, and Crowell 2001). Most states have established neither state-training programs for court personnel nor standardized criteria for case processing and, as a result, screening practices vary substantially among and within states (Feld 1991; Kempf-Leonard and Sample 2000).

Figure 11.8 summarizes the number of girls referred to juvenile courts from 1985 to 2000 for delinquency offenses—person, property, drugs, and public order. Reflecting the arrest trends depicted earlier (Figures 11.1, 11.2, and 11.3), the number of girls referred for offenses against the person almost tripled (2.9) over the fifteen-year period, and referrals for public order offenses (2.4) and drug offenses (2.5) more than doubled. Property crimes, which comprise the largest single component of female delinquency referrals, *only* increased 28 percent overall despite a sharp decrease from their peak in 1996 and 1997. Figure 11.9 shows the number of girls referred to juvenile courts for simple and aggravated

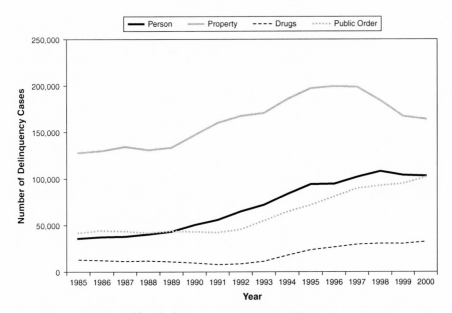

FIGURE 11.8 Number of female delinquency cases, 1985–2000. (*Source:* Stahl, Finnegan, and Kang 2003.)

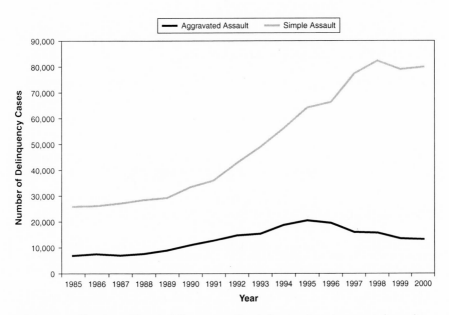

FIGURE 11.9 Number of female delinquency referrals for simple and aggravated assaults, 1985–2000. (*Source:* Stahl, Sickmund, and Snyder 2004.)

assaults between 1985 and 2000. Over this period, the number of girls referred for aggravated assaults increased 95 percent, from around 6,600 to 13,000, and the number of girls referred for simple assaults more than tripled (211 percent), from about 25,700 to 79,800.

Police arrested an estimated 2.4 million juveniles in 2000 (Snyder 2002) and referred an estimated 1.6 million delinquents to juvenile courts. Table 11.3 reports the number of delinquency cases and the number and proportion of females in each offense category in 2000. Girls comprised about one-quarter (24.6 perecent) of total delinquency referrals. Table 11.4 reports that, for both boys and girls, property crimes accounted for the largest proportion of delinquency referrals. Somewhat more than one-quarter (28 percent) of delinquency cases involved Property Crime Index offenses and two-thirds (66 percent) of those cases alleged larceny-theft (e.g., shoplifting). Police referred girls for more

TABLE 11.3   DELINQUENCY CASES, 2000

	Number of Cases	Number of Female Cases	Percentage Female Cases
Total Delinquency	1,633,300	402,200	24.6
Person Offenses	375,600	103,100	27.5
Criminal Homicide	1,700	***	***
Forcible Rape	4,700	***	***
Robbery	22,600	***	***
Aggravated Assault	51,200	13,100	25.6
Simple Assault	255,800	79,800	31.2
Other Violent Sex Offenses	12,500	***	***
Other Person Offenses	27,200	7,300	26.8
Property Offenses	668,600	164,700	24.6
Burglary	108,600	11,400	10.5
Larceny-Theft	303,200	107,400	35.4
Motor Vehicle Theft	38,300	8,500	22.2
Arson	8,300	***	***
Vandalism	106,800	14,400	13.5
Trespassing	49,400	9,200	18.6
Stolen Property Offenses	25,200	3,600	14.3
Other Property Offenses	28,900	9,000	31.1
Drug Law Violations	194,200	32,500	16.7
Public Order Offenses	395,000	101,900	25.8
Obstruction of Justice	179,200	48,400	27
Disorderly Conduct	90,200	27,400	30.4
Weapons Offenses	37,500	4,900	13.1
Liquor Law Violations	27,000	8,100	30.0
Nonviolent Sex Offenses	14,900	***	***
Other Public Order Offenses	46,200	11,000	23.8
Violent Crime Index*	80,100	15,400	19.2
Property Crime Index**	458,300	128,400	28.0

* Includes criminal homicide, forcible rape, robbery, and aggravated assault.

** Includes burglary, larceny-theft, motor vehicle theft, and arson.

*** Too few cases to develop valid national estimate.

Source: OJJDP Statistical Briefing Book (2000).

TABLE 11.4   DELINQUENCY REFERRALS, 2000

Offense Type	Total Referrals	Female Referrals	Percentage Female
Person	375,600	103,079	27.4
Property	668,600	164,705	24.6
Drugs	194,200	32,493	16.7
Public Order	395,000	101,891	25.8
Total	1,633,400	402,168	24.6

Source: Stahl, Finnegan, and Kang (2003).

than one-third (35 percent) of larceny-theft cases. Violent Crime Index referrals involved less than 5 percent of delinquency referrals and aggravated assaults comprised nearly two-thirds (64 percent) of those cases. Girls accounted for less than one-fifth (19 percent) of all Violent Crime Index referrals and one-quarter (26 percent) of aggravated assault referrals. By contrast, girls accounted for nearly one-third (31 percent) of referrals for simple assault. Girls committed too few of the most serious violent crimes (e.g., homicide, rape, and robbery) to provide a basis for valid national estimates. Similarly, we lack reliable national estimates of the number of status offenders referred to juvenile courts.

Once police or others refer a case to juvenile court, prosecutors or intake personnel must decide whether to file a formal petition, to dismiss a case, or to handle it informally. Although legal variables such as offense seriousness and prior referrals strongly influence intake decisions, gender exerts a modest influence on filing decisions (Shelden and Horvath 1987). As in so many areas of gender and juvenile justice administration, there is surprisingly little recent research. For many years, court intake personnel closed about half of delinquency referrals without filing a formal petition. In 2000, prosecutors or court personnel filed formal petitions against 58 percent of youths referred to juvenile courts (Puzzanchera et al. 2004). Of the 42 percent of youths whom court personnel processed informally, many still experienced some type of intervention (Puzzanchera et al. 2004). While court personnel dismissed outright about 40 percent of those cases, most of the remaining youths received informal dispositions similar to those imposed following formal adjudication (Kempf-Leonard and Sample 2000). For example, court personnel placed nearly one-third (33 percent) of nonpetitioned youths on informal probation and required an additional one-quarter (27 percent) to perform community service, pay restitution, or the like (Minor, Hartmann, and Terry 1997).

Subtle racial attitudes may affect intake personnel's decisions whether to file a petition (Bishop and Frazier 1992). For example, probation officers attributed white juveniles' crimes to external environmental factors for which they were not responsible (e.g., dysfunctional families, drug abuse, or peer influences), whereas they attributed black youths' crimes to their own negative attitudes and personality defects (Bridges and Steen 1998). These attributions, in turn, affect staff's risk assessments, filing decisions, and sentence recommendations and mark the beginning of cumulative racial disparities in juvenile justice administration (McCord, Widom, and Crowell 2001).

Gender stereotypes may interact with racial attitudes and subtly influence probation officers' assessments (Gaarder, Rodriguez, and Zatz 2004). Probation officers frequently describe girls as more manipulative, uncooperative, and difficult to work with than boys (Bond-Maupin, Maupin, and Leisenring 2002; Gaarder, Rodriguez, and Zatz 2004). However, they perceived white girls' behavior as self-destructive, resulting from low self-esteem or negative peer influences and recommended placement in treatment-oriented facilities. By contrast, they perceived black girls to be more "criminal," to make inappropriate "lifestyle choices," and to require placement in more punishment-oriented institutions (Miller 1996). A study that included Hispanic girls in the racial mix revealed a similar pattern of racial attribution (Gaarder, Rodriguez, and Zatz 2004). Even when girls reported abuse, probation officers sometimes viewed them as partially responsible for the abuse, using their victimization as an excuse, whining too much, and trying to manipulate the system (Bond-Maupin, Maupin, and Leisenring 2002; Gaarder, Rodriguez, and Zatz 2004).

Figure 11.10 summarizes the proportion of cases in which court personnel or prosecutors filed delinquency petitions against boys and girls from 1985 to 2000. The proportion of cases formally petitioned has increased steadily over those fifteen years *and* prosecutors typically file delinquency petitions against

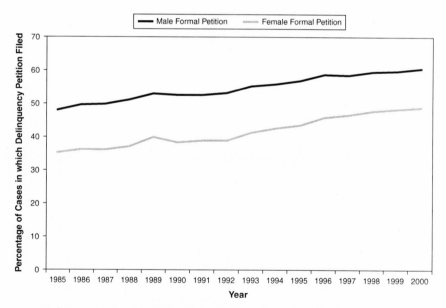

FIGURE 11.10   Male and female percentage of cases resulting in filing of delinquency petition, 1985–2000. (*Source:* Stahl, Finnegan, and Kang 2003.)

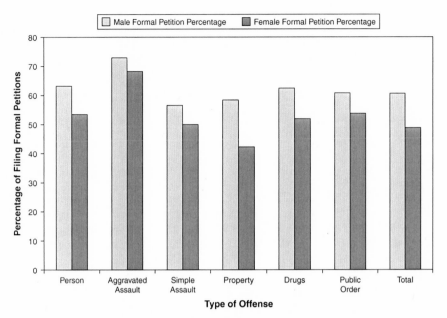

FIGURE 11.11 Filing percentage of formal petitions by gender and type of offense, 2000. (*Source:* Stahl, Finnegan, and Kang 2003.)

boys about 13 percent to 15 percent more frequently than they do against girls. Figure 11.11 compares the rates at which prosecutors filed delinquency petitions against boys and girls in 2000 for various offenses. Overall, they filed delinquency petitions against 61 percent of boys and 49 percent of girls and at higher rates for each type of offense. For youths charged with offenses against the person, they filed petitions about 10 percent more often against boys than girls. Court personnel filed formal petitions at the highest rate against boys and girls accused of aggravated assault (73 percent of boys and 68 percent of girls). Similarly, they charged 57 percent of boys and 50 percent of girls referred for simple assaults. The differences between boys and girls in the rates of filing petitions for assaults were the smallest of any offense category.

Black girls were disproportionately overrepresented in comparison with their makeup of the population among the 402,000 girls referred for delinquencies in 2000. Although black juveniles comprised about 16 percent of the juvenile population and Asian/Pacific Islanders and Native American juveniles accounted for another 5 percent, as Table 11.5 indicates, police referred larger proportions of black girls than white girls to juvenile courts for all categories of crimes except drug offenses. White girls made up about two-thirds (67 percent) of all delinquency referrals, black girls comprised 29 percent, and girls of other races the remaining 4 percent. Compared with girls of color, white girls comprised a larger proportion of drug referrals (86 percent) and a smaller proportion of referrals for offenses against the person (59 percent).

TABLE 11.5   GIRLS' RATES OF REFERRAL AND PETITIONS BY RACE, 2000

Referral Offense	Offense for Which Referred (%)			Proportion of Formal Petitions Filed (%)		
	White	Black	Other	White	Black	Other
Person	59.2	37.8	3.0	50.2	58.4	51.8
Property	68.2	27.3	4.5	40.3	46.8	41.2
Drugs	85.8	11.3	2.8	49.9	65:3	57.0
Public Order	68.6	28.1	3.3	52.1	57.2	55.5
Total	67.4	28.9	3.7	46.6	53.8	47.6

Source: Stahl, Finnegan, and Kang (2003).

A relationship exists between the seriousness of an offense and the decision to file a delinquency petition, and prosecutors filed the highest proportion of petitions for offenses against the person. Some variations in rates of filing petitions against girls by race and offense contribute to the overrepresentation of minority females in the juvenile justice system. Recall from Figure 11.11 that prosecutors filed petitions against 49 percent of all girls and against 53 percent of those charged with offenses against the person. Table 11.5 reports the rates at which court personnel filed petitions by race and offense. Courts petitioned white girls at rates somewhat lower than they did black girls (47 percent versus 54 percent). Court personnel filed petitions against black girls about 8 percent more frequently than they did white girls charged with offenses against the person. Although white girls constituted the vast majority (86 percent) of girls referred to courts for drug offenses, courts filed petitions against half (50 percent) of them as contrasted with nearly two-thirds (65 percent) of black girls. Although white girls report higher rates of drug usage than do girls of other races, courts filed petitions against them for drug involvement less frequently (Acoca and Dedel 1998). Black girls comprise about 17 percent of the youth population, 29 percent of all juveniles referred for delinquency, and 32 percent of those against whom petitions were filed. Although differences in filing rates by race are small for some offense categories, successive discretionary decisions accumulate and contribute to disproportionate overrepresentation of minority youths and black females in the justice system (McCord, Widom, and Crowell 2001). Race and gender have separate effects, and white girls are the primary beneficiaries of the justice system's leniency (MacDonald and Chesney-Lind 2001; Miller 1996).

Waiver of Girls to Criminal Courts

Three generic types of laws to transfer youths to criminal court—judicial waiver, prosecutorial "direct file," and legislative exclusion of offenses from juvenile court jurisdiction—vest the jurisdictional determination in the judicial, executive, or legislative branches (Snyder and Sickmund 1999; Torbet et al. 1996).[5] Although the largest number of states use judicial waiver to make transfer decisions, over the past two decades prosecutorial "direct file" and offense exclusion laws actually account for the largest number of chronological juveniles tried in criminal courts (Bishop et al. 1996; Feld 2000). We lack systematic data about the numbers and characteristics of youths waived by methods other than those initiated by a transfer motion filed in juvenile court.

For a tiny fraction of juveniles, filing a delinquency petition also may initiate the process to waive judicially a youth to criminal court. Of the roughly 1.5 million annual delinquency referrals over the past fifteen years, only about 0.6 percent resulted in a judicial waiver to criminal court (Puzzanchera et al. 2004; Stahl, Finnegan, and Kang 2003). The percentage of juveniles judicially waived has declined steadily from its peak in 1991 (0.8 percent) and now accounts for the disposition of about 0.3 percent of all delinquency referrals. In part, the decrease in judicial waivers reflects the broader shift of transfer discretion from judges to prosecutors (Torbet et al. 1996). As Table 11.6 indicates, prosecutors charged the largest proportion of judicially waived juveniles with offenses against the person and the smallest proportion with public order and property offenses. In 2000, judges transferred proportionally four times as many boys as girls and by roughly similar ratios in each offense category. In 2000, juvenile court judges transferred an estimated total of 370 girls for criminal prosecution, and the numbers and proportions of girls transferred by race are too small for any meaningful comparisons. Judges transferred girls of all races charged with similar crimes at similar rates (Stahl, Finnegan, and Kang 2003).

We know very little about the "criminal court careers" of transferred girls or how they resemble or differ from transferred boys (Feld 1998; Acoca and Dedel 1998). One study examined twenty-two waived girls convicted and sentenced as adults (Gaarder and Belknap 2002). It reported that two-thirds of transferred girls committed serious crimes, but one-quarter had no prior record, nearly half had received no previous juvenile court placements prior to their transfer and sentences to prison, and nothing distinguished them from girls who remained in the juvenile system (Gaarder and Belknap 2002). Contrary to expectations of "get tough" legislators, transferring and sentencing youths as adults appears to accelerate the frequency and seriousness of reoffending compared with similar

TABLE 11.6   PERCENTAGE OF MALE AND FEMALE JUVENILES WAIVED BY TYPE OF OFFENSE, 2000

	Male	Female
N =	5,211	370
Person	0.8	0.2
Property	0.4	0.1
Drugs	0.5	0.2
Public Order	0.2	0
Total	0.4	0.1

Source: Stahl, Finnegan, and Kang (2003).

youths tried and sentenced as juveniles (Bishop and Frazier 2000; Fagan 1995, 1996). However, transferred girls reoffended less frequently or seriously than did their waived male counterparts following release (Winner et al. 1997).

Detention

After police take a youth into custody, court personnel decide whether to detain her prior to adjudication or disposition. Most statutes authorize judges to detain a youth if she poses a danger to herself or others or is likely to run away or frustrate court processes (e.g., *Schall v. Martin*, 467 U.S. 253 [1984]; Snyder and Sickmund 1999; Frazier and Bishop 1985). Because detention envisions short-term custody for juveniles awaiting trial or disposition, detention facilities typically house a heterogeneous mix of minor and serious offenders, as well as mentally ill youths and others for whom courts lack suitable placements (Wordes and Jones 1998). Courts also use detention facilities for short-term postadjudication sanctions for youths who violated court orders or conditions of probation (i.e., "technical violations") (Beger and Hoffman 1998).

Several studies examine judges' detention decisions and the impact of pretrial detention on subsequent dispositions (Clarke and Koch 1980; Fagan and Guggenheim 1996; Feld 1993; Frazier and Bishop 1985; McCarthy 1987; McCarthy and Smith 1986; McCord, Widom, and Crowell 2001). Although similar legal and demographic variables affect both initial detention decisions and subsequent dispositions, detention *per se* exhibits an independent and aggravating effect on juveniles' sentences (Clarke and Koch 1980; Feld 1993; Frazier and Cochran 1986; Kempf-Leonard and Sample 2000). Placement in pretrial detention increases the likelihood that a court will petition, adjudicate, and sentence a juvenile. A few studies examine the role of gender in detention decisions. On the one hand, judges more often detain delinquents charged with serious offenses and those with prior records and, as a consequence, boys, especially black youths, experience higher rates of detention (Frazier and Bishop 1985). On the other hand, although judges detain proportionally fewer juveniles for minor crimes and status offenses, they detain girls charged with minor offenses more frequently than they do boys (Feld 1989, 1993; Frazier and Cochran 1986). Judges detain female status offenders, especially runaways, more readily than they do males, because of a prevailing paternalistic and protective ethos (Schutt and Dannefer 1988). Girls may spend more time in detention than boys because courts lack alternative placements that would ensure their safety (Beyer et al. 2003; Bond-Maupin, Maupin, and Leisenring 2002).

Although the JJDPA substantially reduced the numbers of status offenders held in detention facilities by the late 1980s (U.S. General Accounting Office 1991), girls still comprised the majority of youths whom courts detained for status offenses (Schwartz, Steketee, and Schneider 1990). Similarly, the number of juveniles in adult jails declined as a result of the JJDPA, but courts still detained female status offenders in lockups more often than boys (Chesney-Lind 1988b;

Schwartz, Harris, and Levi 1988). Critics long have decried conditions of confinement in detention facilities—overcrowding, lack of programs, and poorly trained staff. Because of their fewer numbers, girls' detention facilities frequently suffer from overcrowding and inadequate educational, physical, and psychological services to meet basic needs (e.g., American Bar Association and National Bar Association 2001; Lederman and Brown 2000). Detained girls report that staff use foul and demeaning language, threaten and intimidate them, use unnecessary physical restraints, touch them inappropriately, push and hit them, and conduct strip searches in the presence of male staff (Acoca 1999; Acoca and Dedel 1998).

From 1985 to 2000, court personnel held about one-fifth (20 percent) of all youths in pretrial detention. Even as juvenile crime rates and court referrals increased between the mid-1980s and the mid-1990s, states detained larger proportions of boys than girls, again reflecting boys' greater involvement in serious and violent crime (Kempf-Leonard and Sample 2000; Wordes and Jones 1998). Figure 11.12 indicates that juvenile courts detain girls for all offenses at a rate about 3 percent to 5 percent lower than they do boys, and detention of boys and girls moves consistently in tandem, rising and falling together. Figure 11.13 reports the proportion of boys and girls detained by type of offense in 2000. Courts detain proportionally fewer girls than boys for all types of offenses with the greatest difference for those charged with property offenses and the smallest disparity for those charged with public order violations. Public order violations

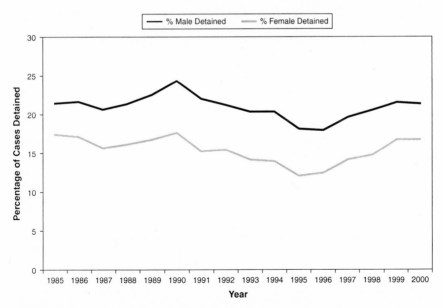

FIGURE 11.12 Percentage of cases in which courts detained male and female juveniles, 1985–2000. (*Source:* Stahl, Finnegan, and Kang 2003.)

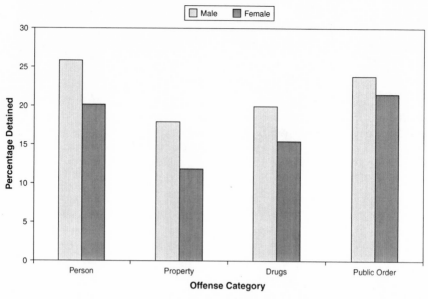

FIGURE 11.13 Percentage of boys and girls detained by offense, 2000. (*Source:* Stahl, Finnegan, and Kang 2003.)

include contempt of court and probation violations, and court personnel, rather than police, more frequently initiate these proceedings.

Table 11.7 reports the numbers and percentages of male and female delinquents detained for various offenses in 2000. Courts detained nearly one-third (31 percent) of all girls for crimes against the person and an additional one-third (33 percent) of girls for public order offenses, the largest gender disparity of any offense category. Because simple assaults comprise the larger proportion of girls' offenses against the person and public order offenses subsume "technical violations" of probation, these gendered differences in detention patterns likely reflect relabeling and bootstrapping practices.

Table 11.8 reports data from the Census of Juveniles in Residential Placement (CJRP). CJRP provides a one-day count of youths in detention facilities and

TABLE 11.7   NUMBERS AND PERCENTAGE OF JUVENILES DETAINED BY GENDER, 2000

	Female N =	Female %	Male N =	Male %
Total	67,041		262,758	
Person	20,732	31	70,373	27
Property	19,381	29	90,332	34
Drugs	5,019	7	32,157	12
Public Order	21,909	33	69,896	27

Source: Stahl, Finnegan, and Kang (2003).

TABLE 11.8   DETAILED OFFENSE PROFILE OF DETAINED JUVENILES BY SEX, 2001

Most Serious Offense	Total	Percentage	Male N =	Male %	Female N =	Female %
Total	27,502	100	22,398	100	5,103	100
Delinquency	26,367	96	21,750	97	4,617	90
Person	8,322	30	6,951	31	1,371	27
Violent Crime Index*	5,286	19	4,701	21	585	11
Other Person	3,036	11	2,250	10	786	15
Property	6,600	24	5,634	25	966	19
Property Crime Index**	5,466	20	4,665	21	801	16
Other Property	1,134	4	969	4	165	3
Drug	2,142	8	1,881	8	261	5
Public Order	2,685	10	2,250	10	435	9
Technical Violation	6,618	24	5,031	22	1,587	31
Status Offense	1,134	4	651	3	486	10

* Includes criminal homicide, violent sexual assault, robbery, and aggravated assault.
** Includes burglary, theft, auto theft, and arson.
Source: Adapted from Sickmund, Sladky, and Kang (2004).

postdisposition placements, rather than annual admission and release data that measure the volume and flow of population through a facility. On October 24, 2001, states held a total of 104,413 juveniles in custody—nearly three-quarters (73 percent) in residential placements and about one-quarter (26 percent) in detention facilities (Sickmund, Sladky, and Kang 2004, tables 8 and 11). CJRP detention data suggest three different "girl control" strategies—relabeling incorrigibility as simple assault, bootstrapping status offenders via technical violations, and continued confinement of status offenders. States detained about 96 percent of all juveniles for delinquency and about 4 percent for status offenses. States charged nearly one-third (30 percent) of detained juveniles with crimes against the person, an additional one-quarter each with property crimes (24 percent) and technical violations (24 percent), and the remainder with public order offenses (10 percent) or drug crimes (8 percent). Girls accounted for about one-fifth (19 percent) of the total number of juveniles held in detention.

States detained more than four times (4.4) as many boys as girls (22,398 versus 5,103) and held them for different offenses. States detained 97 percent of boys for delinquency compared with 90 percent of girls. Conversely, states detained proportionally three times as many girls as boys for status offenses (10 percent versus 3 percent). Although states held a larger proportion of boys (31 percent) than girls (27 percent) for person offenses, the disparity reflects the greater seriousness of boys' offenses. For example, states detained proportionally twice as many boys (21 percent) as girls (11 percent) for Violent Crime Index offenses. By contrast, states charged 15 percent of girls in detention with other person (i.e., simple assault), as compared with 10 percent of boys. Without controlling for the type of offenses, "[d]etained males had been in the facility an average of 42 days, compared with an average of 32 days for detained females" (Snyder and Sickmund 1999, p. 202).

States detained nearly one-quarter (24 percent) of all youths for technical violations (i.e., probation violations and contempt of court), and this may be an instance of bootstrapping status offenders. Unlike other offenses for which states held roughly one-quarter (26 percent) of youths in detention facilities and three-quarters (74 percent) in residential placements, states confined nearly half (43 percent) of the youths charged with "technical violations" in short-term detention facilities (Sickmund, Sladky, and Kang 2004). Moreover, states detained nearly one-third (31 percent) of girls as contrasted with fewer than one-quarter (22 percent) of boys for technical violations. When states detain youths for technical violations, they hold girls longer in custody than they do boys (23.6 days versus 16.5 days) (Beger and Hoffman 1998).

States detained 1,134 youths for status offenses, about 4 percent of all youths in detention, even though the JJDPA discourages them from doing so (Sickmund, Sladky, and Kang 2004). States detained proportionally three times as many girls as boys (10 percent versus 3 percent) for status offenses, *and* girls comprised about 43 percent of all detained status offenders. During the 1990s, boys comprised a small majority of all youths detained for runaway (60 percent), truancy (54 percent), ungovernability (55 percent), and liquor violations (57 percent) (Puzzanchera et al. 2004; U.S. General Accounting Office 1995a).

Although juvenile courts detained fewer girls than boys, Figure 11.14 reports some disparities in detention of girls of different races (Kempf 1992; Pope and Feyerherm 1990; Wordes, Bynum, and Corley 1994; Wordes and Jones 1998). Overall, juvenile courts detained about 4 percent more girls of color than they did

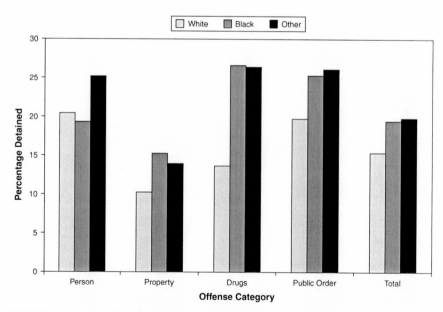

FIGURE 11.14   Detention of girls by race, 2000. (*Source:* Stahl, Finnegan, and Kang 2003.)

white girls with the largest disparity for those charged with drug and public order violations. Although white girls comprised the vast majority of girls (86 percent) referred to courts for drug offenses (see Table 11.5), court personnel filed petitions for drug offenses against a larger proportion of black girls (65 percent) than white girls (50 percent), and juvenile courts detained proportionally twice as many black girls (27 percent) charged with drug offenses as they did white girls (14 percent).

Adjudication

After the state files a delinquency petition, a youth must admit or deny the allegations (i.e., plead guilty or not guilty). If she admits the allegation, then the case proceeds for disposition. If she denies the allegation, then the court conducts an adjudicatory hearing (i.e., trial) to decide her guilt or innocence. Adjudicatory hearings occur in only a small fraction of delinquency cases (Feld 1993). "Adjudication" is a juvenile justice euphemism for conviction or a finding of guilt. However, even if a child pleads guilty or the prosecutor proves her guilt beyond a reasonable doubt, the court may still withhold adjudication. Nonadjudication does not mean that the court found the child innocent, but rather that it refrained from making a formal finding of delinquency. States' terminologies differ—continuance without a finding, continuance for dismissal, adjournment in contemplation of dismissal, or the like (Sanborn and Salerno 2005). A juvenile court judge may decline to adjudicate a youth delinquent if she contemplates a nominal disposition or dismissal or to protect her record, and they do not adjudicate the majority of youths who appear before them. Whether a judge decides to adjudicate a youth delinquent, in turn, may affect the severity of the disposition.

The rate of adjudication has risen steadily over the past fifteen years and judges consistently adjudicate boys delinquent about 10 percent more often than they do girls (Stahl, Finnegan, and Kang 2003). By 2000, juvenile courts formally adjudicated delinquent 41 percent of boys and 31 percent of girls and adjudicated more boys than girls in every offense category (Stahl, Finnegan, and Kang 2003). Juvenile court judges adjudicated about 4 percent more girls of color delinquent than they did white girls charged with similar offenses, a racial pattern that is consistent with other research on justice administration (e.g., MacDonald and Chesney Lind 2001; Poe-Yamagata and Butts 1996).

Juveniles' Procedural Rights at Adjudication

Since the Supreme Court decided *In re Gault* (1967), delinquents theoretically enjoy most of the criminal procedural rights of adult defendants, except for the right to a jury trial (*McKeiver v. Pennsylvania* 1970). However, the "law in action" diverges significantly from the "law on the books" (Feld 1993, 1999). Although *Gault* held that juveniles had a constitutional right to counsel, juvenile courts in many states convict many delinquents without giving them an attorney (Burruss and Kempf-Leonard 2002; Feld 1988, 1989, 1993; U.S. General Accounting Office 1995b). Observational studies in many jurisdictions strongly question the quality of representation that juveniles receive (American Bar Association 1995; Celeste and Puritz 2003; Cooper, Puritz, and Shang 1998). The types of legal services delivery system and attorney payment schedule adversely affect the quality of representation (American Bar Association 1995). Girls interviewed about their lawyers expressed dissatisfaction with their representation, felt that attorneys did not familiarize themselves with their cases, did not listen to or respect them, and did not exert themselves on their behalf (Acoca and Dedel 1998).

The only study to examine gender differences in rates of representation reports that lawyers represented girls less often than boys, especially females charged with serious crimes and property crimes (Feld 1989, 1993). In Minnesota, attorneys appeared for 47 percent of boys, but only 41 percent of girls, in juvenile court proceedings (Feld 1989, 1993). However, girls charged with "other delinquency" (i.e., public order offenses and technical violation) and status offenses enjoyed somewhat higher rates of representation than did boys facing similar charges (Feld 1989, 1993). Unfortunately, studies of the impact of lawyers in juvenile courts consistently report that youths represented by counsel receive more severe dispositions than do those who appear without lawyers (Feld 1988, 1989, 1993; Burruss and Kempf-Leonard, 2002).[6] Girls who have higher rates of representation than do boys charged with minor and status offenses also experience higher rates of home-removal.

Gault only addressed the constitutional rights of delinquents (i.e., youths charged with crimes and who faced possible institutional confinement). Status offenders enjoy fewer procedural rights than do juveniles charged with delinquency offenses (Dalby 1994; Feld 2004; Smith 1992). If states charge status offenders with noncriminal misconduct and do not initially incarcerate them in delinquency institutions, then they may use less formal procedures including a lower standard of proof, less stringent evidentiary standards, and more limited access to an attorney (Feld 1993, 2004). Youths charged with noncriminal misconduct do not enjoy the privilege against self-incrimination available to delinquents (e.g., *In re Spalding*, 332 A.2d 246 [Md. 1975]; [Smith 1992]).

Delinquency Dispositions

Delinquency statutes give juvenile court judges a wide array of sentencing options: dismissal, continuance without a finding, restitution or fine, probation with or without conditions or supervision, out-of-home placement in a public or private residential facility or group home, or confinement in a county or state training school or other secure public or private setting. Probationary dispositions may be informal and voluntary or court ordered with or without conditions or terms of supervision. Probation orders typically command a juvenile to obey laws, observe curfew, attend school, remain at home or in a court-ordered placement, and report to a probation officer. Failure to comply with conditions of probation (e.g., violating curfew, truanting from school, or absenting from a court-ordered placement) constitutes "technical violations" for which a judge may impose a short-term sanction, such as placement in a detention facility, or revoke the probation and impose a more stringent disposition.

Boys commit most of the serious delinquency, and most evaluations of juvenile court sentencing practices focus on them. More sentencing research has focused on racial disparities rather than gender differences (Feld 1999; McCord, Widom, and Crowell 2001). Some research on gender bias focuses on "chivalrous" or lenient treatment of delinquent girls to explain juvenile courts' tendency to sentence them less severely than boys. Other analysts invoke "protectionist" or "paternalistic" explanations to account for juvenile courts' tendency to intervene more stringently in the lives of sexually active females and status offenders (Chesney-Lind 1977, 1988a; Johnson and Scheuble 1991; Schlossman 1977; Schlossman and Wallach 1978). One study argued that "paternalistic" gender expectations may result in more severe sentencing of girls than boys for less serious violations, such as status offenses, whereas "chivalrous" attitudes may produce greater leniency for girls than for boys who commit more serious crimes (Johnson and Scheuble 1991). Sentencing research conducted prior to the 1980s consistently reported a gender double standard. Juvenile courts petitioned, detained, and incarcerated more girls than boys charged with status offenses, but sentenced males charged with delinquency more severely than they did females (Bishop and Frazier 1992). For example, juvenile courts confined more boys than girls charged with similar offenses and gave more girls probation or dismissal (Johnson and Scheuble 1991). More recent studies report fewer gender differences in sentencing status offenders (Clarke and Koch 1980; Corley, Cernkovich, and Giordano 1989; Teilman and Landry 1981; U.S. General Accounting Office 1995a). The United States General Accounting Office (1995a) reports that "there were only relatively minor differences in the percentages of female and male status offenders detained, adjudicated, and placed ... [and] analyses ... in seven states generally did not indicate any significant gender-based differences in the processing of female and male status offenders" (p. 9).

Bishop and Frazier (1992) analyzed juvenile courts' use of contempt power to sanction status offenders who violated a court order and reported differential gender treatment and "bootstrapping." For example, the likelihood that a judge would incarcerate a male status offender increased from 3.9 percent for those not found in contempt to 4.4 percent for those found in contempt, whereas if the court subsequently found a female status offender in contempt, the risk of her confinement of increased from 1.8 percent to 63.2 percent. "In short, females referred to juvenile court for contempt following an earlier adjudication for a status offense receive harsher judicial dispositions than their male counterparts" (Bishop and Frazier 1992, p. 1183).

One study examined the separate effects of gender and race on girls' sentences and reported that white females charged with drug violations initially received more lenient dispositions than either black or white males or black females, but once they accumulated several prior adjudications, judges sentenced them more severely than boys (Horowitz and Pottieger 1991). Other studies suggest that while girls, particularly white girls, enjoy initial leniency in petitioning and adjudication, "the court's benevolence declines as girls enter the disposition stage" with minority females at a particular disadvantage (MacDonald and Chesney-Lind 2001, p. 188).

Once juvenile courts adjudicate a youth delinquent, some type of formal response becomes very likely. Over the past fifteen years, juvenile courts have removed more than one-quarter (28 percent) of those adjudicated delinquent from their home, placed more than half (57 percent) on probation, imposed other sanctions such as fines or restitution on more than one in ten (11 percent), and dismissed fewer than one in twenty (4 percent) cases (Stahl, Finnegan, and Kang 2003). During this period, judges removed boys from their homes more often than girls (29 percent versus 22 percent), and, conversely, they placed a larger proportion of girls than boys on probation (62 percent versus 56 percent) (Stahl, Finnegan, and Kang 2003). These long-term, average differences reflect both changes in practice over time and differences in the seriousness of boys' and girls' delinquency.

Table 11.9 reports the proportion of boys and girls who received out-of-home placement and probationary dispositions in 2000 when charged with similar offenses. Overall, states placed less than one-fifth of girls (19 percent) compared with more than one-quarter of boys (25 percent) out of home or in secure facilities. A similar disparity occurs within each individual offense category, with the greatest discrepancy for boys and girls convicted of property crimes (24 percent versus 15 percent) and the smallest gender difference for those convicted of public order offenses (29 percent versus 23 percent). Significantly, both boys and girls experienced higher rates of out-of-home placements for public order offenses (29 percent and 23 percent) (i.e., "technical violations"), than did youths sentenced for crimes against the person. Conversely, juvenile courts placed a larger proportion of girls on probation than they did boys (68 percent versus 62 percent) across all offense categories. Black girls received somewhat more

TABLE 11.9   PERCENTAGE PLACEMENT AND PROBATION OF BOYS AND GIRLS BY OFFENSE, 2000

	Placed		Probation	
	Male	Female	Male	Female
Total	25.2	18.7	61.8	67.6
Person	26.8	19.5	61.8	69.3
Property	23.6	15.4	63.7	70.2
Drugs	21.1	13.5	61.7	65.7
Public Order	28.8	23.3	58.9	63.5

Source: Stahl, Finnegan, and Kang (2003).

TABLE 11.10   OFFENSE PROFILE OF COMMITTED RESIDENTS BY SEX, 2001

Most Serious Offense	Total	Percentage of Total Confined	Male N =	Male %	Female N =	Female %
Total	76,298	100	66,444	87	9,855	13
Delinquency	72,525	95	64,191	89	8,334	11
Person	26,436	35	23,385	88	3,051	12
Violent Crime Index*	18,321	24	16,920	92	1,401	8
Other Person	8,115	11	6,465	80	1,650	20
Property	22,689	30	20,340	90	2,349	10
Property Crime Index**	18,942	25	17,043	90	1,896	10
Other Property	3,750	5	3,297	88	453	12
Drug	6,891	9	6,225	90	666	10
Public Order	7,713	10	7,053	91	660	9
Technical Violation	8,796	12	7,188	82	1,608	18
Status Offense	3,774	5	2,253	60	1,521	40

* Includes criminal homicide, violent sexual assault, robbery, and aggravated assault.

** Includes burglary, theft, auto theft, and arson.

Source: Adapted from Sickmund, Sladky, and Kang (2004).

(3.2 percent) out-of-home placements or probation dispositions than did white girls and correspondingly fewer lesser sanctions or dismissals (Stahl, Finnegan, and Kang 2003).

Table 11.10 reports the offenses, numbers, and percentages of juveniles in residential custody in total and separately for boys and girls based on data from the CJRP. States committed 76,298 juveniles to residential custody on October 24, 2001, and confined 95 percent for delinquency offenses and 5 percent for status offenses. States held more than one-third (35 percent) of youths for crimes against the person and nearly one-third (30 percent) for property offenses. States confined equal proportions of youths for Violent Crime Index (24 percent) and Property Crime Index (25 percent) offenses.

As a result of cumulative differences in the seriousness of boys' offenses, rates of arrest, petitions, detention, and adjudication, boys comprise the vast majority of all youths (87 percent) and delinquent youths (89 percent) in custody. Boys heavily predominate among youths in custody for Violent Crime Index (92 percent) and Property Crime Index (90 percent) offenses. Girls comprise one-fifth (20 percent) of all youths confined for simple assaults, their largest component of any criminal offense. Proportionally, states are almost twice as likely to confine girls as boys for simple assault (20 percent versus 11 percent). States confined almost one-fifth (18 percent) of all girls for technical violations, proportionally about 50 percent more than boys. Finally, girls account for 40 percent of all youths confined for status offenses. We lack data on juveniles' length of stay or differences between boys' and girls' length of confinement in residential placements. However, an earlier study reported that "[a]mong committed juveniles, the difference between the average time in the facility for males and females was more than three weeks. Committed males had been in the facility more than

6 months on average (189 days), compared with an average of 165 days for committed females" (Snyder and Sickmund 1999, p. 202).

Recall that police arrested and referred girls for aggravated and simple assaults at higher rates than they did for other types of offenses. Juvenile courts detained and processed larger proportions of girls charged with assaults than with other crimes. Following sentencing, girls comprised one-fifth (20 percent) of all youths confined for simple assault, the largest proportion of girls for *any* criminal offense. Table 11.11 relies on CJRP data and reports on juveniles in all residential placements—detention and confinement—in 1997, 1999, and 2001 to highlight the differences between the offenses for which states confine males and females. In 2001, girls comprised 13 percent of all delinquents in confinement and of those confined for violent crimes. Both proportions increased over the three biennial censuses. States confined one-quarter (25 percent) of all delinquent girls for either simple or aggravated assaults. By contrast, states confined boys for a more heterogeneous mix of offenses and only about one in seven (15 percent) for simple or aggravated assaults.

When we examine changes in confinement for assault, we see that in each succeeding biennial census, the proportion of girls as a percentage of all juveniles confined for aggravated and simple assaults increased. Although males comprise 92 percent of all delinquents confined for Violent Crime Index offenses, the proportion of girls confined for aggravated assaults, as a percentage of all delinquents confined for aggravated assaults, increased from 12 percent to 15 percent. Similarly, the proportion of girls confined for simple assaults, as a percentage of

TABLE 11.11   CONFINEMENT OF GIRLS FOR PERSON OFFENSES, 1997–2001

	1997	1999	2001
Total Delinquents in Detention and Residential Placement	98,222	102,958	99,297
Female Proportion of All Delinquents in Confinement	11%	12%	13%
Number of Females Confined for All Person Offenses	3,612	4,365	4,443
Proportion of Delinquent Offenders Confined for All Person Offenses Who Are Female	10%	12%	13%
Number of Females Confined for Simple and Aggravated Assault	2,535	3,147	3,211
Percentage of Total Delinquents Confined for Aggravated Assault Who Are Girls	12%	14%	15%
Percentage of Total Delinquents Confined for Simple Assault Who Are Girls	22%	23%	24%
Percentage of Girls Confined for Simple and Aggravated Assaults as a Proportion of All Girls' Delinquency Confinements	23%	25%	25%
Percentage of Boys Confined for Simple and Aggravated Assaults as a Proportion of All Boys' Delinquency Confinements	16%	16%	15%
Girls' Percentage Aggravated Assaults to All Assaults	45%	45%	40%
Boys' Percentage Aggravated Assaults to All Assaults	62%	60%	54%

Source: Adapted from Sickmund, Sladky, and Kang (2004).

TABLE 11.12 CONFINEMENT OF GIRLS FOR TECHNICAL VIOLATIONS AND STATUS OFFENSES, 1997–2001

	1997	1999	2001
Number of Girls Confined for Technical Violations	2,457	2,976	3,210
Percentage of Total Youths Confined for Technical Violations Who Are Girls	20%	21%	21%
Number of Girls Confined for All Status Offenses	3,234	1,824	2,115
Percentage of Girls Confined for All Status Offenses	47%	39%	41%
Percentage Girls of Total Confined for Runaways	63%	55%	51%
Percentage Girls of Total Confined for Incorrigibility	44%	34%	46%

Source: Adapted from Sickmund, Sladky, and Kang (2004).

all delinquents confined for simple assault, increased from 22 percent to 24 percent. In all three biennia, states confined a majority of all boys convicted of assault for aggravated assaults (62 percent, 60 percent, 54 percent), rather than simple assaults. By contrast, states confined the majority of girls convicted of assaults for simple assaults, rather than aggravated assaults (45 percent, 45 percent, 40 percent). Violent girls may violate gender norms and appear more serious (Schaffner 1999), but as contrasted with the boys, states confine larger proportions of girls for less violent and injurious crimes. The incarceration of larger numbers and proportions of girls for assaults, especially simple assaults, suggests a relabeling of other conduct, such as incorrigibility, to obtain access to secure placement facilities.

Table 11.12 shows that states confine a larger proportion of girls than boys (18 percent versus 11 percent) for "technical violations"—violations of conditions of probation or disobeying a valid court order. Table 11.12 reports that girls comprise about one-fifth (20 percent, 21 percent, 21 percent) of all youths in custody for technical violations. Moreover, the number of girls confined for such violations has increased nearly one-third (31 percent) over six years from 2,457 to 3,210. Although states confine only 5 percent of youths for status offenses, girls constitute nearly half (41 percent) of them and a majority (63 percent, 55 percent, 51 percent) of all juveniles confined for "running away." Although the JJDPA dramatically reduced the overall number of status offenders in confinement, every study of institutionalized youths reports that states incarcerate disproportionately more girls than boys for status offenses. Earlier studies of institutionalized girls reported that states confined from 50 percent (Feld 1977) to 70 percent (Bartollas 1993) to more than 80 percent (Giallombardo 1974) of girls for status offenses.

We observe some differences when we look at the racial composition of male and female juveniles in confinement in 2001. Although minority offenders comprise a disproportionate share of all youths in residential placement, Table 11.13 reports some differences between boys and girls. White girls comprise the largest

TABLE 11.13   RACIAL PROFILE OF YOUTHS IN CUSTODY, 2001

	Male %	Female %
White	38	47
Black	40	35
Hispanic	18	13
Other	4	5

Source: Adapted from Sickmund, Sladky, and Kang (2004).

plurality (47 percent) of females in custody, whereas black boys comprise the largest plurality (40 percent) of males in custody. Although racial disparities exist for both genders, they are somewhat less acute for girls than for boys. Although boys comprised 89 percent of all the youths whom judges committed to facilities, they sentenced a larger proportion of girls to private facilities than they did boys (41 percent versus 34 percent) (Sickmund, Sladky, and Kang 2004). The higher rate of confinement of girls in private facilities reflects, in part, the inadequate number of beds available in public facilities (Kempf-Leonard and Sample 2000). White girls comprise about 46 percent of all females in residential placements, black girls accounted for more than one-third (38 percent), and juveniles of other racial groups comprised the remaining fifth (18 percent) of committed girls.

We have very little current information about the institutional experiences of confined girls, perhaps because institutional review boards (IRBs) pose insuperable barriers to participant-observation studies of incarcerated minors. However, two studies from the 1970s (Feld 1977; Giallombardo 1974) analyzed girls' adaptations to institutional confinement and reported that states confined most girls for status offenses rather than for delinquency. Giallombardo (1974) reported that girls in institutions formed informal family and kinship networks as an expression of their gender roles and as a way of coping with the deprivations of confinement. By contrast, Feld (1977) found few differences between the inmate subcultures in female institutions and those in organizationally comparable male training schools.

A Hidden System and Transinstitutionalization

Because the JJDPA made it more difficult to confine status offenders in delinquency institutions, it provided impetus for courts to refer and parents to commit youths to private-sector psychiatric and chemical dependency treatment facilities. The Supreme Court in *Parham v. J.R.* (442 U.S. 609 [1979]) ruled that parents voluntarily may commit their children to secure facilities for treatment and that the only procedural safeguards youths required were a staff physician's independent evaluation of "the child's mental and emotional condition and need for treatment." As long as hospital personnel determine that a child needs treatment, her parents may commit her without any judicial review or legal recourse (Weithorn 1988).

Private treatment facilities constitute a parallel, hidden system of social control for youths. During the 1980s and early 1990s, many troublesome youths whom juvenile courts previously dealt with as status offenders entered private mental health or substance abuse treatment facilities (Jackson-Beeck, Schwartz, and Rutherford 1987). Females and children whose families' medical insurance benefits included mental health or chemical dependency treatment constituted a growing market for service providers who afforded levels of security comparable to those in public institutions (Schwartz 1989b; Weithorn 1988). Coinciding with the deinstitutionalization of status offenders in the 1970s and 1980s, analysts in several states reported corresponding increases in the number of juvenile admissions, especially females, to private treatment facilities (Chesney-Lind 1988a; Federle and Chesney-Lind 1992; Krisberg et al. 1986; Schwartz 1989a; Weithorn 1988). Physicians diagnosed many youths as suffering from conduct disorders (CDs) or syndromes such as adjustment reactions or Oppositional Defiant Disorder (ODD), many youths whose symptoms include losing temper, initiating physical fights, staying out late without permission, "sexual promiscuity," running away from home overnight at least twice parallel those exhibited by "runaway," "incorrigible," or "ungovernable" youths (Jackson-Beeck, Schwartz, and Rutherford 1987). Psychiatric hospitals' quest for profits, insurance coverage for chemical dependency and inpatient mental health treatment, and malleable diagnostic categories enabled entrepreneurs to "medicalize" adolescent deviance and parents to incarcerate troublesome children without any meaningful judicial supervision (Weithorn 1988).

Although transinstitutionalization of female status offenders into private facilities for treatment of CD, ODD, or substance abuse expanded during the 1980s and 1990s, the more recent advent of "managed care" within the health care system has limited this growth somewhat (Chesney-Lind and Pasko 2004). Analysts attribute the downturn, in part, to more effective medication management and to external review of hospitalization decisions by insurance carriers (U.S. General Accounting Office 1994). To limit costs, HMOs and other managed care service providers increasingly deny approval for inpatient treatment/confinement for primarily behavioral misconduct such as running away or fighting with a parent (Chesney-Lind and Pasko 2004). Unfortunately, private facilities' ability to limit research access and to invoke medical privilege to protect the confidentiality of records preclude systematic evaluations of the numbers, characteristics, or presenting symptoms of adolescent admissions or the effectiveness of their treatment (Kempf-Leonard and Sample 2000; Schwartz 1989a; U.S. General Accounting Office 1994). However, as HMOs restrict parents' ability to commit their daughters for treatment of CDs, they increase pressures to place more girls in public institutions.

One study compared the characteristics of youths whom judges referred to state psychiatric facilities for mental health evaluations with those whom courts committed to correctional facilities (Thomas and Stubbe 1996). The juvenile court referred more than one-fifth (22 percent) of the hospitalized youths for status offense behaviors—running away, truancy, or unruly behavior—for which they could not confine them in training schools. Females comprised more than half (55 percent) of the youths whom judges hospitalized for treatment of their noncriminal misconduct (Thomas and Stubbe 1996). Another study examined juvenile courts' use of mental health placements and the characteristics of youths placed in mental health facilities (Herz 2001). Although placements in mental health facilities and delinquency institutions accounted for a small proportion of all dispositions (14 percent), courts committed white female offenders to mental health placements about eight times more often than they did black males and two and one half times more often than black female or white male offenders (Herz 2001).

Program and Policy Implications

Juvenile courts adapt to broader sociopolitical and legal changes, and organizational maintenance and institutional resilience may explain their continued endurance at least as well as their ability to achieve rehabilitative goals (Schwartz, Weiner, and Enosh 1998; Sutton 1988). The breadth and mutability of juvenile courts' mission provide them with the ability to redefine the boundaries of social control (Sutton 1988) and enable court personnel to maintain operational stability in the face of the delinquent male "crime drop" with an offsetting increase in female cases (Federle 2000). The broad discretion available to juvenile courts allows them to relabel many status offenders as minor delinquents and to "bring status offenders under the jurisdiction of the court at a rate almost as great as had existed prior to the [decriminalization] reform" (Schneider 1984, p. 367). Courtroom observers report that following decriminalization of status offenses, prosecutors charged many girls with criminal-type offenses for the same behavior they previously charged as status offenses (Mahoney and Fenster 1982). After Washington State temporarily decriminalized status offenses, some police and courts "redefined" them as minor criminal offenders so that juvenile courts could retain jurisdiction and dispositional authority over them. "[B]ecause many status offenders are not simply runaways or truants but also engage in delinquent activities, it is possible for many such youths to be 'relabeled' delinquents rather than remain classified as status offenders" (Castallano 1986, p. 496). Our analyses of the changing handling of girls' simple and aggravated assaults strongly suggest that the perceived growth in girls' "violence" may reflect a "criminalization of intra-familial conflicts and aggressive behavior," rather than an actual change in girls' behavior (American Bar Association and National Bar Association 2001, p. 14).

After three decades of deinstitutionalizing status offenders, the juvenile justice system remains committed to protecting and controlling girls, but without responding to their real needs. After Congress passed the JJDPA, neither federal nor state governments created options to ensure that girls who could not or would not stay at home would have access to services and alternatives (Chesney-

Lind and Shelden 2004; Maxson and Klein 1997). The failure to provide adequate social services, in turn, creates substantial pressures to circumvent restrictions on the disposition of status offenders by relabeling, bootstrapping, and trans-institutionalizing them. Confinement of girls appears to be driven by a relabeling of minor forms of girls' violence from "incorrigibility" to simple assault. The malleability of labels threatens to undermine the rationale and progress made in deinstitutionalizing status offenders.

We have identified many gaps in our knowledge about how the juvenile justice system responds to young offenders, especially females. Because of the success of deinstitutionalization efforts, states file far fewer petitions against juveniles for status offenses than they previously did. As a result, we know less now than we did two decades ago about how the juvenile justice system processes status offense–like behaviors. We also know less now than we did twenty years ago about how other agencies, which do not consistently produce data about decision-making and informal dispositions, handle these youths.

Take-Home Points

1. Historically, juvenile courts dealt with girls primarily under its noncriminal status offense jurisdiction and focused on aspects of family conflict: runaway, incorrigibility, "sexual precocity," or being a "stubborn child." However, state and federal legislative changes in the 1970s to promote deinstitutionalization of status offenders made it more difficult for the juvenile justice system to deal with noncriminal misconduct within the traditional rubric. As a result, the problem of girls in conflict with their families remained, even as policy changes restricted judges' access to institutions.

2. Policy changes to "crack down" on youth violence, such as transfer of more youths to criminal court for prosecution as adults and harsher delinquency sentences, and the adoption of mandatory arrest policies for domestic violence, indirectly affected juvenile courts' response to female offenders. Heightened sensitivity to domestic violence combined with prohibitions on incarcerating status offenders may have encouraged police to arrest girls for trivial domestic disturbances. Charging them with simple assaults rather than with status offenses (e.g., incorrigibility or unruliness) enables families, police, and juvenile courts to relabel the same behavior as delinquency and thereby evade the prohibitions of the JJDPA. Changes in patterns of arrests, victim–offender relationships, court processing practices, and confinement of boys and girls charged with simple assault suggest that much of the perceived increases in girls' "violence" over the past two decades may actually reflect a relabeling of status offenders as delinquents.

3. After three decades of deinstitutionalizing status offenders, the juvenile justice system remains committed to protecting and controlling girls, but without providing the resources necessary to respond to their real needs. The failure to provide adequate social services, in turn, creates substantial

pressures to circumvent restrictions on the disposition of status offenders by relabeling, bootstrapping, and transinstitutionalizing them. Confinement of girls appears to be driven by a relabeling of minor forms of girls' violence from "incorrigibility" to simple assault. The malleability of labels threatens to undermine the progress made in deinstitutionalizing status offenders.

4. Many gaps exist in our knowledge about how the juvenile justice system responds to female offenders. As a result of deinstitutionalization efforts, states file far fewer petitions for status offenses than they previously did. As a result, we know less now than we did two decades ago about how the juvenile justice system processes status offense–like behaviors. We know even less about how nonjustice system agencies, such as mental health and chemical dependency treatment facilities, handle these youths because they do not routinely generate data about decision-making and informal dispositions.

Appendix:
Girls Study Group Members

Dr. Margaret A. Zahn, Professor, Department of Sociology, North Carolina State University; Senior Research Scientist, Crime, Violence, and Justice Research Program, RTI International

Dr. Robert Agnew, Professor, Department of Sociology, Emory University

Dr. Elizabeth Cauffman, Assistant Professor, Department of Psychology and Social Behavior, University of California, Irvine

Dr. Meda Chesney-Lind, Professor, Women's Studies Program, University of Hawaii at Manoa

Dr. Gayle Dakof, Associate Research Professor, Department of Epidemiology and Public Health, University of Miami

Dr. Barry Feld, Professor, School of Law, University of Minnesota

Dr. Diana Fishbein, Director, Transdisciplinary Behavioral Science Program, RTI International

Dr. Peggy Giordano, Professor of Sociology, Center for Family and Demographic Research, Bowling Green State University

Dr. Candace Kruttschnitt, Professor, Department of Sociology, University of Toronto

Dr. Jody Miller, Professor, Department of Criminology and Criminal Justice, University of Missouri–St. Louis

Dr. Merry Morash, Professor, School of Criminal Justice, Michigan State University

Dr. Darrell Steffensmeier, Professor, Department of Sociology, Pennsylvania State University

Ms. Giovanna Taormina, Executive Director, Girls Circle Association

Dr. Donna-Marie Winn, Senior Research Scientist, Center for Child and Family Policy, Duke University

Notes

INTRODUCTION

1. The 640,000 number is the total number of estimated arrests of female juveniles in 2006 (the 2006 FBI arrest numbers are from police departments serving 72 percent of the population). The FBI number is adjusted to correct for the missing respondents, using the same procedure the Office of Juvenile Justice and Delinquency Prevention (OJJDP) does when they produce their Juvenile Arrest reports.

CHAPTER 2

1. A case in point is Felson's (1996, 2002) recent analyses of female violence and victimization. He reduces gender differences in victimization rates to biologically based issues of size and strength. Simply, women are small and weak, so they do not fight and are likely to be attacked. Such analyses are reductionistic and do not offer insight into the complex nature of violence.

2. In studies of girls' delinquency, macro-level structural analyses are perhaps the least well developed. However, several recent attempts to examine structural features of gender inequality and their relation to crime and victimization have proven fruitful (Bailey and Peterson 1995; Dugan, Nagin, and Rosenfeld 1999; Peterson and Bailey 1992; Steffensmeier and Haynie 2000b; Whaley 2001). For example, Peterson and Bailey (1992, p. 162) found that "the greater the income gap between males and females, the higher the rape rate" across U.S. cities. Steffensmeier and Haynie (2000b) found that structural disadvantage has a strong impact on rates of homicide for adult women and men and adolescent males, but that "the contexts for homicide among juvenile females are shaped less by adverse economic conditions and conditions of social disorganization" (p. 107). Their analysis did not, however, include direct measures of gender-based structural inequalities (such as gender disparities

in educational attainment, income, and occupational participation). This is an area in which additional research is clearly warranted.

3. Daly's conceptual schema provides a useful means of organizing the primary thematic aspects of feminist research in criminology. We should note that, as with any typology, any single study can address questions within several of these categories. In fact, we see the best work as that which simultaneously addresses multiple aspects and will make note of these overlaps where relevant.

4. Gender is one of the strongest and most persistent known correlates with offending. Historically, this led researchers to use all-male samples. More recently, quantitative research with samples that include both genders includes a dichotomous measure of gender in order to avoid misspecification. Unfortunately, much work does not go beyond this methodological step and thus fails to theorize gender's effects.

5. The fallacy of gender neutrality is demonstrated by the fact that criminologists never draw from all-female samples and assume their findings are generalizable to males. Thus, the notion of gender neutrality is based on the implicit perspective of the male subject (see Daly, 2000).

6. Much early feminist work in criminology correctly critiqued existing theory and research for focusing on men's and boys' crime at the expense of women and girls. Yet, as gender-focused modes of inquiry evolved within the field, the key questions scholars asked concerning female offending and offenders also pointed to the need to "gender" the criminal behavior of men. While the danger in this focus lies in a return to the prefeminist era of placing men back at the center of inquiry (Daly 1998), it is nonetheless the case that criminology has ignored the significance of gender in the study of male offending. Given men's and boys' overrepresentation as offenders, the study of masculinities and crime is an important area for feminist inquiry. Historically, the gendered nature of male offending was assumed (and normalized), but was neither explored nor theorized. Parallel with the growth in the sociological study of masculinity, recent work in feminist criminology has attempted to look at the criminal behavior of men in the context of gendered theories. This approach has enhanced our understanding of male offending.

7. Fill in the blank with any number of variables (for instance, violent, aggressive, assertive, peer-oriented).

CHAPTER 3

1. The other key source of official data, juvenile court statistics, is the focus of Chapter 11. As expected, girls' delinquency trends as reflected in juvenile court statistics parallel the trends observed in the arrest data.

2. See Steffensmeier (1993) for a discussion of these measures. Also see O'Brien (1999).

3. For parsimony and to reduce clutter, we collapse some overlapping offense categories (e.g., fraud, forgery, and embezzlement) and group the categories into five general types of delinquency.

4. For more detail on key elements of our analysis here, see Steffensmeier and others (2005).

5. Note that "weapons use/possession" is not targeted in our analysis (but see Table 3.1). The arrest data show the gender gap narrowing (FP goes from 6 percent to 11 percent) due mainly to sharp declines in weapons arrest rates for male youths since 1990 as compared with stable girls' rates. In contrast, self-report data from the NYRBS show "carrying a weapon" has declined among both girls and boys with the gender gap slightly widening.

6. The three questions asked of twelfth graders were how often during the past twelve months they have (a) "gotten into a serious fight at school or at work," (b) "hurt someone badly enough to need bandages or a doctor," and (c) "hit an instructor or supervisor." The question on hitting an instructor/supervisor is not asked of eighth and tenth graders. We exclude from the assault index an item asking eighth, tenth, and twelfth graders about involvement in a "fight where a group of your friends were against another group" because this item is ambiguous and does not refer to culpability. First, this question is vague enough to encompass a snowball fight among friends as well as gang activity. The other questions ask about specific acts that are more clearly violent in nature (e.g., "hurt someone badly enough to need bandages or a doctor"). Second, involvement in a "group fight" was widespread among both girls and boys, indicating the item likely includes mostly minor incidents that are unlikely to lead to arrest. Third, it is unclear whether the respondent was the aggressor, the victim, or a bystander. Nonetheless, the results for the "group fight" item parallel those for the other items (i.e., essentially no change in the gender gap over the 1980 to 2003 period).

7. The stability of the gender gap, especially over the 1990s, is remarkable in light of the substantial arrest gains by girls for assault and in light of possible self-fulfilling effects on survey sources of the increased legitimacy of girls' violence over the past one to two decades. Recent media and popular representations might encourage adolescent females to see their delinquency and violence, or that of their peers, as more commonplace and hence as less shaming or more acceptable behavior (e.g., less of a violation of "femininity"), increasing their willingness to self-report it. In a similar vein, we might expect victims to be more inclined to report girls as violent offenders, by labeling gray areas of aggressive behavior as "assaultive" that in the past would have been ignored or defined in milder terms.

8. We also examined the effects of individual juvenile ages (i.e., ages twelve to seventeen) on violent offending for both the arrest and the self-report data. Key findings are as follows. First, the gender gap widens a bit with age of juvenile (e.g., FP of arrests and self-reported violence is higher among twelve- to fourteen-year-olds than among fifteen- to seventeen-year-olds). Second, the trend patterns in assault rates and in the gender gap are similar across youth age groups.

9. Although it does not strictly qualify as a longitudinal survey, self-report trend data from the National Youth Survey (NYS) also show constancy in the juvenile gender gap for violent crime. Specifically, the 1967 to 1972 samples and 1977 to 1980 samples revealed similar gender gaps for minor assaults and felony assaults (Canter 1982b); and a matched sample of "high-risk" youths (aged thirteen to seventeen) surveyed in the 1977 NYS and the more recent 1989 Denver Youth Survey revealed constancy in the gender gap for minor assaults and felony assaults. Also, Canter's analysis revealed a sizable difference for aggravated assault in 1980 between the male-to-female self-reported ratio (about 3.5 to 1) and the arrest ratio for self-reported aggravated assault (5.6 to 1). The arrest ratio in 2000 had narrowed to about 3.56 to 1, essentially identical to the 1980 self-reported ratio. These numbers provide additional evidence for a closing of the gap between what girls have always done (and reported, when asked anonymously) and arrest statistics rather than a course change in girls' participation in serious violence.

10. Note that the comparison of "burglary/criminal trespass" trends between arrest and self-report sources is somewhat ambiguous since it assumes that the item measuring "trespassing" in *MTF* is roughly analogous to the sorts of behaviors that can lead to an arrest for burglary. The notion of "unlawful entry" that underlies the charge of burglary can entail a much broader range of behavior considerably beyond the traditional notion of "breaking and entering" a residence or business to steal property or money. Instead, unlawful entry with intent to commit (any) crime can encompass retail theft, theft from a motor vehicle, vandalism of someone's residence or business, physical attack or threat of someone in his/her residence,

being an accomplice or coconspirator to any of these activities, and "holding" or possessing property or money that has been taken in any of these activities.

11. Other self-report evidence suggests that the gender gap in delinquency has stayed fairly stable going back as far as the late 1960s. The NYS, generally recognized as the best of the self-report studies (because of its methodological rigor and national sample), provides information on delinquency trends for male and female adolescents from the late 1960s to the early 1980s. The survey results show increases in some delinquent behaviors (e.g., alcohol and drug use) among both male and female adolescents and decreases in others (e.g., theft and assault) but stable gender differences in delinquency. After reviewing the data, Delbert Elliott and associates conclude that during this time frame, the self-report data "show no significant decline in the [male-to-female] sex ratios on eight specific offenses" (Elliott, Morse, and Huizinga 1987). See also the review of early self-report studies on girls' and boys' delinquency in Steffensmeier and Steffensmeier (1980).

12. The National Institute on Drug Abuse's (NIDA) *Household Drug Abuse Survey* also provides information on self-reported substance use of male and female youths going back to the 1970s. However, because of frequent changes in methodology and item content, it is risky to use the NIDA data for gauging trends in youth drug use.

CHAPTER 4

1. We use the term "gender" throughout to maintain consistency with other chapters in this book. However, it is recognized that "gender" is a social construct, unlike sex, that focuses primarily on constitutional characteristics.

CHAPTER 5

1. A variable is considered a mediator if it transmits the influence of the independent variable to the dependent variable.

2. A moderating effect is the same as an interaction. In this type of situation, the direction or magnitude of the relationship between two variables hinges on the value of a third variable.

3. Sex-by-group interactions also were not significant in multivariate analyses of a variety of crimes that controlled for parents' drug/alcohol abuse, poverty, race, and parental arrest history (Widom and White 1997).

4. Smith and Ireland (2005) also found that sexual abuse was related to self-reported general offending and illicit drug use (but not violent offending or arrests) in early adulthood among females. These findings, however, are based on a bivariate analysis and only fifteen women reported any sexual abuse.

CHAPTER 7

1. Percentages calculated from raw numbers provided in Devoe and others (2003).

2. Little research has been done on the effect of school transitions and delinquency. Alspaugh (1998) finds a significant negative relationship between transition from elementary school to middle school and academic achievement and a positive relationship between transition from middle to high school and dropping out. Others find that transition from elementary to middle school decreases attachment to school (Eccles and Midgley 1989; Simmons and Blyth 1987), participation in extracurricular activities, and perceptions of support from school personnel (Seidman et al. 1994).

Biglan and others (2004) discuss the possible contribution of school transitions to problem behavior. As Eccles and Midgley (1989) discuss, "the organization of most junior high and middle schools runs contrary to the developmental needs of children" during adolescence (Biglan et al. 2004, p. 86). While elementary schools offer supportive social networks and more collaborative environments, middle and junior high schools are more competitive and rigid, with fewer opportunities to participate in decision-making in the school, such as choices regarding school norms and rules. It is likely, therefore, that the transition from the supportive elementary school environment to the disruptive middle school environment and the even more rigid high school environment could increase the probability of delinquency. More research on this relationship, as well as gender differences within this relationship, is needed.

3. Although the outcome of these results is teacher victimization, this is presumably related somewhat to student delinquency in that the delinquent acts being committed by students result at least partially in the victimization of teachers.

CHAPTER 9

1. Psychologists include all behaviors that are intended to harm in the definition of aggression. This means that both direct and indirect (and even covert) aggressions are included. Relational aggression is a particularly insidious form of indirect or social aggression that is intended to harm a girl's or boy's social relationships. Some researchers differentiate between social aggression, which is nonconfrontational and uses a social network to attack a youth without the youth being present, and direct relational aggression, in which a youth is attacked in the presence of others (Xie et al. 2002).

2. Aside from the physical versus relational modes, youths differ in their use of aggression depending on whether they are reacting to others or trying to achieve a purpose, for example, establish control or take something from each other (Little et al. 2003). Four types of aggression—physical aggression used in reaction to an insult or challenge, physical aggression used to achieve some purpose, relational aggression in reaction to an insult or a challenge, and relational aggression to achieve some purpose—have been shown to be distinct and differentially connected to whether youths tend to provoke others, get upset easily, see themselves as victimized by peers, and use coercive strategies to influence other people (Little et al. 2003). It is not a simple matter to untangle the different types of aggression, including physical violence, since in many instances multiple forms are used, or one form develops into another.

3. In a similar example that does not involve fighting, one ethnographic account of African American girls in an urban high school observed that these girls were often stereotyped as "loud" (Fordham 1993). The researcher documented that the girls were surrounded by a definition of femininity that is white and were ignored even when they excelled academically. In response, some African American girls resisted by embracing a style of acting like "those loud black girls," a form of "contrariness" that, while granting them visibility, also "dooms" them academically in the school (Fordham 1993, p. 22).

4. In this study, 16.4 percent had experienced violence from their mothers and 17.1 percent from their fathers.

5. Although the association of aggression with these disorders may be weaker for boys, violent boys should also be assessed and provided with appropriate intervention.

CHAPTER 10

1. However, family poverty was not a significant predictor of gang membership for young women (Thornberry 1997).

2. Recent evidence suggests that girls' supportive relationships in gangs may be stronger in all-female gangs and gangs with a substantial number of female members than in gangs that are numerically or ideologically male-dominated. See Joe Laidler and Hunt (2001); Peterson, Miller, and Esbensen (2001); and Miller and Brunson (2000) regarding the effect of gendered gang structure on member activities and delinquency.

3. This is particularly true because boys in all-male gangs also reported lower rates of gang delinquency than youths in gangs with both male and female membership.

4. Moore (1991) noted that this finding is partly an artifact of the underrepresentation of "square" women in her sample. She noted, "Some such women refused the interview because their husbands would not allow them to discuss their 'deviant' adolescence; others refused because they were afraid that they would be questioned about what they now define as 'deviance'—particularly about sexual activity" (p. 130). Moore concluded, "These views offer a poignant confirmation of the stigma attached to women's gang membership" (p. 130).

CHAPTER 11

Acknowledgments: Meda Chesney-Lind reviewed an earlier version of this chapter and provided several important suggestions and insights. Critiques by Kimberly Kempf-Leonard, Howard Snyder, Anne Stahl, Melissa Sickmund, and Donna Bishop further helped to improve it. I bear responsibility for any remaining deficiencies.

1. The NCJJ and the OJJDP continually update annual data on juvenile justice administration and more recent data are available at http://ojjdp.ncjrs.org/ojstatbb/index.html.

2. For ease of presentation, I round percentages to the nearest whole number, even when reporting decimals in the tables. When comparing boys and girls or girls of different races, I only discuss instances of substantial differences (e.g., about 5 percent) between groups.

3. "Family problems, even some that in past years may have been classified as status offenses (e.g., incorrigibility), can now result in an assault arrest. This logic also explains why violent crime arrests over the past decade have increased proportionately more for juvenile females than males" (Snyder 2002, p. 9).

4. As one probation officer observed, "if you arrest the parents, then you have to shelter the kids. . . . So if the police just make the kids go away and the number of kids being referred to the juvenile court for assaulting their parents or for disorderly conduct or punching walls or doors . . . the numbers have just been increasing tremendously because of that political change" (Gaarder, Rodriguez, and Zatz 2004, p. 565).

5. Judicial waiver statutes allow a juvenile court judge to waive jurisdiction on a discretionary basis after conducting a hearing to determine whether the youth is "amenable to treatment" or poses a threat to public safety. Legislative offense exclusion laws simply remove certain categories of offenses from juvenile court jurisdiction, for example, all youths sixteen years of age or older and charged with murder. With prosecutorial waiver of "direct file," juvenile and criminal courts share concurrent jurisdiction over certain ages and offenses, typically older youths and serious crimes, and prosecutors may exercise their discretion to charge a youth with a crime in either juvenile or criminal court (Snyder and Sickmund 2006; Feld 2000).

6. Several explanations may account for this consistent finding. First, attorney incompetence or structural impediments to effective representation, such as inadequate resources and crushing caseloads, may produce adverse outcomes. Second, judges may predetermine the likely disposition a juvenile will receive and appoint counsel when they anticipate a more severe sentence. Third, judicial hostility to adversarial litigants may garner harsher sentences similar to those received by criminal defendants who insist on a trial rather than plead guilty (Feld 1993; Burrus and Kempf-Leonard 2002).

References

Aalsma, M. C., and D. K. Lapsley. 2001. "A Typology of Adolescent Delinquency: Sex Differences and Implications for Treatment." *Criminal Behavior and Mental Health* 11: 173–191.

AAUW Educational Foundation. 2001. *Hostile Hallways: Bullying, Teasing, and Sexual Harassment in School*. Washington, DC: American Association of University Women Educational Foundation.

Abram, K. M., L. A. Teplin, D. R. Charles, S. L. Longworth, G. M. McClelland, and M. K. Dulcan. 2004. "Posttraumatic Stress Disorder and Trauma in Youth in Juvenile Detention." *Archives of General Psychiatry* 61:403–410.

Achenbach, T. 1991. *Manual for the Youth Self Report and 1991 Profile*. Burlington: University of Vermont, Department of Psychiatry.

Acker, J. 1990. "Hierarchies, Jobs, Bodies: A Theory of Gendered Organizations." *Gender and Society* 4:139–158.

Acoca, L. 1998a. "Defusing the Time Bomb: Understanding and Meeting the Growing Health Care Needs of Incarcerated Women in America." *Crime and Delinquency* 44 (1): 46–69.

———. 1998b. "Outside/Inside: The Violation of American Girls at Home, on the Streets, and in the Juvenile Justice System." *Crime and Delinquency* 44:561–589.

———. 1999. "Investing in Girls: A 21st Century Strategy." *Juvenile Justice* 6:3–13.

Acoca, L., and K. Dedel. 1998. *No Place to Hide: Understanding and Meeting the Needs of Girls in the California Juvenile Justice System*. San Francisco, CA: National Council on Crime and Delinquency.

Adams, M. S., and T. D. Evans. 1996. "Teacher Disapproval, Delinquent Peers, and Self-Reported Delinquency: A Longitudinal Test of Labeling Theory." *Urban Review* 28:199–211.

Adler, P., and P. Adler. 1998. *Peer Power: Preadolescent Culture and Identity*. New Brunswick, NJ: Rutgers University Press.

Agnew, R. 1992. "Foundation for a General Strain Theory of Crime and Delinquency." *Criminology* 30:47–87.

———. 1997. "Stability and Change in Crime Over the Life Course: A Strain Theory Explanation." In *Developmental Theories of Crime and Delinquency,* edited by T. P. Thornberry, 101–132. New Brunswick, NJ: Transaction Publishers.

———. 1999. "A General Strain Theory of Community Differences in Crime Rates." *Journal of Research in Crime and Delinquency* 36:123–155.

———. 2000. "Juvenile Delinquency: Causes and Control." In *Crime, Justice and Law,* 63–90. Los Angeles, CA: Roxbury Publishing Company.

———. 2005a. *Juvenile Delinquency: Causes and Control.* Los Angeles, CA: Roxbury.

———. 2005b. *Why Do Criminals Offend? A General Theory of Crime and Delinquency.* Los Angeles, CA: Roxbury.

———. 2006. *Pressured Into Crime: An Overview of General Strain Theory.* Los Angeles, CA: Roxbury.

Agnew, R., and T. Brezina. 1997. "Relational Problems with Peers, Gender, and Delinquency." *Youth and Society* 29:84–111.

Akers, R. L. 1998. *Social Learning and Social Structure: A General Theory of Crime and Deviance.* Boston, MA: Northeastern University Press.

Akers, R. L., and C. S. Sellers. 2004. *Criminological Theories.* Los Angeles, CA: Roxbury.

Alarid, L. F., V. S. Burton, Jr., and F. T. Cullen. 2000. "Gender and Crime among Felony Offenders: Assessing the Generality of Social Control and Differential Association Theories." *Journal of Research in Crime and Delinquency* 37:171–199.

Alder, C. 1984. "Gender Bias in Juvenile Diversion." *Crime and Delinquency* 30:400–414.

———. 1996. "Introduction." In *And When She Was Bad? Working with Young Women in Juvenile Justice and Related Areas,* edited by C. Alder and M. Baines. Hobart: National Clearinghouse for Youth Studies.

Almgren, G., A. Guest, G. Inmerwahr, and M. Spittel. 1998. "Joblessness, Family Disruption, and Violent Deaths in Chicago: 1970–1990." *Social Forces* 76 (4): 1465–1493.

Alspaugh, J. W. 1998. "Achievement Loss Associated with the Transition to Middle School and High School." *Journal of Educational Research* 92:20–25.

Amato, P. R., and J. G. Gilbreth. 1999. "Nonresident Fathers and Children's Well-Being: A Meta-Analysis." *Journal of Marriage and the Family* 61:557–573.

Amato, P. R., and B. Keith. 1991. "Parental Divorce and the Well-Being of Children: A Meta-Analysis." *Psychological Bulletin* 110:26–46.

American Bar Association. 1995. *A Call for Justice: An Assessment of Access to Counsel and Quality of Representation in Delinquency Proceedings.* Washington, DC: American Bar Association.

American Bar Association and National Bar Association. 2001. *Justice by Gender: The Lack of Appropriate Prevention, Diversion and Treatment Alternatives for Girls in the Juvenile Justice System.* Chicago: American Bar Association and National Bar Association. http://www.abanet.org/crimjust/juvjus/girls.html.

American Psychiatric Association. 1994. *Diagnostic and Statistical Manual of Mental Disorders.* Washington, DC: American Psychiatric Association.

Anderson, B., M. Holmes, and E. Ostresh. 1999. "Male and Female Delinquents' Attachments and Effects on Severity of Self-Reported Delinquency." *Criminal Justice and Behavior* 26:435–452.

Anderson, E. 1999. *Code of the Street: Decency, Violence, and the Moral Life of the Inner City.* New York: Norton.

Anderson, M., J. Kaufman, T. R. Simon, L. Barrios, L. Paulozzi, G. Ryan, R. Hammond, W. Modzeleski, T. Feucht, and L. Potter. 2001. "School-Associated Violent Deaths in the United States, 1994–1999." *Journal of the American Medical Association* 286:2695–2702.

Angold, A., E. J. Costello, and C. M. Worthman. 1998. "Puberty and Depression: The Roles of Age, Pubertal Status and Pubertal Timing." *Psychological Medicine* 28:51–61.

Angold, A., A. Erkanli, H. L. Egger, and E. J. Costello. 2000. "Stimulant Treatment for Children: A Community Perspective." *Journal of the American Academy of Child and Adolescent Psychiatry* 39:975–984; discussion 984–994.

Angold, A., A. Erkanli, E. M. Farmer, J. A. Fairbank, B. J. Burns, and G. Keeler. 2002. "Psychiatric Disorder, Impairment and Service Use in Rural African American and White Youth." *Archives of General Psychiatry* 59:893–901.

Arborelius, L., M. J. Owens, P. M. Plotsky, and C. B. Nemeroff. 1999. "The Role of Corticotropin-Releasing Factor in Depression and Anxiety Disorders." *Journal of Endocrinology* 160:1–12.

Arcia, E., and C. K. Conners. 1998. "Gender Differences in ADHD?" *Journal of Developmental and Behavioral Pediatrics* 19:77–83.

Artz, S. 1997. "On Becoming an Object." *Journal of Child and Youth Care* 11:17–37.

———. 1998a. *Sex, Power, and the Violent School Girl.* Toronto, Canada: Trifolium Books.

———. 1998b. "Where Have All the School Girls Gone? Violent Girls in the School Yard." *Child and Youth Care Forum* 27:77–109.

———. 2000. "Considering Adolescent Girls' Use of Violence: A Researcher's Reflections on Her Inquiry." *B.C. Counselor* 22:45–54.

———. 2004. "Revisiting the Moral Domain: Using Social Interdependence Theory to Understand Adolescent Girls' Perspectives on the Use of Violence." In *Girls and Aggression: Contributing Factors and Intervention Principles,* edited by M. M. Moretti, C. L. Odgers, and M. A. Jackson, 101–113. New York: Kluwer Academic/Plenum Publishers.

Aseltine, R. H., Jr. 1995. "A Reconsideration of Parental and Peer Influences on Adolescent Deviance." *Journal of Health and Social Behavior* 36:103–121.

Asher, S. R., and J. D. Coie. 1990. *Peer Rejection in Childhood.* New York: Cambridge University Press.

Attar, B., N. G. Guerra, and P. H. Tolan. 1995. "Neighborhood Disadvantage, Stressful Life Events, and Adjustment in Elementary School Children." *Journal of Clinical Child Psychology* 23:391–400.

Bailey, W. C., and R. D. Peterson. 1995. "Gender Inequality and Violence against Women: The Case of Murder." In *Crime and Inequality,* edited by J. Hagan and R. D. Peterson, 174–205. Stanford, CA: Stanford University Press.

Barak, G. 1998. *Integrating Criminologies.* Boston, MA: Allyn and Bacon.

Barbaresi, W. J., S. K. Katusic, R. C. Colligan, V. S. Pankratz, A. L. Weaver, K. J. Weber, D. A. Mrazek, and S. J. Jacobsen. 2002. "How Common Is Attention-Deficit/Hyperactivity Disorder? Incidence in a Population-Based Birth Cohort in Rochester, Minn." *Archives of Pediatric and Adolescent Medicine* 156:217–224.

Barkley, R. A. 1998. *Attention-Deficit Disorder: A Handbook for Diagnosis and Treatment.* New York: Guilford Press.

Bartollas, C. 1993. "Little Girls Grown Up: The Perils of Institutionalization." In *Female Criminality: The State of the Art,* edited by C. Culliver, 469–482. New York: Garland Press.

Bartusch, D. J., and R. L. Matsueda. 1996. "Gender, Reflected Appraisals, and Labeling: A Cross-Group Test of an Interactionist Theory of Delinquency." *Social Forces* 75:145–177.

Baskin, D. R., and I. B. Sommers. 1997. *Casualties of Community Disorder: Women's Careers in Violent Crime.* New York: Westview Press.

———. 1998. *Casualties of Community Disorder: Women's Careers in Violent Crime.* New York: Westview Press.

Batchelor, S., and M. Burman. 2001. "Discussing Violence: Let's Hear It from the Girls." *Probation Journal* 48:125–134.

Battin, S. R., K. G. Hill, R. D. Abbott, R. F. Catalano, and J. D. Hawkins. 1998. "The Contribution of Gang Membership to Delinquency beyond Delinquent Friends." *Criminology* 36: 93–115.

Battistich, V., and A. Hom. 1997. "The Relationship between Students' Sense of their School as a Community and Their Involvement in Problem Behaviors." *American Journal of Public Health* 87:1997–2001.

Baumrind, D. 1966. "Effects of Authoritative Control on Child Behavior." *Child Development* 37:887–907.

———. 1996. "The Discipline Controversy." *Family Relations: Journal of Applied Family and Child Studies* 45:405–414.

Bays, J. 1990. "Substance Abuse and Child Abuse: Impact of Addiction on the Child." *Pediatric Clinics of North America* 37:881–904.

Becker, K. B., and L. A. McCloskey. 2002. "Attention and Conduct Problems in Children Exposed to Family Violence." *American Journal of Orthopsychiatry* 72:83–91.

Beckett, K. 1997. *Making Crime Pay: Law and Order in Contemporary American Politics*. New York: Oxford University Press.

Beger, R. R., and H. Hoffman. 1998. "The Role of Gender in Detention Dispositioning of Juvenile Probation Violators." *Journal of Crime and Justice* 21:173–188.

Beitchman, J. H., K. J. Zucker, J. E. Hood, G. A. daCosta, D. Akman, and E. Cassavia. 1992. "A Review of the Long-Term Effects of Child Sexual Abuse." *Child Abuse and Neglect* 16:101–118.

Belknap, J., M. Dunn, and K. Holsinger. 1997. "Moving Toward Juvenile Justice and Youth-Serving Systems that Address the Distinct Experience of the Adolescent Female." Gender Specific Work Group Report to the Governor. Columbus, OH: Office of Criminal Justice Services.

Bell, C. C., and E. J. Jenkins. 1993. "Community Violence and Children on Chicago's Southside." *Psychiatry: Interpersonal and Biological Processes* 56:46–54.

Belsky, J., L. Steinberg, and P. Draper. 1991. "Childhood Experience, Interpersonal Development, and Reproductive Strategy and Evolutionary Theory of Socialization." *Child Development* 62:647–670.

Bennett, L., and S. Fineran. 1998. "Sexual and Severe Physical Violence among High School Students: Power Beliefs, Gender, and Relationship." *American Journal of Orthopsychiatry* 68:645–652.

Bensley, L. S., S. J. Spieker, J. Van Eenwyk, and J. Schoder. 1999. "Self-Reported Abuse History and Adolescent Problem Behaviors. II. Alcohol and Drug Use." *Journal of Adolescent Health* 24:173–180.

Berger, R. J. 1989. "Female Delinquency in the Emancipation Era: A Review of the Literature." *Sex Roles* 21:374–399.

Berndt, T. J. 1982. "The Features and Effects of Friendship in Early Adolescence." *Child Development* 64:544–555.

Best, C. L., B. S. Dansky, and D. G. Kilpatrick. 1992. "Medical Students' Attitudes about Female Rape Victims." *Journal of Interpersonal Violence* 7:175–188.

Bettie, J. 2000. "Women Without Class: Chicas, Cholas, Trash, and the Presence/Absence of Class Identity." *Signs: Journal of Women in Culture and Society* 26:1–35.

Betz, C. L. 1995. "Childhood Violence: A Nursing Concern." *Issues in Comprehensive, Pediatric Nursing* 18:149–161.

Beyer, M., G. Blair, S. Katz, S. Simkins, and A. Steinberg. 2003. "A Better Way to Spend $500,000: How the Juvenile Justice System Fails Girls." *Wisconsin Women's Law Journal* 18:51–75.

Biederman, J., S. V. Faraone, E. Mick, S. Williamson, T. E. Wilens, T. J. Spencer, W. Weber, J. Jetton, I. Kraus, J. Pert, and B. Zallen. 1999. "Clinical Correlates of ADHD in Females:

Findings from a Large Group of Girls Ascertained from Pediatric and Psychiatric Referral Sources." *Journal of the American Academy of Child and Adolescent Psychiatry* 38: 966–975.

Biederman, J., E. Mick, S. V. Faraone, E. Braaten, A. Doyle, T. Spencer, T. E. Wilens, E. Frazier, and M. A. Johnson. 2002. "Influence of Gender on Attention Deficit Hyperactivity Disorder in Children Referred to a Psychiatric Clinic." *American Journal of Psychiatry* 159:36–42.

Biglan, A., P. A. Brennan, S. L. Foster, and H. D. Holder. 2004. *Helping Adolescents at Risk: Prevention of Multiple Problem Behaviors.* New York: Guilford Press.

Billy, J. O. G., and J. R. Udry. 1985. "The Influence of Male and Female Best Friends on Adolescent Sexual Behavior." *Adolescence* 20:21–32.

———. 2005. "The Role of Race and Ethnicity in Juvenile Justice Processing." In *Our Children, Their Children: Confronting Racial and Ethnic Differences in American Juvenile Justice,* edited by D. F. Hawkins and K. Kempf-Leonard, 23–82. Chicago: University of Chicago Press.

Bishop, D. M., and C. Frazier. 1992. "Gender Bias in Juvenile Justice Processing: Implications of the JJDP Act." *Journal of Criminal Law and Criminology* 82:1162–1186.

———. 2000. "Consequences of Transfer" in *Changing Borders of Juvenile Justice: Transfer of Adolescents to the Criminal Courts,* edited by J. Fagan and F. E. Zimring, 227–276. Chicago: University of Chicago Press.

Bishop, D. M., C. Frazier, L. Lanza-Kaduce, and L. Winner. 1996. "The Transfer of Juveniles to Criminal Court: Does It Make a Difference?" *Crime and Delinquency* 42:171–191.

Bjerregaard, B., and C. Smith. 1993. "Gender Differences in Gang Participation, Delinquency, and Substance Use." *Journal of Quantitative Criminology* 4:329–355.

Bjorkvist, K. 1994. "Sex Differences in Physical, Verbal, and Indirect Aggression: A Review of Recent Research." *Sex Roles* 30:177–188.

Blackwell, B. S., and S. Eschholz. 2002. "Sex Differences and Rational Choice: Traditional Tests and New Directions." In *Rational Choice and Criminal Behavior,* edited by A. R. Piquero and S. G. Tibbetts, 109–136. New York: Routledge.

Bloom, B. E., ed. 2003. *Gendered Justice: Addressing Female Offenders.* Durham, NC: Carolina Academic Press.

Bloom, B., B. Owen, E. P. Deschenes, and J. Rosenbaum. 2002a. "Improving Juvenile Justice for Females: A Statewide Assessment in California." *Crime and Delinquency* 4:526–552.

———. 2002b. "Moving Toward Justice for Female Juvenile Offenders in the New Millennium." *Journal of Contemporary Criminal Justice* 18:37–56.

Blum, J., M. Ireland, and R. W. Blum. 2003. "Gender Differences in Juvenile Violence: A Report from Add Health." *Journal of Adolescent Health* 32:234–240.

Blumstein, A. 1996. "Youth Violence, Guns, and the Illicit-Drug Industry." *Journal of Criminal Law and Criminology* 86:10–36.

Blumstein, A., and J. Wallman. 2000. "The Recent Rise and Fall of American Violence." In *The Crime Drop in America,* edited by A. Blumstein and J. Wallman. New York: Cambridge University Press.

———. 2005. *The Crime Drop in America.* 2nd ed. Cambridge: Cambridge University Press.

Bond-Maupin, L., J. R. Maupin, and A. Leisenring. 2002. "Girls' Delinquency and the Justice Implications of Intake Workers' Perspectives." *Women and Criminal Justice* 13:51–77.

Bonny, A. E., M. T. Britto, B. K. Klostermann, R. W. Hornung, and G. B. Slap. 2000. "School Disconnectedness: Identifying Adolescents at Risk." *Pediatrics* 106:1017–1021.

Born, L., A. Shea, and M. Steiner. 2002. "The Roots of Depression in Adolescent Girls: Is Menarche the Key?" *Current Psychiatry Reports* 4:449–460.

Bottcher, J. 1995. "Gender As Social Control: A Qualitative Study of Incarcerated Youths and their Siblings in Greater Sacramento." *Justice Quarterly* 12:33–58.

———. 2001. "Social Practices of Gender: How Gender Relates to Delinquency in the Everyday Lives of High-Risk Youth." *Criminology* 39:893–932.

Bourgois, P. 1995. *In Search of Respect: Selling Crack in el Barrio.* Cambridge: Cambridge University Press.

Bowker, A. 2004. "Predicting Friendship Stability during Early Adolescence." *Journal of Early Adolescence* 24:85–112.

Bowker, L. H., H. S. Gross, and M. W. Klein. 1980. "Female Participation in Delinquent Gang Activities." *Adolescence* 15:509–519.

Bowker, L. H., and M. W. Klein. 1983. "The Etiology of Female Juvenile Delinquency and Gang Membership: A Test of Psychological and Social Structural Explanations." *Adolescence* 18:739–751.

Braithwaite, J. 1989. *Crime, Shame and Reintegration.* Cambridge: Cambridge University Press.

Breslau, N., H. D. Chilcoat, E. S. Susser, T. Matte, K. Y. Liang, and E. L. Peterson. 2001. "Stability and Change in Children's Intelligence Quotient Scores: A Comparison of Two Socioeconomically Disparate Communities." *American Journal of Epidemiology* 154:711–777.

Bridges, G. S., and S. Steen. 1998. "Racial Disparities in Official Assessments of Juvenile Offenders: Attributional Stereotypes as Mediating Mechanisms." *American Sociological Review* 63:554–570.

Brier, N. 1995. "Predicting Antisocial Behavior in Youngsters Displaying Poor Academic Achievement: A Review of Risk Factors." *Journal of Developmental and Behavioral Pediatrics* 16:271–276.

Britton, D. M. 2000. "Feminism in Criminology: Engendering the Outlaw." *Annals of the American Academy of Political and Social Science* 571:57–76.

Broidy, L. M. 1995. "Direct Supervision and Delinquency: Assessing the Adequacy of Structural Proxies." *Journal of Criminal Justice* 23:541–554.

———. 2001. "A Test of General Strain Theory." *Criminology* 39:9–36.

Broidy, L. M., and R. Agnew. 1997. "Gender and Crime: A General Strain Theory Perspective." *Journal of Research in Crime and Delinquency* 34:275–306.

Broidy, L., E. Cauffman, D. L. Espelage, P. Mazerolle, and A. Piquero. 2003a. "Sex Differences in Empathy and Its Relation to Juvenile Offending." *Violence and Victims* 18:503–516.

Broidy, L. M., D. S. Nagin, R. E. Tremblay, J. E. Bates, B. Brame, K. A. Dodge, D. Fergusson, J. L. Horwood, R. Loeber, R. Laird, D. R. Lynam, T. E. Moffitt, G. S. Pettit, and F. Vitaro. 2003b. "Developmental Trajectories of Childhood Disruptive Behaviors and Adolescent Delinquency: A Six-Site, Cross-National Study." *Developmental Psychology* 39:222–245.

Brooks-Gunn, J., G. J. Duncan, and J. L. Aber. 1997a. *Neighborhood Poverty, Vol. 1: Context and Consequences for Children.* New York: Russell Sage Foundation.

———. 1997b. *Neighborhood Poverty, Vol. 2: Policy Implications in Studying Neighborhoods.* New York: Russell Sage Foundation.

Brooks-Gunn, J., G. J. Duncan, P. K. Klebanov, and N. Sealand. 1993. "Do Neighborhoods Influence Child and Adolescent Behavior?" *American Journal of Sociology* 99:335–395.

Brooks-Gunn, J., J. Graber, and R. L. Paikoff. 1994. "Studying Links between Hormones and Negative Affect: Models and Measures." *Journal of Adolescent Research* 4:469–486.

Brooks-Gunn, J., P. K. Klebanov, and G. J. Duncan. 1996. "Ethnic Differences in Children's Intelligence Test Scores: Role of Economic Deprivation, Home Environment, and Maternal Characteristics." *Child Development* 67:396–408.

Brown, B. S., and A. R. Mills. 1987. *Youth at High Risk for Substance Abuse.* Rockville, MD: U.S. Department of Health and Human Services, National Institute on Drug Abuse.

Brown, L. M. 1998. *Raising their Voices: The Politics of Girls' Anger.* Cambridge, U.K.: Harvard University Press.

———. 2003. *Girlfighting.* New York: New York University Press.

Brown, L. M., and C. Gilligan. 1992. *Meeting at the Crossroads: Women's Psychology and Girls' Development.* New York: Harvard University Press.

———. 1993. *Meeting at the Crossroads: Women's Psychology and Girls' Development.* New York: Ballantine.

Brown, W. K. 1978. "Black Female Gangs in Philadelphia." *International Journal of Offender Therapy and Comparative Criminology* 21:221–228.

Browne, A., and E. Lichter. 2001. "Imprisonment in the United States." In *Encyclopedia of Women and Gender. Vol. A–K,* edited by J. Worrall, 611–623. London: Academic Press.

Browne, K. D., and C. E. Hamilton. 1998. "Physical Violence between Young Adults and their Parents: Associations with a History of Child Maltreatment." *Journal of Family Violence* 13:59–79.

Bryk, A. S., and M. E. Driscoll. 1988. *The School as Community: Shaping Forces and Consequences for Students and Teachers.* Madison, WI: University of Wisconsin, National Center on Effective Secondary Schools.

Buka, S. L., T. L. Stichick, I. Birdthistle, and F. J. Earls. 2001. "Youth Exposure to Violence: Prevalence, Risks, and Consequences." *American Journal of Orthopsychiatry* 71:298–310.

Burket, R. C., M. W. Sajid, M. Wasiak, and W. C. Myers. 2005. "Personality Comorbidity in Adolescent Females with ADHD." *Journal of Psychiatric Practitioners* 11:131–136.

Burman, M. 2003. "Challenging Conceptions of Violence: A View from the Girls." *Sociology Review* 13:2–6.

Burman, M., J. Brown, and S. Batchelor. 2003. "'Taking it to Heart': Girls and the Meanings of Violence." In *The Meaning of Violence,* edited by A. Stanko, 71–89. New York: Routledge.

Burruss, G. W., Jr., and K. Kempf-Leonard. 2002. "The Questionable Advantage of Defense Counsel in Juvenile Court." *Justice Quarterly* 19:37–67.

Bursik, R. J., and H. G. Grasmick. 1993a. *Neighborhoods and Crime: The Dimensions of Effective Community Control.* New York: Lexington Books.

———. 1993b. "Neighborhood Opportunities for Criminal Behavior." In *Neighborhoods and Crime: The Dimensions of Effective Community Control.* New York: Lexington Books.

Burton, L. M., K. W. Allison, and D. Obeidallah. 1995. "Social Context and Adolescence: Perspectives on Development among Inner-City African American Teens." In *Pathways through Adolescence: Individual Development in Relation to Social Contexts,* edited by L. J. Crockett and A. C. Crouter, 119–138. Hillsdale, NJ: Lawrence Erlbaum Associates.

Burton, V. S., F. T. Cullen, T. D. Evans, L. F. Alarid, and R. G. Dunaway. 1998. "Gender, Self Control, and Crime." *Journal of Research in Crime and Delinquency* 35:123–147.

Caetano, S. C., J. P. Hatch, P. Brambilla, R. B. Sassi, M. Nicoletti, A. G. Mallinger, E. Frank, D. J. Kupfer, M. S. Keshavan, and J. C. Soares. 2004. "Anatomical MRI Study of Hippocampus and Amygdala in Patients with Current and Remitted Major Depression." *Psychiatry Research* 132:141–147.

Cairns, R. B., and B. D. Cairns. 1994. *Lifelines and Risks: Pathways of Youth in Our Time.* New York: Cambridge University Press.

Cairns, R. B., B. D. Cairns, H. J. Neckerman, L. L. Ferguson, and J. L. Gariepy. 1989. "Growth and Aggression: I. Childhood to Early Adolescence." *Developmental Psychology* 25:320–330.

Cairns, R. B., B. D. Cairns, H. J. Neckerman, S. D. Gest, and J. Gariepy. 1988. "Social Networks and Aggressive Behavior: Peer Support or Peer Rejection?" *Developmental Psychology* 24:815–823.

Cairns, R. B., M. C. Leung, L. Buchanan, and B. D. Cairns. 1995. "Friendships and Social Networks in Childhood and Adolescence: Fluidity, Reliability, and Interrelations." *Child Development* 66:1330–1345.

Campbell, A. 1984. *The Girls in the Gang.* New York: Basil Blackwell.

———. 1987. "Self Definition by Rejection: The Case of Gang Girls." *Social Problems* 34: 451–466.

———. 1990. "Female Participation in Gangs." In *Gangs in America,* edited by R. C. Huff, 163–182. Newbury Park, CA: SAGE Publications.

———. 1991. *The Girls in the Gang.* Cambridge, U.K.: Basil Blackwell.

———. 1993. *Men, Women and Aggression.* New York: Basic Books.

Canter, R. J. 1982a. "Family Correlates of Male and Female Delinquency." *Criminology* 20: 149–167.

———. 1982b. "Sex Differences in Self-Report Delinquency." *Criminology* 20:373–393.

Capaldi, D. M., H. K. Kim, and J. W. Shortt. 2004. "Women's Involvement in Aggression in Young Adult Romantic Relationships: A Developmental Systems Model." In *Aggression, Antisocial Behavior, and Violence among Girls,* edited by M. Putallaz and K. Bierman, 223–241. New York: Guilford Press.

Caplan, P. J., M. Crawford, J. S. Hyde, and J. T. E. Richardson. 1997. *Gender Differences in Human Cognition.* New York: Oxford University Press.

Carr, M. B., and T. A. Vandiver. 2001. "Risk and Protective Factors among Youth Offenders." *Adolescence* 36:409–426.

Carr, P. J. 2003. "The New Parochialism: The Implications of the Beltway Case for Arguments Concerning Informal Social Control." *American Journal of Sociology* 108:1249–1291.

Carter, C. S., and M. Altemus. 1997. "Integrative Functions of Lactational Hormones in Social Behavior and Stress Management." *Annals of the New York Academy of Sciences* 807: 164–174.

Caspi, A., and E. S. Herbener. 1990. "Continuity and Change: Assortative Marriage and the Consistency of Personality in Adulthood." *Journal of Personality and Social Psychology* 58:250–258.

Caspi, A., D. Lynam, T. E. Moffitt, and P. A. Silva. 1993. "Unraveling Girls' Delinquency: Biological, Dispositional, and Contextual Contributions to Adolescent Misbehavior." *Developmental Psychology* 29:19–30.

Caspi, A., and T. E. Moffitt. 1991. "Individual Differences Are Accentuated During Periods of Social Change: The Sample Case of Girls at Puberty." *Journal of Personality and Social Psychology* 61:157–168.

Castallano, T. C. 1986. "The Justice Model in the Juvenile Justice System: Washington State's Experience." *Law and Policy* 8:479–506.

Catalano, R. F., and J. D. Hawkins. 1996. "The Social Development Model: A Theory of Antisocial Behavior." In *Delinquency and Crime: Current Theories,* edited by J. D. Hawkins, 149–197. New York: Cambridge University Press.

Cauffman, E. 2004. "A Statewide Screening of Mental Health Symptoms among Juvenile Offenders in Detention." *Journal of the American Academy of Child and Adolescent Psychiatry* 43:430–439.

Cauffman, E., S. S. Feldman, J. Waterman, and H. Steiner. 1998. "Posttraumatic Stress Disorder among Female Juvenile Offenders." *Journal of the American Academy of Child and Adolescent Psychiatry* 37:1209–1216.

Cauffman, E., and T. Grisso. 2005. "Mental Health Issues among Minority Offenders in the Juvenile Justice System." In *Our Children, Their Children: Confronting Racial and Ethnic Differences in American Juvenile Justice,* edited by D. F. Hawkins and K. Kempf-Leonard, 391–412. Chicago: University of Chicago Press.

Celeste, G., and P. Puritz. 2003. "The Children Left Behind: Assessment of Access to Counsel and Quality of Representation in Delinquency Proceedings in Louisiana." *Southern Law Review* 30:398–501.

Cepeda, A., and A. Valdez. 2003. "Risk Behaviors among Young Mexican American Gang-Associated Females: Sexual Relations, Partying, Substance Use, and Crime." *Journal of Adolescent Research* 18:90–106.

Cernkovich, S. A., and P. C. Giordano. 1979. "Delinquency, Opportunity, and Gender." *Journal of Criminal Law and Criminology* 70:145–151.

———. 1987. "Family Relationships and Delinquency." *Criminology* 25:295–321.

———. 1992. "School Bonding, Race, and Delinquency." *Criminology* 30:261–291.

Cernkovich, S. A., P. C. Giordano, and M. D. Pugh. 1985. "Chronic Offenders: The Missing Cases in Self-Report Delinquency Research." *Journal of Criminal Law and Criminology* 76:705–732.

Chamberlain, P. 2003. *Treating Chronic Juvenile Offenders: Advances Made through the Oregon Multidimensional Treatment Foster Care Model.* Washington, DC: American Psychological Association.

Champion, H. L. O., and R. H. Durant. 2001. "Exposure to Violence and Victimization and the Use of Violence by Adolescents in the United States." *Minerva Pediatrics* 53: 189–197.

Charmandari, E., T. Kino, E. Souvatzoglou, and G. P. Chrousos. 2003. "Pediatric Stress: Hormonal Mediators and Human Development." *Hormone Research* 59 (4): 161–179.

Chermack, S. T., S. F. Stoltenberg, B. E. Fuller, and F. C. Blow. 2000. "Gender Differences in the Development of Substance-Related Problems: The Impact of Family History of Alcoholism, Family History of Violence and Childhood Conduct Problems." *Journal of Studies on Alcohol* 61:845–852.

Chesney-Lind, M. 1977. "Paternalism and the Female Status Offender." *Crime and Delinquency* 23:121–130.

———. 1988a. "Girls and Status Offenses: Is Juvenile Justice Still Sexist?" *Criminal Justice Abstracts* 20:144–165.

———. 1988b. "Girls in Jail." *Crime and Delinquency* 34:156–168.

———. 1989. "Girls' Crime and Woman's Place: Toward a Feminist Model of Female Delinquency." *Crime and Delinquency* 35:5–29.

———. 1993. "Girls, Gangs and Violence: Anatomy of a Backlash." *Humanity and Society* 17:321–344.

———. 1997. *The Female Offender: Girls, Women, and Crime.* Thousand Oaks, CA: SAGE Publications.

———. 1999. "Girls and Violence: An Overview." In *Youth Violence: Prevention, Intervention and Social Policy,* edited by D. J. Flannery and C. H. Huff, 171–200. Washington, DC: American Psychiatric Press.

———. 2001. "Are Girls Closing the Gender Gap in Violence?" *Criminal Justice* (Spring): 18–23.

———. 2002. "Criminalizing Victimization: The Unintended Consequences of Pro-Arrest Policies for Girls and Women." *Criminology and Public Policy* 2:81–90.

Chesney-Lind, M., and M. Belknap. 2004. "Trends in Delinquent Girls' Aggression and Violent Behavior: A Review of the Evidence." In *Aggression, Antisocial Behavior and Violence among Girls: A Developmental Perspective,* edited by M. Puytallaz and P. Bierman, 203–222. New York: Guilford Press.

Chesney-Lind, M., and J. Hagedorn. 1999. *Female Gangs in America: Essays on Girls, Gangs and Gender.* Chicago: Lake View Press.

Chesney-Lind, M., and V. V. Paramore. 2001. "Are Girls Getting More Violent? Exploring Juvenile Robbery Trends." *Journal of Contemporary Criminal Justice* 17:142–166.

Chesney-Lind, M., and L. Pasko. 2004. *The Female Offender: Girls, Women and Crime.* Thousand Oaks, CA: SAGE Publications.

Chesney-Lind, M., and R. G. Shelden. 1997. *Girls, Delinquency, and Juvenile Justice.* Pacific Grove, CA: Brooks/Cole.

———. 2004. *Girls, Delinquency and Juvenile Justice.* Belmont: Thompson/Wadsworth.

Chesney-Lind, M., R. G. Shelden, and K. A. Joe. 1996. "Girls, Delinquency, and Gang Membership." In *Gangs in America,* edited by C. R. Huff, 185–204. Thousand Oaks, CA: SAGE Publications.

Chessler, P. 2001. *Women's Inhumanity to Women.* New York: Nation Books.

Children and Family Justice Center. 2005. *Education on Lockdown: The Schoolhouse to Jailhouse Track.* Evanston, IL: Northwestern University School of Law.

Cho, M. M., A. C. DeVries, J. R. Williams, and C. S. Carter. 1999. "The Effects of Oxytocin and Vasopressin on Partner Preferences in Male and Female Prairie Voles (*Microtus ochrogaster*)." *Behavioral Neuroscience* 113:1071–1079.

Claes, M., and R. Simard. 1992. "Friendship Characteristics of Delinquent Adolescents." *International Journal of Adolescence and Youth* 3:287–301.

Clarke, A. R., R. J. Barry, R. McCarthy, and M. Selikowitz. 2001. "Age and Sex Effects in the EEG: Differences in Two Subtypes of Attention-Deficit/Hyperactivity Disorder." *Clinical Neurophysiology* 112:815–826.

Clarke, S. H., and G. G. Koch. 1980. "Juvenile Court—Therapy or Crime Control, and Do Lawyers Make a Difference?" *Law and Society Review* 14:263–308.

Cloward, R. A., and F. F. Piven. 1979. "Hidden Protest: The Channeling of Female Innovation and Resistance." *Signs: Journal of Women in Culture and Society* 4:651–669.

Cocozza, J. J. 1991. *Responding to the Mental Health Needs of Youth in the Juvenile Justice System.* Seattle, WA: The National Coalition for the Mentally Ill in the Criminal Justice System.

Cocozza, J. J., and K. R. Skowyra. 2000. "Youth with Mental Health Disorders: Issues and Emerging Responses." *Juvenile Justice* 7:3–13.

Cohen, A. K. 1955. *Delinquent Boys: The Culture of the Gang.* New York: Free Press.

Cohen, J. A., E. Deblinger, A. P. Mannarino, and R. Steer. 2004. "A Multisite Randomized Trial for Children with Sexual Abuse–Related PTSD Symptoms." *Journal of the American Academy of Child and Adolescent Psychiatry* 43:393–402.

Cohen, J. A., and A. P. Mannarino. 1998. "Interventions for Sexually Abused Children: Initial Treatment Outcome Findings." *Child Maltreatment* 3:17–27.

Cohen, L. E., and M. Felson. 1979. "Social Change and Crime Rate Trends: A Routine Activity Approach." *American Sociological Review* 44:588–608.

Coie, J. D., K. A. Dodge, and J. B. Kupersmidt. 1990. "Peer Group Behavior and Social Status." In *Peer Rejection in Childhood,* edited by S. Asher and J. D. Coie, 17–59. Cambridge: Cambridge University Press.

Coker, A. L., D. L. Richter, R. F. Valois, R. E. McKeown, C. Z. Garrison, and M. L. Vincent. 1994. "Correlates and Consequences of Early Initiation of Sexual Intercourse." *Journal of School Health* 64:372–377.

Collins, D. W., and D. Kimura. 1997. "A Large Sex Difference on a Two-Dimensional Mental Rotation Task." *Behavioral Neuroscience* 111:845–849.

Collins, W. A., and B. Laursen. 1999. *Relationships as Developmental Contexts: The Minnesota Symposia on Child Psychology.* Mahwah, NJ: Lawrence Erlbaum Associates.

Colvin, M. 2000. *Crime and Coercion.* New York: St. Martin's Press.

Comings, D. E., D. Muhleman, J. P. Johnson, and J. P. MacMurray. 2002. "Parent-Daughter Transmission of the Androgen Receptor Gene as an Explanation of the Effect of Father Absence on Age of Menarche." *Child Development* 73:1046–1051.

Community Research Associates. 1998. *Juvenile Female Offenders: A Status of the States Report.* Washington, DC: ODDJP.

Connell, R. W. 2002. *Gender*. Cambridge, U.K.: Polity Press.

Cookston, J. T. 1999. "Parental Supervision and Family Structure: Effects on Adolescent Problem Behaviors." *Journal of Divorce and Remarriage* 32:107–122.

Cooley, C. H. 1902/1992. *Human Nature and the Social Order*. New Brunswick, NJ: Transaction.

Cooper, N. L., P. Puritz, and W. Shang. 1998. "Fulfilling the Promise of In re Gault: Advancing the Role of Lawyers for Children." *Wake Forest Law Review* 33:651–679.

Corley, C. J., S. Cernkovich, and P. Giordano. 1989. "Sex and the Likelihood of Sanction." *Journal of Criminal Law and Criminology* 80:540–556.

Corneau, M., and N. Lanctot. 2004. "Mental Health Outcomes of Adjudicated Males and Females: The Aftermath of Juvenile Delinquency and Problem Behaviour." *Criminal Behaviour and Mental Health* 14:251–262.

Cornish, D., and R. Clarke. 1986. *The Reasoning Criminal: Rational Choice Perspectives on Offending*. New York: Springer-Verlag.

Corsaro, W. A., and D. Eder. 1990. "Children's Peer Cultures." *Annual Review of Sociology* 16:197–220.

Costello, B. J., and H. J. Mederer. 2003. "A Control Theory of Gender Difference in Crime and Delinquency." In *Control Theories of Crime and Delinquency*, edited by C. L. Britt and M. R. Gottfredson, 77–107. New Brunswick, NJ: Transaction.

Costello, E. J., S. Mustillo, A. Erkland, G. Keeler, and A. Angold. 2003. "Prevalence and Development of Psychiatric Disorders in Childhood and Adolescence." *Archives of Clinical Psychiatry* 60:833–844.

Costello, E. J., M. Sung, C. Worthman, and A. Angold. 2007. "Pubertal Maturation and the Development of Alcohol Use and Abuse." *Drug and Alcohol Dependence* 88S:S50–S59.

Costello, J. C. 2003. "'Wayward and Noncompliant' People with Mental Disabilities: What Advocates of Involuntary Outpatient Commitment Can Learn from the Juvenile Court Experience with Status Offense Jurisdiction." *Psychology, Public Policy, and Law* 9: 233–257.

Costello, J. C., and N. L. Worthington. 1981. "Incarcerating Status Offenders—Attempts to Circumvent the Juvenile Justice and Delinquency Prevention Act." *Harvard Civil Rights Civil Liberties Law Review* 16:41–81.

Cota-Robles, S., and W. Gamble. 2006. "Parent–Adolescent Processes and Reduced Risk for Delinquency: The Effect of Gender for Mexican American Adolescents." *Youth and Society* 37:375–392.

Cottler, L. B., W. M. Compton, D. Mager, E. L. Spitznagel, and J. Aleksandar. 1992. "Posttraumatic Stress Disorder among Substance Users from the General Population." *American Journal of Psychiatry* 149:664–670.

Cottrell, B., and P. Monk. 2004. "Adolescent-to-Parent Abuse." *Journal of Family Issues* 25:1072–1095.

Cozby, P. C. 1973. "Self-Disclosure: A Literature Review." *Psychological Bulletin* 79:73–91.

Craig, W. M. 1998. "The Relationship among Bullying, Victimization, Depression, Anxiety, and Aggression in Elementary School Children." *Personality and Individual Differences* 24:123–140.

Crawford, M. 1995. *Talking Difference: On Gender and Language*. Thousand Oaks, CA: SAGE Publications.

Crick, N. R., M. A. Bigbee, and C. Howes. 1996. "Gender Differences in Children's Normative Beliefs about Aggression: How Do I Hurt Thee? Let Me Count the Ways." *Child Development* 67:1003–1014.

Crick, N. R., and J. K. Grotpeter. 1995. "Relational Aggression, Gender, and Social-Psychological Adjustment." *Child Development* 66:710–722.

Crick, N. R., N. E. Werner, J. F. Casas, K. M. O'Brien, D. A. Nelson, J. K. Grotpeter, and K. M. Markon. 1999. "Childhood Aggression and Gender: A New Look at an Old Problem." In *Nebraska Symposium on Motivation,* edited by D. Bernstein, 75–141. Lincoln: University of Nebraska.

Crosnoe, R., K. G. Erickson, and S. M. Dornbusch. 2002. "Protective Functions of Family Relationships and School Factors on the Deviant Behavior of Adolescent Boys and Girls." *Youth and Society* 33:515–544.

Csikszentmihalyi, M., and R. Larson. 1984. *Being Adolescent: Conflict and Growth in the Teen-age Years.* New York: Basic Books.

Cullen, F. T. 1994. "Social Support as an Organizing Concept for Criminology: Presidential Address to the Academy of Criminal Justice Sciences." *Justice Quarterly* 11:527–559.

Cullen, F. T., and R. Agnew. 2003. *Criminological Theory: Past to Present.* Los Angeles, CA: Roxbury Publishing Company.

Cummings, A. L., and A. W. Leschied. 2002. "Aggressive Adolescent Girls: A Qualitative Analysis of their Verbal and Physical Aggression." In *Research and Treatment for Aggression with Adolescent Girls,* edited by A. L. Cummings and A. W. Leschied, 57–76. Lewiston: Edwin Mellen Press.

Curran, D. J. 1984. "Myth of the 'New' Female Delinquent." *Crime and Delinquency* 30: 386–399.

Curry, G. D. 1997. "Selected Statistics on Female Gang Involvement." In *Fifth Joint National Conference on Gangs, Schools, and Communities.* Orlando, FL.

———. 1998. "Female Gang Involvement." *Journal of Research in Crime and Delinquency* 35:100–118.

———. 1999. "Responding to Female Gang Involvements." In *Female Gangs in America,* edited by M. Chesney-Lind and J. Hagedorn, 133–153. Chicago: Lake View Press.

Curry, G. D., R. A. Ball, and R. J. Fox. 1994. "Gang Crime and Law Enforcement Recordkeeping." In *Research in Brief.* Washington, DC: National Institute of Justice.

Curry, G. D., and S. H. Decker. 1998. *Confronting Gangs: Crime and Community.* Los Angeles, CA: Roxbury Publishing Company.

Curtis, R. L., Jr., P. Leung, E. Sullivan, K. Eschbach, and M. Stinson. 2001. "Outcomes of Child Sexual Contacts: Patterns of Incarcerations from a National Sample." *Child Abuse and Neglect* 25:719–736.

Cymbalisty, B. Y., S. Z. Schuck, and J. A. Dubeck. 1975. "Achievement Level, Institutional Adjustment and Recidivism among Juvenile Delinquents." *Journal of Community Psychology* 3:289–294.

D'Unger, A. V., K. C. Land, and P. L. McCall. 2002. "Sex Differences in Age Patterns of Delinquent/Criminal Careers: Results from Poisson Latent Class Analyses of the Philadelphia Cohort Study." *Journal of Quantitative Criminology* 18:349–375.

D'Unger, A. V., K. C. Land, P. L. McCall, and D. S. Nagi. 1998. "How Many Latent Classes of Delinquency/Criminal Careers? Results from Mixed Poisson Regression Analysis." *American Journal of Sociology* 103:1593–1630.

Dalby, C. 1994. "Gender Bias Towards Status Offenders: A Paternalistic Agenda Carried Out through the JJDPA." *Law and Inequality Journal* 12:429, 438–440.

Daley, T. C., S. E. Whaley, M. D. Sigman, M. P. Espinosa, and C. Neumann. 2003. "IQ on the Rise: The Flynn Effect in Rural Kenyan Children." *Psychological Science* 14:215–219.

Daly, K. 1992. "Women's Pathways to Felony Court: Feminist Theories of Lawbreaking and Problems of Representation." *Southern California Review of Law and Women's Studies* 2:11–52.

———. 1994. *Gender, Crime, and Punishment.* New Haven, CT: Yale University Press.

———. 1998. "Gender, Crime and Criminology." In *The Handbook of Crime and Justice,* edited by M. Tonry, 85–108. Oxford: Oxford University Press.

———. 2000. "Feminist Theoretical Work in Criminology." *DivisioNews. Newsletter of the Division of Women and Crime, American Society of Criminology* (August). http://www .ou.edu/soc/dwc/newsletter.htm.

Daly, K., and M. Chesney-Lind. 1988. "Feminism and Criminology." *Justice Quarterly* 5: 497–535.

Daly, K., and L. Maher. 1998. "Crossroads and Intersections: Building from Feminist Critique." In *Criminology at the Crossroads: Feminist Readings in Crime and Justice,* edited by K. Daly and L. Maher, 1–17. Oxford: Oxford University Press.

Datesman, S. K., F. R. Scarpitti, and R. M. Stephenson. 1975. "Female Delinquency—An Application of Self and Opportunity Theories." *Journal of Researching in Crime and Delinquency* 12:107–123.

Davies, P. T., and M. Windle. 1997. "Gender-Specific Pathways between Maternal Depressive Symptoms, Family Discord, and Adolescent Adjustment." *Developmental Psychology* 33: 657–668.

De Coster, S., K. Heimer, and S. M. Wittrock. 2006. "Neighborhood Disadvantage, Social Capital, Street Context, and Youth Violence." *Sociological Quarterly* 47:723–753.

Deblinger, E., and M. E. Runyon. 2005. "Understanding and Treating Feelings of Shame in Children Who Have Experienced Maltreatment." *Child Maltreatment* 10 (4): 364–376.

Deblinger, E., R. A. Steer, and J. Lippmann. 1999. "Maternal Factors Associated with Sexually Abused Children's Psychosocial Adjustment." *Child Maltreatment* 4:13–20.

Decker, S. H. 1985. "Systematic Analysis of Diversion—Net Widening and Beyond." *Journal of Criminal Justice* 13:207–216.

Decker, S. H., S. Pennell, and A. Caldwell. 1996. *Arrestees and Guns: Monitoring the Illegal Firearms Market.* Washington, DC: Final Report submitted to the National Institute of Justice.

Decker, S. H., and B. Van Winkle. 1996. *Life in the Gang.* Cambridge: Cambridge University Press.

Dembo, R., L. Williams, E. Berry, and E. Wish. 1988. "Physical Abuse, Sexual Victimization and Illicit Drug Use: Replication of a Structural Analysis among a New Sample of High Risk Youths." Paper presented at the annual meeting of the American Society of Criminology.

Demuth, S. 2004. "Understanding the Delinquency and Social Relationships of Loners." *Youth and Society* 35:366–392.

Demuth, S., and S. L. Brown. 2004. "Family Structure, Family Processes, and Adolescent Delinquency: The Significance of Parental Absence Versus Parental Gender." *Journal of Research in Crime and Delinquency* 41:58–81.

Deschenes, E. P., and F. A. Esbensen. 1999a. "Violence among Girls: Does Gang Membership Make a Difference?" In *Female Gangs in America: Essays on Girls, Gangs and Gender,* edited by M. Chesney-Lind and J. M. Hagedorn, 277–294. Chicago: Lake View Press.

———. 1999b. "Violence and Gangs: Gender Differences in Perceptions and Behavior." *Journal of Quantitative Criminology* 15:63–96.

Devoe, J. F., K. Peter, P. Kaufman, S. A. Ruddy, A. K. Miller, M. Planty, T. D. Snyder, and M. R. Rand. 2003. *Indicators of School Crime and Safety: 2003.* Washington, DC: National Center for Education Statistics and Bureau of Justice.

Deykin, E. Y., and S. L. Buka. 1997. "Prevalence and Risk Factors for Posttraumatic Stress Disorder among Chemically Dependent Adolescents." *American Journal of Psychiatry* 154:752–757.

Dick, D. M., R. J. Rose, R. J. Viken, and J. Kaprio. 2000. "Pubertal Timing and Substance Use: Associations between and within Families across Late Adolescence." *Developmental Psychology* 36:180–189.

Dickens, W. T., and J. R. Flynn. 2001. "Heritability Estimates Versus Large Environmental Effects: The IQ Paradox Resolved." *Psychological Review* 108:346–369.

Dietrich, L. C. 1998. *Chicana Adolescents: Bitches, 'Ho's, and Schoolgirls.* Westport, CT: Praeger.

Dishion, T. J., D. W. Andrews, and L. Crosby. 1995. "Antisocial Boys and Their Friends in Early Adolescence: Relationship Characteristics, Quality, and Interactional Process." *Child Development* 66:139–151.

Dixon, A., P. Howie, and J. Starling. 2004. "Psychopathology in Female Juvenile Offenders." *Journal of Child Psychology and Psychiatry* 45:1150–1158.

Dornfield, M., and C. Kruttschnitt. 1992. "Do the Stereotypes Fit? Mapping Gender-Specific Outcomes and Risk Factors." *Criminology* 30 (3): 397–419.

Draper, P., and J. Belsky. 1990. "Personality Development in the Evolutionary Perspective." *Journal of Personality* 58:141–161.

Dugan, L., D. S. Nagin, and R. Rosenfeld. 1999. "Explaining the Decline in Intimate Partner Homocide: The Effects of Changing Domesticity, Women's Status, and Domestic Violence Resources." *Homicide Studies* 3:187–214.

Duncan, G. J., J. P. Connell, P. K. Klebanov, J. Brooks-Gunn, G. J. Duncan, and J. L. Aber. 1997. "Conceptual and Methodological Issues in Estimating Causal Effects and Family Conditions on Individual Development." In *Context and Consequences for Children,* vol. 1, 219–250. New York: Russell Sage Foundation.

DuRant, R., C. Cadenhead, R. A. Pendergrast, G. Slavens, and C. W. Linder. 1994. "Factors Associated with the Use of Violence among Urban Black Adolescents." *American Journal of Public Health* 84:612–617.

DuRant, R., A. Getts, C. Cadenhead, and E. Woods. 1995. "The Association between Weapon-Carrying and the Use of Violence among Adolescents Living in or around Public Housing." *Journal of Adolescent Health* 17:376–380.

Durlauf, S. 2004. "Neighborhood Effects Part I: Cities and Urban Systems: From Theory to Facts." In *Handbook of Regional and Urban Economics,* vol. 4, edited by J. V. Henderson and J.-F. Thisse, 2173–2242. Amsterdam: Elsevier.

Eccles, J. S., and B. L. Barber. 1999. "Student Council, Volunteering, Basketball, or Marching Band: What Kind of Extracurricular Involvement Matters?" *Journal of Adolescence Research* 14:10–43.

Eccles, J. S., and C. Midgley. 1989. "Stage/Environment Fit: Developmentally Appropriate Classrooms for Early Adolescents." In *Research on Motivation in Education,* vol. 3, edited by R. E. Ames and C. Ames, 139–186. New York: Academic Press.

Eder, D., C. Evans, and S. Parker. 1995. *School Talk: Gender and Adolescent Culture.* New Brunswick, NJ: Rutgers University Press.

Edleson, J. L. 1999. "Children's Witnessing of Adult Domestic Violence." *Journal of Interpersonal Violence* 14:839–870.

Eggers, T. Z. 1998. "The 'Becca Bill' Would Not Have Saved Becca: Washington State's Treatment of Young Female Offenders." *Journal of Law and Inequality* 16:219–258.

Egley, A., Jr., and A. K. Major. 2004. *Highlights of the 2002 National Youth Gang Survey.* Washington, DC: Department of Justice.

Einstadter, W., and S. Henry. 1995. *Criminological Theory: An Analysis of Its Underlying Assumptions.* Fort Worth, TX: Harcourt Brace College Publishers.

Eitle, D. J. 2002. "Exploring a Source of Deviance-Producing Strain for Females Perceived Discrimination and General Strain Theory." *Journal of Criminal Justice* 30:429–442.

Eitle, D. J., and R. J. Turner. 2002. "Exposure to Community Violence and Young Adult Crime: The Effects of Witnessing Violence, Traumatic Victimization, and Other Stressful Life Events." *Journal of Research in Crime and Delinquency* 39:214–237.

Elliott, D. S., S. S. Ageton, and R. Canter. 1979. "Integrated Theoretical Perspective on Delinquent Behavior." *Journal of Crime and Delinquency* 16:3–27.

Elliott, D. S., D. Huizinga, and S. S. Ageton. 1985. *Explaining Delinquency and Drug Use.* Beverly Hills, CA: SAGE Publications.

Elliott, D. S., D. Huizinga, and S. W. Menard. 1989. *Multiple Problem Youth: Delinquency, Substance Abuse, and Mental Health Problems.* New York: Springer-Verlag.

Elliott, D. S., S. Menard, B. Rankin, A. Elliott, D. Huizinga, and W. J. Wilson. 2006. *Good Kids from Bad Neighborhoods: Successful Development in Social Context.* New York: Cambridge University Press.

Elliott, D. S., B. Morse, and D. Huizinga. 1987. "Self Reported Violent Offending: A Descriptive Analysis of Juvenile Violent Offenders and their Offending Careers." *Journal of Interpersonal Violence* 1:472–514.

Elliott, D. S., W. J. Wilson, D. Huizinga, R. J. Sampson, A. Elliott, and B. Rankin. 1996. "The Effects of Neighborhood Disadvantage on Adolescent Development." *Journal of Crime and Delinquency* 33:389–426.

Ellis, B. J. 2004. "Timing of Pubertal Maturation in Girls: An Integrated Life History Approach." *Psychological Bulletin* 130:920–958.

Ellis, B. J., and J. Garber. 2000. "Psychosocial Antecedents of Variation in Girls' Pubertal Timing: Maternal Depression, Stepfather Presence, and Marital and Family Stress." *Child Development* 71:485–501.

Ellis, B. J., S. McFadyen-Ketchum, K. A. Dodge, G. S. Pettit, and J. E. Bates. 1999. "Quality of Early Family Relationships and Individual Differences in the Timing of Pubertal Maturation in Girls: A Longitudinal Test of an Evolutionary Model." *Journal of Personality and Social Psychology* 77:387–401.

Emler, N., S. Reicher, and A. Ross. 1987. "The Social Context of Delinquent Conduct." *Journal of Child Psychology and Psychiatry* 28:99–109.

English, K. 1993. "Self-Reported Crime Rates of Women Prisoners." *Journal of Quantitative Criminology* 9:357–382.

Erez, E. 1987. "Situational or Planned Crime and the Criminal Career." In *Boy to Man, from Delinquency to Crime,* edited by M. E. Wolfgang, T. P. Thornberry, and R. M. Figlio, 122–133. Chicago: University of Chicago Press.

Ernst, M., L. L. Liebenauer, A. C. King, G. A. Fitzgerald, R. M. Cohen, and A. J. Zametkin. 1994. "Reduced Brain Metabolism in Hyperactive Girls." *Journal of the American Academy of Child and Adolescent Psychiatry* 33 (6): 858–868.

Esbensen, F. A., and E. P. Deschenes. 1998. "Multisite Examination of Youth Gang Membership: Does Gender Matter?" *Criminology* 36:799–828.

Esbensen, F. A., E. P. Deschenes, and L. T. Winfree. 1999. "Differences between Gang Girls and Gang Boys: Results from a Multi-Site Survey." *Youth and Society* 31:27–53.

Esbensen, F. A., and D. Huizinga. 1991. "Juvenile Victimization and Delinquency." *Youth and Society* 23:202–228.

———. 1993. "Gangs, Drugs, and Delinquency in a Survey of Urban Youth." *Criminology* 31:565–589.

Esbensen, F. A., D. Huizinga, and A. W. Weiher. 1993. "Gang and Non-Gang Youth: Differences in Explanatory Factors." *Journal of Contemporary Criminal Justice.* 9:94–116.

Esbensen, F. A., and L. T. Winfree. 1998. "Race and Gender Differences between Gang and Nongang Youths: Results from a Multisite Survey." *Justice Quarterly* 15:505–526.

Espelage, D. L., E. Cauffman, L. Broidy, A. R. Piquero, P. Mazerolle, and H. Steiner. 2003. "A Cluster-Analytic Investigation of MMPI Profiles of Serious Male and Female Juvenile Offenders." *Journal of the American Academy of Child and Adolescent Psychiatry* 42: 770–777.

Everett, S. A., and J. H. Price. 1995. "Students' Perceptions of Violence in the Public Schools: The MetLife Survey." *Journal of Adolescent Health* 17:345–352.

Eyre, S. L., V. Hoffman, and S. G. Millstein. 1998. "The Gamesmanship of Sex: A Model Based on African American Adolescent Accounts." *Medical Anthropology Quarterly* 12:467–489.

Fagan, A. A. 2003. "The Short- and Long-Term Effects of Adolescent Violent Victimization Experienced within the Family and Community." *Violence and Victims* 18:445–459.

Fagan, J. 1990. "Social Processes of Delinquency and Drug Use among Urban Gangs." In *Gangs in America*, edited by C. R. Huff, 173–219. Newbury Park, CA: SAGE Publications.

Fagan, J. A. 1995. "Separating the Men from the Boys: The Comparative Advantage of Juvenile versus Criminal Court Sanctions on Recidivism among Adolescent Felony Offenders." In *A Sourcebook of Serious, Violent and Chronic Juvenile Offenders*, edited by J. C. Howell, B. Krisberg, J. D. Hawkins, et al., 238–260. Thousand Oaks, CA: SAGE Publications.

———. 1996. "The Comparative Advantage of Juvenile versus Criminal Court Sanctions on Recidivism among Adolescent Felony Offenders." *Law and Policy* 18:77–114.

Fagan, J. A., and M. Guggenheim. 1996. "Preventive Detention and the Judicial Prediction of Dangerousness for Juveniles: A Natural Experiment." *Journal of Criminal Law and Criminology* 86:415–448.

Farand, L., F. Chagnon, J. Renaud, and M. Rivard. 2004. "Completed Suicides among Quebec Adolescents Involved with Juvenile Justice and Child Welfare Services." *Suicide and Life Threatening Behavior* 34:24–35.

Farrell, A. D., and S. E. Bruce. 1997. "Impact of Exposure to Community Violence on Violent Behavior and Emotional Distress among Urban Adolescents." *Journal of Clinical Child Psychology* 26:2–14.

Farrington, D. P. 1989. "Early Predictors of Adolescent Aggression and Adult Violence." *Violence* 4:79–100.

———. 1994. "Early Developmental Prevention of Juvenile Delinquency." *Criminal Behaviour and Mental Health* 4:209–227.

Farrington, D. P., B. Gallagher, L. Morley, R. J. Ledger, and D. J. West. 1986. "Unemployment, School Leaving, and Crime." *British Journal of Criminology* 26:335–356.

Farrington, D., and D. West. 1993. "Criminal, Penal, and Life Histories of Chronic Offenders, Risk and Protective Factors and Early Identification." *Criminal Behavior and Mental Health* 3:492–523.

Fauth, R. C., T. R. Leventhal, and J. Brooks-Gunn. 2005. "Early Impacts of Moving from Poor to Middle-Class Neighborhoods on Low-Income Youth." *Applied Developmental Psychology* 26:415–439.

Federal Bureau of Investigation (FBI). 2003. *Uniform Crime Reports: Crime in the United States—2003*. Washington, DC: U.S. Department of Justice.

Federal Bureau of Investigation (FBI). 2004. *Uniform Crime Reports: Crime in the United States (1979–2003)*. Washington, DC: U.S. Department of Justice.

Federle, K. H. 1990. "The Abolition of the Juvenile Court: A Proposal for the Preservation of Children's Legal Rights." *Journal of Contemporary Law* 16:23–51.

———. 2000. "The Institutionalization of Female Delinquency." *Buffalo Law Review* 48:881–908.

Federle, K. H., and M. Chesney-Lind. 1992. "Special Issues in Juvenile Justice: Gender, Race, and Ethnicity." In *Juvenile Justice and Public Policy: Toward a National Agenda*, edited by I. Schwartz, 165–195. New York: Lexington Books.

Feiring, C., S. Miller, and C. M. Cleland. 2007. "Potential Pathways from Stigmatization and Internalizing Symptoms to Delinquency in Sexually Abused Youth." *Child Maltreatment* 12:220–232.

Feitel, B., N. Margetson, J. Chamas, and C. Lipman. 1992. "Psychosocial Background and Behavioral and Emotional Disorders of Homeless and Runaway Youth." *Hospital and Community Psychiatry* 43:155–159.

Feld, B. C. 1977. *Neutralizing Inmate Violence: Juvenile Offenders in Institutions.* Cambridge, U.K.: Ballinger Publishing.

———. 1988. "Juvenile Court Meets the Principle of Offense: Punishment, Treatment, and the Difference It Makes." *Boston University Law Review* 68:821–915.

———. 1989. "Right to Counsel in Juvenile Court: An Empirical Study of When Lawyers Appear and the Difference They Make." *Journal of Criminal Law and Criminology* 79: 1185–1346.

———. 1991. "Justice by Geography: Urban, Suburban, and Rural Variations in Juvenile Justice Administration." *Journal of Criminal Law and Criminology* 82:156–210.

———. 1993. *Justice for Children: The Right to Counsel and Juvenile Courts.* Boston, MA: Northeastern University Press.

———. 1998. "Juvenile and Criminal Justice Systems' Responses to Youth Violence." *Crime and Justice* 24:189–261.

———. 1999. *Bad Kids: Race and the Transformation of the Juvenile Court.* New York: Oxford University Press.

———. 2000. "Legislative Exclusion of Offenses from Juvenile Court Jurisdiction: A History and Critique." In *The Changing Borders of Juvenile Justice: Transfer of Adolescents to the Criminal Court,* edited by J. A. Fagan and F. E. Zimring, 83–144. Chicago: University of Chicago Press.

———. 2003. *Race, Politics, and Juvenile Justice: The Warren Court and the Conservative "Backlash."* Minnesota Law Review.

———. 2004. *Cases and Materials on Juvenile Justice Administration.* St. Paul, MN: West Publishing.

Felson, M. 1998. *Crime and Everyday Life.* Thousand Oaks, CA: Pine Forge Press.

Felson, R. B. 1996. "Big People Hit Little People: Sex Differences in Physical Power and Interpersonal Violence." *Criminology* 34:433–452.

———. 2002. *Violence and Gender Reexamined.* Washington, DC: American Psychological Association.

Felson, R. B., A. E. Liska, S. J. South, and T. L. McNulty. 1994. "The Subculture of Violence and Delinquency: Individual Versus School Context Effects." *Social Forces* 73:155–173.

Fendrich, M. C. 1991. "Institutionalization and Parole Behavior: Assessing the Influence of Individual and Family Characteristics." *Journal of Community Psychology* 19:109–122.

Fenstermaker, S., and C. West. 2002. *Doing Gender, Doing Difference: Inequality, Power, and Institutional Change.* New York: Routledge.

Ferguson, A. A. 2000. *Bad Boys: Public Schools in the Making of Black Masculinity.* Ann Arbor: University of Michigan Press.

Fergusson, D. M., and L. J. Horwood. 1995. "Early Disruptive Behavior, IQ, and Later School Achievement and Delinquent Behavior." *Journal of Abnormal Child Psychology* 23:183–199.

———. 2002. "Male and Female Offending Trajectories." *Development and Psychopathology* 14:159–177.

Figueira-McDonough, J. 1992. "Community Structure and Female Delinquency Rates: A Heuristic Discussion." *Youth and Society* 24:3–30.

Fishbein, D. 2000. "The Importance of Neurobiological Research to the Prevention of Psychopathology." *Preventive Science* 1:89–106.

———. 2001. *Behavioral Perspectives in Criminology.* Belmont, CA: Wadsworth.

Fisher, P. A., M. R. Gunnar, P. Chamberlain, and J. B. Reid. 2000. "Preventive Intervention for Maltreated Preschool Children: Impact on Children's Behavior, Neuroendocrine Activity, and Foster Parent Functioning." *Journal of the American Academy of Child and Adolescent Psychiatry* 39:1356–1364.

Fishman, L. T. 1995. "The Vice Queens: An Ethnographic Study of Black Female Gang Behavior." In *The Modern Gang Reader,* edited by M. W. Klein, C. L. Maxson, and J. Miller, 83–92. Los Angeles, CA: Roxbury Publishing Company.

Fitzpatrick, K. M. 1997. "Aggression and Environmental Risk among Low-Income African-American Youth." *Journal of Adolescent Health* 21:172–178.

Flannery, D. J. 1997. "School Violence: Risk, Preventive Intervention, and Policy. ERIC Clearinghouse on Urban Education (ED 416 272)." In *Urban Diversity Series No. 109.* New York: Teachers College.

Fleisher, M. S. 1998. *Dead End Kids: Gang Girls and the Boys They Know.* Madison: Wisconsin University Press.

Fleisher, M. S., and J. L. Krienert. 2004. "Life-Course Events, Social Networks, and the Emergence of Violence among Female Gang Members." *Journal of Comparative Psychology* 32: 607–622.

Fleming, C. B., R. F. Catalano, M. L. Oxford, and T. W. Harachi. 2002. "A Test of Generalizability of the Social Development Model across Gender and Income Groups with Longitudinal Data from the Elementary School Development Period." *Journal of Quantitative Criminology* 18:423–439.

Flouir, E., and A. Buchanan. 2002. "Father Involvement in Childhood and Trouble with the Police in Adolescence: Findings from the 1958 British Cohort." *Journal of Interpersonal Violence* 17:698–701.

Fordham, S. 1993. "'Those Loud Black Girls': (Black) Women, Silence, and Gender 'Passing' in the Academy." *Anthropological and Education Quarterly* 24 (1): 3–32.

Forehand, R., and D. J. Jones. 2003. "Neighborhood Violence and Coparent Conflict: Interactive Influence on Child Psychosocial Adjustment." *Journal of Abnormal Child Psychology* 31:591–604.

Foster, H., J. Hagan, and J. Brooks-Gunn. 2004. "Age, Puberty, and Exposure to Intimate Partner Violence in Adolescence." *Annals of the New York Academy of Sciences* 1036:151–166.

Franke, T. M., A. L. T. Huynh-Hohnbaum, and Y. Chung. 2002. "Adolescent Violence: With Whom They Fight and Where." *Journal of Ethnic and Cultural Diversity in Social Work* 11:133–158.

Frazier, C. E., and D. M. Bishop. 1985. "Pretrial Detention of Juveniles and Its Impact on Case Dispositions." *Journal of Criminal Law and Criminology* 76:1132–1152.

Frazier, C. E., and J. K. Cochran. 1986. "Detention of Juveniles: Its Effect on Subsequent Juvenile Court Processing Decisions." *Youth and Society* 17:286–305.

Friedman, J., and D. P. Rosenbaum. 1988. "Social Control Theory: The Salience of Components by Age, Gender, and Type of Crime." *Journal of Quantitative Criminology* 4:363–381.

Fuentes, A. 1998. "The Crackdown on Kids." *The Nation,* June 15/22:20–22.

Funk, S. J. 1999. "Risk Assessment for Juveniles on Probation: A Focus on Gender." *Criminal Justice and Behavior* 26:44–68.

Gaarder, E., and J. Belknap. 2002. "Tenuous Borders: Girls Transferred to Adult Court." *Criminology* 40:481–517.

Gaarder, E., N. Rodriguez, and M. S. Zatz. 2004. "Criers, Liars, and Manipulators: Probation Officers' View of Girls." *Justice Quarterly* 21:547–578.

Gabel, K., and D. Johnston. 1995. *Children of Incarcerated Parents.* New York: Lexington Books.

Galen, B. R., and M. K. Underwood. 1997. "A Developmental Investigation of Social Aggression among Children." *Developmental Psychology* 33:589–600.

Galloway, D., R. Martin, and B. Wilcox. 1985. "Persistent Absence from School and Exclusion from School: The Predictive Power of School and Community Variables." *British Educational Research Journal* 11:51–61.

Ganzer, V. J., and I. G. Sarason. 1973. "Variables Associated with Recidivism among Juvenile Delinquents." *Journal of Consulting and Clinical Psychology* 40:1–5.

Garbarino, J. 2000. "The Effects of Neighborhood Violence on Children." In *Child Psychology,* edited by L. Batter and C. Tamis-Lemonda, 412–425. Philadelphia, PA: Psychology Press.

Garland, A. F., R. L. Hough, K. M. McCabe, M. Yeh, P. A. Wood, and G. A. Aarons. 2001. "Prevalence of Psychiatric Disorders in Youths across Five Sectors of Care." *Journal of the American Academy of Child and Adolescent Psychiatry* 40:409–418.

Garland, D. 2001. *The Culture of Control: Crime and Social Order in Contemporary Society.* Chicago: University of Chicago Press.

Gaub, M., and C. L. Carlson. 1997. "Gender Differences in ADHD: A Meta-Analysis and Critical Review." *Journal of the American Academy of Child and Adolescent Psychiatry* 36:1036–1045.

Ge, X., G. H. Brody, R. D. Conger, and R. L. Simons. 2006. "Pubertal Transition and African American Children's Internalizing and Externalizing Symptoms." *Journal of Youth and Adolescence* 35:528–537.

Ge, X., G. H. Brody, R. D. Conger, R. L. Simons, and V. M. Murry. 2002. "Contextual Amplification of Pubertal Transition Effects on Deviant Peer Affiliation and Externalizing Behavior among African American Children." *Developmental Psychology* 38:42–54.

Ge, X., R. D. Conger, and G. H. Elder, Jr. 1996. "Coming of Age Too Early: Pubertal Influences on Girls' Vulnerability to Psychological Distress." *Child Development* 67:3386–3400.

———. 2001. "The Relationship between Pubertal Status and Psychological Distress in Adolescent Boys." *Journal of Research on Adolescence* 11:49–70.

Ge, X., R. D. Conger, F. O. Lorenz, and R. L. Simons. 1994. "Parents' Stressful Life Events and Adolescent Depressed Mood." *Journal of Health and Social Behavior* 35:28–44.

Gecas, V., and M. Seff. 1990. "Social Class and Self-Esteem: Psychological Centrality, Compensation, and the Relative Effects of Work and Home." *Social Psychology Quarterly* 53: 165–173.

Gershoff, E. T. 2002. "Corporal Punishment by Parents and Associated Child Behaviors and Experiences: A Meta-Analytic and Theoretical Review." *Psychological Bulletin* 128:539–579.

Gershon, J. 2002. "A Meta-Analytic Review of Gender Differences in ADHD." *Journal of Attention Disorders* 5:143–154.

Giallombardo, R. 1974. *The Social World of Imprisoned Girls: A Comparative Study of Institutions for Juvenile Delinquents.* New York: John Wiley and Sons.

Gil, A. G., W. A. Vega, and R. J. Turner. 2002. "Early and Mid-Adolescence Risk Factors for Later Substance Abuse by African-Americans and European Americans." *Public Health Reports* 117:S15–S30.

Gilfus, M. 1992. "From Victims to Survivors to Offenders: Women's Routes to Entry and Immersion into Street Crime." *Women and Criminal Justice* 4:63–89.

Gilligan, C. 1982. *In a Different Voice: Psychological Theory and Women's Development.* Cambridge, U.K.: Harvard University Press.

Giordano, P. C. 1978. "Girls, Guys, and Gangs: The Changing Social Context of Female Delinquency." *Journal of Criminal Law and Criminology* 69:126–132.

———. 1995. "Wider Circle of Friends in Adolescence." *American Journal of Sociology* 101:661–697.

Giordano, P. C., and S. A. Cernkovich. 1979. "On Complicating the Relationship between Liberation and Delinquency." *Social Problems* 26:467–481.

———. 1997. "Gender and Antisocial Behavior." In *Handbook of Antisocial Behavior,* edited by D. Stoff and J. Breiling, 496–510. New York: Wiley.

Giordano, P. C., S. A. Cernkovich, and A. DeMaris. 1993. "The Family and Peer Relationships of Black Adolescents." *Journal of Marriage and the Family* 55:277–287.

Giordano, P. C., S. A. Cernkovich, and D. Holland. 2003. "Changes in Friendship Over the Life Course: Implications for Desistance from Crime." *Criminology* 41:293–327.

Giordano, P. C., S. A. Cernkovich, and M. D. Pugh. 1986. "Friendships and Delinquency." *American Journal of Sociology* 91:1170–1202.

Giordano, P. C., S. A. Cernkovich, and J. Rudolph. 2002. "Gender, Crime, and Desistance: Toward a Theory of Cognitive Transformation." *American Journal of Sociology* 107:990–1064.

Giordano, P. C., M. A. Longmore, and W. D. Manning. 2001. "On the Nature and Developmental Significance of Adolescent Romantic Relationships." In *Sociological Studies of Children and Youth,* vol. 8, edited by D. A. Kinney, 109–137. New York: Elsevier Science Ltd.

———. 2006. "Gender and the Meanings of Adolescent Romantic Relationships: A Focus on Boys." *American Sociological Review* 71:260–287.

Giordano, P. C., T. J. Millhollin, S. A. Cernkovich, M. D. Pugh, and J. L. Rudolph. 1999. "Delinquency, Identity, and Women's Involvement in Relationship Violence." *Criminology* 37: 17–40.

Giordano, P. C., and S. Mohler-Rockwell. 2001. "Differential Association Theory and Female Crime." In *Of Crime and Criminality: The Use of Theory in Everyday Life,* edited by S. Simpson, 3–24. Thousand Oaks, CA: Pine Forge Press.

Giordano, P. C., R. D. Schroeder, and S. A. Cernkovich. 2007. "Emotions and Crime over the Life Course: A Neo-Meadian Perspective on Criminal Continuity and Change." *American Journal of Sociology* 112: 1603–1661.

Girls Inc. 1996. *Prevention and Parity: Girls in Juvenile Justice.* Indianapolis, IN: Girls Incorporated National Resource Center.

Glueck, S., and E. Glueck. 1934. *Five Hundred Delinquent Women.* New York: Alfred A. Knopf.

———. 1950. *Unraveling Juvenile Delinquency.* Cambridge, U.K.: The Commonwealth Fund.

Goering, J., and J. D. Fiens. 2003. *Choosing a Better Life? Evaluation of the Moving to Opportunity Social Experiment.* Washington, DC: Urban Institute Press.

Goldstein, N. E., D. H. Arnold, J. Weil, C. M. Mesiarik, D. Peuschold, T. Grisso, and D. Osman. 2003. "Comorbid Symptom Patterns in Female Juvenile Offenders." *International Journal of Law and Psychiatry* 26:565–582.

Goodwin, M. H. 1990. *He-Said-She-Said: Talk as Social Organization among Black Children.* Bloomington, IN: Indiana University Press.

Gottfredson, D. C. 2001. *Delinquency and Schools.* Cambridge: Cambridge University Press.

Gottfredson, D. C., and C. S. Koper. 1996. "Race and Sex Differences in the Prediction of Drug Use." *Journal of Consulting and Clinical Psychology* 64:305–314.

Gottfredson, D. C., D. B. Wilson, and S. S. Najaka. 2002. "School-Based Crime Prevention." In *Evidence-Based Crime Prevention,* edited by L. W. Sherman, D. Farrington, B. Welsh, et al., 56–164. London: Routledge.

Gottfredson, G. D. 1981. "Schooling and Delinquency." In *New Directions in the Rehabilitation of Criminal Offenders,* edited by S. E. Martin, L. B. Sechrest, and R. Redner, 424–469. Washington, DC: National Academy Press.

Gottfredson, G. D., and D. C. Gottfredson. 1985. *Victimization in Schools.* New York: Plenum.

Gottfredson, G. D., D. C. Gottfredson, A. A. Payne, and N. C. Gottfredson. 2005. "School Climate Predictors of School Disorder: Results from a National Study of Delinquency Prevention in Schools." *Journal of Research in Crime and Delinquency* 42:412–444.

Gottfredson, M., and T. Hirschi. 1990. *A General Theory of Crime.* Palo Alto, CA: Stanford University Press.

Gove, W. R., and T. R. Herb. 1974. "Stress and Mental Illness among the Young: A Comparison of the Sexes." *Social Forces* 83:256–265.

Graber, J. A., J. Brooks-Gunn, and M. P. Warren. 1995. "The Antecedents of Menarcheal Age: Heredity, Family Environment, and Stressful Life Events." *Child Development* 66:346–359.

———. 1999. "The Vulnerable Transition: Puberty and the Development of Eating Pathology and Negative Mood." *Womens' Health Issues* 9:107–114.

———. 2006. "Pubertal Effects on Adjustment in Girls: Moving from Demonstrating Effects to Identifying Pathways." *Journal of Youth and Adolescence* 35:391–401.

Graber, J. A., P. M. Lewinsohn, J. R. Seeley, and J. Brooks-Gunn. 1997. "Is Psychopathology Associated with the Timing of Pubertal Development?" *Journal of the American Academy of Child and Adolescent Psychiatry* 36:1768–1776.

Grant, L. 1984. "Black Females 'Place' in the Desegregated Classrooms." *Sociology of Education* 57:98–111.

Griffiths, V. 1995. *Adolescent Girls and Their Friends: A Feminist Ethnography.* Aldershot, U.K.: Avebury.

Grisso, T., R. Barnum, K. E. Fletcher, E. Cauffman, and D. Peuschold. 2001. "Massachusetts Youth Screening Instrument for Mental Health Needs of Juvenile Justice Youths." *Journal of the American Academy of Child and Adolescent Psychiatry* 40:541–548.

Hadley, M. 2003. "Relational, Indirect, Adaptive, or Just Mean: Recent Work on Aggression in Adolescent Girls—Part I." *Studies in Gender and Sexuality* 4:367–394.

———. 2004. "Relational, Indirect, Adaptive, or Just Mean: Recent Studies on Aggression in Adolescent Girls—Part II." *Studies in Gender and Sexuality* 5:331–350.

Hagan, J. 1990. "The Structuration of Gender and Deviance: A Power-Control Theory of Vulnerability to Crime and the Search for Deviant Role Exits." *Canadian Review of Sociology and Anthropology* 27:137–156.

Hagan, J., and H. Foster. 2003. "S/He's a Rebel: Toward a Sequential Stress Theory of Delinquency and Gendered Pathways to Disadvantage in Emerging Adulthood." *Social Forces* 82:53–86.

Hagan, J., A. R. Gillis, and J. Simpson. 1985. "The Class Structure of Gender and Delinquency: Toward a Power-Control Theory of Common Delinquent Behavior." *American Journal of Sociology* 90:1151–1178.

Hagan, J., P. J. Hirschfield, and C. Shedd. 2002. "Shooting at Tilden High: Causes and Consequences." In *Deadly Lessons: Understanding Lethal School Violence,* edited by M. H. Moore, C. V. Petrie, A. A. Braga, et al., 143–174. Washington, DC: National Research Council.

Hagan, J., and B. McCarthy. 1997. *Mean Streets: Youth Crime and Homelessness.* Cambridge: Cambridge University Press.

Hagan, J., J. H. Simpson, and A. R. Gillis. 1979. "The Sexual Stratification of Social Control: A Gender-Based Perspective on Crime and Delinquency." *British Journal of Sociology* 30: 25–38.

Hagan, J., J. Simpson, and A. R. Gillis. 1998. "Feminist Scholarship, Relational and Instrumental Control, and a Power-Control Theory of Gender and Delinquency." *British Journal of Sociology* 34:301–336.

Hagedorn, J. M. 1998. *People and Folks: Gangs, Crime, and the Underclass in a Rustbelt City.* Chicago: Lake View Press.

Hagedorn, J. M., and M. L. Devitt. 1999. "Fighting Female: The Social Construction of Female Gangs." In *Female Gangs in America*, edited by M. Chesney-Lind and J. Hagedorn, 256–276. Chicago: Lake View Press.

Hall, W. 2004. "Violence among Girls on Upswing." *Patriot News*, April 21, 2004, A1, A8.

Hampson, E. 1990. "Variations in Sex-Related Cognitive Abilities across the Menstrual Cycle." *Brain and Cognition* 14:26–43.

Handler, J. F., and J. Zatz. 1982. *Neither Angels nor Thieves: Studies in Deinstitutionalization of Status Offenders.* Washington, DC: National Academy Press.

Hansen, D. M., R. W. Larson, and J. B. Dworkin. 2003. "What Adolescents Learn in Organized Youth Activities: A Survey of Self-Reported Developmental Experiences." *Journal of Research on Adolescence* (Blackwell Publishing Limited) 13:25–55.

Hanson, S. L., and R. S. Kraus. 1998. "Women, Sport, and Science: Do Female Athletes Have an Advantage?" *Sociology of Education* 71:93–110.

Harris, A. R. 1977. "Sex and Theories of Deviance: Toward a Functional Theory of Deviant Typescripts." *American Sociological Review* 42:8–16.

Harris, J. 1998. *The Nurture Assumption: Why Children Turn out the Way They Do.* New York: Free Press.

Hart, C. H., D. A. Nelson, C. Robinson, S. F. Olsen, and M. K. McNeilly-Choque. 1998. "Overt and Relational Aggression in Russian Nursery School–Age Children: Parenting Style and Marital Linkages." *Developmental Psychology* 34:687–697.

Hawkins, D. F., M. W. Arthur, R. F. Catalano, M. Tonry, and D. P. Farrington. 1995. "Preventing Substance Abuse." In *Building A Safer Society: Strategic Approaches to Crime Prevention. Vol. 19: Crime and Justice: A Review of the Research,* edited by M. Tonry and D. Farrington, 343–427. Chicago: University of Chicago Press.

Hawkins, D. F., and K. Kempf-Leonard. 2005. *Our Children, Their Children: Confronting Racial and Ethnic Differences in American Juvenile Justice.* Edited by D. F. Hawkins and K. Kempf-Leonard. Chicago: University of Chicago Press.

Hawkins, J. D., and R. F. Catalano, Jr. 1993. *Risk-Focused Prevention Using the Social Development Strategy.* Seattle, WA: Developmental Research and Programs, Inc.

Hawkins, J. D., and D. M. Lishner. 1987. "Schooling and Delinquency." In *Handbook on Crime and Delinquency Prevention,* edited by E. H. Johnson, 179–221. New York: Greenwood.

Hay, C. 2003. "Family Strain, Gender, and Delinquency." *Sociological Perspectives* 46:107–135.

Haynie, D. 2001. "Delinquent Peers Revisited: Does Network Structure Matter?" *American Journal of Sociology* 106:1013–1057.

———. 2002. "Friendship Networks and Delinquency: The Relative Nature of Peer Delinquency." *Journal of Quantitative Criminology* 18:99–134.

———. 2003. "Contexts of Risks? Explaining the Link between Girls' Pubertal Development and Their Delinquency Involvement." *Social Forces* 82:355–397.

Haynie, D. L., P. C. Giordano, W. D. Manning, and M. A. Longmore. 2005. "Adolescent Romantic Relationships and Delinquency Involvement." *Criminology* 43:177–210.

Hayward, C. 2003. *Gender Differences at Puberty.* Cambridge: Cambridge University Press.

Hayward, C., J. D. Killen, D. M. Wilson, L. D. Hammer, I. F. Litt, H. C. Kraemer, F. Haydel, A. Varady, and C. B. Taylor. 1997. "Psychiatric Risk Associated with Early Puberty in Adolescent Girls." *Journal of American Child and Adolescent Psychiatry* 36:255–262.

Heide, K. 1992. *Why Kids Kill Parents: Child Abuse and Adolescent Homicide.* Columbus: Ohio State University.

Heimer, K. 1995. "Gender, Race and the Pathways to Delinquency: An Interactionist Explanation." In *Crime and Inequality,* edited by J. Hagan and R. D. Peterson, 140–173. Stanford, CA: Stanford University Press.

———. 1996. "Gender, Interaction, and Delinquency: Testing a Theory of Differential Social Control." *Social Psychology Quarterly* 59:39–61.

Heimer, K., and S. De Coster. 1999. "The Gendering of Violent Delinquency." *Criminology* 27:277–313.

Heimer, K., and R. Matsueda. 1994. "Role-Taking, Role Commitment, and Delinquency: A Theory of Differential Social-Control." *American Sociological Review* 59:365–390.

Heinze, H. J., P. A. Toro, and K. A. Urberg. 2004. "Antisocial Behavior and Affiliation with Deviants Peers." *Journal of Clinical Child and Adolescent Psychology* 33:336–346.

Hellman, D. A., and S. Beaton. 1986. "The Pattern of Violence in Urban Public Schools: The Influence of School and Community." *Journal of Research in Crime and Delinquency* 23: 102–127.

Henggeler, S. W., J. Edwards, and C. M. Borduin. 1987. "The Family Relations of Female Juvenile Delinquents." *Journal of Abnormal Child Psychology* 15:199–209.

Hennessey, M., J. D. Ford, K. Mahoney, S. J. Ko, and C. B. Siegfried. 2004. *Trauma among Girls in the Juvenile Justice System.* Los Angeles, CA: National Child Traumatic Stress Network.

Hennington, C., J. N. Hughes, T. A. Cavell, and B. Thompson. 1998. "The Role of Relational Aggression in Identifying Aggressive Boys and Girls." *Journal of Psychology* 36:457–477.

Henriques, Z. W., and N. Manam-Rupert. 2001. "Living on the Outside: African American Women Before, During, and After Imprisonment." *Prison Journal* 81:6–19.

Herman-Giddens, M. E., and E. J. Slora. 1997. "Secondary Sexual Characteristics of Young Girls Seen in Office Practice: A Study from the Paediatric Research in Office Settings Network." *Pediatrics* 88:505–512.

Hermann, D., and T. Parente. 1996. *Retraining Cognition: Techniques and Application.* Baltimore, MD: Aspen Publishers.

Herrenkohl, T., E. Maguin, K. Hill, J. Hawkins, R. Abbott, and R. Catalano. 2000. "Developmental Risk Factors for Youth Violence." *Journal of Adolescent Health* 26:176–186.

Herrera, V. M., and L. A. McCloskey. 2001. "Gender Differences in the Risk for Delinquency among Youth Exposed to Family Violence." *Child Abuse and Neglect* 25:1037–1051.

———. 2003. "Sexual Abuse, Family Violence, and Female Delinquency: Findings from a Longitudinal Study." *Violence and Victims* 18:319–334.

Herz, D. C. 2001. "Understanding the Use of Mental Health Placements by the Juvenile Justice System." *Journal of Emotional and Behavioral Disorders* 9:172–181.

Hetherington, E., and J. Kelly. 2002. *For Better or for Worse: Divorce Reconsidered.* New York: W.W. Norton and Company.

Hey, S. 1997. *The Company She Keeps: Ethnography of Girls' Friendship.* Buckingham: Open University Press.

Hill, G. D., and E. M. Crawford. 1990. "Women, Race, and Crime." *Criminology* 28:601–626.

Hinshaw, S. P., D. R. Blachman, D. J. Bell, S. L. Foster, and E. J. Mash. 2005. "Attention-Deficit/ Hyperactivity Disorder in Girls." In *Handbook: Of Behavioral and Emotional Problems in Girls,* edited by D. Bell, S. L. Foster, and E. J. Mash, 117–147. New York: Kluwer Academic/ Plenum Publishers.

Hinshaw, S. P., E. T. Carte, N. Sami, J. J. Treuting, and B. A. Zupan. 2002. "Pre-Adolescent Girls with Attention Deficit/Hyperactivity Disorder: II. Neuropsychological Performance in Relation to Subtypes and Individual Classification." *Journal of Consulting and Clinical Psychology* 70:1099–1111.

Hirschi, T. 1969. *Causes of Delinquency.* Berkeley and Los Angeles: University of California Press.

Hofferth, S. L., L. Reid, and F. L. Mott. 2001. "The Effects of Early Childbearing on Schooling Over Time." *Family Planning Perspectives* 33:259–267.

Holsinger, K., and A. Holsinger. 2005. "Differential Pathways to Violence and Self-Injurious Behavior: African American and White Girls in the Juvenile Justice System." *Journal of Research in Crime and Delinquency* 42:211–242.

Hornberger, S., T. Martin, and J. Collins. 2006. *Integrating Systems of Care: Improving Quality of Care for the Most Vulnerable Children and Families.* Washington, DC: Child Welfare League of America.

Horowitz, R., and A. Pottieger. 1991. "Gender Bias in Juvenile Justice Handling of Serious Crime-Involved Youth." *Journal of Research in Crime and Delinquency* 28:75–100.

Hotte, J. P., and S. Rafman. 1992. "The Specific Effects of Incest on Prepubertal Girls from Dysfunctional Families." *Child Abuse and Neglect* 16 (2): 273–283.

Howell, J. 2003. *Preventing and Reducing Juvenile Delinquency: A Comprehensive Framework.* London: SAGE Publications.

Howing, P. T., J. S. Wodarski, P. D. Kurtz, J. M. Gaudin, and E. M. Herbst. 1990. "Child Abuse and Delinquency: The Empirical and Theoretical Links." *Social Work* 35:244–249.

Hubbard, D. J., and T. C. Pratt. 2002. "A Meta-Analysis of the Predictors of Delinquency among Girls." *Journal of Offender Rehabilitation* 34:1–13.

Huebner, A. J., and S. C. Betts. 2002. "Exploring the Utility of Social Control Theory for Youth Development: Issues of Attachment, Involvement, and Gender." *Youth and Society* 34: 123–145.

Huff, C. R. 1989. "Youth Gangs and Public Policy." *Crime and Delinquency* 35:524–538.

———. 1993. "Gangs in the United States." In *The Gang Intervention Handbook,* edited by A. P. Goldstein, R. C. Huff, and C. R. Huff, 3–20. Champaign, IL: Research Press.

Huizinga, D., R. Loeber, and T. Thornberry. 2000. *Co-Occurrence of Delinquency and Other Problem Behaviors.* OJJDP Juvenile Justice Bulletin. Washington, DC: U.S. Department of Justice.

Huizinga, D., A. W. Weiher, R. Espiritu, and F. Esbensen. 2003. "Delinquency and Crime: Some Highlights from the Denver Youth Survey." In *Taking Stock of Delinquency,* edited by T. P. Thornberry and M. D. Krohn, 47–91. New York: Kluwer Academic.

Hulanicka, B. 1986. "Effects of Psychological and Emotional Factors on Age at Menarche." *Materialy i Prace Antropologiczne* 107:45–80.

———. 1989. "Age at Menarche of Girls from Disturbed Families." *Humanbiologia, Budapest* 19:173–177.

Hulanicka, B., L. Gronkiewicz, and J. Koniarek. 2001. "Effect of Familial Distress on Growth and Maturation of Girls: A Longitudinal Study." *American Journal of Human Biology* 13: 771–776.

Hunt, G., and K. Joe Laidler. 2001. "Situations of Violence in the Lives of Girl Gang Members." *Health Care for Women International* 22:363–384.

Hunt, G., K. Joe Laidler, and K. Evans. 2002. "The Meaning and Gendered Culture of Getting High: Gang Girls and Drug Issues." *Contemporary Drug Problems* 29:375–415.

Hunt, G., K. Joe Laidler, and K. MacKenzie. 2000. "'Chillin', Being Dogged and Getting Buzzed': Alcohol in the Lives of Female Gang Members." *Drugs: Education, Prevention and Policy* 7:331–353.

———. 2005. "Moving into Motherhood: Gang Girls and Controlled Risk." *Youth and Society* 36:333–373.

Ingoldsby, E. M., and D. S. Shaw. 2002. "Neighborhood Contextual Factors and Early Starting Antisocial Pathways." *Clinical Child and Family Psychology Review* 5:21–55.

Insel, T. R., J. T. Winslow, Z. Wang, and L. J. Young. 1998. "Oxytocin, Vasopressin, and the Neuroendocrine Basis of Pair Bond Formation." *Advances in Experimental Medicine and Biology* 449:215–224.

Ireland, T. O., C. A. Smith, and T. P. Thornberry. 2002. "Developmental Issues in the Impact of Child Maltreatment on Later Delinquency and Drug Use." *Criminology* 40:359–399.

Iscoe, I., M. Williams, and J. Harvey. 1964. "Age, Intelligence, and Sex as Variables in the Conformity Behavior of Negro and White Children." *Child Development* 35:451–460.

Jackson-Beeck, M., I. Schwartz, and A. Rutherford. 1987. "Trends and Issues in Juvenile Confinement for Psychiatric and Chemical Dependency Treatment." *International Journal of Law and Psychiatry* 10:153–165.

Jacob, J. C. 2006. "Male and Female Youth Crime in Canadian Communitites: Assessing the Applicability of Social Disorganization Theory." *Canadian Journal of Criminology and Criminal Justice* 48:31–60.

Jaffe, P., D. Wolfe, and S. K. Wilson. 1990. *Children of Battered Women. Developmental Clinical Psychology and Psychiatry*, vol. 21. Newbury Park, CA: SAGE Publications.

James, S. E., J. Johnson, and C. Raghavan. 2004. "I Couldn't Go Anywhere: Contextualizing Violence and Drug Abuse: A Social Network Study." *Violence Against Women* 10:991–1014.

Janus, M., A. Burgess, and A. McCormack. 1987. "Histories of Sexual Abuse in Adolescent Males." *Adolescence* 22:405–417.

Jargowsky, P. A. 1997. *Poverty and Place*. New York: Russell Sage Foundation.

Jarjoura, G. R. 1993. "Does Dropping Out of School Enhance Delinquent Involvement? Results from a Large-Scale National Probability Sample." *Criminology* 31:149–172.

———. 1996. "The Conditional Effects of Social Class on the Dropout Delinquency Relationship." *Journal of Research in Crime and Delinquency* 33:232–255.

Jasper, A., C. Smith, and S. Bailey. 1998. "One Hundred Girls in Care Referred to an Adolescent Forensic Mental Health Service." *Journal of Adolescence* 21:555–568.

Jencks, C., and S. E. Mayer. 1990. "The Social Consequences of Growing Up in a Poor Neighborhood." In *Inner City Poverty in the United States*, edited by L. Lynn and M. McGeary, 111–186. Washington, DC: National Academy Press.

Jenkins, P. H. 1997. "School Delinquency and the School Social Bond." *Journal of Research in Crime and Delinquency* 34:337–367.

Jensen, G. F. 2003. "Gender Variation in Delinquency: Self-Image, Beliefs and Peers as Mediating Mechanisms." In *Social Learning Theory and the Explanation of Crime: A Guide for the New Century*, vol. 11, edited by R. L. Akers and G. F. Jensen, 151–178. New Brunswick, NJ: Transaction Books.

Jensen, G. F., and M. L. Erickson. 1978. "The Social Meaning of Sanctions." In *Crime, Law and Sanctions: Theoretical Perspectives*, edited by M. D. Krohn and R. I. Akers, 119–136. Beverly Hills, CA: SAGE Publications.

Jensen, G. F., and R. Eve. 1976. "Sex Differences in Delinquency." *Criminology* 13:427–448.

Jezova, D., E. Jurankova, A. Mosnarova, M. Kriska, and I. Skultetyova. 1996. "Neuroendocrine Response During Stress with Relation to Gender Differences." *Acta Neurobiol* 56:779–785.

Jiwani, Y., N. Janovicek, A. Cameron, H. Berman, and Y. Jiwani. 2002. "Erased Realities: The Violence of Racism in the Lives of Immigrant and Refugee Girls of Colour." In *In the Best Interests of the Girl Child*, edited by H. Berman and Y. Jiwani, 45–88. London, Ontario, Canada: The Alliance of Five Research Centres on Violence.

Joe, K. A., and M. Chesney-Lind. 1995. "Just Every Mother's Angel: An Analysis of Ethnic and Gender Variation in Youth Gang Membership." *Gender and Society* 9:408–431.

———. 1999. "'Just Every Mother's Angel': An Analysis of Gender and Ethnic Variations in Youth Gang Membership. Female Gangs." In *America: Essays on Girls, Gangs and Gender*, edited by M. Chesney-Lind and J. Hagedorn, 210–231. Chicago: Lake View Press.

Joe Laidler, K. A., and G. Hunt. 1997. "Violence and Social Organization in Female Gangs." *Social Justice* 24:148–169.

———. 2001. "Accomplishing Femininity among the Girls in the Gang." *British Journal of Criminology* 41:656–678.

Johnson, B. M. 2002. *Friendships among Delinquent Adolescent Girls: Why Do Some Select Males as their Closest Friends?* Los Angeles, CA: University of California.

Johnson, D. R., and L. K. Scheuble. 1991. "Gender Bias in the Disposition of Juvenile Court." *Criminology* 29:677–699.

Johnson, R. E. 1979. *Juvenile Delinquency and Its Origins.* Cambridge: Cambridge University Press.

Jones, N. 2004. "'It's Not Where You Live, It's How You Live': How Young Women Negotiate Conflict and Violence in the Inner City." *Annals of the American Academy of Political and Social Science* 595:49–62.

Junger-Tas, J., D. Ribeaud, and M. Cruyff. 2004. "Juvenile Delinquency and Gender." *European Journal of Criminology* 1:333–375.

Kaltiala-Heino, R., M. Marttunen, P. Rantanen, and M. Rimpela. 2003. "Early Puberty Is Associated with Mental Health Problems in Middle Adolescence." *Social Sciences and Medicine* 57:1055–1064.

Kandel, D. B. 1978. "Homophily, Selection, and Socialization in Adolescent Deviance: An Algebra of Interpersonal Influences." *Journal of Drug Issues* 26:289–315.

Kandel, D., and M. Davies. 1991. "Friendship Networks, Intimacy, and Illicit Drug Use in Young Adulthood: A Comparison of Two Competing Theories." *Criminology* 29:441–467.

Kanter, R. M. 1977. "Some Effects of Proportions of Group Life: Skewed Sex Ratios and Responses to Token Women." *American Journal of Sociology* 82:965–990.

Kaprio, J., A. Rimpela, T. Winter, R. J. Viken, M. Rimpela, and R. J. Rose. 1995. "Common Genetic Influences on BMI and Age at Menarche." *Human Biology: An International Record of Research* 67:739–753.

Kataoka, S. H., B. T. Zima, D. A. Dupre, K. A. Moreno, X. Yang, and J. T. McCracken. 2001. "Mental Health Problems and Service Use among Female Juvenile Offenders: Their Relationship to Criminal History." *Journal of the American Academy of Child and Adolescent Psychiatry* 40:549–555.

Katz, J. 1988. *Seductions of Crime: Moral and Sensual Attractions in Doing Evil.* New York: Basic Books.

Katz, L., J. Kling, and J. Liebman. 2001. "Moving to Opportunity in Boston: Early Results of a Randomized Mobility Experiment." *Quarterly Journal of Economics* 116 (2): 607–654.

Katz, R. 2000. "Explaining Girls' and Women's Crime and Desistance in the Context of Their Victimization Experiences: A Developmental Test of Revised Strain Theory and the Life Course Perspective." *Violence Against Women* 6:633–661.

Kaufman, J., and C. S. Widom. 1999. "Childhood Victimization, Running Away, and Delinquency." *Journal of Research in Crime and Delinquency* 30:347–370.

Kaufman, P., C. Xianglei, S. Choy, K. Peter, S. Ruddy, A. Miller, J. Fleury, K. Chandler, M. Planty, and M. Rand. 2001. *Indicators of School Crime and Safety: 2001.* Washington, DC: U.S. Departments of Education and Justice.

Kavanagh, K., and H. Hops. 1994. "Good Girls? Bad Boys? Gender and Development as Contexts for Diagnosis and Treatment." *Advances in Clinical Child Psychology* 16:45–79.

Keenan, K., R. Loeber, and S. Green. 1999. "Conduct Disorder in Girls." *Clinical Child and Family Psychology Review* 2:3–19.

Keenan, K., M. Stouthamer-Loeber, and R. Loeber. 2004. "Developmental Approaches to Studying Conduct Problems in Girls." In *The Development and Treatment of Girlhood Aggression,* edited by D. J. Pepler, K. C. Madsen, C. Webster, et al., 29–46. Mahwah, NJ: Lawrence Erlbaum Associates.

Kellam, S. G., C. H. Brown, and J. B. Fleming. 1983. "Relationship of First-Grade Social Adaptation to Teenage Drinking, Drug-Use, and Smoking." *Digest of Alcoholism Theory and Application* 2 (2): 20–24.

Keller, T. E., R. F. Catalano, K. P. Haggerty, and C. B. Fleming. 2002. "Parent Figure Transitions and Delinquency and Drug Use among Early Adolescent Children of Substance Abusers." *American Journal of Drug and Alcohol Abuse* 28:399–427.

Kelley, B. T., T. P. Thornberry, and C. A. Smith. 1997. *In the Wake of Childhood Maltreatment.* Juvenile Justice Bulletin (August 1977). Washington, DC: U.S. Department of Justice.

Kelling, G., and C. Coles. 1996. *Fixing Broken Windows: Restoring Order and Reducing Crime in our Communities.* New York: Touchstone.

Kempf, K. L. 1992. *The Role of Race in Juvenile Justice Processing in Pennsylvania.* Shippensburg, PA: Center for Juvenile Justice Training and Research.

Kempf-Leonard, K., and L. L. Sample. 2000. "Disparity Based on Sex: Is Gender Specific Treatment Warranted?" *Justice Quarterly* 17:89–128.

Kendall-Tackett, K. A., L. M. Williams, and D. Finkelhor. 1993. "Impact of Sexual Abuse on Children: A Review and Synthesis of Recent Empirical Studies." *Psychological Bulletin* 113:164–180.

Kim, J. E., E. M. Hetherington, and D. Reiss. 1999. "Associations among Family Relationships, Antisocial Peers, and Adolescents' Externalizing Behaviors: Gender and Family Type Differences." *Child Development* 70:1209–1030.

Kim, J. Y. S., and M. Fendrich. 2002. "Gender Differences in Juvenile Arrestees' Drug Use, Self-Reported Dependence, and Perceived Need for Treatment." *Psychiatric Services* 55: 70–75.

Kim, K., and P. K. Smith. 1998. "Childhood Stress, Behavioral Symptoms and Mother–Daughter Pubertal Development." *Journal of Adolescence* 21:231–240.

King, J. 1998. "Attention-Deficit Hyperactivity Disorder and the Stress Response." *Biological Psychiatry* 44:72–74.

Kirschbaum, C., B. M. Kudielka, J. Gaab, N. C. Schommer, and D. H. Hellhammer. 1999. "Impact of Gender, Menstrual Cycle Phase and Oral Contraceptives on the Hypothalamic-Pituitary-Adrenal Axis." *Psychosomatic Medicine* 64:154–162.

Klein, L. C., and E. J. Corwin. 2002. "Seeing the Unexpected: How Sex Differences in Stress Responses May Provide a New Perspective on the Manifestation of Psychiatric Disorders." *Current Psychiatry Reports* 4:441–448.

Klein, M. W. 1979. "Deinstitutionalization and Diversion of Juvenile Offenders: A Litany of Impediments." *Crime and Justice: An Annual Review of Research* 1:145–201.

———. 1995. *The American Street Gang: Its Nature, Prevalence and Control.* New York: Oxford University Press.

———. 2001. "Foreword." In *One of the Guys: Girls, Gangs and Gender,* edited by J. Miller, ix–xii. New York: Oxford University Press.

Klepinger, D. H., S. Lundberg, and R. D. Plotnick. 1995. "Adolescent Fertility and the Educational Attainment of Young Women." *Family Planning Perspectives* 27:23–28.

Kling, J., J. Liebman, and L. Katz. Forthcoming. "Experimental Analysis of Neighborhood Effects." *Econometrica.*

Kling, J., J. Ludwig, and L. Katz. 2005. "Neighborhood Effects on Crime for Female and Male Youth: Evidence from a Randomized Housing-Voucher Experiment." *Quarterly Journal of Economics* 120:87–130.

Koester, S., and J. Schwartz. 1993. "Crack, Gangs, Sex, and Powerlessness: A View from Denver." In *Crack Pipe as Pimp: An Ethnographic Investigation for Sex-for-Crack Exchanges,* edited by M. S. Ratner, 187–201. New York: Lexington Books.

Komter, A. 1989. "Hidden Power in Marriage." *Gender and Society* 14:42–72.

Konopka, G. 1966. *The Adolescent Girl in Conflict.* Englewood Cliffs, NJ: Prentice-Hall.

Koppelman, J. 2004. "Children with Mental Disorders: Making Sense of Their Needs and the Systems that Help Them." *National Health Policy Forum* 799:1–24.

Krause, W., and M. D. McShane. 1994. "A Deinstitutionalization Retrospective: Relabeling the Status Offender." *Journal of Crime and Justice* 17:45–67.

Krisberg, B., I. Schwartz, P. Lisky, and J. Austin. 1986. "The Watershed of Juvenile Justice Reform." *Crime and Delinquency* 32:5–38.

Krivo, L. J., and R. D. Peterson. 1996. "Extremely Disadvantaged Neighborhoods and Urban Crime." *Social Forces* 75:619–650.

Krohn, M. D. 1999. "Social Learning Theory: The Continuing Development of a Perspective." *Theoretical Criminology* 3:462–476.

Krohn, M. D., and J. L. Massey. 1980. "Social Control and Delinquent Behavior: An Examination of the Elements of the Social Bond." *Sociological Quarterly* 25:529–543.

Kroneman, L., R. Loeber, and A. E. Hipwell. 2004. "Is Neighborhood Context Differently Related to Externalizing Problems and Delinquency for Girls Compared with Boys?" *Clinical Child and Family Psychology Review* 7:109–122.

Kruttschnitt, C. 1996. "Contributions of Quantitative Methods to the Study of Gender and Crime, or Bootstrapping Our Way into the Theoretical Thicket." *Journal of Quantitative Criminology* 12:135–161.

———. 2001. "Gender and Violence." In *Women, Crime and Criminal Justice,* edited by C. M. Renzetti and L. Goodstein, 77–92. Los Angeles, CA: Roxbury Publishing Company.

———. 2002. With the assistance of G. Gartner and K. Ferraro. "Women's Involvement in Serious Interpersonal Violence." *Aggression and Violent Behavior* 7:529–565.

Kubrin, C. E., and R. Weitzer. 2003. "New Directions in Social Disorganization Theory." *Journal of Research in Crime and Delinquency* 40:374–402.

Kudielka, B. M., A. Buske-Kirschbaum, D. H. Hellhammer, and C. Kirschbaum. 2004. "Differential Heart Rate Reactivity and Recovery after Psychosocial Stress (TSST) in Healthy Children, Younger Adults, and Elderly Adults: The Impact of Age and Gender." *International Journal of Behavioral Medicine* 11:116–121.

LaGrange, T. C., and R. A. Silverman. 1999. "Low Self Control and Opportunity: Testing the General Theory of Crime as an Explanation for Gender Differences in Delinquency." *Criminology* 37:41–72.

Lahey, B. B., S. H. Goodman, and I. D. Waldman. 1999. "Relation of Age of Onset to Die Type and Severity of Child and Adolescent Conduct Problems." *Journal of Abnormal Child Psychology* 27:247–260.

Laitinen-Krispijn, S., J. Van der Ende, A. A. J. M. Hazebroek-Kampschreur, and F. C. Verhulst. 1999. "Pubertal Maturation and the Development of Behavioural and Emotional Problems in Early Adolescence." *Acta Psychiatrica Scandinavica* 99:16–25.

Lamb, S. 2001. *The Secret Lives of Girls.* New York: Free Press.

Lanctot, N., and M. Le Blanc. 2002. "Explaining Deviance by Adolescent Females." In *Crime and Justice: A Review of Research,* vol. 29, edited by M. Tonry, 113–202. Chicago: University of Chicago Press.

Lane, T. W., and G. E. Davis. 1987. "Child Maltreatment and Juvenile Delinquency: Does a Relationship Exist?" In *Prevention of Delinquent Behavior,* edited by J. D. Burchard and S. N. Burchard, 122–138. Beverly Hills, CA: SAGE Publications.

Larson, R., M. Richards, B. Sims, and J. Dworkin. 2001. "How Urban African-American Young Adolescents Spend Their Time: Time Budgets for Location, Activities, and Companionship." *American Journal of Community Psychology* 29:565–597.

Lauderback, D., J. Hansen, and D. Waldorf. 1992. "'Sisters Are Doin' It for Themselves: A Black Female Gang in San Francisco." *Gang Journal* 1:57–72.

Laundra, K. H., G. Kieger, and S. J. Bahr. 2002. "A Social Developmental Model of Serious Delinquency: Examining Gender Differences." *Journal of Primary Prevention* 22:389–407.

Lauritsen, J., and N. White. 2001. "Putting Violence in Its Place: The Influence of Race, Ethnicity, Gender, and Place on the Risk for Violence." *Criminology and Public Policy* 1:37–59.

Lederman, C. S., and E. N. Brown. 2000. "Entangled in the Shadows: Girls in the Juvenile Justice System." *Buffalo Law Review* 48:909–925.

Lederman, C. S., G. A. Dakof, M. A. Larrea, and H. Li. 2004. "Characteristics of Adolescent Females in Juvenile Detention." *International Journal of Law and Psychiatry* 27:321–337.

Leek, M. M. 1991. "Genetic Narcissism in the Family Unit: Genetic Similarity Theory as an Extension of Hamilton's Rule into the Human Domain." PhD thesis, University of Sheffield.

Leiter, J., K. A. Myers, and M. T. Zingraff. 1994. "Substantiated and Unsubstantiated Cases of Child Maltreatment: Do Their Consequences Differ?" *Social Work Research* 18:67–82.

Leitz, L. 2003. "Girl Fights: Exploring Females' Resistance to Educational Structures." *International Journal of Sociology and Social Policy* 23:15–43.

Lemert, C., and M. Winter. 2000. *Crime and Deviance: Essays and Innovations of Edwin Lemert.* Lanhan, MD: Rowman and Littlefield.

Lempers, J. D., and D. Clark-Lempers. 1990. "Family Economic Stress, Maternal and Paternal Support and Adolescent Distress." *Journal of Adolescence* 13 (3): 217–229.

Lenssen, V. S., T. Doreleijers, M. van Dijk, and C. Hartman. 2000. "Girls in Detention: What Are Their Characteristics? A Project to Explore and Document the Character of This Target Group and the Significant Ways in Which It Differs from One Consisting of Boys." *Journal of Adolescence* 23:287–303.

Leonard, E. 1982. *Women, Crime, and Society: A Critique of Theoretical Criminology.* New York: Longman.

Leschied, A., A. Cummings, M. Van Brunschot, A. Cunningham, and A. Saunders. 2000. *Female Adolescent Aggression: A Review of the Literature and the Correlates of Aggression (User Report No. 2000–2004).* Ottawa, Canada: Solicitor General Canada.

Leve, L. D., and P. Chamberlain. 2004. "Female Juvenile Offenders: Defining an Early Onset Pathway for Delinquency." *Journal of Child and Family Studies* 13:439–452.

Levene, K. S., M. M. Walsh, and L. K. Augimeri. 2004. "Linking Identification and Treatment of Early Risk Factors for Female Delinquency." In *Girls and Aggression: Contributing Factors and Intervention Principles.* Vol. 19 of *Perspectives in Law and Psychology,* edited by M. M. Moretti, C. L. Odgers, and M. A. Jackson, 147–163. New York: Kluwer Academic/Plenum Publishers.

Leventhal, T., and J. Brooks-Gunn. 2000. "The Neighborhoods They Live in: The Effects of Neighborhood Residence on Child and Adolescent Outcomes." *National Health Policy Forum* 126:309–337.

Lipsey, M. W., and J. H. Derzon. 1998. "Predictors of Violent or Serious Delinquency in Adolescence and Early Adulthood: A Synthesis of Longitudinal Research." In *Serious and Violent Juvenile Offenders: Risk Factors and Successful Interventions,* edited by R. Loeber and D. P. Farrington, 86–105. Thousand Oaks, CA: SAGE Publications.

Lipsitt, P. D., S. L. Buka, and L. P. Lipsitt. 1990. "Early Intelligence Scores and Subsequent Delinquency: A Prospective Study." *American Journal of Family Therapy* 18 (2): 197–208.

Liska, A., and M. Reed. 1985. "Ties to Conventional Institutions and Delinquency: Estimating Reciprocal Effects." *American Sociological Review* 50:547–560.

Little, T. D., S. M. Jones, C. C. Henrich, and P. H. Hawley. 2003. "Disentangling the 'Whys' from the 'Whats' of Aggressive Behavior." *International Journal of Behavioral Development* 27:122–133.

Liu, R. X. 2004. "Parent–Youth Conflict and School Delinquency/Cigarette Use: The Moderating Effects of Gender and Associations with Achievement-Oriented Peers." *Sociological Inquiry* 74:271–297.

Liu, X., and H. Kaplan. 1999. "Explaining the Gender Differences in Adolescent Antisocial Behavior: A Longitudinal Test of Mediating Mechanisms." *Criminology* 37:195–215.

Lloyd, D., J. G. Bachman, P. M. O'Malley, and J. E. Schulenberg. 2007. *Monitoring the Future: A Continuing Study of American Youth (12th-Grade Survey), 2006.* Conducted by University of Michigan, Institute for Social Research, Survey Research Center. ICPSR20022-v.2. Ann Arbor, MI: Inter-university Consortium for Policital and Social Research [producer and distributor], 12–13.

Lockwood, D. 1996. "Violence and Violence Prevention among African American Middle School Children." Working Paper No. 06-1, Consortium of Negotiation and Conflict Resolution: Consortium of Georgia Universities for the Advancement of Conflict Resolution Theory and Education, Savannah, GA.

———. 1997. *Violence among Middle and High School Students: Analysis and Implications for Prevention.* Washington, DC: Department of Justice, Office of Justice Programs, National Institute of Justice.

Loeber, R., and D. P. Farrington. 2001. *Child Delinquents: Development, Intervention, and Service Needs.* Thousand Oaks, CA: SAGE Publications.

Loeber, R., D. P. Farrington, M. Stouthamer-Loeber, T. E. Moffitt, A. Caspi, and D. Lynam. 2001. "Male Mental Health Problems, Psychopathy and Personality Traits: Key Findings from the First 14 Years of the Pittsburgh Youth Study." *Clinical Child and Family Psychology Review* 4:273–297.

Loeber, R., K. Keenan, and Q. Zhang. 1997. "Boys' Experimentation and Persistence in Developmental Pathways toward Serious Delinquency." *Journal of Child and Family Studies* 5: 321–357.

Loeber, R., and M. Stouthamer-Loeber. 1986. "Family Factors as Correlates and Predictors of Conduct Problems and Juvenile Delinquency." In *Crime and Justice*, vol. 7, edited by M. Tonry and N. Morris. Chicago: University of Chicago Press.

Luster, T., and S. A. Small. 1997. "Sexual Abuse History and Number of Sex Partners among Female Adolescents." *Family Planning Perspectives* 29:204–211.

Lynam, D., T. Moffitt, and M. Stouthamer-Loeber. 1993. "Explaining the Relation between IQ and Delinquency: Class, Race, Test Motivation, School Failure or Self-Control?" *Journal of Abnormal Psychology* 2:187–196.

Lynch, M., and D. Cicchetti. 1998. "An Ecological-Transactional Analysis of Children and Contexts: The Longitudinal Interplay among Child Maltreatment, Community Violence, and Children's Symptomatology." *Developmental Psychopathology* 10:235–227.

Ma, X., L. L. Stewin, and D. L. Mah. 2001. "Bullying in School: Nature, Effects and Remedies." *Research Paper in Education* 16:247–270.

Maccoby, E. E. 1998. *The Two Sexes: Growing Up Apart, Coming Together.* London: Belknap Press.

Maccoby, E. E., M. Putallaz, and K. L. Bierman. 2004. "Aggression in the Context of Gender Development." In *Aggression, Antisocial Behavior, and Violence among Girls*, edited by M. Putallaz and K. L. Bierman, 3–22. New York: Guilford Press.

MacDonald, J. M., and M. Chesney-Lind. 2001. "Gender Bias and Juvenile Justice Revisited." *Crime and Delinquency* 47:173–195.

MacDonald, J. M., and A. R. Gover. 2005. "Concentrated Disadvantage and Youth-on-Youth Homicide." *Homicide Studies* 9:30–54.

MacDonald, M. P. 1999. *All Souls.* New York: Ballantine Books.

MacMaster, F. P., and V. Kusumakar. 2004. "MRI Study of the Pituitary Gland in Adolescent Depression." *Journal of Psychiatric Research* 38:231–236.

Magnusson, D. 1988. *Individual Development from an Interactional Perspective: A Longitudinal Study.* Hillsdale, NJ: Lawrence Erlbaum Associates.

Magnusson, D., L. R. Bergman, L. N. Robins, and M. Rutter. 1990. "A Pattern Approach to the Study of Pathway from Childhood to Adulthood." In *Straight and Devious Pathways from Childhood to Adulthood,* edited by L. N. Robins and M. Rutter, 101–115. New York: Cambridge University Press.

Magnusson, D., and A. Ohman. 1987. *Psychopathology: An Interactional Perspective (Personality, Psychopathology, and Psychotherapy).* New York: Academic Press.

Maguin, E., and R. Loeber. 1996. "Academic Performance and Delinquency." In *Crime and Justice: A Review of Research,* vol. 20, edited by M. Tonry, 145–264. Chicago: University of Chicago Press.

Maguire, K., and A. L. Pastore. 1997. *Bureau of Justice Statistics Sourcebook of Criminal Justice Statistics, 1996.* Washington, DC: Bureau of Justice Statistics.

Maher, L. 1997. *Sexed Work: Gender, Race and Resistance in a Brooklyn Drug Market.* Oxford: Clarendon Press.

Maher, L., and R. Curtis. 1992. "Women on the Edge: Crack Cocaine and the Changing Contexts of Street-Level Sex Work in New York City." *Crime, Law and Social Change* 18: 221–258.

Mahoney, A. R., and C. Fenster. 1982. "Female Delinquents in a Suburban Court." In *Judge, Lawyer, Victim, Thief: Women, Gender Roles and Criminal Justice,* edited by N. H. Rafter and E. A. Stanko, 22–54. Boston, MA: Northeastern University Press.

Mahoney, J., and B. Cairns. 1997. "Do Extracurricular Activities Protect Against Early School Dropout?" *Developmental Psychology* 13:241–253.

Mahoney, J. L., R. B. Cairns, and T. W. Farmer. 2003. "Promoting Interpersonal Competence and Educational Success through Extracurricular Activity Participation." *Journal of Educational Psychology* 95:409–418.

Mahoney, J. L., and H. Stattin. 2000. "Leisure Time Activities and Adolescent Anti-Social Behavior: The Role of Structure and Social Context." *Journal of Adolescence* 23:113–127.

Mahoney, K., J. D. Ford, S. J. Ko, and C. B. Siegfried. 2004. *Trauma Focused Interventions for Youth in the Juvenile Justice System.* Los Angeles, CA: National Child Traumatic Stress Network.

Maki, P. M., J. B. Rich, and R. S. Rosenbaum. 2002. "Implicit Memory Varies across the Menstrual Cycle: Estrogen Effects in Young Women." *Neuropsychologia* 40:518–529.

Males, M. 1996. *The Scapegoat General Ion: American's War on Adolescents.* Monroe, ME: Common Courage Press.

Manchester, D., A. Hodgkinson, and T. Casey. 1997. "Prolonged, Severe Behavioural Disturbance Following Traumatic Brain Injury: What Can Be Done?" *Brain Injury* 11 (8): 605–617.

Manlove, J. 1998. "The Influence of High-School Dropout and School Disengagement on the Risk of School-Age Pregnancy." *Journal of Research on Adolescence* 8:187–220.

Manning, W. D., and K. L. Lamb. 2003. "Adolescent Well-Being in Cohabiting, Married, and Single-Parent Families." *Journal of Marriage and the Family* 65:876–893.

Marcus, R. F. 1996. "The Friendships of Delinquents." *Adolescence* 31:145–158.

Margolin, G., and E. B. Gordis. 2000. "The Effects of Family and Community Violence on Children." *Annual Review of Psychology* 51:445–479.

Markowitz, F. E. 2001. "Extending Social Disorganization Theory: Modeling the Relationships between Cohesion, Disorder, and Fear." *Criminology* 39:293–320.

Martin, C. A., T. H. Kelly, M. K. Rayens, B. R. Brogli, A. Brenzel, J. W. Smith, and H. A. Omar. 2002. "Sensation Seeking, Puberty, and Nicotine, Alcohol and Marijuana Use in Adolescence." *Journal of the American Academy of Child and Adolescent Psychiatry* 41:1495–1502.

Martin, R. 1997. "'Girls Don't Talk about Garages!' Perceptions of Conversation in Same- and Cross-Sex Friendships." *Personal Relationships* 4:115–130.

Maskin, M. 1974. "A Comparison of Graduate and Recidivist WISC IQ Scores in a Delinquency Treatment Program for Girls." *Journal of Clinical Psychology* 30:319–320.

Mason, W. A., and M. Windle. 2002. "Gender, Self-Control and Informal Social Control in Adolescence, A Test of Three Models of the Continuity of Delinquent Behavior." *Youth and Society* 33:479–514.

Mason, W. A., L. Zimmerman, and W. Evans. 1998. "Sexual and Physical Abuse among Incarcerated Youth: Implications for Sexual Behavior, Contraceptive Use, and Teenage Pregnancy." *Child Abuse and Neglect* 22:987–995.

Massey, D. S., and N. A. Denton. 1993. *American Apartheid: Segregation and the Making of the Underclass.* Cambridge, U.K.: Harvard University Press.

Matsueda, R. 1992. "Reflected Appraisals, Parental Labeling, and Delinquency: Specifying a Symbolic Interactionist Theory." *American Journal of Sociology* 97:1577–1611.

Matsueda, R., and K. Anderson. 1998. "The Dynamics of Delinquent Peers and Delinquent Behavior." *Criminology* 36:269–308.

Maxson, C. L., and M. W. Klein. 1995. "Investigating Gang Structures." *Journal of Gang Research* 3:33–40.

———. 1997. *Responding to Troubled Youth.* New York: Oxford University Press.

Maxson, C., and M. Whitlock. 2001. *Gangs in America.* 3rd ed. Edited by C. R. Huff. Thousand Oaks, CA: SAGE Publications.

May, J. C., M. R. Delgado, R. E. Dahl, V. A. Stenger, N. D. Ryan, and J. A. Fiez. 2004. "Event-Related Functional Magnetic Resonance Imaging of Reward Related Brain Circuitry in Children and Adolescents." *Biological Psychiatry* 55:359–366.

Mayer, J. 1994. "Girls in the Maryland Juvenile Justice System: Findings of the Female Population Taskforce." Presentation to the Gender Specific Services Training Group. Minneapolis, MN.

Mazerolle, P., and J. Maahs. 2000. "General Strain and Delinquency: An Alternative Examination of Conditioning Influences." *Justice Quarterly* 17:753–778.

McBurnett, K., A. Raine, M. Stouthamer-Loeber, R. Loeber, A. M. Kumar, M. Kumar, and B. B. Lahey. 2005. "Mood and Hormone Responses to Psychological Challenge in Adolescent Males with Conduct Problems." *Biological Psychiatry* 57:1109–1116.

McCabe, K. M., A. E. Lansing, A. Garland, and R. Hough. 2002. "Gender Differences in Psychopathology, Functional Impairment, and Familial Risk Factors among Adjudicated Delinquents." *Journal of the American Academy of Child and Adolescent Psychiatry* 41:860–867.

McCarthy, B. 1987. "Preventive Detention and Pretrial Custody in Juvenile Court." *Journal of Criminal Justice* 15:185–200.

McCarthy, B., D. Felmlee, and J. Hagan. 2004. "Girl Friends Are Better: Gender, Friends, and Crime among School and Street Youth." *Criminology* 42:805–835.

McCarthy, B., and J. Hagan. 1999. "In the Company of Women: A Structural Elaboration of a Power-Control Theory of Gender and Delinquency." *Criminology* 37:761–788.

———. 2005. "Danger, Deterrence, and the Decision to Offend." *Social Forces* 83:1065–1096.

McCarthy, B., and B. Smith. 1986. "The Conceptualization of Discrimination in the Juvenile Justice Process: The Impact of Administrative Factors and Screening Decisions on Juvenile Court Dispositions." *Criminology* 24:41–64.

McCarthy, M., and M. Altemus. 1997. "Central Nervous System Actions of Oxytocin and Modulation of Behavior in Humans." *Molecular Medicine Today* 1:269–275.

McClanahan, S. 1999. "Father Absence and the Welfare of Children." In *Coping with Divorce, Single Parenting, and Remarriage: A Risk and Resiliency Perspective*, edited by E. M. Hetherington, 117–146. Mahwah, NJ: Lawrence Erlbaum Associates.

McCluskey, J. D., S. P. Varano, B. M. Huebner, and T. S. Bynum. 2004. "Who Do You Refer? The Effects of a Policy Change on Juvenile Referrals." *Criminal Justice Policy Review* 15: 437–461.

McCord, J. 1991. "The Cycle of Crime and Socialization Practices." *Journal of Criminal Law and Criminology* 82:211–228.

McCord, J., C. S. Widom, and N. A. Crowell. 2001. *Juvenile Crime, Juvenile Justice*. Washington, DC: National Academy Press.

McCurley, C., and H. N. Snyder. 2004. *Victims of Violent Juvenile Crime*. Washington, DC: Juvenile Justice Bulletin. Office of Juvenile Justice and Delinquency Prevention, National Institute of Justice.

McEwen, B. S. 2003. "Mood Disorders and Allostatic Load." *Biological Psychiatry* 54 (3): 200–207.

McGee, Z. T. 2003. "Community Violence and Adolescent Development." *Journal of Contemporary Criminal Justice* 19:293–314.

McGivern, R. F., J. P. Huston, D. Byrd, T. King, G. J. Siegle, and J. Reilly. 1997. "Sex Differences in Visual Recognition Memory: Support for a Sex-Related Difference in Attention in Adults and Children." *Brain and Cognition* 34:323–336.

McGloin, J. M., and T. C. Pratt. 2003. "Cognitive Ability and Delinquent Behavior among Inner-City Youth: A Life-Course Analysis of Main, Mediating, and Interaction Effects." *International Journal of Offender Therapy and Comparative Criminology* 47:253–271.

McGloin, J. M., T. C. Pratt, and J. Maahs. 2004. "Rethinking the IQ–Delinquency Relationship: A Longitudinal Analysis of Multiple Theoretical Models." *Justice Quarterly* 21:603–665.

McKnight, L., and A. Loper. 2002. "The Effect of Risk and Resilience Factors on the Prediction of Delinquency in Adolescent Girls." *School Psychology International* 23:186–198.

McNulty, T. L., and P. E. Bellair. 2003a. "Explaining Racial and Ethnic Differences in Adolescent Violence: Structural Disadvantage, Family Well-Being, and Social Capital." *Justice Quarterly* 20:1–31.

———. 2003b. "Explaining Racial and Ethnic Differences in Serious Adolescent Violent Behavior." *Criminology* 41:709–746.

Mead, G. 1934. *Mind, Self and Society from the Standpoint of a Social Behaviorist*. Chicago: University of Chicago Press.

Mears, D., M. Ploeger, and M. Warr. 1998. "Explaining the Gender Gap in Delinquency: Peer Influence and Moral Evaluations of Behavior." *Journal of Research in Crime and Delinquency* 35:251–266.

Menard, S., and B. Morse. 1986. "IQ and Delinquency: A Response to Harry and Minor." *American Journal of Sociology* 91 (4): 962–968.

Messer, J., B. Maughan, D. Quinton, and A. Taylor. 2004. "Precursors and Correlates of Criminal Behaviour in Women." *Criminal Behaviour and Mental Health* 14:82–107.

Messerschmidt, J. 1993. *Masculinities and Crime*. Lanham, MD: Rowman and Littlefield.

———. 1995. "From Patriarchy to Gender: Feminist Theory, Criminology and the Challenge of Diversity." In *International Feminist Perspectives in Criminology: Engendering a Discipline*, edited by N. Rafter and F. Heidensohn, 167–188. Buckingham: Open University Press.

———. 2004. *Flesh and Blood: Adolescent Gender Diversity and Violence*. Lanham, MD: Rowman and Littlefield.

Messner, S. F., M. D. Krohn, and A. E. Liska. 1989. *Theoretical Integration in the Study of Deviance and Crime: Problems and Prospects*. Albany: State University of New York Press.

Messner, S. F., L. E. Raffalovich, and R. McMillan. 2001. "Economic Deprivation and Changes in Homicide Arrest Rates for White and Black Youths, 1967–1998: A National Time-Series Analysis." *Criminology* 39:591–614.

Messner, S. F., and R. Rosenfeld. 2007. *Crime and the American Dream*. 4th ed. Belmont, CA: Wadsworth.

Miethe, T. D., and R. F. Meier. 1994. *Crime and Its Social Context*. Albany: State University of New York Press.

Miller, B. C., M. C. Norton, T. Curtis, E. J. Hill, P. Schvancveldt, and M. H. Young. 1997. "The Timing of Sexual Intercourse among Adolescents: Family, Peer and Other Antecedents." *Youth and Society* 29:54–83.

Miller, E. 1986. *Street Woman*. Philadelphia, PA: Temple University Press.

Miller, J. 1996. "An Examination of Disposition Decision-Making for Delinquent Girls." In *The Intersection of Race, Gender and Class in Criminology*, edited by M. D. Schwartz and D. Milovanovic, 219–246. New York: Garland Press.

———. 1998. "Up It Up: Gender and the Accomplishment of Street Robbery." *Criminology* 36:37–66.

———. 2001. *One of the Guys: Girls, Gangs, and Gender*. New York: Oxford University Press.

———. 2002a. "On Gang Girls, Gender and a Structured Action Theory." *Theoretical Criminology* 6:461–476.

———. 2002b. "The Strengths and Limits of 'Doing Gender' for Understanding Street Crime." *Criminology* 6:433–460.

Miller, J., and R. K. Brunson. 2000. "Gender Dynamics in Youth Gangs: A Comparison of Male and Female Accounts." *Justice Quarterly* 17:801–830.

Miller, J., and S. H. Decker. 2001. "Young Women and Gang Violence: An Examination of Gender, Street Offending and Violent Victimization in Gangs." *Justice Quarterly* 18:115–140.

Miller, J., and C. W. Mullins. 2006. "Taking Stock: The Status of Feminist Theories in Criminology." In *The Status of Criminology Theory*, edited by F. T. Cullen, J. P. Wright, and M. Coleman, 217–250. New Brunswick, NJ: Transaction.

Miller, J., and N. A. White. 2003. "Gender and Adolescent Relationship Violence: A Contextual Examination." *Criminology* 41:1207–1248.

Miller, W. 1973. "The Molls." *Society* 11:32–35.

———. 1975. *Violence by Youth Gangs and Youth Groups as a Crime Problem in Major American Cities*. Washington, DC: Government Printing Office.

Miller-Johnson, M., P. R. Constanzo, J. D. Coie, M. R. Rose, D. C. Browne, and C. Johnson. 2003. "Peer Social Structure and Risk-Taking Behaviors among African American Early Adolescents." *Journal of Youth and Adolescence* 32:375–384.

Minor, K. I., D. J. Hartmann, and S. Terry. 1997. "Predictors of Juvenile Court Actions and Recidivism." *Crime and Delinquency* 43:328–344.

Miranda, K. M. 2003. *Homegirls in the Public Sphere*. Austin: University of Texas Press.

Moffitt, T. E. 1993. "Adolescence Limited and Life Course Persistent Antisocial Behavior: A Developmental Taxonomy." *Psychological Review* 100:674–701.

Moffit, T. E., A. Caspi, J. Belsky, and P. A. Silva. 1992. "Childhood Experience and the Onset of Menarche: A Test of a Sociobiological Model." *Child Development* 63:47–58.

Moffitt, T. E., A. Caspi, M. Rutter, and P. A. Silva. 2001. *Sex Differences in Antisocial Behavior: Conduct Disorder, Delinquency, and Violence in the Dunedin Longitudinal Study*. Cambridge: Cambridge University Press.

Moffitt, T. E., and P. A. Silva. 1988. "IQ and Delinquency: A Direct Test of the Differential Detection Hypothesis." *Journal of Abnormal Psychology* 97:330–333.

Molidar, C. D. 1996. "Female Gang Members: A Profile of Aggression and Victimization." *Social Work* 41:251–257.

Molidor, C., and R. Tolman. 1998. "Gender and Contextual Factors in Adolescent Dating Violence." *Violence Against Women* 4:180–195.

Molnar, B. E., A. Browne, M. Cerda, and S. L. Buka. 2005. "Violent Behavior by Girls Reporting Violent Victimization: A Prospective Study." *Archives of Pediatric and Adolescent Medicine* 159:731–739.

Molnar, B. E., M. Cerda, A. Roberts, and S. Buka. Forthcoming. "Neighborhood Resources: Effects on Aggressive and Delinquent Behaviors among Urban Youth." *American Journal of Public Health.*

Moore, J. W. 1991. *Going Down to the Barrio: Homeboys and Homegirls in Change.* Philadelphia, PA: Temple University Press.

Moore, J. W., and J. Hagedorn. 1996. "What Happens to the Girls in the Gang?" In *Gangs in America,* edited by C. R. Huff, 205–218. Thousand Oaks, CA: SAGE Publications.

———. 2001. *Female Gangs: A Focus on Research.* Bulletin. Washington, DC: U.S. Department of Justice, Office of Justice Programs, Office of Juvenile Justice and Delinquency Prevention.

Morash, M. 1986. "Gender, Peer Group Experiences, and Seriousness of Delinquency." *Journal of Research in Crime and Delinquency* 23:46–67.

———. 1999. "A Consideration of Gender in Relation to Social Learning and Social Structure: A General Theory of Crime and Deviance." *Theoretical Criminology* 3:451–462.

Morenoff, J. D., R. J. Sampson, and S. W. Raudenbush. 2001. "Neighborhood Inequality, Collective Efficacy, and the Spatial Dynamics of Homicide." *Criminology* 39:517–560.

Morris, A. 1987. *Women, Crime, and Justice.* New York: Basil Blackwell.

Morris, R. E., C. J. Baker, M. Valentine, and A. J. Pennisi. 1998. "Variations in HIV Risk Behaviors of Incarcerated Juveniles during a Four-Year Period: 1989–1992." *Journal of Adolescent Health* 23:39–48.

Moss, H., M. M. Vanyukov, and C. S. Martin. 1995. "Salivary Cortisol Responses and the Risk for Substance Use in Prepubertal Boys." *Biological Psychiatry* 38:547–555.

M.T.A. Group Co-operative. 1999. "A 14-Month Randomized Clinical Trial of Treatment Strategies for Attention-Deficit Hyperactivity Disorder." *Archives of General Psychiatry* 56:1073–1086.

Mullins, C. W., and R. Wright. 2003. "Gender, Social Networks, and Residential Burglary." *Criminology* 41:813–839.

Mullins, C. W., R. Wright, and B. A. Jacobs. 2004. "Gender, Streetlife and Criminal Retaliations." *Criminology* 42:911–940.

Myers, W. C., R. C. Burket, W. B. Lyles, and L. Stone. 1990. "DSM-III Diagnoses and Offenses in Committed Female Juvenile Delinquents." *American Academy of Psychiatry and Law* 18:47–54.

Myin-Germeys, I., L. Krabbendam, P. Delespaul, and J. van Os. 2004. "Sex Differences in Emotional Reactivity to Daily Life Stress in Psychosis." *Journal of Clinical Psychiatry* 65:805–809.

Najaka, S. S., D. C. Gottfredson, and D. B. Wilson. 2001. "A Meta-Analytic Inquiry into the Relationship between Selected Risk Factors and Problem Behavior." *Prevention Science* 2:257–271.

Natale, M., R. E. Gur, and R. C. Gur. 1983. "Hemispheric Asymmetries in Processing Emotional Expressions." *Neuropsychologia* 21:555–565.

National Center for Juvenile Justice. 2005. *Juvenile Arrest Rates by Offense, Sex, and Race.* http://ojjdp.ncjrs.org/ojstatbb/crime/excel/JAR_20050228.xls.

National Council on Crime and Delinquency. 1975. "Jurisdiction Over Status Offenders Should Be Removed from the Juvenile Court: A Policy Statement." *Crime and Delinquency* 21:97–99.

———. 2007. "And Justice for Some. Differential Treatment of Youth of Color in the Justice System." www.nccd-crc.org/need/pubs/2007jan_justice_for_some.pdf (accessed February 1, 2007).

National Research Council. 1993. "Understanding Child Abuse and Neglect. Panel on Research on Child Abuse and Neglect." Commission on Behavioral and Social Sciences and Education. National Research Council. Washington, DC: National Academy Press.

Ness, C. 2004. "Why Girls Fight: Female Youth Violence in the Inner City." *Annals of the American Academy of Political and Social Science* 595:32–48.

Neville, K. A., and J. L. Walker. 2005. "Precocious Pubarche Is Associated with SGA, Prematurity, Weight Gain, and Obesity." *Archives of Disease in Childhood* 90:258–261.

Newburn, T., and E. Stanko. 1994. *Just Boys Doing Business: Men, Masculinities and Crime.* London: Routledge.

Norland, S., R. C. Wessel, and N. Shover. 1981. "Masculinity and Delinquency." *Criminology* 19:421–433.

Nurge, D. 1998. "Female Gangs and Cliques in Boston: What's the Difference?" Paper presented at the annual meeting of the American Society of Criminology, Washington, DC.

O'Brien, R. M. 1999. "Measuring the Convergence/Divergence of 'Serious Crime' Arrest Rates for Males and Females." *Journal of Quantitative Criminology* 15:97–114.

O'Brien, R. M., J. Stockard, and L. Isaacson. 1999. "The Enduring Effects of Cohort Characteristics on Age-Specific Homicide Rates, 1960–1995." *American Journal of Sociology* 104:1061–1095.

Obeidallah, D. A., R. T. Brennan, J. Brooks-Gunn, and F. Earls. 2004. "Links between Pubertal Timing and Neighborhood Contexts: Implications for Girls' Violent Behavior." *Journal of the American Academy of Child and Adolescent Psychiatry* 43:1460–1468.

Obeidallah, D. A., and F. J. Earls. 1999. *Adolescent Girls: The Role of Depression in the Development of Delinquency.* Washington, DC: U.S. Department of Justice, Office of Justice Programs, National Institute of Justice.

Odgers, C. L., and M. M. Moretti. 2002. "Aggressive and Antisocial Girls: Research Update and Future Research Challenges." *International Journal of Forensic Mental Health* 2 (1): 17–33.

Odgers, C. L., M. G. Schmidt, and N. D. Reppucci. 2004. "Reframing Violence Risk Assessment for Female Juvenile Offenders." In *Girls and Aggression: Contributing Factors and Intervention Principles,* edited by M. M. Moretti, C. L. Odgers, and M. A. Jackson, 195–210. New York: Kluwer Academic/Plenum Publishers.

Office of Juvenile Justice and Delinquency Prevention (OJJDP). 1996. *Female Offenders in the Juvenile Justice System—Statistics Summary.* Washington, DC: OJJDP.

———. 2000. *Statistical Briefing Book.* Washington, DC: OJJDP. http://ojjdp.ncjrs.org/ojstatbb/court/JCSCF_Display.asp?ID=qa06601&year=2000&group=1&type=1.

Offord, D. R., M. H. Boyle, and Y. A. Racine. 1989. "Ontario Child Health Study: Correlates of Conduct Disorder." *Journal of the American Academy of Child and Adolescent Psychiatry* 28:856–860.

Offord, D. R., and M. F. Poushinsky. 1981. "School Performance, IQ and Female Delinquency." *International Journal of Social Psychiatry* 27:53–62.

Olweus, D. 1993. *Bullying at School: What We Know and What We Can Do.* Oxford, U.K.: Blackwell.

Orenstein, P. 1994. *Schoolgirls.* New York: Doubleday.

Orr, D. P., and G. M. Ingersoll. 1995. "The Contribution of Level of Cognitive Complexity and Pubertal Timing to Behavioral Risk in Young Adolescents." *Pediatrics* 95:528–533.

Orr, L., J. D. Feins, R. Jacob, E. Beecroft, L. Sanbonmatsu, and L. F. Katz. 2003. *Moving to Opportunity for Fair Housing Demonstration Interim Impacts Evaluation*. Washington, DC: U.S. Department of Housing and Urban Development, Office of Policy Research and Development. http://search.ebscohost.com/login.aspx?direct=true&db=psyhref&AN=MOFHDIIME.ORR.USDEPARTMENTOFHOUSINGANDU.BJJC.

Osgood, D. W., L. D. Johnston, P. M. Malley, and J. G. Bachman. 1988. "The Generality of Deviance in Late Adolescence and Early Adulthood." *American Sociological Review* 53: 81–93.

Osgood, D., Wayne, J. K. Wilson, J. G. Bachman, P. M. O'Malley, and L. D. Johnston. 1996. "Routine Activities and Individual Deviant Behavior." *American Sociological Review* 61: 635–655.

Osofsky, J. D. 1995. "The Effects of Exposure to Violence on Young Children." *American Psychology* 50:782–788.

Ostroff, C. 1992. "The Relationship between Satisfaction, Attitudes and Performance: An Organizational Level Analysis." *Journal of Applied Psychology* 77:963–974.

Ousey, G. C., and M. Lee. 2002. "Examining the Conditional Nature of the Illicit Drug Market–Homicide Relationship: A Partial Test of the Theory of Contingent Causation." *Criminology* 40:73–102.

Ouston, J. 1984. "Delinquency, Family Background and Educational Attainment." *British Journal of Criminology* 24:2–26.

Pagani, L. S., R. E. Tremblay, D. Nagin, M. Zoccolillo, F. Vitaro, and P. McDuff. 2004. "Risk Factor Models for Adolescent Verbal and Physical Aggression toward Mothers." *International Journal of Behavioral Development* 28:528–537.

Paikoff, R., and J. Brooks-Gunn. 1991. "Do Parent–Child Relationships Change during Puberty?" *Psychological Bulletin* 110:47–66.

Paquette, J. A., and M. K. Underwood. 1999. "Gender Differences in Young Adolescents' Experiences of Peer Victimization: Social and Physical Aggression." *Merrill-Palmer Quarterly* 45:242–266.

Patchin, J. W., B. M. Huebner, J. D. McCluskey, S. P. Varano, and T. S. Bynum. 2006. "Exposure to Community Violence and Childhood Delinquency." *Crime and Delinquency* 52: 307–332.

Patterson, G. R., L. Crosby, and S. Vuchinich. 1992. "Predicting Risk for Early Police Arrest." *Journal of Quantitative Criminology* 8:335–355.

Pattillo, M. E. 1998. "Sweet Mothers and Gangbangers: Managing Crime in a Black Middle-Class Neighborhood." *Social Forces* 76:747–774.

Pattillo-McCoy, M. 1999. *Black Picket Fences: Privilege and Peril among the Black Middle Class*. Chicago: University of Chicago Press.

Paulson, M. J., R. H. Coombs, and M. A. Richardson. 1990. "School Performance, Academic Aspirations and Drug Use among Children and Adolescents." *Journal of Drug Education* 20:289–303.

Payne, A. A., and D. C. Gottfredson. 2005. "Gender- and Race-Based Outcomes in the Effect of School-Related Factors on Delinquency and Victimization." Thesis manuscript, Villanova University.

Payne, A. A., D. C. Gottfredson, and G. D. Gottfredson. 2003. "Schools as Communities: The Relationships among Communal School Organization, Student Bonding, and School Disorder." *Criminology* 41:1301–1327.

Pepler, D., and W. Craig. 1999. "Aggressive Girls: Development of Disorder and Outcomes." Report No. 57, Toronto, ON: York University.

Pepler, D., W. Craig, A. Yuile, and J. Connolly. 2004. "Girls Who Bully: A Developmental and Relational Perspective." In *Aggression, Antisocial Behavior, and Violence among Girls: A Developmental Perspective,* edited by M. Putallaz and K. L. Bierman, 90–109. New York: Guilford Press.

Peters, R. J., S. R. Tortolero, R. C. Addy, C. Markham, S. L. Escobar-Chaves, M. F. Fernandez-Esquer, and G. S. Yacoubian. 2003. "The Relationship between Sexual Abuse and Drug Use: Findings from Houston's Safer Choices 2 Program." *Journal of Drug Education* 33:49–59.

Peterson, D., J. Miller, and F. Esbensen. 2001. "The Impact of Sex Composition on Gangs and Gang Member Delinquency." *Criminology* 39:411–439.

Peterson, R., and W. C. Bailey. 1992. "Rape and Dimensions of Gender Socioeconomic Inequality in U.S. Metropolitan Areas." *Journal of Research in Crime and Delinquency* 29:162–177.

Peterson, R. L., J. Larson, and R. Skiba. 2001. "School Violence Prevention: Current Status and Policy Recommendations." *Law and Policy* 23:345–371.

Piquero, A., and T. Brezina. 2001. "Testing Moffitt's Account of Adolescence-Limited Delinquency." *Criminology* 39:353–370.

Piquero, A., and R. Paternoster. 1998. "An Application of Stafford and Warr's Reconceptualization of Deterrence to Drinking and Driving." *Journal of Research in Crime and Delinquency* 35:3–39.

Piquero, A. R., and S. G. Tibbetts. 2002. *Rational Choice and Criminal Behavior.* New York: Routledge.

Piquero, N. L., A. R. Gover, J. M. MacDonald, and A. R. Piquero. 2005. "The Influence of Delinquent Peers on Delinquency: Does Gender Matter?" *Youth and Society* 36:251–275.

Piquero, N. L., and M. Sealock. 2004. "Gender and General Strain Theory: A Preliminary Test of Broidy and Agnew's Gender/GST Hypotheses." *Justice Quarterly* 21:125–158.

Platt, A. M. 1977. *The Child Savers: The Invention of Delinquency.* Chicago: University of Chicago Press.

Pleydon, A. P., and J. G. Schner. 2001. "Female Adolescent Friendship and Delinquent Behavior." *Adolescence* 36:189–205.

Plotsky, P. M., M. J. Owens, and C. B. Nemeroff. 1998. "Psychoneuroendocrinology of Depression—Hypothalamic-Pituitary-Adrenal Axis." *Psychiatric Clinics of North America* 21:293–307.

Poe-Yamagata, E., and J. A. Butts. 1996. *Female Offenders in the Juvenile Justice System.* Pittsburgh, PA: National Center for Juvenile Justice.

Polk, K. 1984. "Juvenile Diversion: A Look at the Record." *Crime and Delinquency* 30:648–659.

Pollack, S. 1993. "Opening the Window on a Very Dark Day: A Programme Evaluation of a Peer-support Team at the Kingston Prison for Women." *Forum on Corrections Research* 6:36–38.

Pope, C. E., and W. H. Feyerherm. 1990. "Minority Status and Juvenile Justice Processing: An Assessment of the Research Literatures." *Criminal Justice Abstracts* 22:327–335.

Portillos, E. L. 1999. "Women, Men and Gangs: The Social Construction of Gender in the Barrio." In *Female Gangs in America: Essays on Girls, Gangs and Gender,* edited by M. Chesney-Lind and J. M. Hagedorn, 232–244. Chicago: Lake View Press.

Poulin, A. 1996. "Female Delinquents: Defining their Place in the Justice System." *Wisconsin Law Review* 541–575.

Pratt, T. C., M. G. Turner, and A. R. Piquero. 2004. "Parental Socialization and Community Context: A Longitudinal Analysis of the Structural Sources of Low Self-Control." *Journal of Research in Crime and Delinquency* 41:219–243.

Price, C., and J. Kunz. 2003. "Rethinking the Paradigm of Juvenile Delinquency as Related to Divorce." *Journal of Divorce and Remarriage* 39:109–133.

Putallaz, M., J. Kupersmidt, C. L. Grimes, K. DeNero, and J. D. Coie. 1999. "Overt and Relational Aggression: Aggressors, Victims, and Gender." In *Social Relationships and Two Forms of Aggression: Gender Considerations.* Albuquerque, NM.

Puzzanchera, C., T. Finnegan, and W. Kang. 2005. *Easy Access to Juvenile Populations.* http://www.ojjdp.ncjrs.org/ojstatbb/ezapop/.

Puzzanchera, C., A. Stahl, T. Finnegan, N. Tierney, and H. Snyder. 2003. *Juvenile Court Statistics 1999.* Washington, DC: Office of Juvenile Justice and Delinquency Prevention.

———. 2004. *Juvenile Court Statistics 2000.* Pittsburgh, PA: National Center for Juvenile Justice.

Quicker, J. 1983. *Homegirls: Characterizing Chicana Gangs.* San Pedro, CA: International University Press.

Quinn, P., and S. Wigal. 2004. "Perceptions of Girls and ADHD: Results from a National Survey." *Medscape General Medicine* 6:2.

Quinton, D., A. Pickles, B. Maughan, and M. Rutter. 1993. "Partners, Peers and Pathways. Assortative Pairing and Continuities in Conduct Disorder." *Development and Psychopathology* 54:763–783.

Raber, J. 1998. "Detrimental Effects of Chronic Hypothalamic-Pituitary-Adrenal Axis Activation." *Molecular Neurobiology* 18:1–22.

Rankin, J. 1980. "School Factors and Delinquency: Interaction by Age and Sex." *Social Science Research* 64:420–434.

Razzino, B. F., S. C. Ribirdy, K. Grant, J. R. Ferrari, B. S. Bowden, and J. Zeisz. 2004. "Gender-Related Processed and Drug Use: Self-Expression with Parents, Peers Group Selection, and Achievement Motivation." *Adolescence* 39:167–178.

Reebye, P., M. M. Moretti, V. J. Wiebe, and J. C. Lessard. 2000. "Symptoms of Posttraumatic Stress Disorder in Adolescents with Conduct Disorder: Sex Differences and Onset Patterns." *Canadian Journal of Psychiatry* 45:746–751.

Reese, L. E., E. M. Vera, T. R. Simon, and R. M. Ikeda. 2000. "The Role of Families and Care Givers as Risk and Protective Factors in Preventing Youth Violence." *Clinical Child and Family Psychological Review* 3:61–77.

Reiboldt, W. 2001. "Adolescent Interactions with Gangs, Family, and Neighborhoods." *Journal of Family Issues* 22:211–242.

Reiss, A. J. 1986. "Co-Offender Influences on Criminal Careers." In *Criminal Careers and Career Criminals.*, edited by A. Blumstein, J. Cohen, J. A. Roth, et al., 121–160. Washington, DC: National Academy Press.

Reitsma-Street, M., S. Artz, and J. A. Winterdyk. 2000. "Girls and Crime." In *Issues and Perspectives on Young Offenders in Canada,* edited by J. A. Winterdyk, 61–87. Toronto, Canada: Harcourt.

Resnick, M., P. Bearman, R. Blum, K. Bauman, K. Harris, J. Jones, J. Tabor, T. Beuhring, R. Sieving, M. Shew, M. Ireland, L. Bearinger, and J. Udry. 1997. "Protecting Adolescents from Harm: Findings from the National Longitudinal Study on Adolescent Health." *Journal of the American Medical Association* 27:823–830.

Resnick, M., L. J. Harris, and R. W. Blum. 1993. "Impact of Caring and Connectedness on Adolescent Health and Well-Being." *Journal of Pediatric Child Health* 29:1–9.

Reynolds, W. M., and H. F. Johnston. 1994. "The Nature and Study of Depression in Children and Adolescents." In *Handbook of Depression in Children and Adolescents,* edited by R. M. Reynolds and H. F. Johnston, 3–17. New York: Plenum.

Richards, P., and C. A. Tittle. 1981. "Gender and Perceived Chances of Arrest." *Social Forces* 59:1182.

Richie, B. 1996. *Compelled to Crime: The Gender Entrapment of Battered Black Women*. New York: Routledge.

Rieder, J., and S. M. Coupey. 1999. "Update on Pubertal Development." *Current Opinion in Obstetrics and Gynecology* 11:457–462.

Rivera, B., and C. S. Widom. 1990. "Childhood Victimization and Violent Offending." *Violence and Victims* 5:19–35.

Robbers, M. 2004. "Revisiting the Moderating Effect of Social Support on Strain: A Gendered Test." *Sociological Inquiry* 74:546–569.

Roberts, R. E., C. R. Roberts, and Y. Xing. 2006. "Prevalence of Youth-Reported DSM-IV Psychiatric Disorders among African, European, and Mexican American Adolescents." *Journal of American Child and Adolescent Psychiatry* 45:1329–1337.

Robertson, A. A., P. L. Dill, J. Husain, and C. Undesser. 2004. "Prevalence of Mental Illness and Substance Abuse Disorders among Incarcerated Juvenile Offenders in Mississippi." *Child Psychiatry and Human Development* 35:55–74.

Robertson, R. G., R. G. Bankier, and L. Schwartz. 1987. "The Female Offender: A Canadian Study." *Canadian Journal of Psychiatry* 32:749–755.

Roelfsema, F., G. van den Berg, M. Frolich, J. D. Veldhuis, A. van Eijk, M. M. Buurman, and B. H. Etman. 1993. "Sex-Dependent Alterations in Cortisol Response to Endogenous Adrenocorticotropin." *Journal of Clinical Endocrinology and Metabolics* 77:234–240.

Rohde, P., J. Noell, and L. Ochs. 1999. "IQ Scores among Homeless Older Adolescents: Characteristics of Intellectual Performance and Associations with Psychosocial Functioning." *Journal of Adolescence* 22:319–328.

Rosario, M., S. Salzinger, R. S. Feldman, and D. S. Ng-Mak. 2003. "Community Violence Exposure and Delinquent Behaviors among Youth: The Moderating Role of Coping." *Journal of Community Psychology* 31:489–512.

Rosay, A. B., D. C. Gottfredson, T. A. Armstrong, and M. A. Harmon. 2000. "Invariance of Measures of Prevention Program Effectiveness: A Replication." *Journal of Quantitative Criminology* 16:341–367.

Rose, C. C., B. A. Glaser, G. B. Calhoun, and J. M. Bates. 2004. "Assessing the Parents of Juvenile Offenders: A Preliminary Validation Study of the Juvenile Offender Parent Questionnaire." *Child and Family Behavior Therapy* 26:25–43.

Rosenbaum, J. L., and J. Lasley. 1990. "School, Community Context, and Delinquency: Rethinking the Gender Gap." *Justice Quarterly* 7:493–513.

Rosenbloom, S. R., and N. Way. 2004. "Experiences of Discrimination among African American, Asian American, and Latino Adolescents in an Urban School." *Youth and Society* 35:420–451.

Rosso, I. M., C. M. Cintron, and R. J. Steingard. 2005. "Amygdala and Hippocampus Volumes in Pediatric Major Depression." *Biological Psychiatry* 57:21–26.

Rothman, D. 1980. *Conscience and Convenience: The Asylum and Its Alternatives in Progressive America*. Boston, MA: Little, Brown.

Rothwell, N. A., G. W. LaVigna, and T. J. Willis. 1999. "A Non-Aversive Rehabilitation Approach for People with Severe Behavioural Problems Resulting from Brain Injury." *Brain Injury* 13 (7): 521–533.

Rountree, P. W., and B. D. Warner. 1999. "Social Ties and Crime: Is the Relationship Gendered?" *Criminology* 37:789–814.

Rowe, D. C. 2002. *Biology and Crime*. Los Angeles, CA: Roxbury.

Rowe, D. C., and D. P. Farrington. 1997. "The Familial Transmission of Criminal Convictions." *Criminology* 35:177–201.

Rowe, D., A. Vazsonyi, and D. Flannery. 1995. "Sex Differences: Do Means and Within-Sex Variation Have Similar Causes?" *Journal of Research in Crime and Delinquency* 32:84–100.

Rubin, H. T. 1985. *Juvenile Justice: Policy, Practice and Law*. 2nd ed. New York: Random House.

Rucklidge, J. J., and R. Tannock. 2001. "Psychiatric, Psychosocial and Cognitive Functioning of Female Adolescents with ADHD." *Journal of Academy of Child and Adolescent Psychiatry* 40:530–540.

Russ, H. 2004. "The War on Catfights." *City Limits* (February): 19–22.

Rutter, M., H. Giller, and A. Hagell. 1998. *Antisocial Behavior by Young Children*. New York: Cambridge University Press.

Ryder, J. A. 2007. "I Wasn't Really Bonded with My Family: Attachment, Loss and Violence among Adolescent Female Offenders." *Critical Criminology* 15: 19–40.

Ryerson, E. 1978. *The Best Laid Plans—America's Juvenile Court Experiment*. New York: Hill and Wang.

Rys, G., and G. Bear. 1997. "Relational Aggression and Peer Relations: Gender and Developmental Issues." *Merrill-Palmer Quarterly* 43:87–106.

Sagrestano, L., S. H. McCormick, R. L. Paikoff, and G. N. Holmbeck. 1999. "Pubertal Development and Parent–Child Conflict in Low-Income African-American Adolescents." *Journal of Research on Adolescence* 9:85–107.

Sale, E., S. Sambrano, J. F. Springer, and C. W. Turner. 2003. "Risk, Protection, and Substance Use in Adolescents: A Multi-Site Model." *Journal of Drug Education* 33:91–105.

Salzinger, S., R. S. Feldman, D. S. Ng-Mak, E. Mojica, T. Stockhammer, and M. Rosario. 2002a. "Effects of Partner Violence and Physical Child Abuse on Child Behavior: A Study of Abused and Comparison Children." *Journal of Family Violence* 27:23–51.

Salzinger, S., R. S. Feldman, T. Stockhammer, and J. Hood. 2002b. "An Ecological Framework for Understanding Risk for Exposure to Community Violence and the Effects of Exposure on Children and Adolescents." *Aggression and Violence Behavior* 7:423–451.

Sampson, R. J. 1987. "Urban Black Violence: The Effect of Male Joblessness and Family Disruption." *American Journal of Sociology* 93:348–382.

Sampson, R. J., and W. B. Groves. 1989. "Community Structure and Crime: Testing Social-Disorganization Theory." *American Journal of Sociology* 94:774–802.

Sampson, R. J., and J. Laub. 1993. *Crime in the Making: Pathways and Turning Points through Life*. Cambridge, U.K.: Harvard University Press.

Sampson, R. J., and J. D. Morenoff. 1997. "Ecological Perspectives on the Neighborhood Context of Urban Poverty: Past and Present." In *Neighborhood Poverty*. Vol. 2 of *Policy Implications in Studying Neighborhoods,* edited by J. Brooks-Gunn, G. J. Duncan, and J. L. Aber, 1–22. New York: Russell Sage Foundation.

Sampson, R. J., J. D. Morenoff, and T. Gannon-Rowley. 2002. "Assessing 'Neighborhood Effects': Social Processes and New Directions in Research." *Annual Review of Sociology* 51:443–478.

Sampson, R. J., J. D. Morenoff, and S. Raudenbush. 2005. "Social Anatomy of Racial and Ethnic Disparities in Violence." *American Journal of Public Health* 95:224–232.

Sampson, R. J., and W. J. Wilson. 1995. "Toward a Theory of Race, Crime, and Urban Inequality." In *Crime and Inequality,* edited by J. Hagan and R. Peterson. Stanford, CA: Stanford University Press.

Sanborn, J. B., Jr., and A. W. Salerno. 2005. *Juvenile Justice System: Law and Process*. Los Angeles, CA: Roxbury Publishing.

Saner, H., and P. Ellickson. 1996. "Concurrent Risk Factors for Adolescent Violence." *Journal of Adolescent Health* 19:94–103.

Sanislow, C. A., C. M. Grillo, D. C. Fehon, S. R. Axelrod, and T. H. McGlashan. 2003. "Correlates of Suicide Risk in Juvenile Detainees and Adolescent Inpatients." *Journal of the American Academy of Child and Adolescent Psychiatry* 42:234–240.

Savin-Williams, R., and T. Berndt. 1990. "Chapter 11. Friendship and Peer Relations." In *At the Threshold: The Developing Adolescent*, edited by S. S. Feldman and G. R. Elliott, 277–307. Cambridge, U.K.: Harvard University Press.

Scaramella, L., R. Conger, R. Spoth, and R. Simons. 2002. "Evaluation of a Social-Contextual Model of Delinquency: A Cross-Study Replication." *Child Development* 73:175–195.

Scarpa, A. 2003. "Community Violence Exposure in Young Adults." *Trauma, Violence, and Abuse* 4:210–227.

Schaefer, A., F. Collette, P. Philippot, L. M. van der Linden, S. Laureys, and G. Delfiore. 2003. "Neural Correlates of 'Hot' and 'Cold' Emotional Processing: A Multilevel Approach to the Functional Anatomy of Emotion." *NeuroImage* 18:938–949.

Schaffner, L. 1999. "Violence and Female Delinquency: Gender Transgressions and Gender Invisibility." *Berkeley Women's Law Journal* 14:40–50.

Schalet, A., G. Hunt, and K. Joe Laidler. 2003. "Respectability and Autonomy: The Articulation and Meaning of Sexuality among the Girls in the Gang." *Journal of Contemporary Ethnography* 32:108–143.

Schlossman, S. L. 1977. *Love and the American Delinquent: The Theory and Practice of "Progressive" Juvenile Justice 1825–1920*. Chicago: University of Chicago Press.

Schlossman, S., and R. B. Cairns. 1994. "Problem Girls: Observations on Past and Present." In *Children in Time and Place: Intersecting Historical and Developmental Insights*, edited by J. Modell, R. D. Parke, and J. Elder, 110–130. New York: Cambridge University Press.

Schlossman, S. L., and S. Wallach. 1978. "The Crime of Precocious Sexuality: Female Delinquency in the Progressive Era." *Harvard Educational Review* 48:65–94.

Schneider, A. L. 1984. "Divesting Status Offenses from Juvenile Court Jurisdiction." *Crime and Delinquency* 30:347–370.

Schuck, A. M., and C. S. Widom. 2005. "Understanding the Role of Neighborhood Context in the Long-Term Criminal Consequences of Child Maltreatment." *American Journal of Community Psychology* 36:207–222.

Schur, E. 1984. *Labeling Women Deviant: Gender, Stigma, and Social Control*. New York: Random House.

Schutt, R. K., and D. Dannefer. 1988. "Detention Decisions in Juvenile Cases: JINS, JDs, and Gender." *Law and Society Review* 22:509–520.

Schwartz, I. M. 1989a. "Hospitalization of Adolescents for Psychiatric and Substance Abuse Treatment." *Journal of Adolescent Health Care* 10:1–6.

———. 1989b. *(In)Justice for Juveniles: Rethinking the Best Interests of the Child*. Lexington, MA: Lexington Books.

Schwartz, I. M., L. Harris, and L. Levi. 1988. "The Jailing of Juveniles in Minnesota: A Case Study." *Crime and Delinquency* 34:133–149.

Schwartz, I. M., M. W. Steketee, and V. W. Schneider. 1990. "Federal Juvenile Justice Policy and the Incarceration of Girls." *Crime and Delinquency* 36:511–520.

Schwartz, I. M., N. A. Weiner, and G. Enosh. 1998. "Nine Lives and Then Some: Why the Juvenile Court Will Not Roll Over and Die." *Wake Forest Law Review* 33:533–552.

Schwartz, M. D., and D. Milovanovic. 1996. *Race, Gender, and Class in Criminology: The Intersection*. New York: Garland Publishing.

Seeman, M. V. 1997. "Psychopathology in Women and Men Focus on Female Hormones." *American Journal of Psychiatry* 154:1641–1647.

Seidlitz, L., and E. Diener. 1998. "Sex Differences in the Recall of Affective Experiences." *Journal of Personality and Social Psychology* 74:262–271.

Seidman, E., L. R. Allen, J. L. Aber, C. Mitchell, and J. Feinman. 1994. "The Impact of School Transitions in Early Adolescence on the Self-System and Perceived Social-Context of Poor Urban Youth." *Child Development* 65:507–522.

Seydlitz, R. 1991. "The Effects of Age and Gender on Parental Control and Delinquency." *Youth and Society* 23:175–201.

Shaffer, J. N., and R. B. Ruback. 2002. *Violent Victimization as a Risk Factor for Violent Offending among Juveniles.* Washington, DC: Office of Juvenile Justice and Delinquency Prevention.

Shansky, R. M., C. Glavis-Bloom, D. Lerman, P. McRae, C. Benson, K. Miller, L. Cosand, T. L. Horvath, and A. F. Arnsten. 2004. "Estrogen Mediates Sex Differences in Stress-Induced Prefrontal Cortex Dysfunction." *Molecular Psychiatry* 9:531–538.

Shaw, C. R., and H. D. McKay. 1942a. *Juvenile Delinquency and Urban Areas.* Chicago: University of Chicago Press.

———. 1942b. *Labeling Women Deviant.* New York: Random House.

Shelden, R. G., and J. A. Horvath. 1987. "Intake Processing in a Juvenile Court: A Comparison of Legal and Nonlegal Variables." *Juvenile and Family Court Journal* 38:13–19.

Shelton, D. 2001. "Emotional Disorders in Young Offenders." *Journal of Nursing Scholarship* 33:259–263.

———. 2004. "Experiences of Detained Young Offenders in Need of Mental Health Care." *Journal of Nursing Scholarship* 36:129–133.

Sherman, L. W. 1993. "Defiance, Deterrence and Irrelevance: A Theory of the Criminal Sanction." *Journal of Research in Crime and Delinquency* 30:445–473.

Shover, N., S. Norland, J. James, and W. Thornton. 1979. "Gender Roles and Delinquency." *Social Forces* 58:162–175.

Sickmund, M., T. J. Sladky, and W. Kang. 2004. *Census of Juveniles in Residential Placement Databook.* http://www.ojjdp.ncjrs.org/ojstatbb.cjrp/.

Siegel, J. A., and L. M. Williams. 2003. "The Relationship between Child Sexual Abuse and Female Delinquency and Crime: A Prospective Study." *Journal of Research in Crime and Delinquency* 40:71–94.

Siegel, J. M., C. S. Aneshensel, B. Taub, D. P. Cantwell, and A. K. Driscoll. 1998. "Adolescent Depressed Mood in a Multiethnic Sample." *Journal of Youth and Adolescence* 27:413–427.

Sikes, G. 1997. *Eight Ball Chicks.* New York: Anchor Books.

Silverstein, B., and R. Krate. 1975. *Children of the Dark Ghetto: A Developmental Psychology.* New York: Praeger.

Silverthorn, P., P. J. Frick, and R. Reynolds. 2001. "Timing of Onset and Correlates of Severe Conduct Problems in Adjudicated Girls and Boys." *Journal of Psychopathological and Behavioral Assessment* 23:171–181.

Silverthorn, P. and J. Frick. 1999. "Developmental Pathways to Antisocial Behavior: The Delayed-Onset Pathway in Girls." *Development and Psychopathology* 11:101–126.

Simmel, G. 1950. *The Sociology of Georg Simmel.* Edited by K. H. Wolfe. New York: The Free Press.

Simmons, R. 2002. *Odd Girl Out: The Hidden Culture of Aggression in Girls.* San Diego, CA: Harcourt.

Simmons, R. G., and D. A. Blyth. 1987. *Moving into Adolescence: The Impact of Pubertal Change and School Context.* Hawthorne, NY: Aldine de Gruyter.

Simon, J. 1997. "Governing through Crime." In *The Crime Conundrum: Essays on Criminal Justice,* edited by L. M. Friedman and G. Fisher, 171–190. Boulder, CO: Westview Press.

Simons, R. L., C. Johnson, J. Beaman, R. Conger, and L. B. Whitbeck. 1996. "Parents and Peer Group as Mediators of the Effect of Community Structure on Adolescent Problem Behavior." *American Journal of Community Psychology* 24:145–171.

Simons, R. L., R. L. Miller, and S. M. Aigner. 1980. "Contemporary Theories of Deviance and Female Delinquency: An Empirical Test." *Journal of Research in Crime and Delinquency* 17:42–57.

Simons, R., E. Stewart, L. Gordon, R. Conger, and G. Elder. 2002. "A Test of Life-Course Explanations for Stability and Change in Antisocial Behavior from Adolescence to Young Adulthood." *Criminology* 40:401–434.

Simpson, S. S. 1991. "Caste, Class and Violent Crime: Explaining Difference in Female Offending." *Criminology* 29:115–135.

———. 2000. "Gendered Theory and Single Sex Research." In *Divisio-News*. http://search .ebscohost.com/login.aspx?direct=true&db=psyhref&AN=2002.06707.0020010.

Simpson, S. S., and L. Elis. 1995. "Doing Gender: Sorting Out the Caste and Crime Conundrum." *Criminology* 33:47–81.

Simpson, S. S., and C. Gibbs. 2005. "Making Sense of Intersections: Does Quantitative Analysis Enlighten or Obfuscate?" In *New Directions in the Study of Gender, Offending and Victimization*, edited by C. Kruttschknitt and K. Heimer, 269–302. New York: New York University Press.

Singer, M. I., T. M. Anglin, L. Y. Song, and L. Lunghofer. 1995. "Adolescent's Exposure to Violence and Associated Symptoms of Psychological Trauma." *Journal of the American Medical Association* 273:447–482.

Singer, S., and M. Levine. 1988. "Power-Control Theory, Gender, and Delinquency: A Partial Replication with Additional Evidence on the Effects of Peers." *Criminology* 26:627–648.

Sinha, R. 2001. "How Does Stress Increase Risk of Drug Abuse and Relapse?" *Psychopharmacology* 158:343–359.

Sizonenko, P. C. 1987. "Normal Sexual Maturation." *Pediatrician* 14 (4): 191–201.

Smart, C. 1976. *Women Crime and Criminology: A Feminist Critique*. Boston, MA: Routledge and Kegan Paul.

Smith, C. A., and T. O. Ireland. 2005. "Developmental Consequences of Maltreatment among Young Women in the Rochester Youth Development Study." *Criminology* 38 (1): 67–102.

Smith, C., and T. P. Thornberry. 1995. "The Relationship between Childhood Maltreatment and Adolescent Involvement in Delinquency." *Criminology* 57:451–481.

Smith, D. A. 1979. "Sex and Deviance: An Assessment of Major Sociological Variables." *Sociological Quarterly* 20:183–196.

Smith, D. K., L. D. Leve, and P. Chamberlain. 2006. "Adolescent Girls' Offending and Health-Risking Sexual Behavior: The Predictive Role of Trauma." *Child Maltreatment* 11:346–353.

Smith, D. A., and R. Paternoster. 1987. "The Gender Gap in Theories of Deviance: Issues and Evidence." *Criminology* 24:140–172.

Smith, E. M. 1992. "In a Child's Best Interests: Juvenile Status Offenders Deserve Procedural Due Process." *Journal of Law and Inequality* 10:253–284.

Snell, T. 1994. *Women in Prison: Survey of State Prison Inmates, 1991*. Washington, DC: U.S. Department of Justice, Office of Justice Programs, Bureau of Justice Statistics.

Snyder, H. N. 2002. *Juvenile Arrests 2000*. Washington, DC: Office of Juvenile Justice and Delinquency Prevention (NCJ191729).

———. 2004. *Juvenile Arrests 2002*. Washington, DC: Juvenile Justice Bulletin.

Snyder, H. N., C. Puzzanchera, and W. Kang. 2005. "Easy Access to FBI Arrest Statistics 1994–2002." http://search.ebscohost.com/login.aspx?direct=true&db=psyhref&AN=2006 .03928.011007.

Snyder, H. N., and M. Sickmund. 1999. *Juvenile Offenders and Victims: 1999 National Report*. Washington, DC: U.S. Department of Justice, Office of Juvenile Justice and Delinquency Prevention.

———. 2000. *Challenging the Myths*. Washington, DC: U.S. Department of Justice, Office of Juvenile Justice and Delinquency Prevention.

―――. 2006. *Juvenile Offenders and Victims: 2006 National Report.* Washington, DC: U.S. Department of Justice, Office of Justice Programs, Office of Juvenile Justice and Delinquency Prevention.

Sommers, I., and D. R. Baskin. 1993. "The Situational Context of Violent Female Offending." *Journal of Research in Crime and Delinquency* 30:136–162.

Song, L., M. Singer, and T. Anglin. 1998. "Violence Exposure and Emotional Trauma as Contributors to Adolescents' Violent Behaviors." *Archives of Pediatric and Adolescent Medicine* 152:531–536.

South, S. J., and K. D. Crowder. 1997. "Escaping Distressed Neighborhoods: Individual, Community and Metropolitan Influences." *Journal of Sociology* 102:1040–1048.

Spergel, I., and D. Curry. 1993. "The National Youth Gang Survey: A Research and Developmental Process." In *The Gang Intervention Handbook,* edited by A. P. Goldstein and C. R. Huff, 359–400. Champaign, IL: Research Press.

Spohn, R. E. 2000. "Gender Differences in the Effect of Child Maltreatment on Criminal Activity over the Life Course." In *Families, Crime and Criminal Justice,* vol. 2, edited by G. L. Fox and M. L. Benson, 207–231. Stamford, CA: JAI Press.

Stahl, A., T. Finnegan, and W. Kang. 2003. *Easy Access to Juvenile Court Statistics: 1985–2000.* http://ojjdp.ncjrs.org/ojstatbb/ezajcs/.

Stahl, A., M. Sickmund, and H. N. Snyder. 2004. "Statistics on Violent Girls in the Juvenile Justice System: Facts, Myths, and Implications." Paper presented at the annual meeting of the American Society of Criminology, Nashville, TN.

Stattin, H., and D. Magnusson. 1990. *Pubertal Maturation in Female Development.* Vol. 2 of *Paths Through Life.* Hillsdale, NJ: Lawrence Erlbaum Associates.

Steffensmeier, D. J. 1983. "Organization Properties and Sex-Segregation in the Underworld: Building a Sociological Theory of Sex Differences in Crime." *Social Forces* 61:1010–1032.

―――. 1993. "National Trends in Female Arrests, 1960–1990: Assessment and Recommendations for Research." *Journal of Quantitative Criminology* 9:411–441.

Steffensmeier, D. J., and E. Allan. 1996. "Gender and Crime: Toward a Gendered Theory of Female Offending." *Annual Review of Sociology* 22:459–487.

―――. 2000. "Looking for Patterns: Gender, Age, and Crime." In *Criminology: A Contemporary Handbook,* edited by J. Sheley, 83–113. Belmont, CA: Wadsworth.

Steffensmeier, D. J., and L. Broidy. 2001. "Explaining Female Offending." In *Women, Crime, and Criminal Justice: Original Feminist Readings,* edited by C. Renzetti and L. Goodstein, 111–134. Los Angeles, CA: Roxbury Press.

Steffensmeier, D. J., and M. Harer. 1999. "Making Sense of Recent U.S. Crime Trends, 1980–1998: Age Composition Effects and Other Explanations." *Research in Crime and Delinquency* 36:235–274.

Steffensmeier, D. J. and D. Haynie. 2000a. "Gender, Structural Disadvantage, and Urban Crime: Do Macrosocial Variables Also Explain Female Offending Rates?" *Criminology* 38:403–438.

―――. 2000b. "The Structural Sources of Urban Female Violence in the United States: A Macrolevel Gender-Disaggregated Analysis of Adult and Juvenile Offending Rates." *Homicide Studies: An Interdisciplinary and International Journal* 4:107–134.

Steffensmeier, D. J., and J. Schwartz. 2004. "Trends in Female Criminality: Is Crime Still a Man's World?" In *The Criminal Justice System and Women: Offenders, Victims, and Workers,* edited by B. R. Price and N. J. Sokoloff, 95–111. New York: McGraw Hill.

Steffensmeier, D. J., J. Schwartz, H. Zhong, and J. Ackerman. 2005. "An Assessment of Recent Trends in Girls' Violence Using Diverse Longitudinal Sources." *Criminology* 43:355–406.

Steffensmeier, D. J., and R. H. Steffensmeier. 1980. "Trends in Female Delinquency." *Criminology* 18:62–85.

Steffensmeier, D. J., and R. M. Terry. 1986. "Institutional Sexism in the Underworld." *Sociological Inquiry* 56:304–323.

Steffensmeier, D. J., and J. Ulmer. 2005. *Confessions of a Dying Thief: Understanding Criminal Careers and Illegal Enterprise*. New Brunswick, NJ: Transaction Aldine.

Stein, N. 1999. *Classrooms and Courtrooms: Facing Sexual Harassment from K–12 Schools*. New York: Teachers College Press.

Steinberg, L., I. Blatt-Eisengart, and E. Elizabeth Cauffman. 2006. "Patterns of Competence and Adjustment among Adolescents from Authoritative, Authoritarian, Indulgent, and Neglectful Homes: A Replication in a Sample of Serious Juvenile Offenders." *Journal of Research on Adolescence* 16:47–58.

Steinberg, L., N. S. Mounts, S. D. Lamborn, and S. M. Dornbusch. 1991. "Authoritative Parenting and Adolescent Adjustment across Varied Ecological Niches." *Journal of Research on Adolescence* 1:19–36.

Steinhart, D. J. 1996. "Status Offenses." *The Future of Children, The Juvenile Court* 6:86–99.

Stewart, E. A., R. L. Simons, and R. D. Conger. 2002. "Assessing Neighborhood and Social Psychological Influences on Childhood Violence in an African-American Sample." *Criminology* 40:801–830.

Stewart, E. A., R. L. Simons, R. D. Conger, and C. Scaramella. 2002. "Beyond the Interactional Relationship between Delinquency and Parenting Practices: The Contribution of Legal Sanctions." *Journal of Research in Crime and Delinquency* 39:36–59.

Stice, E., K. Presnell, and S. K. Bearman. 2001. "Relation of Early Menarche to Depression, Eating Disorders, Substance Abuse, and Comorbid Psychopathology among Adolescent Girls." *Developmental Psychology* 37:608–619.

Stiffman, A. R. 1989. "Physical and Sexual Abuse in Runaway Youths." *Child Abuse and Neglect* 13:417–426.

Stouthamer-Loeber, M., R. Loeber, E. Wei, D. P. Farrington, and P. O. H. Wikstrom. 2002. "Risk and Promotive Effects in the Explanation of Persistent Serious Delinquency in Boys." *Journal of Consulting and Clinical Psychology* 70:111–123.

Straus, M., and R. J. Gelles. 1990. "How Violent Are American Families? Estimates from the National Family Violence Resurvey and Other Studies." In *Physical Violence in American Families: Risk Factors and Adaptations to Violence in 8145 Families*, 95–112. Piscataway, NJ: Transaction Books.

Stroud, L. R., P. Salovey, and E. S. Epel. 2002. "Sex Differences in Stress Responses: Social Rejection versus Achievement Stress." *Biological Psychiatry* 15:318–327.

Sutherland, E. 1934. *Principles of Criminology*. Philadelphia, PA: Lippincott.

Sutton, J. R. 1988. *Stubborn Children: Controlling Delinquency in the United States, 1640–1981*. Berkeley: University of California Press.

Svensson, R. 2003. "Gender Differences in Adolescent Drug Use." *Youth and Society* 34: 300–329.

Swart, W. J. 1991. "Female Gang Delinquency: A Search for 'Acceptably Deviant Behavior.'" *Mid-American Review of Sociology* 15:43–52.

Swinford, S. P., A. DeMaris, S. A. Cernkovich, and P. C. Giordano. 2000. "Harsh Physical Discipline in Childhood and Violence in Later Romantic Involvements: The Mediating Role of Problem Behaviors." *Journal of Marriage and the Family* 62:508–519.

Talbott, E., D. Celinska, J. Simpson, and M. G. Coe. 2002. "'Somebody Else Making Somebody Else Fight': Aggression and the Social Context among Urban Adolescent Girls." *Exceptionality* 10:203–220.

Tanenhause, D. S. 2004. *Juvenile Justice in the Making.* New York: Oxford University Press.

Tanner, J., S. Davies, and W. O'Grady. 1999. "Whatever Happened to Yesterday's Rebels? Longitudinal Effects of Youth Delinquency on Education and Employment." *Social Problems* 46:250–274.

Tapper, K., and M. Boulton. 2000. "Social Representations of Physical, Verbal, and Indirect Aggression in Children: Sex and Age Differences." *Aggressive Behavior* 26:442–454.

Tarter, R., M. Vanyukov, P. Giancola, M. Dawes, T. Blackson, A. Mezzich, and D. Clark. 1999. "Etiology of Early Age Onset Substance Abuse: A Maturational Perspective." *Developmental Psychopathology* 11:657–683.

Taylor, C. S. 1993. *Girls, Gangs, Women and Drugs.* East Lansing: Michigan State University.

Taylor, S., M. Kemeny, G. Reed, J. Bower, and T. Gruenewald. 2000. "Psychological Resources, Positive Illusions, and Health." *American Psychology* 55:99–109.

Tedeschi, J., and R. Felson. 1994. *Violence, Aggression and Coercive Actions.* Washington, DC: American Psychological Association.

Teicher, M. H., S. L. Anderson, and A. Polcari. 2003. "The Neurobiological Consequences of Early Stress and Childhood Maltreatment." *Neuroscience and Biobehavioral Reviews* 27:33–44.

Teilman, K., and P. Landry. 1981. "Gender Bias in Juvenile Justice." *Journal of Research in Crime and Delinquency* 18:47–80.

Teplin, L., K. Abram, G. M. McClelland, M. K. Dulcan, and A. A. Mericle. 2002. "Psychiatric Disorders in Youth in Detention." *Archives of General Psychiatry* 59:1133–1143.

Thomas, G., M. P. Farrell, and G. M. Barnes. 1996. "The Effects of Single-Mother Families and Nonresident Fathers on Delinquency and Substance Abuse in African-American and White Adolescents." *Journal of Marriage and the Family* 58:884–894.

Thomas, J., and D. Stubbe. 1996. "A Comparison of Correctional and Mental Health Referrals in the Juvenile Court." *Psychiatry Law* 24:379–400.

Thomas, W. I. 1923a. *The Unadjusted Girl.* New York: Harper.

———. 1923b. *The Unadjusted Girl, with Cases and Standpoint for Behavior Analysis.* Boston, MA: Little Brown and Company.

Thornberry, T. P. 1987. "Toward an Interactional Theory of Delinquency." *Criminology* 25: 863–891.

———. 1997. "Membership in Youth Gangs and Involvement in Serious and Violent Offending." In *Serious and Violent Juvenile Offenders: Risk Factors and Successful Interventions,* edited by R. Loeber and D. P. Farrington, 147–166. Thousand Oaks, CA: SAGE Publications.

———. 1999. Personal correspondence, April 2.

Thornberry, T. P., F. Esbensen, and W. B. Van Kammen. 1993. "Commitment to School and Delinquency." In *Urban Delinquency and Substance Abuse,* edited by D. Huizinga, R. Loeber, and T. P. Thornberry, 10/1–10/26. Washington, DC: U.S. Department of Justice, Office of Juvenile Justice and Delinquency Prevention.

Thornberry, T. P., A. Freeman-Gallant, A. J. Lizotte, M. D. Krohn, and C. A. Smith. 2003. "Linked Lives: The Intergenerational Transmission of Antisocial Behavior." *Journal of Abnormal Child Psychology* 31:171–184.

Thornberry, T. P., and M. D. Krohn. 2005. "Applying Interactional Theory to the Explanation of Continuity and Change in Antisocial Behavior." In *Integrated Developmental and Life-Course Theories of Offending,* edited by D. P. Farrington, 183–209. New Brunswick, NJ: Transaction Publishers.

Thornberry, T. P., M. Krohn, A. Lizotte, and D. Chard-Wierschem. 1993. "The Role of Juvenile Gangs in Facilitating Delinquent Behavior." *Journal of Research in Crime and Delinquency* 30:75–85.

Thornberry, T. P., A. Lizotte, M. Krohn, M. Farnworth, and S. J. Jang. 1991. "Testing Interactional Theory: An Examination of Reciprocal Causal Relationships among Family, School, and Delinquency." *Journal of Criminal Law and Criminology* 82:3–35.

———. 1994. "Delinquent Peers, Beliefs, and Delinquent Behavior: A Test of Interactional Theory." *Criminology* 32:47–83.

Thornberry, T. P., M. Moore, and R. L. Christenson. 1985. "The Effect of Dropping Out of School on Subsequent Criminal Behavior." *Criminology* 23:3–18.

Thorne, B. 1994. *Gender Play: Girls and Boys in School.* New Brunswick, NJ: Rutgers University Press.

Thrasher, F. 1927. *The Gang: A Study of 1,313 Gangs in Chicago.* Chicago: University of Chicago Press.

Tibbetts, S. G., and D. C. Herz. 1996. "Gender Differences in Factors of Social Control and Rational Choice." *Deviant Behavior* 17:183–208.

Tibbetts, S. G., and A. R. Piquero. 1999. "The Influence of Gender, Low Birth Weight, and Disadvantaged Environment in Predicting Early Onset of Offending: A Test of Moffitt's Interactional Hypothesis." *Criminology* 37:843–877.

Timmons-Mitchell, J., C. Brown, S. C. Schulz, S. E. Webster, L. A. Underwood, and W. E. Semple. 1997. "Comparing the Mental Health Needs of Female and Male Incarcerated Juvenile Delinquents." *Behavioral Sciences and the Law* 15:195–202.

Tittle, C. 1995. *Control Balance: Toward a General Theory of Deviance.* Boulder, CO: Westview Press.

Tolan, P., N. Guerra, and P. Kendall. 1995. "A Developmental-Ecological Perspective on Anti-Social Behavior in Children and Adults: Towards a Unified Risk and Intervention Framework." *Journal of Consulting and Clinical Psychology* 63:579–584.

Tolone, W. L., and C. R. Tieman. 1990. "Drugs, Delinquency and 'Nerds': Are Loners Deviant?" *Journal of Drug Education* 20:153–162.

Tomada, G., and B. H. Schneider. 1997. "Relational Aggression, Gender, and Peer Acceptance." *Developmental Psychology* 33:601–609.

Tong, R. P. 1998. *Feminist Thought.* Edited by C. West and S. Fenstermaker. Boulder, CO: Westview Press.

Tonry, M. 2004. *Thinking about Crime: Sense and Sensibility in American Penal Culture.* New York: Oxford University Press.

Torbet, P., R. Gable, H. Hurst, I. Montgomery, L. Szymanski, and D. Thomas. 1996. *State Responses to Serious and Violent Juvenile Crime.* Washington, DC: OJJDP.

Torpy, D. J., and G. P. Chrousos. 1996. "The Three-Way Interactions between the Hypothalamic-Pituitary-Adrenal and Gonadal Axes and the Immune System." *Baillieres Clinical Rheumatology* 19:181–198.

Treloar, S., and N. Martin. 1990. "Age at Menarche as a Fitness Trait: Nonadditive Genetic Variance Detected in a Large Twin Sample." *American Journal of Human Genetics* 47:137–148.

Tremblay, R. E., B. Masse, D. Perron, M. Le Blanc, A. E. Schwartzman, and J. E. Ledingham. 1992. "Early Disruptive Behavior, Poor School Achievement, Delinquent Behavior, and Delinquent Personality: Longitudinal Analyses." *Journal of Consulting and Clinical Psychology* 60:64–72.

Triplett, R. A., and G. R. Jarjoura. 1994. "Theoretical and Empirical Specification of a Model of Informal Labeling." *Journal of Quantitative Criminology* 10:241–276.

Tyler, K. A. 2002. "Social and Emotional Outcomes of Childhood Sexual Abuse: A Review of Recent Research." *Aggression and Violent Behavior* 7:567–589.

U.S. General Accounting Office. 1991. *Noncriminal Juveniles: Detentions Have Been Reduced but Better Monitoring Is Needed.* Washington, DC: U.S. General Accounting Office.

———. 1994. *Admission of Minors with Preadult Disorders to Private Psychiatric Hospitals.* Washington, DC: U.S. General Accounting Office.

———. 1995a. *Minimal Gender Bias Occurred in Processing Noncriminal Juveniles.* Washington, DC: U.S. General Accounting Office.

———. 1995b. *Representation Rates Varied as Did Counsel's Impact on Court Outcomes.* Washington, DC: U.S. General Accounting Office.

Udry, J. R. 2000. "Biological Limits of Gender Construction." *American Sociological Review* 65:443–457.

Underwood, M. K. 2003a. "The Comity of Modest Manipulation, the Importance of Distinguishing Bad Behaviors." *Merrill-Palmer Quarterly* 49:373–389.

———. 2003b. *Social Aggression among Girls.* New York: Guilford Press.

Underwood, M., B. Galen, and J. Paquette. 2001. "Top Ten Challenges for Understanding Gender and Aggression in Children: Why Can't We All Just Get Along?" *Social Development* 10:249–266.

Urberg, K. A., S. Shyu, and J. Liang. 1990. "Peer Influence in Adolescent Cigarette Smoking." *Addictive Behaviors* 15:247–255.

Valentine Foundation and Women's Way. 1990. *A Conversation about Girls.* Bryn Mawr, PA: Valentine Foundation.

Van Beest, M., and C. Baerveldt. 1999. "The Relationship between Adolescents' Social Support from Parents and from Peers." *Adolescence* 34:193–201.

van Goozen, S. H., W. Matthys, P. T. Cohen-Kettenis, C. Gispen-de Wied, V. M. Wiegant, and H. van Engeland. 1998. "Salivary Cortisol and Cardiovascular Activity during Stress in Oppositional-Defiant Disorder Boys and Normal Controls." *Biological Psychiatry* 43: 531–539.

van Weissenbruch, M. M., M. J. Engelbregt, M. A. Veening, and H. A. Delemaare–van de Waal. 2005. "Fetal Nutrition and Timing of Puberty." *Endocrine Development* 8:15–33.

Vanyukov, M. M., H. B. Moss, J. A. Plail, T. B. Blackson, A. C. Mezzich, and R. E. Tarter. 1993. "Antisocial Symptoms in Preadolescent Boys and in Their Parents: Association with Cortisol." *Psychiatric Research* 6:9–17.

Venkatesh, S. A. 1998. "Gender and Outlaw Capitalism: A Historical Account of the Black Sisters of the United 'Girl Gang.'" *Signs* 23 (3): 681–709.

Vermeiren, R. 2003. "Psychopathology and Delinquency in Adolescents: A Descriptive and Developmental Perspective." *Clinical Psychology Review* 23:277–318.

Walrath, C., M. Ybarra, E. W. Holden, B. Manteuffel, R. Santiago, and P. Leaf. 2003. "Female Offenders Referred for Community-Based Mental Health Service as Compared with Other Service-Referred Youth: Correlates of Conviction." *Journal of Adolescence* 26: 45–61.

Ward, D. A., and C. R. Tittle. 1994. "IQ and Delinquency: A Test of Two Competing Explanations." *Journal of Quantitative Criminology* 10:189–212.

Warr, M. 1996. "Organization and Instigation in Delinquent Groups." *Criminology* 34:11–37.

———. 2002. *Companions in Crime.* New York: Cambridge University Press.

Warr, M., and M. Stafford. 1991. "The Influence of Delinquent Peers—What They Think or What They Do." *Criminology* 29:851–866.

Wasserman, G. A., P. S. Jensen, S. J. Ko, J. Cocozza, E. Trupin, A. Angold, E. Cauffman, and T. Grisso. 2003a. "Mental Health Assessments in Juvenile Justice: Report on the Consensus Conference." *Journal of the American Academy of Child and Adolescent Psychiatry* 42 (7): 751–761.

Wasserman, G. A., K. Keenan, R. E. Tremblay, J. D. Coie, T. I. Herrenkohl, R. Loeber, and D. Petechuk. 2003b. *Risk and Protective Factors of Child Delinquency.* Washington, DC:

Department of Justice, Office of Justice Programs, Office of Juvenile Justice and Delinquency Prevention.

Wasserman, G. A., L. S. McReynolds, S. J. Ko, L. M. Katz, and J. Schwank. 2005. "Gender Differences in Psychiatric Disorder for Youths in Juvenile Probations." *American Journal of Public Health* 95:131–137.

Wattenberg, W. 1956. "Differences between Girl and Boy Repeaters." *Journal of Educational Psychology* 47:137–146.

Wattenberg, W. W., and F. Saunders. 1954. "Sex Differences among Juvenile Offenders." *Sociology and Social Research* 39:24–31.

Watts, W. D., and A. M. Ellis. 1993. "Sexual Abuse and Drinking and Drug Abuse: Implications for Prevention." *Journal of Drug Education* 23:183–200.

Webster, D., P. Gainer, and H. Champion. 1993. "Weapon-Carrying among Inner-City Junior High School Students: Defensive Behavior versus Aggressive Delinquency." *American Journal of Public Health* 83:1604–1608.

Weichold, K., R. K. Silbereisen, and E. Schmitt-Rodermund. 2003. "Short-Term and Long-Term Consequences of Early versus Late Physical Maturation in Adolescents." In *Gender Differences at Puberty,* edited by C. Hayward, 241–276. New York: Cambridge University Press.

Weis, J. G. 1989. "Family Violence Research Methodology and Design." In *Crime and Justice: A Review of Research,* vol. 11, edited by L. Ohlin and M. Tonry, 117–162. Chicago: University of Chicago Press.

Weithorn, J. 1988. "Mental Hospitalization for Troublesome Youth: An Analysis of Skyrocketing Admission Rates." *Stanford Law Review* 40:773–838.

Wells, E., and J. Rankin. 1991. "Families and Delinquency: A Meta-Analysis of the Impact of Broken Homes." *Social Problems* 38:71–93.

Welsh, L. A., F. X. Archambault, M. Janus, and S. W. Brown. 1995. *Running for Their Lives: Physical and Sexual Abuse of Runaway Adolescents.* New York: Garland.

Welsh, W. N., J. R. Greene, and P. H. Jenkins. 1999. "School Disorder: The Influence of Individual, Institutional and Community Factors." *Criminology* 37:73–116.

West, C., and S. Fenstermaker. 1995. "Doing Difference." *Gender and Society* 9:8–37.

West, C., and D. Zimmerman. 1987. "Doing Gender." *Gender and Society* 1:125–151.

West, D. J., and D. P. Farrington. 1977. *The Delinquent Way of Life.* London: Heinemann.

Whaley, R. B. 2001. "The Paradoxical Relationship between Gender Equality and Rape: Toward a Refined Theory." *Gender and Society* 15:531–555.

White, J. L., T. E. Moffitt, and P. A. Silva. 1989. "A Prospective Replication of the Protective Effects of IQ in Subjects at High Risk for Juvenile Delinquency." *Journal of Consulting and Clinical Psychology* 57:719–724.

Wichstrom, L. 2000. "Psychological and Behavioral Factors Unpredictive of Disordered Eating: A Prospective Study of the General Adolescent Population in Norway." *International Journal of Eating Disorders* 28:33–42.

Widom, C. 1989a. "Child Abuse, Neglect, and Violent Criminal Behavior." *Criminology* 2: 251–271.

———. 1989b. "The Cycle of Violence." *Science* 244:160–166.

———. 1991. "Childhood Victimization: Risk Factor for Delinquency." In *Adolescent Stress: Causes and Consequences,* edited by M. E. Colten and S. Gore, 201–221. New York: Aldine De Gruyter.

———. 1995. *Victims of Childhood Sexual Abuse–Later Criminal Consequences.* Research in Brief. Washington, DC: U.S. Department of Justice, National Institute of Justice.

Widom, C. S., and M. G. Maxfield. 2001. *An Update on the "Cycle of Violence."* Research in Brief. Washington, DC: U.S. Department of Justice, National Institute of Justice.

Widom, C. S., N. A. Weiner, and M. E. Wolfgang. 1989. "The Intergenerational Transmission of Violence." In *Pathways to Criminal Violence*, 137–201. Newbury Park, CA: SAGE Publications.

Widom, C. S., and H. R. White. 1997. "Problem Behaviours in Abused and Neglected Children Grown Up: Prevalence and Co-occurrence of Substance Abuse, Crime and Violence." *Criminal Behaviour and Mental Health* 7:287–310.

Wiesner, M., and H. K. Kim. 2006. "Co-Occurring Delinquency and Depressive Symptoms of Adolescent Boys and Girls: A Dual Trajectory Modeling Approach." *Developmental Psychology* 42:1220–1235.

Wikstrom, P. H., and R. Loeber. 2000. "Do Disadvantaged Neighborhoods Cause Well-Adjusted Children to Become Adolescent Delinquents? A Study of Male Juvenile Serious Offending, Individual Risk and Protective Factors, and Neighborhood Context." *Criminology* 38:1109–1142.

Wilcox, P., and R. R. Clayton. 2001. "A Multilevel Analysis of School Based Weapon Possession." *Justice Quarterly* 18:509–541.

Williams, C. L. 2000. "Preface." *Annals of the American Academy of Political and Social Science* 571:8–13.

Wilson, B. A. 1997. "Cognitive Rehabilitation: How It Is and How It Might Be." *Journal of the International Neuropsychological Society* 3 (5): 487–496.

Wilson, J. W. 1996. *When Work Disappears. The World of the New Urban Poor.* New York: Alfred A. Knopf.

Winfree, T., K. Fuller, T. Vigil, and G. Mays. 1992. "The Definition and Measurement of Gang Status: Policy Implications for Juvenile Justice." *Juvenile and Family Court Journal* 43: 29–37.

Winner, L., L. Lanza-Kaduce, D. M. Bishop, and C. E. Frazier. 1997. "The Transfer of Juveniles to Criminal Court: Reexamining Recidivism Over the Long Term." *Crime and Delinquency* 43:548–563.

Wiseman, R. 2002. *Queen Bees and Wannabees: Helping Your Daughter Survive Cliques, Gossip, Boyfriends, and Other Realities of Adolescence.* New York: Crown Publishers.

Wolfe, D. A., K. Scott, C. Wekerle, and A. Pittman. 2001. "Child Maltreatment: Risk of Adjustment Problems and Dating Violence in Adolescence." *Journal of the American Academy of Child and Adolescent Psychiatry* 40:282–289.

Wolfgang, M. E., T. P. Thornberry, and R. Figlio. 1987. *From Boy to Man, from Delinquency to Crime.* Chicago: University of Chicago Press.

Wolpaw, J., and J. Ford. 2004. *Assessing Exposure to Psychological and Post-Traumatic Stress in the Juvenile Justice Population.* Washington, DC: Juvenile Justice Working Group of the National Child Traumatic Stress Network.

Wong, W. K., and D. G. Cornell. 1999. "PIQ>VIQ Discrepancy as a Correlate of Social Problem Solving and Aggression in Delinquent Adolescent Males." *Journal of Psychoeducational Assessment* 17:104–112.

Wood, J., D. W. Foy, C. A. Goguen, R. Pynoos, and C. B. James. 2002. "Violence Exposure and PTSD among Delinquent Girls." *Journal of Aggression, Maltreatment and Trauma* 6: 109–126.

Worcel, S., S. Shields, and C. Paterson. 1999. "'She Looked at Me Crazy': Escalation of Conflict through Telegraphed Emotion." *Adolescence* 34:689–697.

Wordes, M., T. Bynum, and C. Corley. 1994. "Locking Up Youth: The Impact of Race on Detention Decisions." *Journal of Crime and Delinquency* 31:149–165.

Wordes, M., and S. M. Jones. 1998. "Trends in Juvenile Detention and Steps toward Reform." *Crime and Delinquency* 44:544–560.

World Health Organization. 2000. *What about Boys? A Literature Review on Health and Development of Adolescent Boys.* Washington, DC: Department of Child and Adolescent Health and Development.

Wright, B. R., A. C. Entner, T. E. Moffitt, and P. A. Silva. 2001. "The Effects of Social Ties on Crime Vary by Criminal Propensity: A Life-Course Model of Interdependence." *Criminology* 37:175–194.

Wright, K., and K. Wright. 1994. *Family Life, Delinquency and Crime: A Policymaker's Guide.* Washington, DC: Office of Juvenile Justice and Delinquency Prevention.

Wright, R., and S. Decker. 1994. *Burglars on the Job: Streetlife and Residential Break-ins.* Boston, MA: Northeastern University Press.

———. 1997. *Armed Robbers in Action: Stick Ups and Street Culture.* Boston, MA: Northeastern University Press.

Xie, H., B. D. Cairns, and R. B. Cairns. 2005. "The Development of Aggressive Behaviors among Girls: Measurement Issues, Social Functions, and Differential Trajectories." In *The Development and Treatment of Girlhood Aggression,* edited by D. J. Pepler, K. C. Madsen, C. Webster, et al., 105–136. Mahwah, NJ: Lawrence Erlbaum Associates.

Xie, H., D. J. Swift, B. D. Cairns, and R. B. Cairns. 2002. "Aggressive Behaviors in Social Interaction and Developmental Adaptation: A Narrative Analysis of Interpersonal Conflicts during Early Adolescence." *Social Development* 11:205–224.

Youniss, J., and J. Smollar. 1985. *Adolescent Relations with Mother, Father and Friends.* Chicago: University of Chicago Press.

Zahn-Waxler, C. 1993. "Warriors and Worriers: Gender and Psychopathology." *Development and Psychopathology* 5:79–90.

Zahn-Waxler, C. 2000. "The Development of Empathy, Guilt, and Internalization of Distress: Implications for Gender Differences in Internalizing and Externalizing Problems." In *Anxiety, Depression, and Emotion,* edited by R. Davidson, 222–265. New York: Oxford University Press.

Zimring, F. E. 1998. *American Youth Violence.* New York: Oxford University Press.

———. 2006. *The Great American Crime Decline.* New York: Oxford University Press.

Zimring, F. E., and G. Hawkins. 1997. *Crime Is Not the Problem: Lethal Violence in America.* New York: Oxford University Press.

Zingraff, M. T., J. Leiter, M. C. Johnson, and K. A. Myers. 1994. "The Mediating Effect of School Performance on the Maltreatment-Delinquency Relationship." *Journal of Research in Crime and Delinquency* 31:62–91.

Zingraff, M. T., J. Leiter, J. A. Myers, and M. C. Johnsen. 1993. "Child Maltreatment and Youthful Problem Behavior." *Criminology* 31:173–202.

Zweig, J., A. Sayer, L. J. Crockett, and J. R. Vicary. 2002. "Adolescent Risk Factors for Sexual Victimization." *Journal of Adolescent Research* 17:586–603.

Contributors

Robert Agnew is Samuel Candler Dobbs Professor of Sociology at Emory University in Atlanta. His research focuses on the causes of delinquency, particularly general strain theory, and his recent publications include *Why Do Criminals Offend? A General Theory of Crime and Delinquency* and *Pressured into Crime: An Overview of General Strain Theory.*

Angela Browne has done research on the short- and long-term effects of child physical and sexual abuse, patterns of assault and homicide in couple relationships, and pathways to perpetration of violence by women and girls since 1979. She consults to prisons for women and to juvenile justice, as well as to state and government agencies, and was Associate Director of the Harvard Youth Violence Prevention Center. Dr. Browne is based in Washington, D.C., where she is a policy liaison on crime, violence, and justice issues.

Meda Chesney-Lind, PhD, is Professor of Women's Studies at the University of Hawaii at Manoa. Nationally recognized for her work on women and crime, her books include *Girls, Delinquency and Juvenile Justice; The Female Offender: Girls, Women and Crime; Female Gangs in America; Invisible Punishment;* and *Girls, Women and Crime.* She has just finished a book on trends in girls' violence, entitled *Beyond Bad Girls: Gender, Violence, and Hype.*

Gayle A. Dakof, PhD, is a Research Associate Professor at the University of Miami Miller School of Medicine, Department of Epidemiology and Public Health, Center for Treatment Research on Adolescent Drug Abuse. She is a Senior Trainer of an adolescent evidence-based practice (EBP): Multidimensional Family Therapy (MDFT) and is currently the Principal Investigator on two NIDA-funded drug court studies.

Barry C. Feld is Centennial Professor of Law, University of Minnesota Law School, where he has taught since 1972. He has written eight books and more than seventy law review, book chapters, and criminology articles on juvenile justice administration with a special emphasis on serious young offenders, procedural justice in juvenile court, and youth sentencing policy.

Diana H. Fishbein has a joint PhD in criminology and psychobiology from Florida State University and completed a NIH postdoctoral fellowship in neuroscience at the University of Maryland, School of Medicine. She currently is a Senior Fellow in behavioral neuroscience and Director of the Transdisciplinary Behavioral Science Program at RTI International. Her publications include four books and numerous chapters, monographs, scientific articles, and policy papers.

Peggy C. Giordano is Distinguished Research Professor of Sociology at Bowling Green State University. Her research has centered on adolescent girls and women, and explores the role of basic social network processes in the etiology of criminal onset as well as desistance.

Denise C. Gottfredson is a Professor at the University of Maryland Department of Criminal Justice and Criminology. She received a PhD in Social Relations from The Johns Hopkins University, where she specialized in Sociology of Education. Dr. Gottfredson's research interests include delinquency and delinquency prevention, and particularly the effects of school environments on youth behavior. Dr. Gottfredson has recently completed randomized experiments to test the effectiveness of the Baltimore City Drug Treatment Court and the Strengthening Families Program in Washington, D.C. She is currently directing a randomized trial of the effects of structured after-school programming on the development of problem behavior.

Candace Kruttschnitt is a Professor in the Department of Sociology at the University of Toronto. Her recent books include *Marking Time in the Golden State: Women's Imprisonment in California* (with Rosemary Gartner, 2005) and *Gender and Crime: Patterns in Victimization and Offending* (with Karen Heimer, 2006).

Jody Miller is Professor of Criminology and Criminal Justice at the University of Missouri–St. Louis. She is author of *Getting Played: African American Girls, Urban Inequality, and Gendered Violence* (2008) and *One of the Guys: Girls, Gangs, and Gender* (2001).

Shari Miller, PhD, is a Senior Research Scientist at RTI International. Dr. Miller has over a decade of experience in basic risk and protective research on youth violence and delinquency and in the development, implementation, and evaluation of community-based prevention efforts. She is the recipient of a Career Development Award by the National Institute of Mental Health (NIMH) on violence and delinquency by girls. Through this award, Dr. Miller has been conducting quantitative and qualitative studies to better understand the nature, antecedents, course, and mechanisms of violence and delinquency in girls.

Merry Morash is a Professor at the School of Criminal Justice, Michigan State University. She is the author of *Understanding Gender, Crime and Justice* (2006), and has published numerous articles on women offenders, gender and policing, and domestic violence. She is Director of the Michigan Victim Assistance Academy, which educates professionals who work with crime victims, and the Michigan Regional Community Policing Institute, which advances organizational change to support community policing.

Christopher W. Mullins is an Assistant Professor in the Center for the Study of Crime, Delinquency, and Corrections at Southern Illinois University–Carbondale. His research focuses on violence, especially interconnections between street culture, gender and street violence, and violence by nation-states and paramilitary groups. He is the author of three books and more than a dozen articles and book chapters.

Allison Ann Payne is an Assistant Professor in the Department of Sociology and Criminal Justice at Villanova University. Her research interests include juvenile delinquency, school-based delinquency prevention, and program evaluation. She received her PhD from the University of Maryland, Department of Criminology and Criminal Justice, and has published in *Criminology, The Journal of Research in Crime and Delinquency, Prevention Science,* and *Deviant Behavior.*

Jennifer Schwartz is an Assistant Professor of Sociology at Washington State University. Her research focuses on gender and crime; stratification, family structure, communities, and crime; and how social change impinges on trends in crime and social control. She is also interested in methodological issues related to crime measurement.

Darrell Steffensmeier is a Professor of Sociology and Crime/Law/Justice at Pennsylvania State University. He is past president of the International Association for the Study of Organized Crime, a Fellow of the American Society of Criminology, and has been the recipient of numerous NSF awards for funded research. His recent book (with Jeffery Ulmer), *Confessions of a Dying Thief: Understanding Criminal Careers and Illegal Enterprise* (2005) was the 2006 recipient of the Hindelang Award for outstanding scholarship from the American Society of Criminology.

Donna-Marie Winn is a Licensed Clinical Psychologist who is known both nationally and internationally for her expertise in developing evidence-based programs and tools to help children and young adults grow socially, emotionally, and academically. Dr. Winn is an Investigator at the FPG Child Development Center at the University of North Carolina, Chapel Hill. She is also a Senior Research Scientist in the Department of Sociology and in the Center for Demography and Ethnographic Studies at Duke University. Over the past twenty years, Dr. Winn has worked with many schools, community-based organizations, adults, families, and children.

Margaret A. Zahn is Professor of Sociology at North Carolina State University and Past President and Fellow of the American Society for Criminology. She is Principal Investigator of the Girls Study Group. She has received multiple grants to study violence in a variety of settings and has published extensively in the area. She is the co-editor of several books including *Homicide: A Sourcebook of Social Research* (with M. Dwayne Smith) and *Violence: From Theory to Research* (with Henry Brownstein and Shelly Jackson).

Index